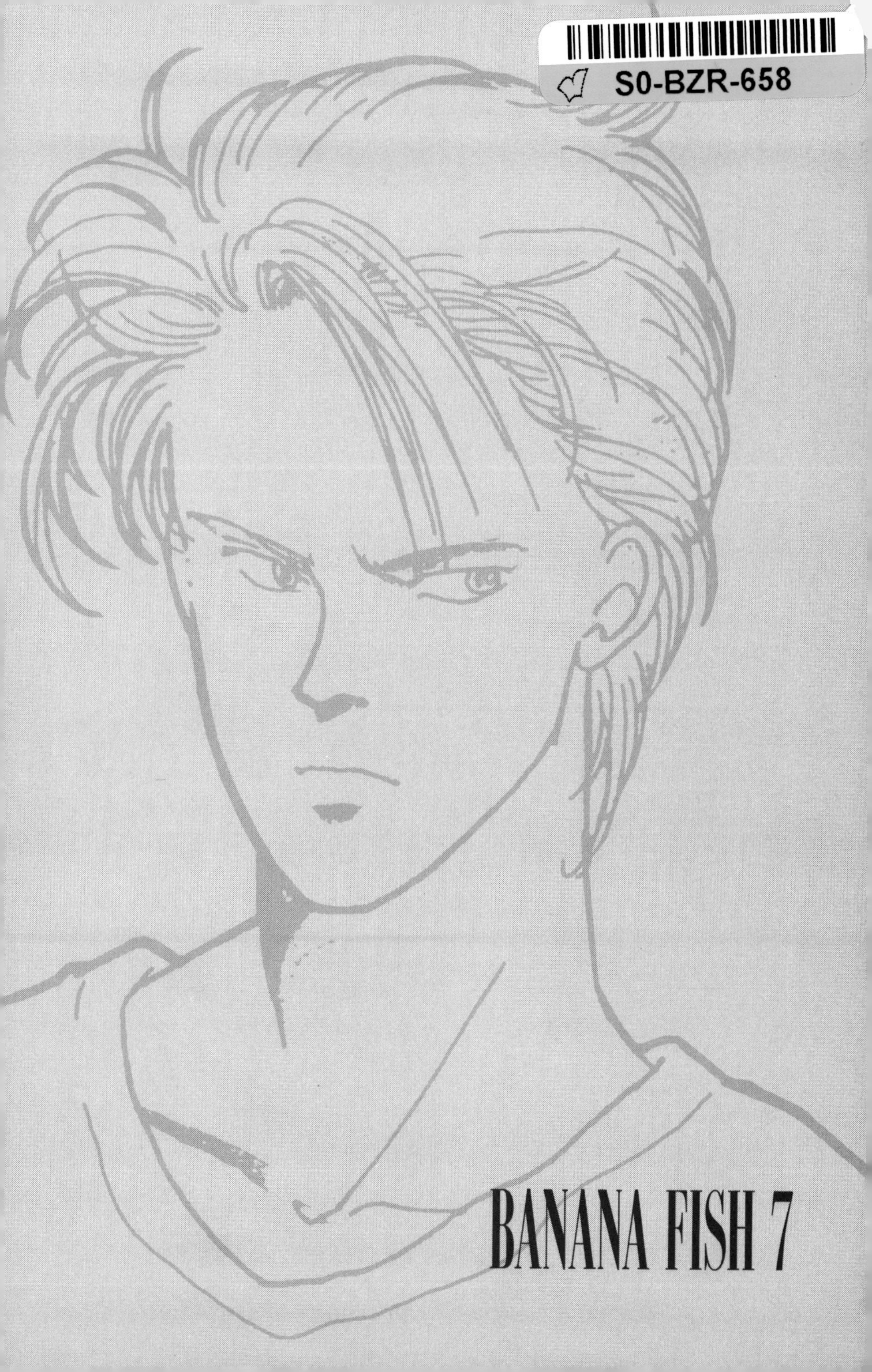

BANANA FISH 7

This volume contains the BANANA FISH installments from PULP Vol. 5, No. 11 through Vol. 6, No. 6, in their entirety.

STORY & ART BY
AKIMI YOSHIDA

ENGLISH ADAPTATION BY
AKEMI WEGMULLER

Translation/Yuji Oniki
Touch-Up Art & Lettering/Cato
Cover Design/Izumi Evers
Editor/Carl Gustav Horn

Managing Editor/Annette Roman
VP of Sales & Marketing/Rick Bauer
VP of Editorial/Hyoe Narita
Publisher/Seiji Horibuchi

For Advertising Rates or Media Kit, Contact:
Elena Ontiveros; (415) 546-7073 Ext. 111 (elena@viz.com)
Viz Communications, Inc.
Attn. Sales & Marketing
PO Box 77010
San Francisco, CA 94107

Printed in Canada

Published by Viz Communications, Inc.
P.O. Box 77010 · San Francisco, CA 94107

10 9 8 7 6 5 4 3 2 1
First printing, November 2002

Visit us at www.viz.com, www.pulp-mag.com, www.animerica-mag.com, and store.viz.com

BANANA FISH

STORY AND ART BY AKIMI YOSHIDA

PULP GRAPHIC NOVEL

vol. 7

THE STORY THUS FAR...

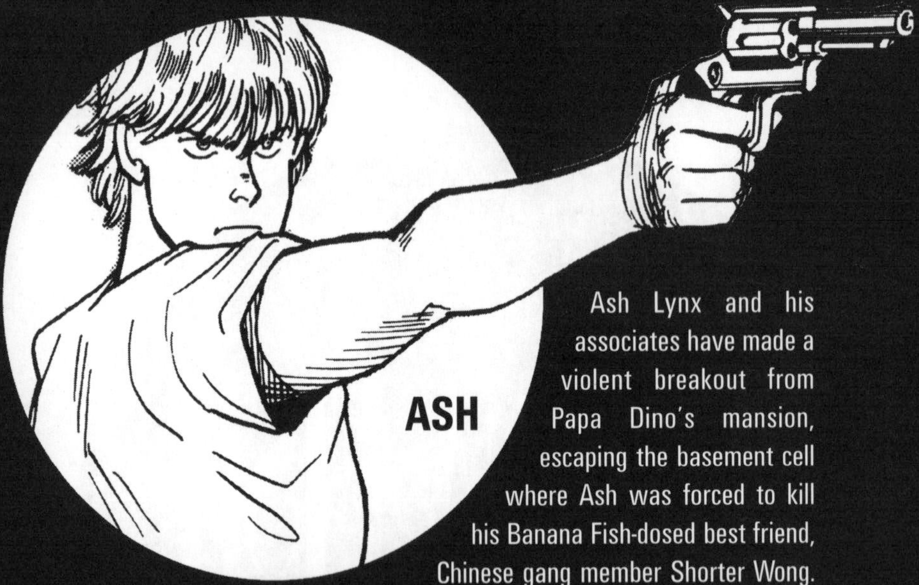
ASH

Ash Lynx and his associates have made a violent breakout from Papa Dino's mansion, escaping the basement cell where Ash was forced to kill his Banana Fish-dosed best friend, Chinese gang member Shorter Wong. They had help leaving the scene from Shorter's boys and his lieutenant, the vicious Sing, who tried to get revenge on Ash—and got swatted aside like a fly. Ash burns down the house with its drug lab, slaughters the guards, and kills one of the two Dawsons, the brother doctors who alone can synthesize Banana Fish. All the public hears of the story in the media is that a shocking arson and home-invasion robbery has hit respectable millionaire and donor to youth charities, Dino Golzine...Now Eiji has holed up with Ash in one of his gang's flophouses, where they await the arrival of their friendly 'hood arms dealer, while Max and Ibé have barged in on the middle-class domesticity of Charlie, an ally on the NYPD. They have news to break to his girlfriend Nadia—Shorter's younger sister...

Eiji Okumura

Young athlete and ward of Eiji; this pure-hearted teen has grown close to Ash and is willing to fight for him, but Ash wants him far away for his own good.

Max Lobo

A reporter himself on the trail of "Banana Fish," with personal knowledge of the drug through Ash's brother Griff, who was in his unit.

Shunichi Ibé

Old photojournalist friend of Max's who brought Eiji with him to NYC do to a story on Ash's gang; now linked to his fate.

Lee Yut-Lung

Youngest brother of a powerful crime family, this master poisoner seeks the downfall of his siblings, whom he blames for their mother's death.

Sing Soo-Ling

This cunning, deadly lil' G became boss of Shorter's gang after he died. He realizes he doesn't know the whole story, yet feels he must take revenge.

Arthur

Took over Ash's old territories, but only with Dino's heavily-armed support; Dino is letting him in on his plans, but regrets he lacks Ash's sense of refinement.

"Papa" Dino Golzine

The urbane, social-climbing Corsican crime lord has a taste for young boys and a lust to be a political kingmaker.

THE STORY THUS FAR...

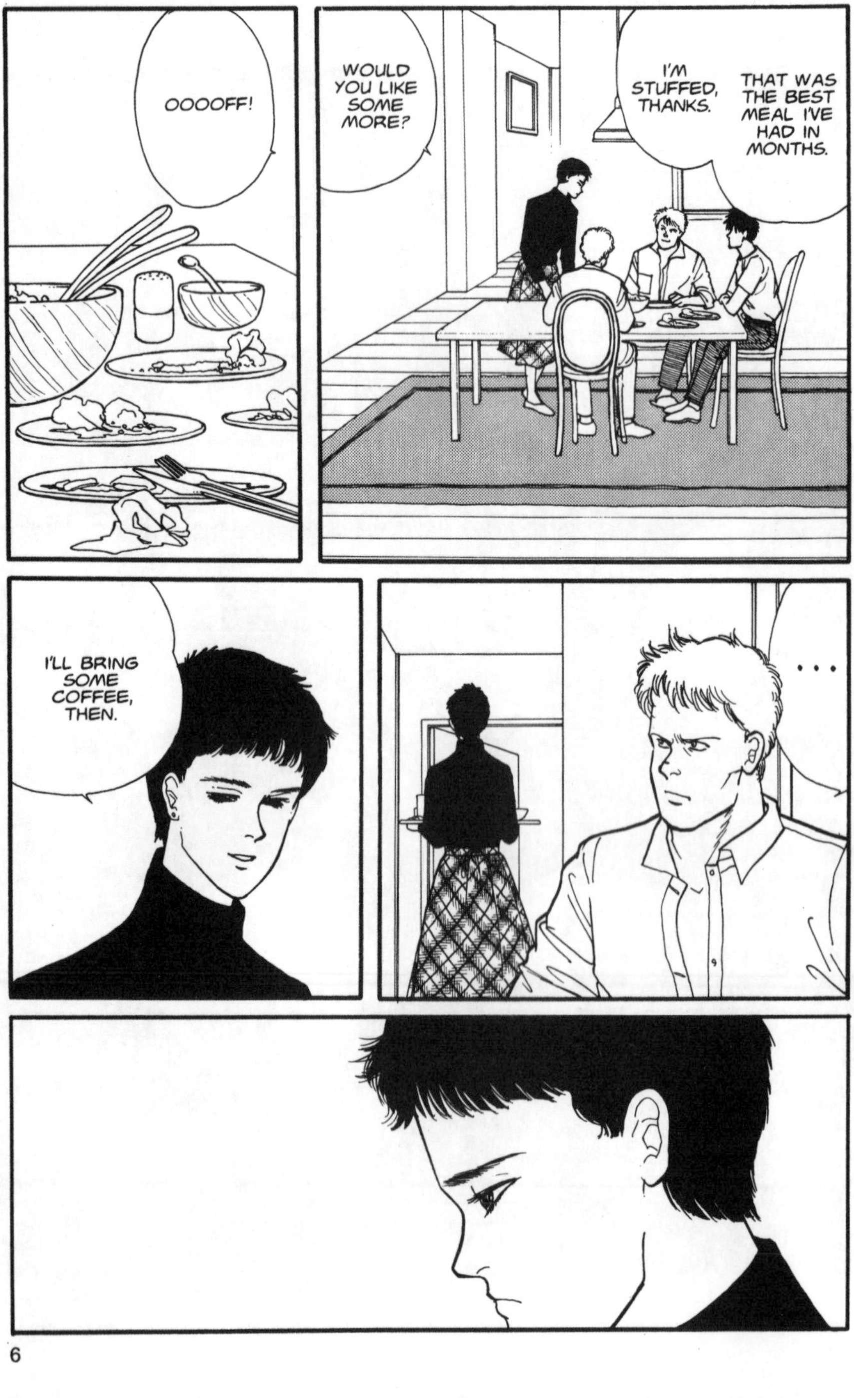
OOOOFF!
WOULD YOU LIKE SOME MORE?
I'M STUFFED, THANKS.
THAT WAS THE BEST MEAL I'VE HAD IN MONTHS.
I'LL BRING SOME COFFEE, THEN.
...

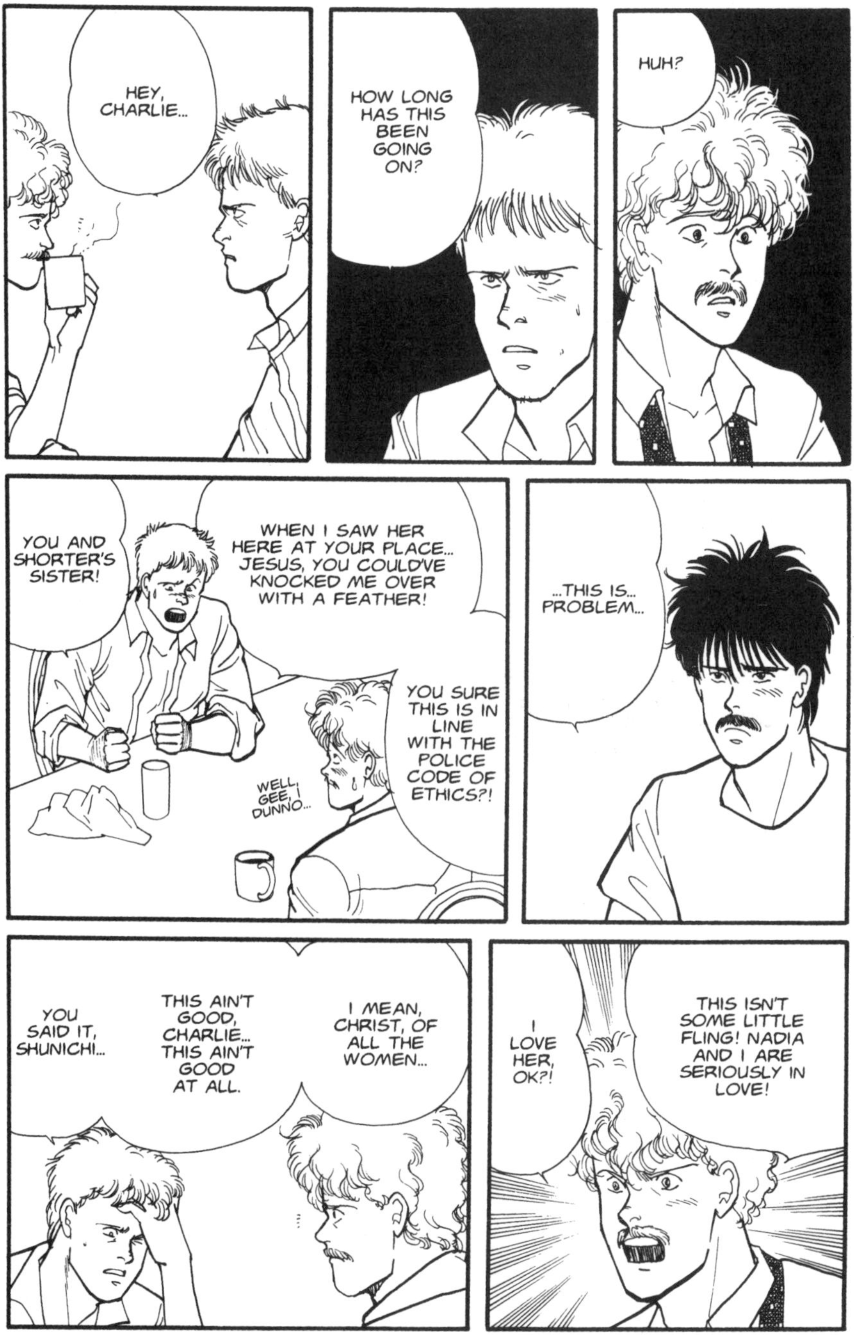
HEY, CHARLIE...
HOW LONG HAS THIS BEEN GOING ON?
HUH?
YOU AND SHORTER'S SISTER!
WHEN I SAW HER HERE AT YOUR PLACE... JESUS, YOU COULD'VE KNOCKED ME OVER WITH A FEATHER!
WELL, GEE, I DUNNO...
YOU SURE THIS IS IN LINE WITH THE POLICE CODE OF ETHICS?!
...THIS IS... PROBLEM...
YOU SAID IT, SHUNICHI...
THIS AIN'T GOOD, CHARLIE... THIS AIN'T GOOD AT ALL.
I MEAN, CHRIST, OF ALL THE WOMEN...
I LOVE HER, OK?!
THIS ISN'T SOME LITTLE FLING! NADIA AND I ARE SERIOUSLY IN LOVE!

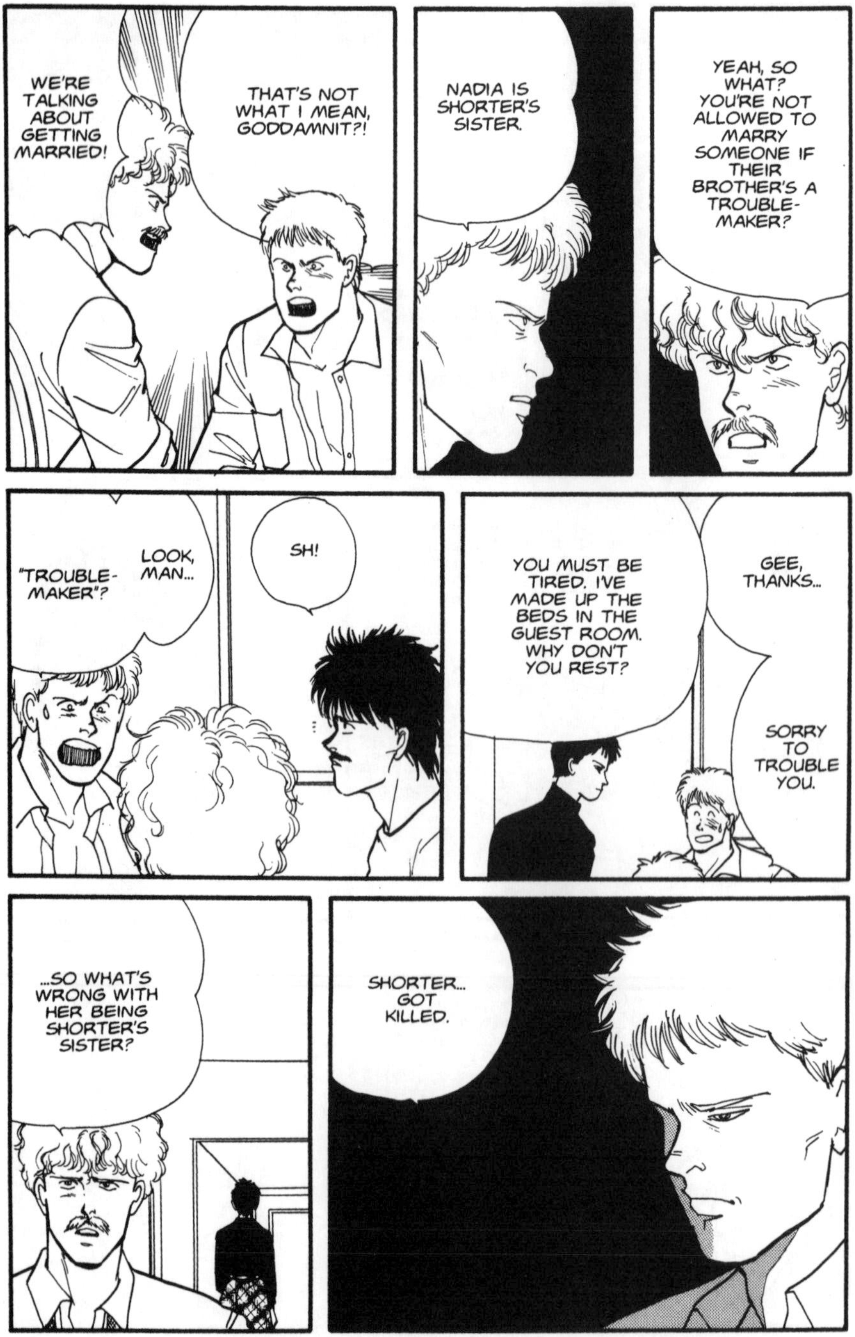

WE'RE TALKING ABOUT GETTING MARRIED!
THAT'S NOT WHAT I MEAN, GODDAMNIT?!
NADIA IS SHORTER'S SISTER.
YEAH, SO WHAT? YOU'RE NOT ALLOWED TO MARRY SOMEONE IF THEIR BROTHER'S A TROUBLE-MAKER?
"TROUBLE-MAKER"?
LOOK, MAN...
SH!
YOU MUST BE TIRED. I'VE MADE UP THE BEDS IN THE GUEST ROOM. WHY DON'T YOU REST?
GEE, THANKS...
SORRY TO TROUBLE YOU.
...SO WHAT'S WRONG WITH HER BEING SHORTER'S SISTER?
SHORTER... GOT KILLED.

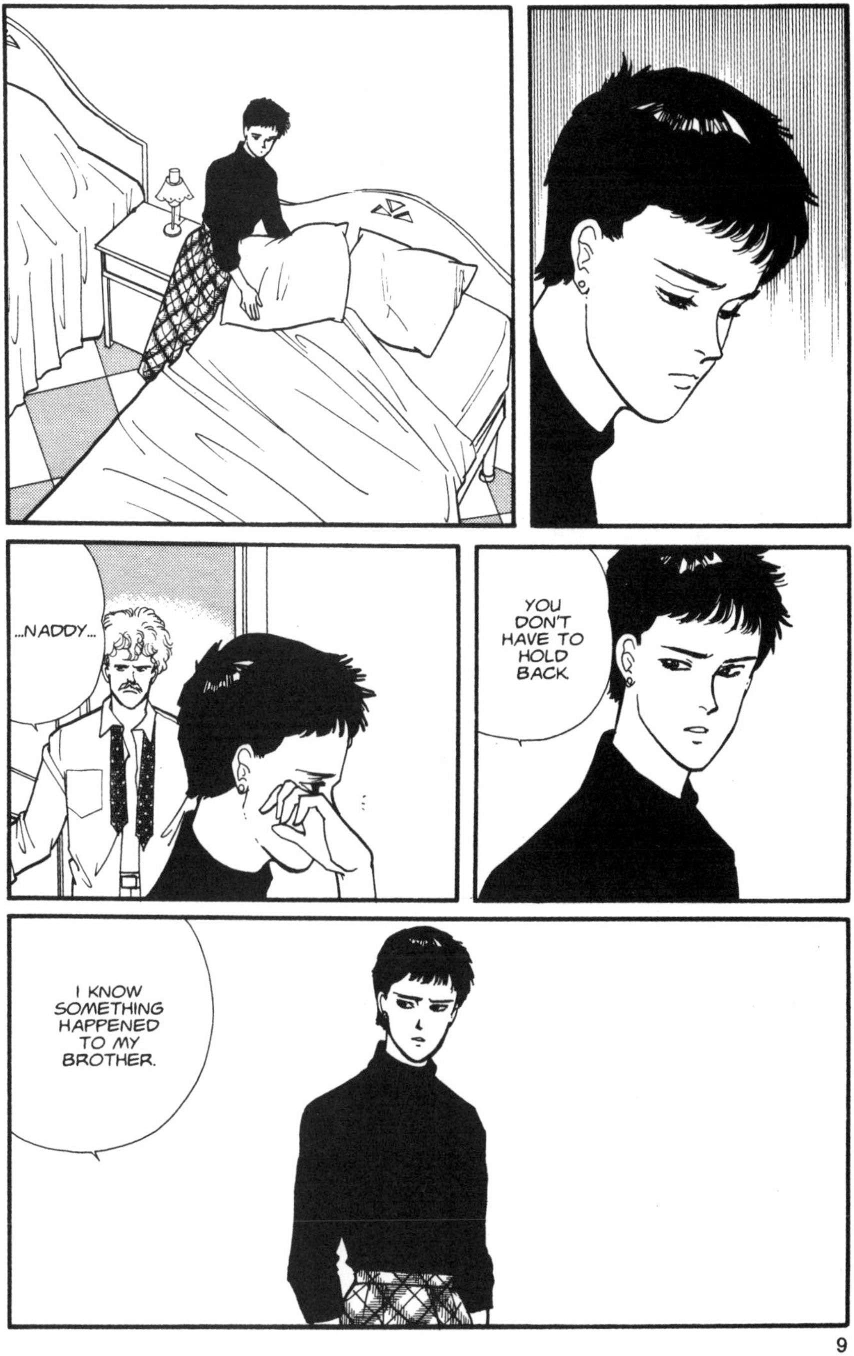
...NADDY...
YOU DON'T HAVE TO HOLD BACK.
I KNOW SOMETHING HAPPENED TO MY BROTHER.

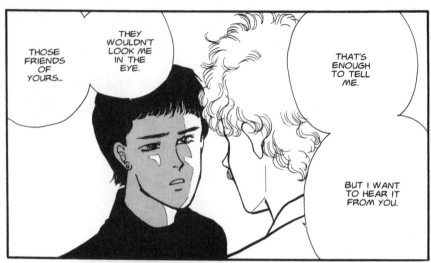

THOSE FRIENDS OF YOURS...

THEY WOULDN'T LOOK ME IN THE EYE.

THAT'S ENOUGH TO TELL ME.

BUT I WANT TO HEAR IT FROM YOU.

...HE'S DEAD, ISN'T HE?

NADIA...

...I WAS AFRAID THIS WOULD HAPPEN SOME DAY...

EVER SINCE HE FELL IN WITH THAT CROWD...

...

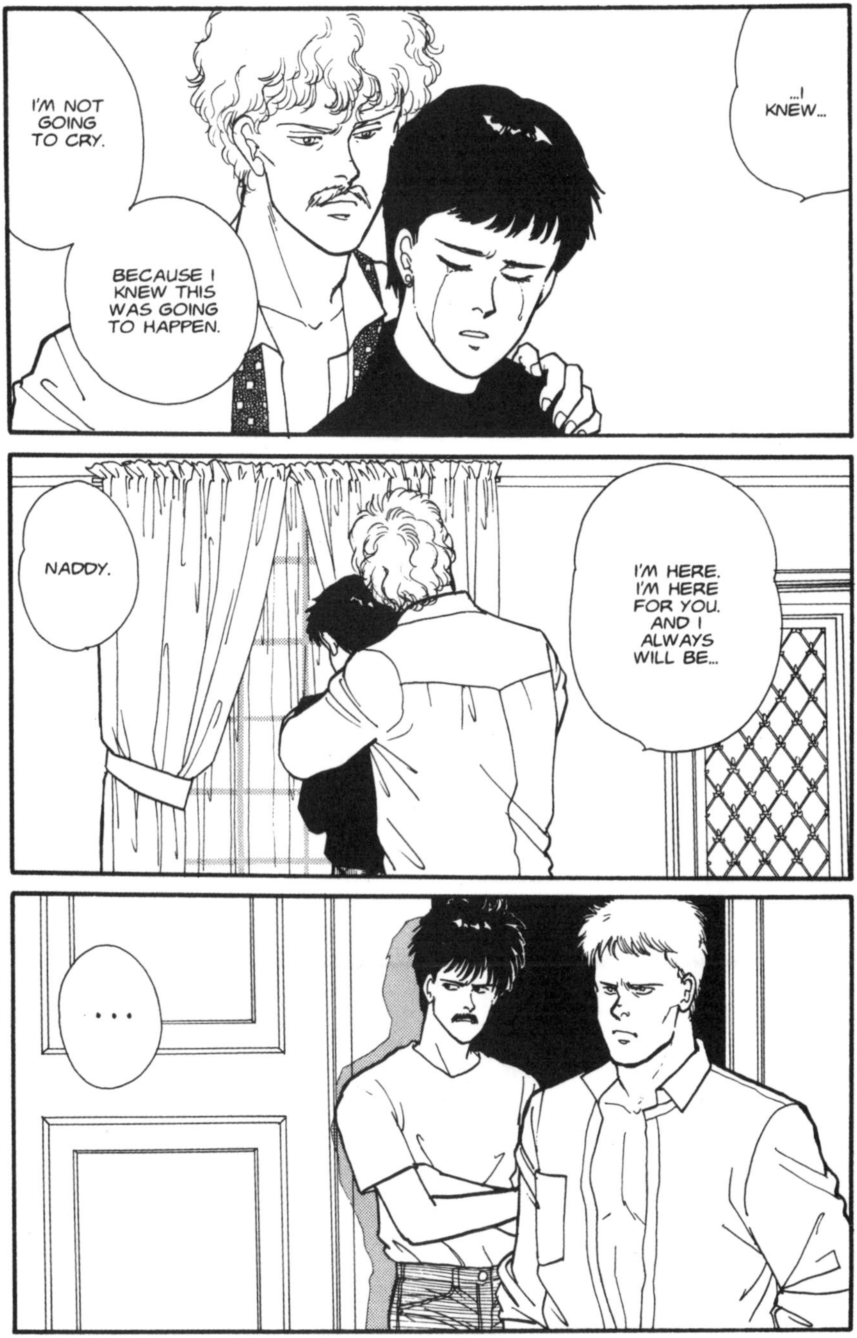
I'M NOT GOING TO CRY.
BECAUSE I KNEW THIS WAS GOING TO HAPPEN.
...I KNEW...
NADDY.
I'M HERE. I'M HERE FOR YOU. AND I ALWAYS WILL BE...
...

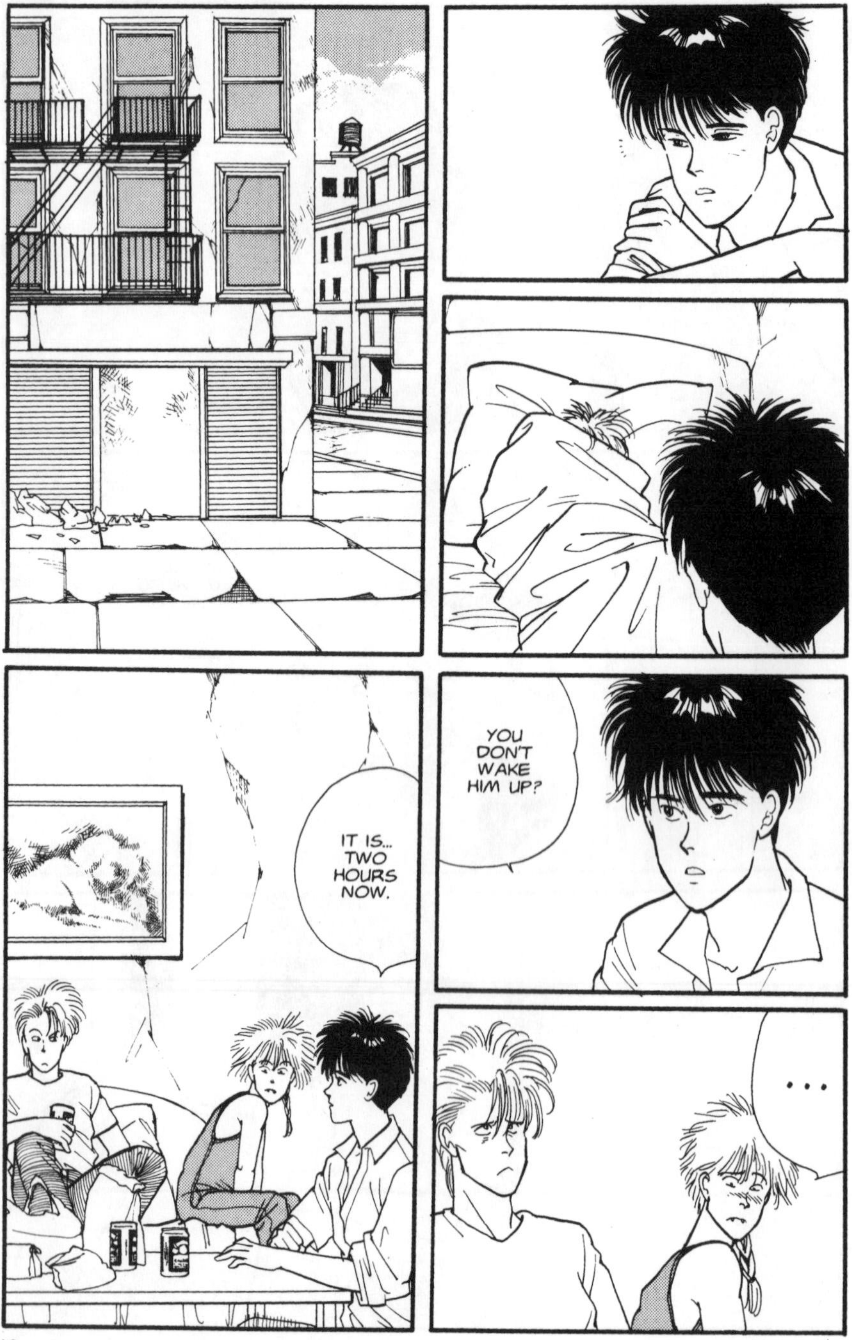
IT IS... TWO HOURS NOW.
YOU DON'T WAKE HIM UP?
...

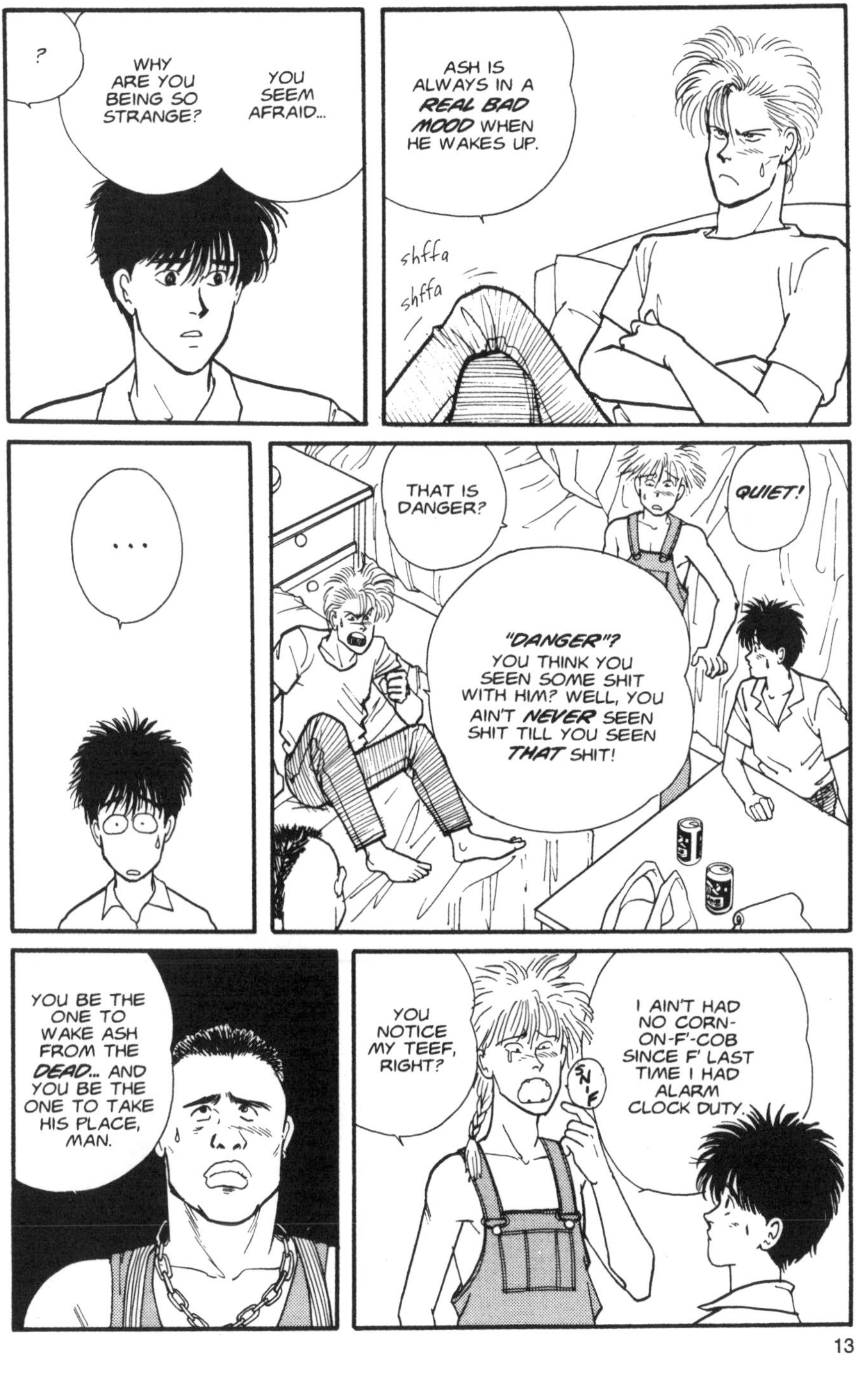
?
WHY ARE YOU BEING SO STRANGE?
YOU SEEM AFRAID...
ASH IS ALWAYS IN A REAL BAD MOOD WHEN HE WAKES UP.
shffa
shffa
...
THAT IS DANGER?
QUIET!
"DANGER"? YOU THINK YOU SEEN SOME SHIT WITH HIM? WELL, YOU AIN'T NEVER SEEN SHIT TILL YOU SEEN THAT SHIT!
YOU BE THE ONE TO WAKE ASH FROM THE DEAD... AND YOU BE THE ONE TO TAKE HIS PLACE, MAN.
YOU NOTICE MY TEEF, RIGHT?
SNIF
I AIN'T HAD NO CORN-ON-F'-COB SINCE F' LAST TIME I HAD ALARM CLOCK DUTY.

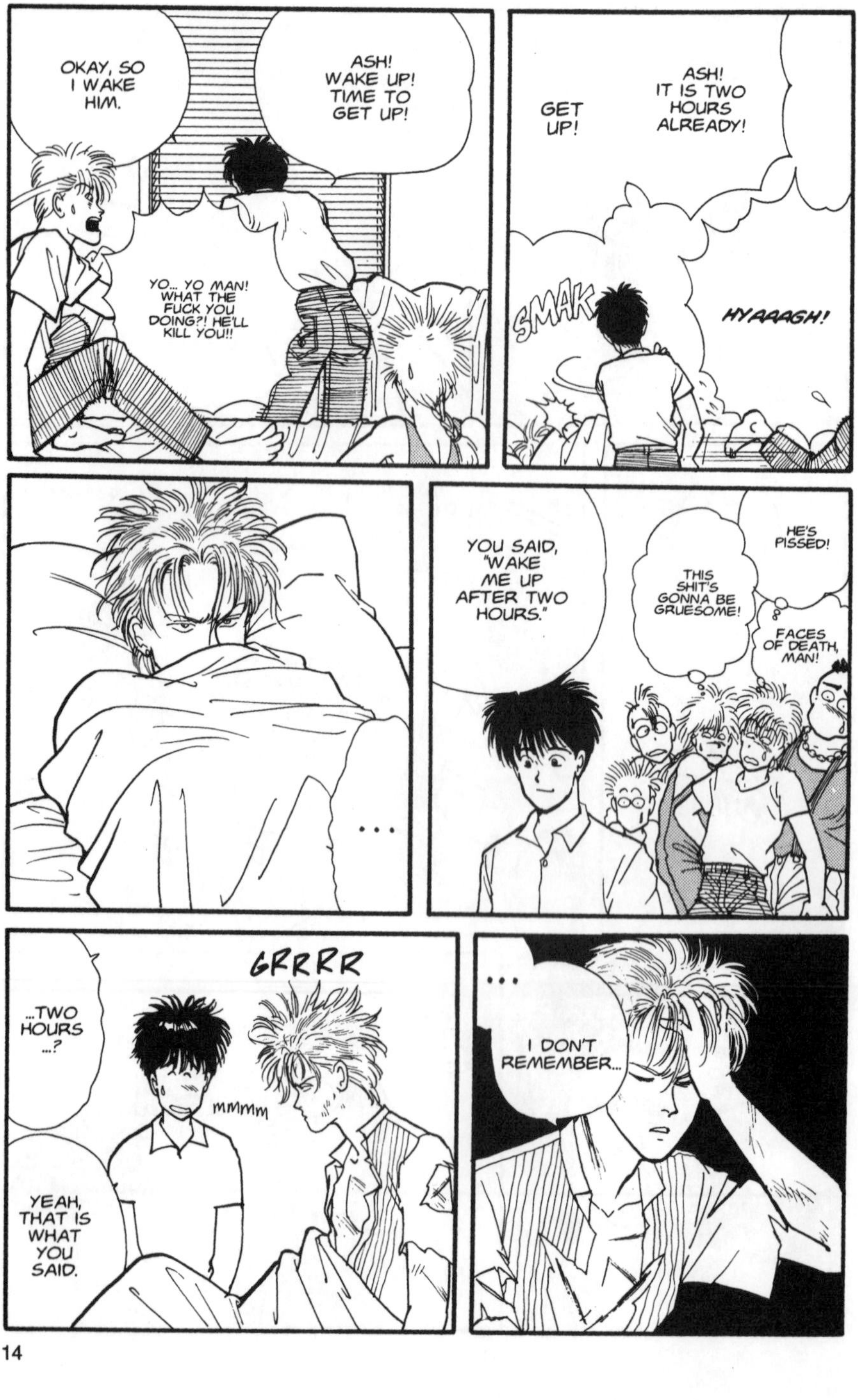
OKAY, SO I WAKE HIM.
ASH! WAKE UP! TIME TO GET UP!
YO... YO MAN! WHAT THE FUCK YOU DOING?! HE'LL KILL YOU!!
GET UP!
ASH! IT IS TWO HOURS ALREADY!
SMAK
HYAAAGH!
...
YOU SAID, "WAKE ME UP AFTER TWO HOURS."
THIS SHIT'S GONNA BE GRUESOME!
HE'S PISSED!
FACES OF DEATH, MAN!
GRRRR
...TWO HOURS ...?
MMMM
YEAH, THAT IS WHAT YOU SAID.
...
I DON'T REMEMBER...

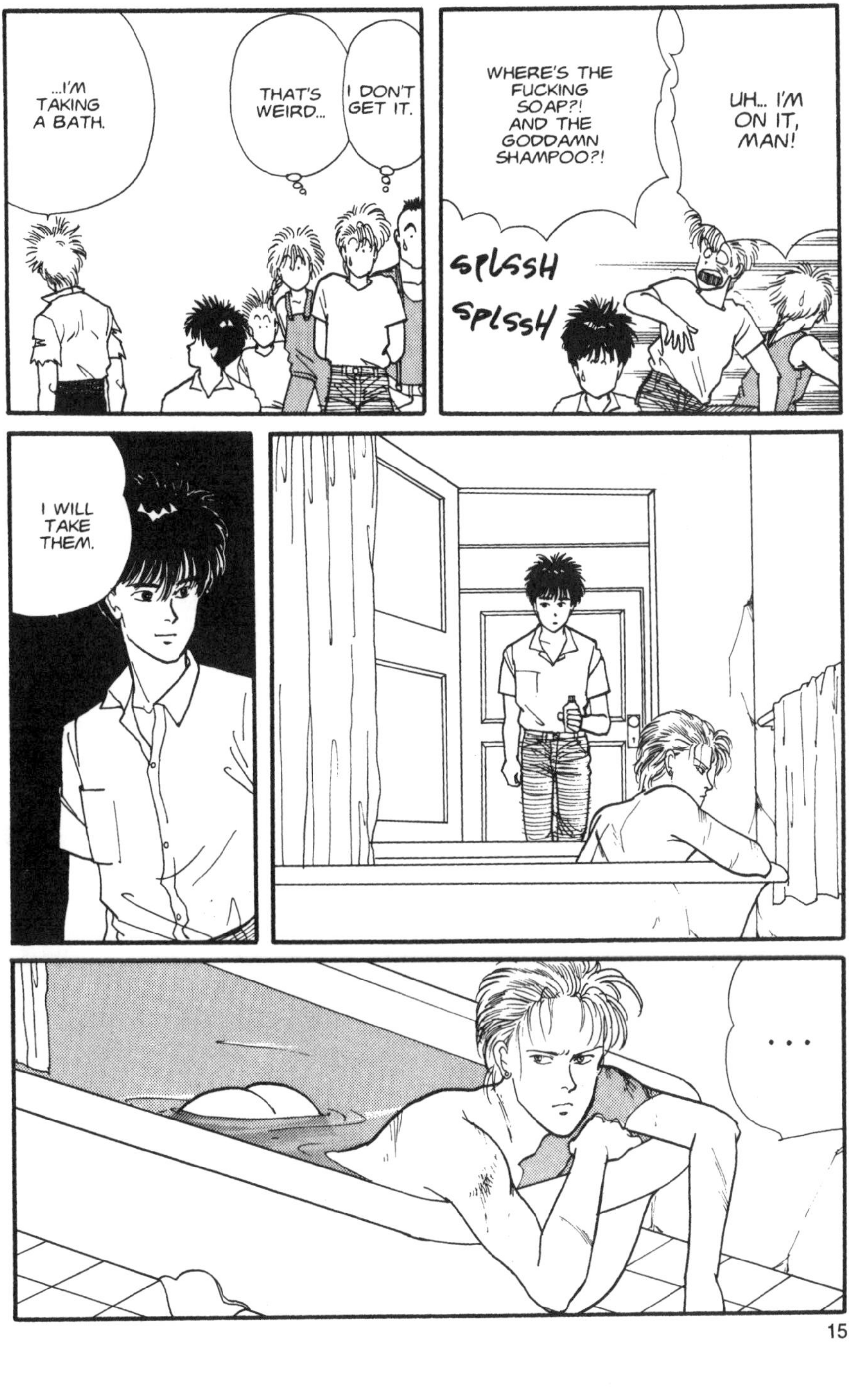
...I'M TAKING A BATH.
THAT'S WEIRD...
I DON'T GET IT.
WHERE'S THE FUCKING SOAP?! AND THE GODDAMN SHAMPOO?!
UH... I'M ON IT, MAN!
SPLSSH
SPLSSH
I WILL TAKE THEM.
. . .

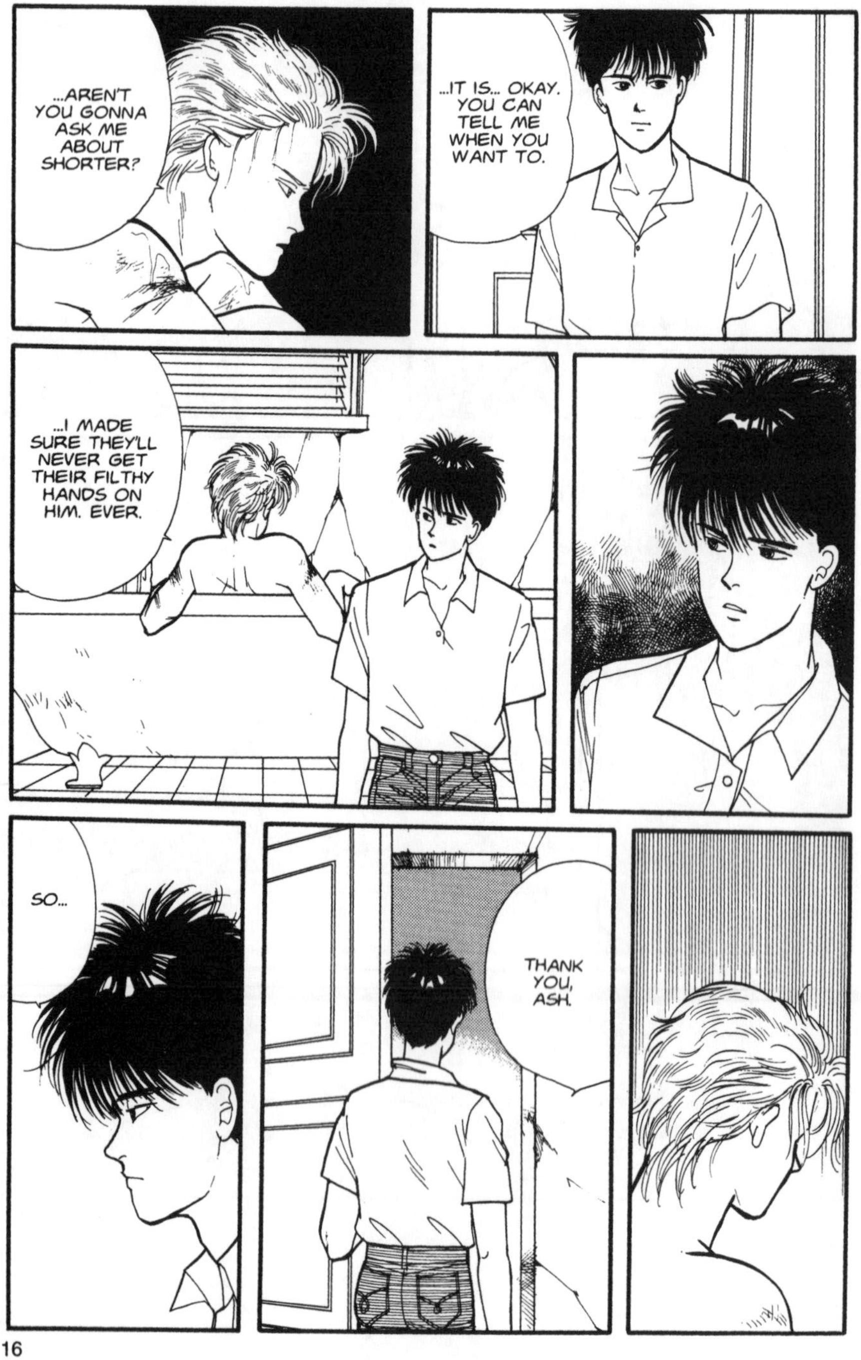
...AREN'T YOU GONNA ASK ME ABOUT SHORTER?
...IT IS... OKAY. YOU CAN TELL ME WHEN YOU WANT TO.
...I MADE SURE THEY'LL NEVER GET THEIR FILTHY HANDS ON HIM. EVER.
SO...
THANK YOU, ASH.

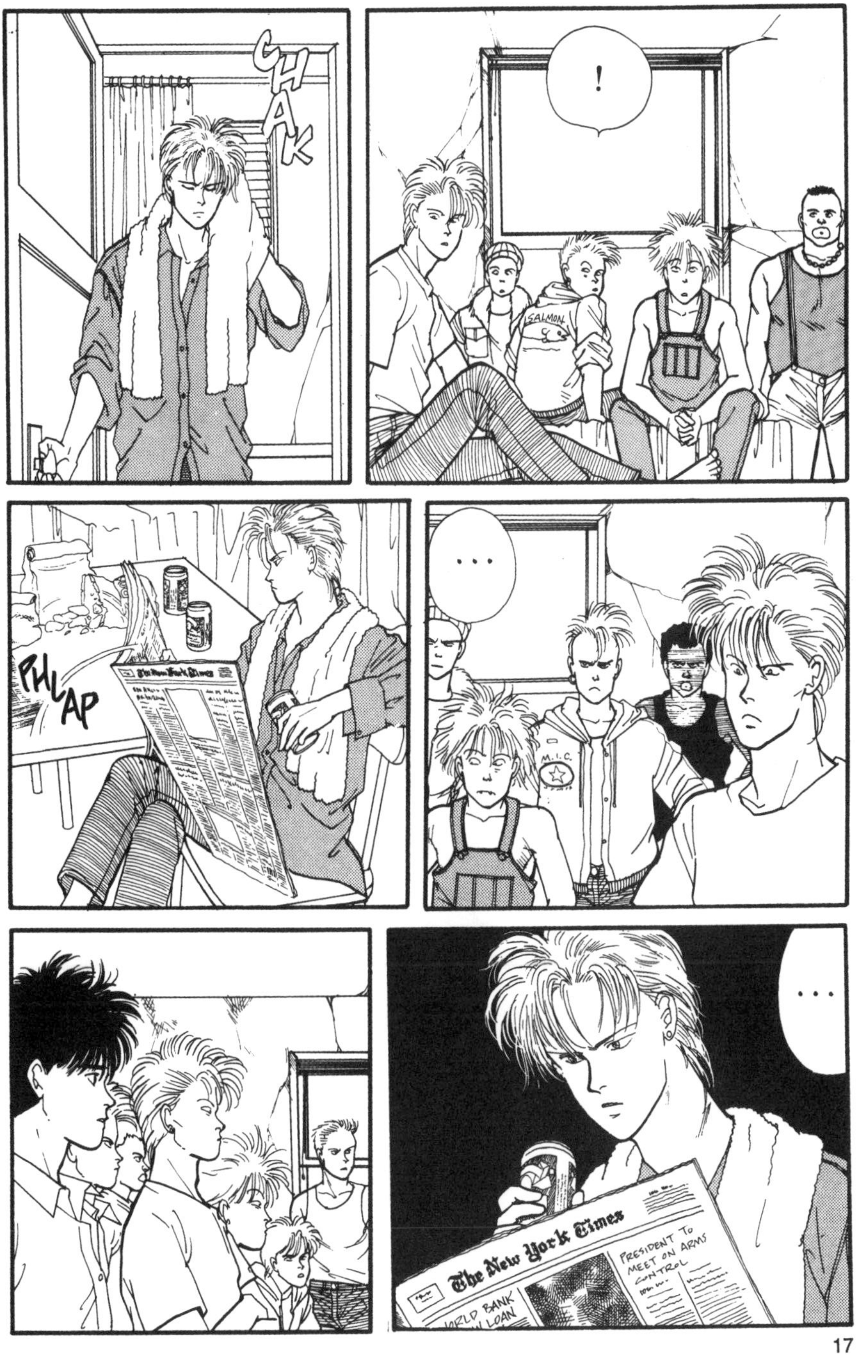
CHAK
!
PHLAP
...
The New York Times
PRESIDENT TO
MEET ON ARMS
CONTROL
...

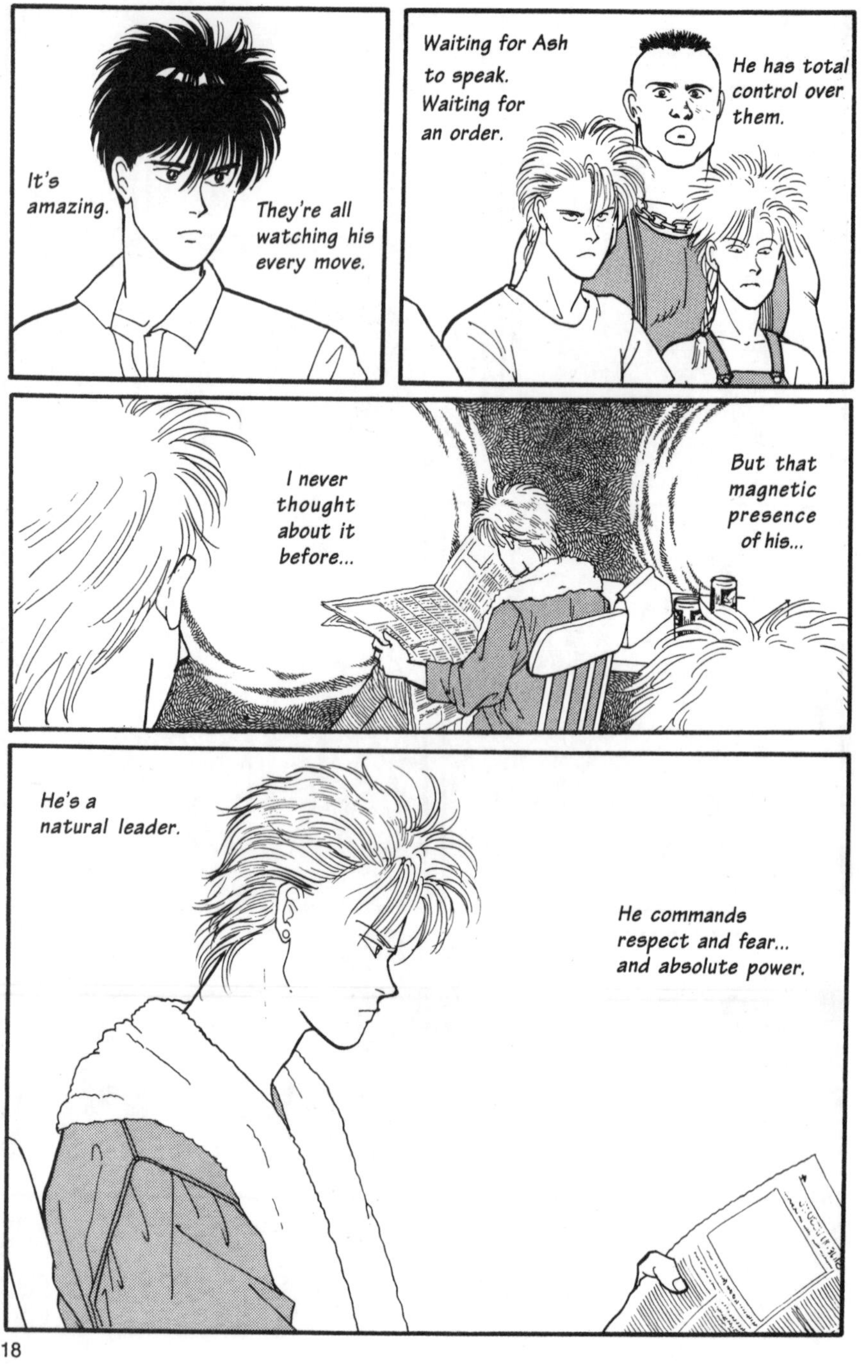
It's amazing.
They're all watching his every move.
Waiting for Ash to speak. Waiting for an order.
He has total control over them.
I never thought about it before...
But that magnetic presence of his...
He's a natural leader.
He commands respect and fear... and absolute power.

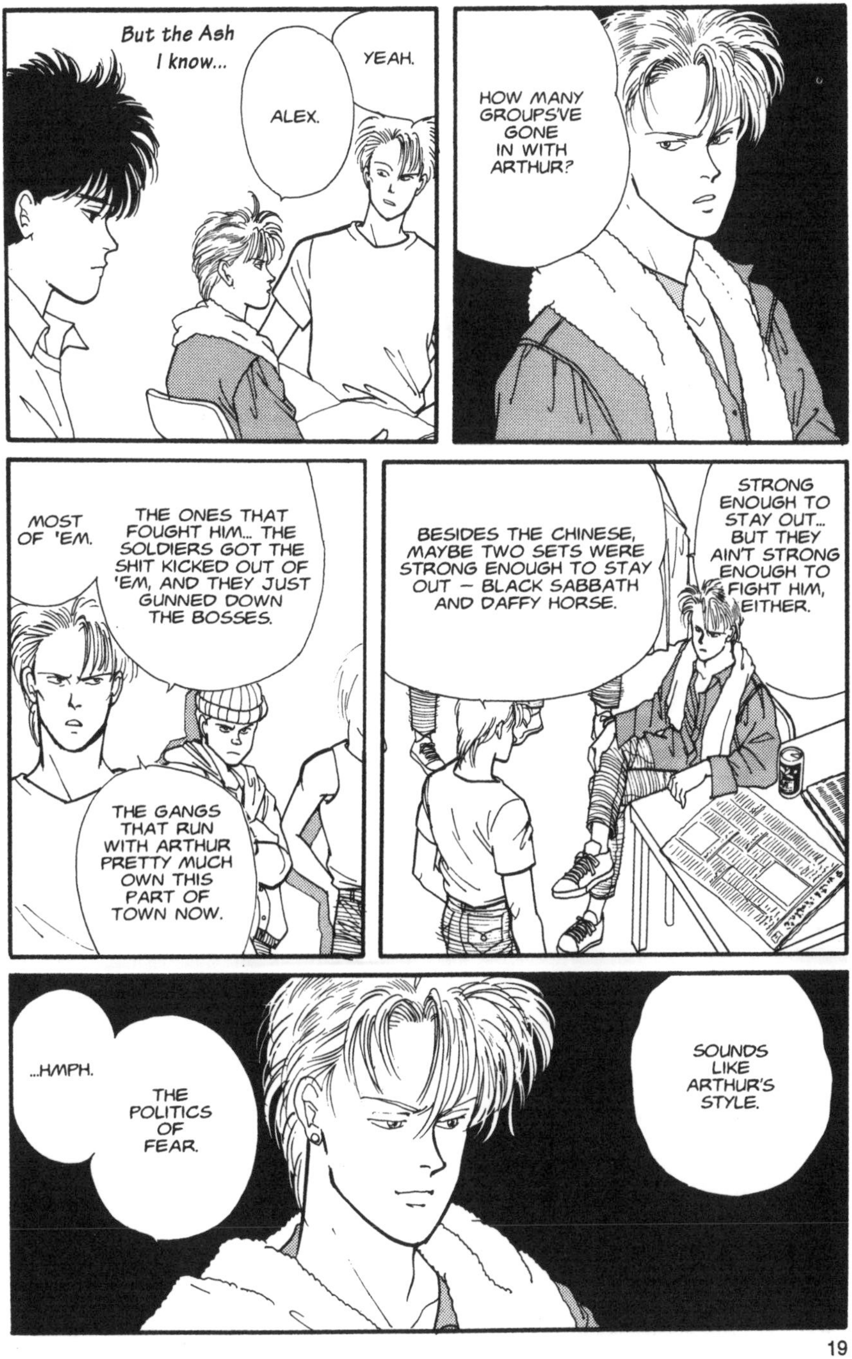
But the Ash I know...
ALEX.
YEAH.
HOW MANY GROUPS'VE GONE IN WITH ARTHUR?
MOST OF 'EM.
THE ONES THAT FOUGHT HIM... THE SOLDIERS GOT THE SHIT KICKED OUT OF 'EM, AND THEY JUST GUNNED DOWN THE BOSSES.
THE GANGS THAT RUN WITH ARTHUR PRETTY MUCH OWN THIS PART OF TOWN NOW.
BESIDES THE CHINESE, MAYBE TWO SETS WERE STRONG ENOUGH TO STAY OUT — BLACK SABBATH AND DAFFY HORSE.
STRONG ENOUGH TO STAY OUT... BUT THEY AIN'T STRONG ENOUGH TO FIGHT HIM, EITHER.
...HMPH.
THE POLITICS OF FEAR.
SOUNDS LIKE ARTHUR'S STYLE.

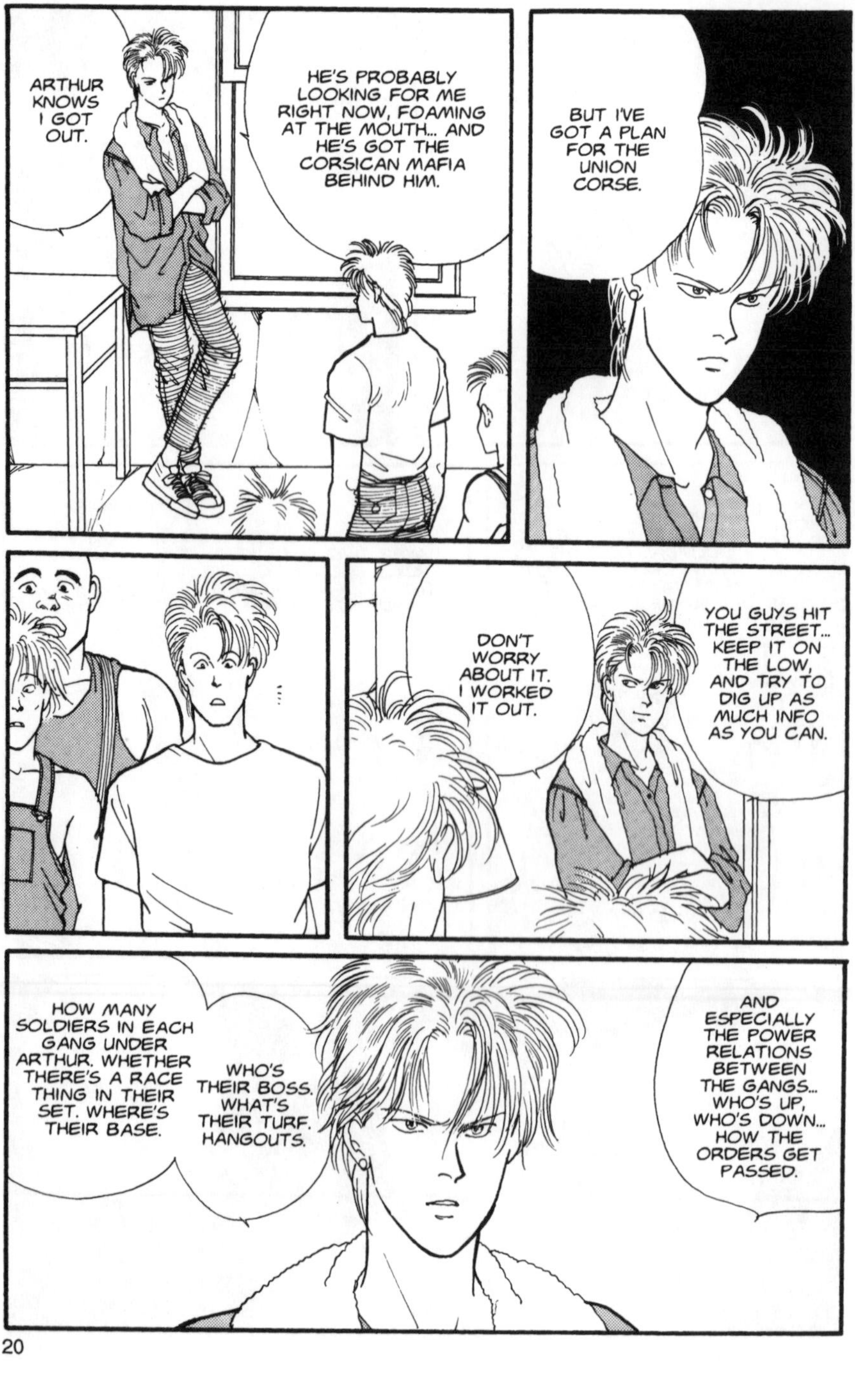
ARTHUR KNOWS I GOT OUT.
HE'S PROBABLY LOOKING FOR ME RIGHT NOW, FOAMING AT THE MOUTH... AND HE'S GOT THE CORSICAN MAFIA BEHIND HIM.
BUT I'VE GOT A PLAN FOR THE UNION CORSE.
...
DON'T WORRY ABOUT IT. I WORKED IT OUT.
YOU GUYS HIT THE STREET... KEEP IT ON THE LOW, AND TRY TO DIG UP AS MUCH INFO AS YOU CAN.
HOW MANY SOLDIERS IN EACH GANG UNDER ARTHUR. WHETHER THERE'S A RACE THING IN THEIR SET. WHERE'S THEIR BASE.
WHO'S THEIR BOSS. WHAT'S THEIR TURF. HANGOUTS.
AND ESPECIALLY THE POWER RELATIONS BETWEEN THE GANGS... WHO'S UP, WHO'S DOWN... HOW THE ORDERS GET PASSED.

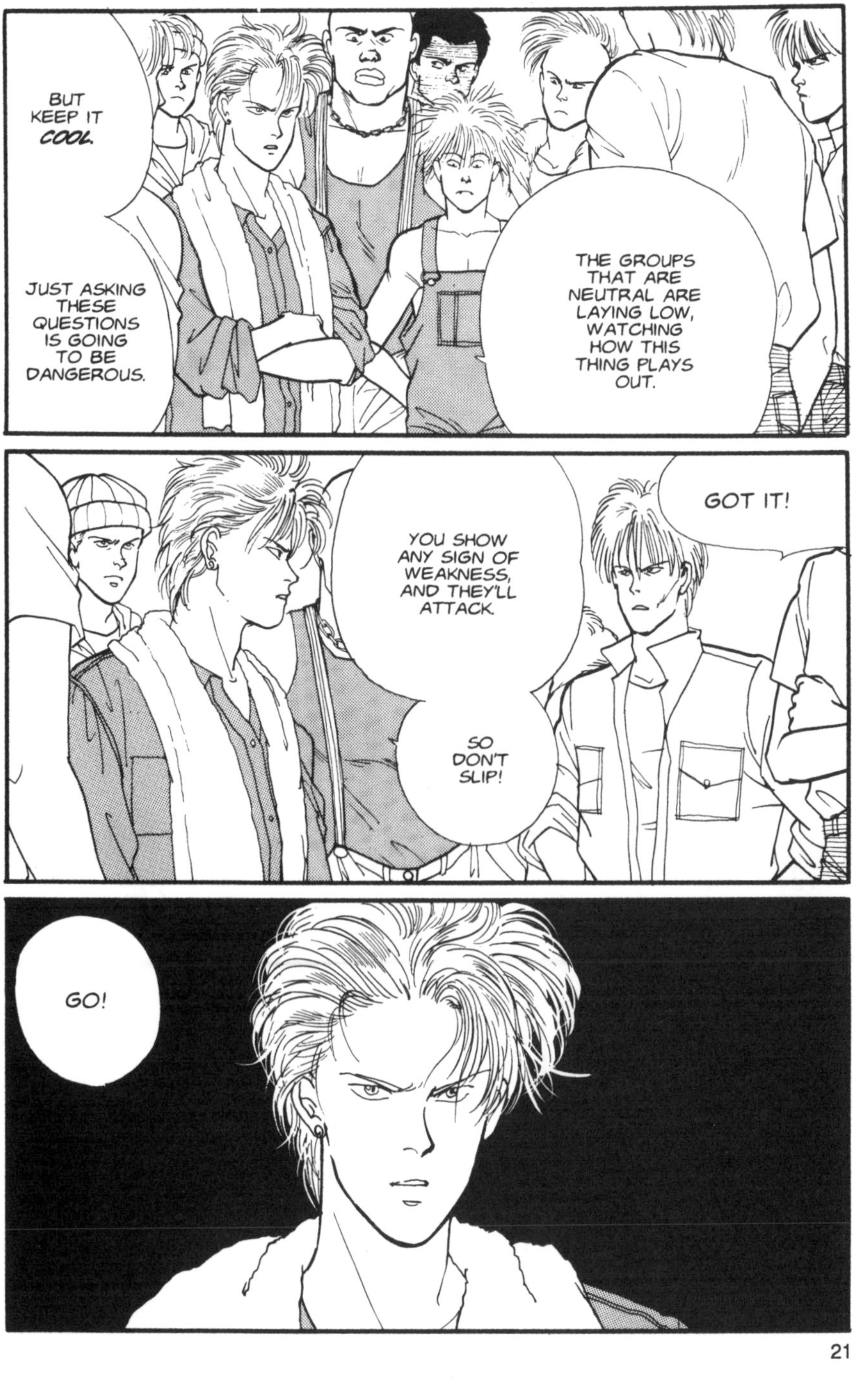
BUT KEEP IT COOL.
JUST ASKING THESE QUESTIONS IS GOING TO BE DANGEROUS.
THE GROUPS THAT ARE NEUTRAL ARE LAYING LOW, WATCHING HOW THIS THING PLAYS OUT.
YOU SHOW ANY SIGN OF WEAKNESS, AND THEY'LL ATTACK.
SO DON'T SLIP!
GOT IT!
GO!

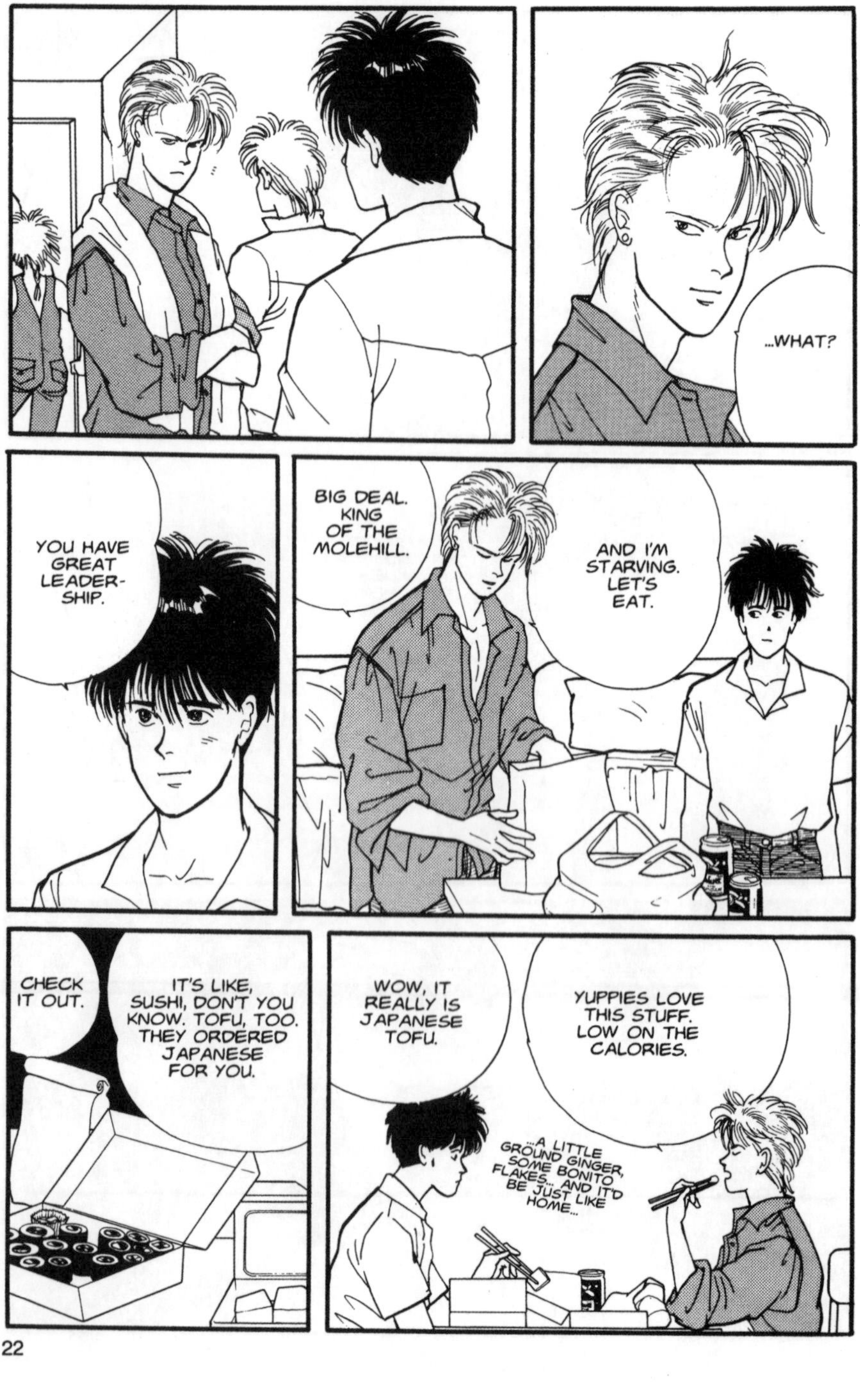
...WHAT?
YOU HAVE GREAT LEADER-SHIP.
BIG DEAL. KING OF THE MOLEHILL.
AND I'M STARVING. LET'S EAT.
CHECK IT OUT.
IT'S LIKE, SUSHI, DON'T YOU KNOW. TOFU, TOO. THEY ORDERED JAPANESE FOR YOU.
WOW, IT REALLY IS JAPANESE TOFU.
YUPPIES LOVE THIS STUFF. LOW ON THE CALORIES.
...A LITTLE GROUND GINGER, SOME BONITO FLAKES... AND IT'D BE JUST LIKE HOME...

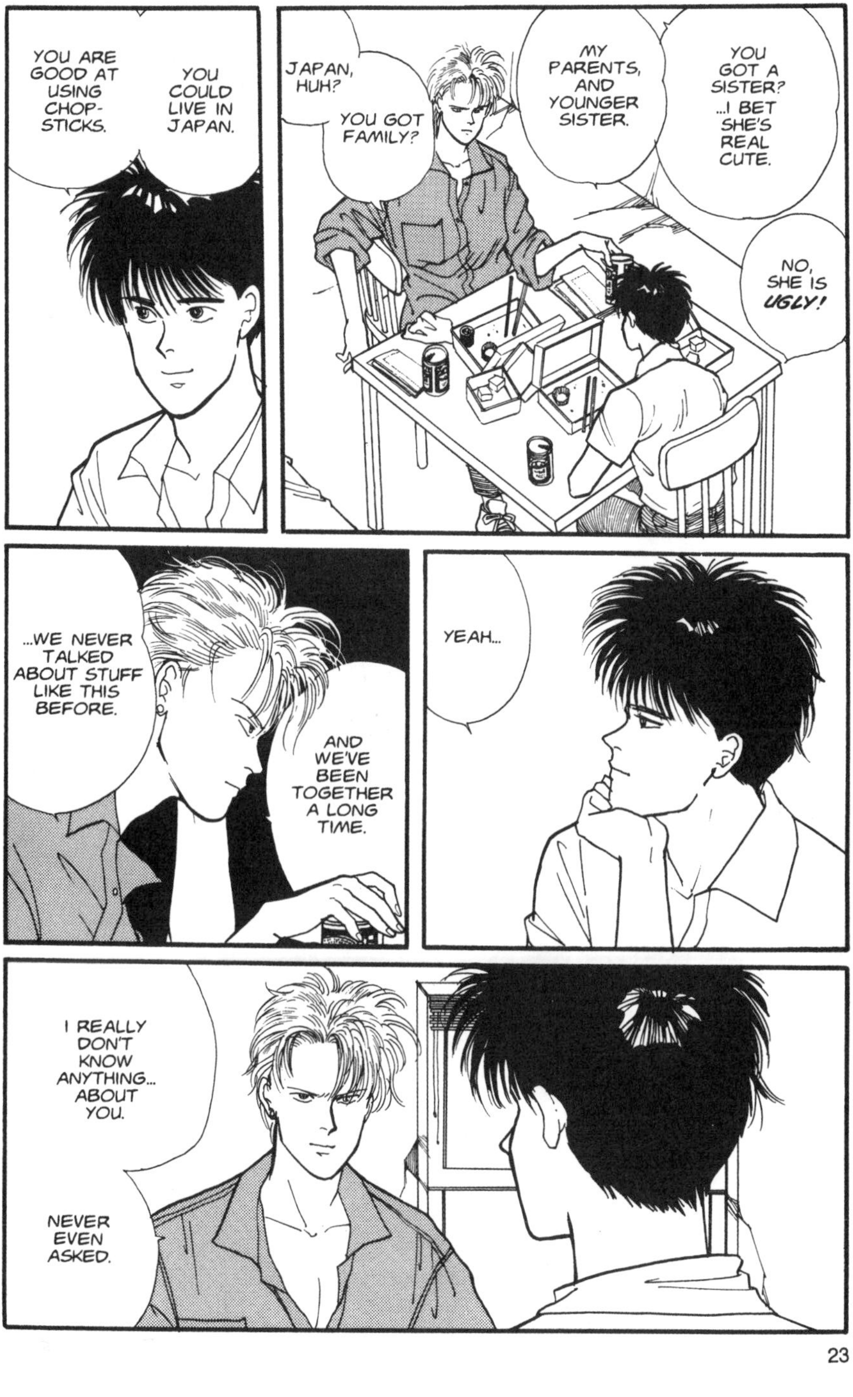
YOU ARE GOOD AT USING CHOP-STICKS.
YOU COULD LIVE IN JAPAN.
JAPAN, HUH?
YOU GOT FAMILY?
MY PARENTS, AND YOUNGER SISTER.
YOU GOT A SISTER? ...I BET SHE'S REAL CUTE.
NO, SHE IS *UGLY!*
...WE NEVER TALKED ABOUT STUFF LIKE THIS BEFORE.
AND WE'VE BEEN TOGETHER A LONG TIME.
YEAH...
I REALLY DON'T KNOW ANYTHING... ABOUT YOU.
NEVER EVEN ASKED.

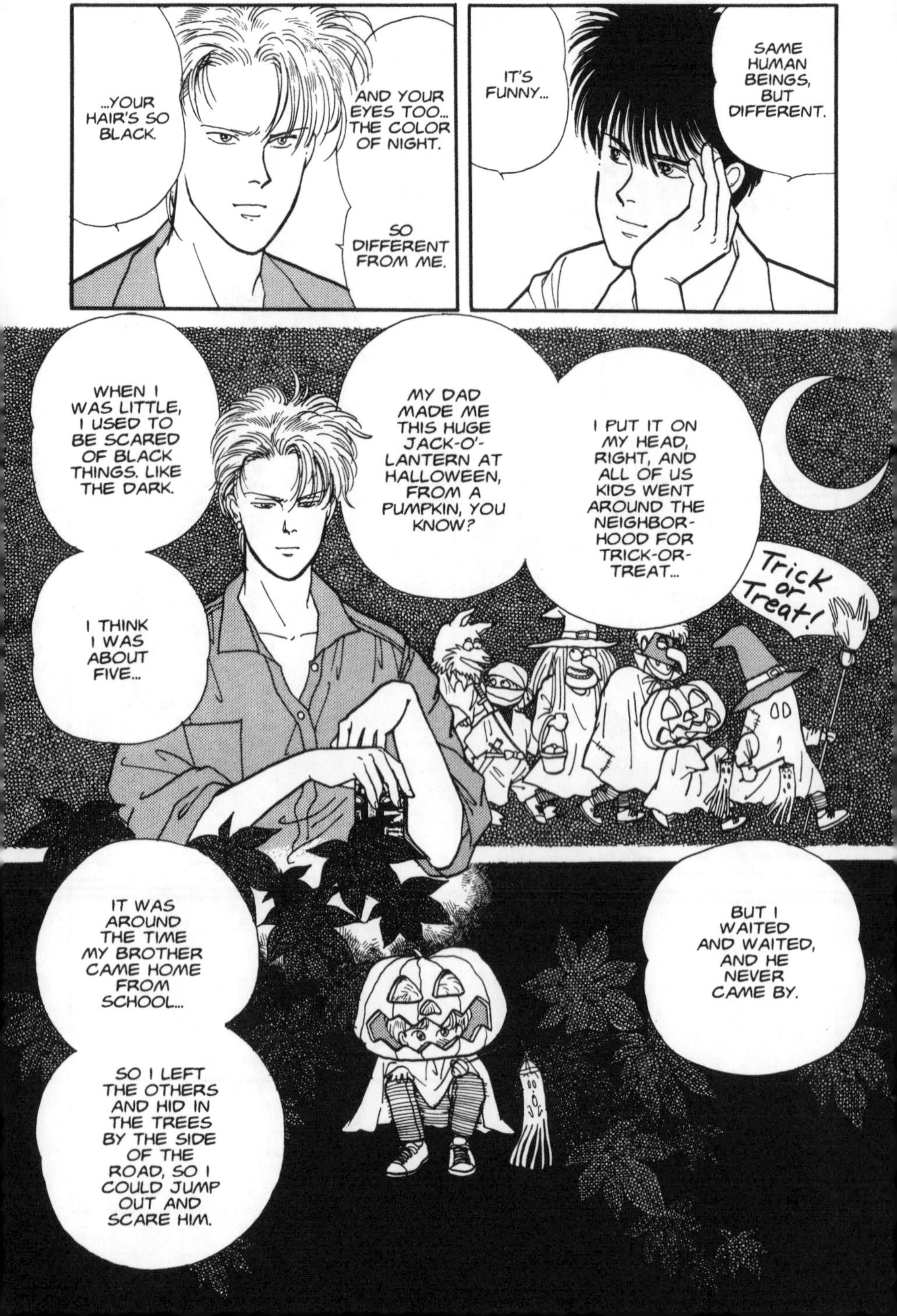
...YOUR HAIR'S SO BLACK.
AND YOUR EYES TOO... THE COLOR OF NIGHT.
SO DIFFERENT FROM ME.
IT'S FUNNY...
SAME HUMAN BEINGS, BUT DIFFERENT.
WHEN I WAS LITTLE, I USED TO BE SCARED OF BLACK THINGS. LIKE THE DARK.
I THINK I WAS ABOUT FIVE...
MY DAD MADE ME THIS HUGE JACK-O'-LANTERN AT HALLOWEEN, FROM A PUMPKIN, YOU KNOW?
I PUT IT ON MY HEAD, RIGHT, AND ALL OF US KIDS WENT AROUND THE NEIGHBOR-HOOD FOR TRICK-OR-TREAT...
Trick or Treat!
IT WAS AROUND THE TIME MY BROTHER CAME HOME FROM SCHOOL...
SO I LEFT THE OTHERS AND HID IN THE TREES BY THE SIDE OF THE ROAD, SO I COULD JUMP OUT AND SCARE HIM.
BUT I WAITED AND WAITED, AND HE NEVER CAME BY.

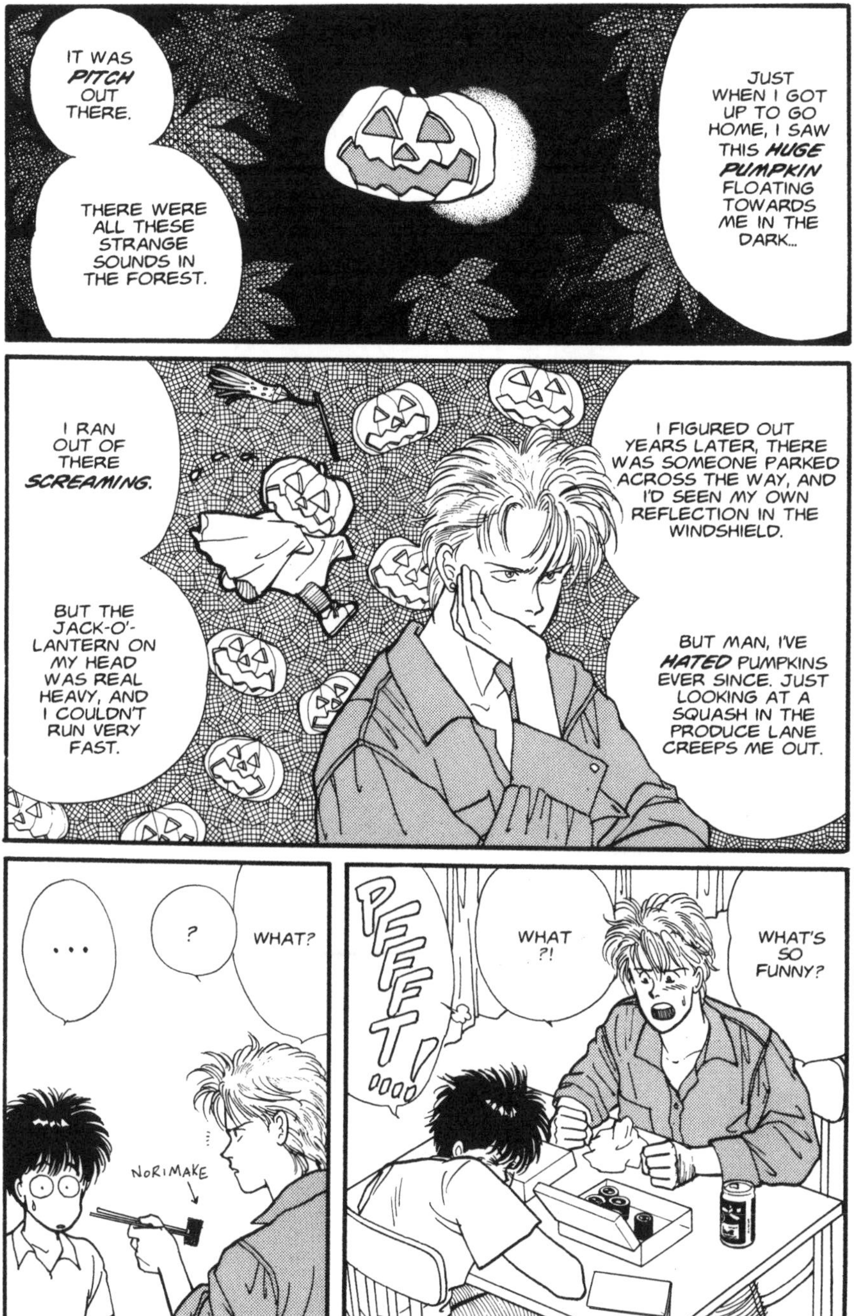

IT WAS PITCH OUT THERE.
THERE WERE ALL THESE STRANGE SOUNDS IN THE FOREST.
JUST WHEN I GOT UP TO GO HOME, I SAW THIS HUGE PUMPKIN FLOATING TOWARDS ME IN THE DARK...
I RAN OUT OF THERE SCREAMING.
BUT THE JACK-O'-LANTERN ON MY HEAD WAS REAL HEAVY, AND I COULDN'T RUN VERY FAST.
I FIGURED OUT YEARS LATER, THERE WAS SOMEONE PARKED ACROSS THE WAY, AND I'D SEEN MY OWN REFLECTION IN THE WINDSHIELD.
BUT MAN, I'VE HATED PUMPKINS EVER SINCE. JUST LOOKING AT A SQUASH IN THE PRODUCE LANE CREEPS ME OUT.
...
?
WHAT?
NORIMAKE
PFFFT!
WHAT ?!
WHAT'S SO FUNNY?

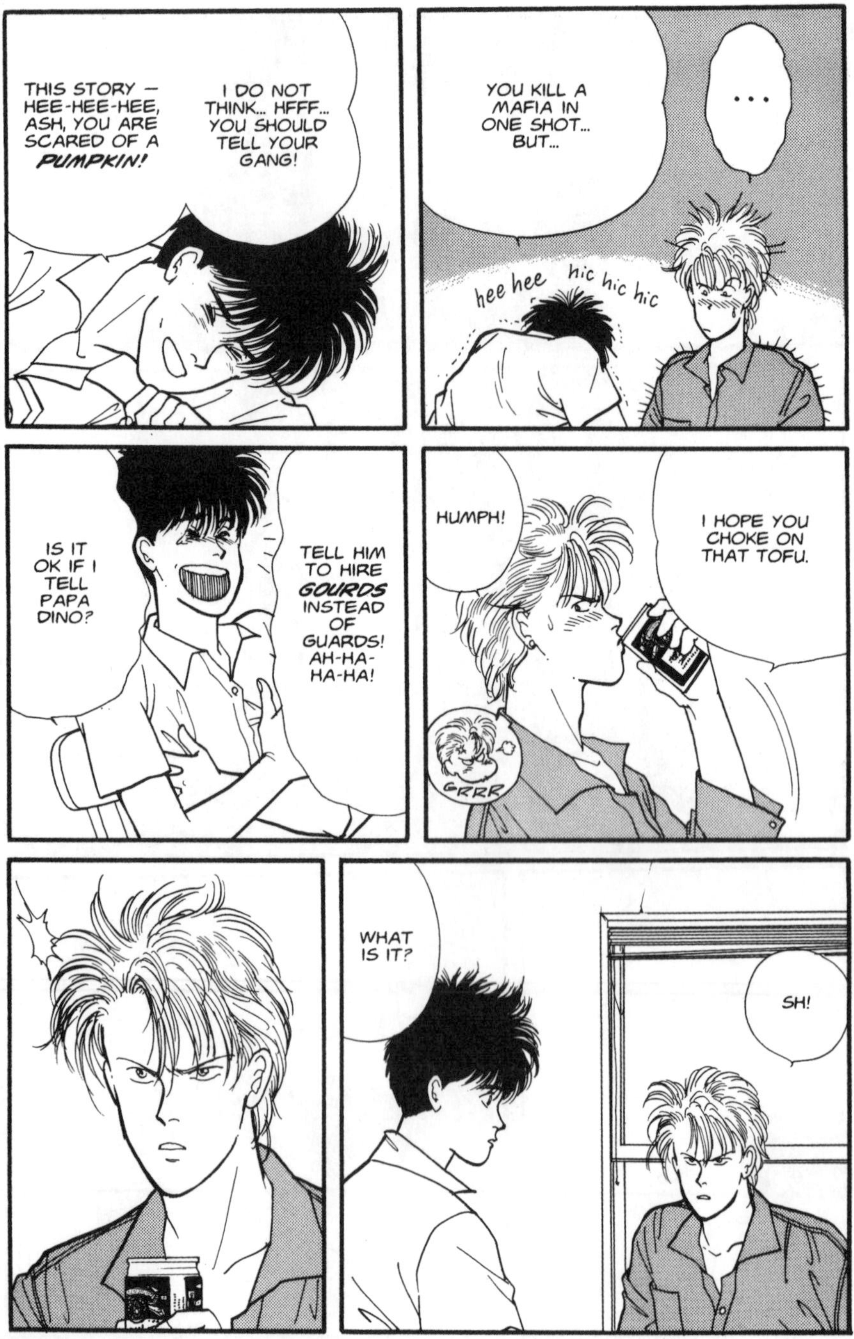
THIS STORY — HEE-HEE-HEE, ASH, YOU ARE SCARED OF A PUMPKIN!
I DO NOT THINK... HFFF... YOU SHOULD TELL YOUR GANG!
YOU KILL A MAFIA IN ONE SHOT... BUT...
...
hee hee
hic hic hic
IS IT OK IF I TELL PAPA DINO?
TELL HIM TO HIRE GOURDS INSTEAD OF GUARDS! AH-HA-HA-HA!
HUMPH!
I HOPE YOU CHOKE ON THAT TOFU.
GRRR
WHAT IS IT?
SH!

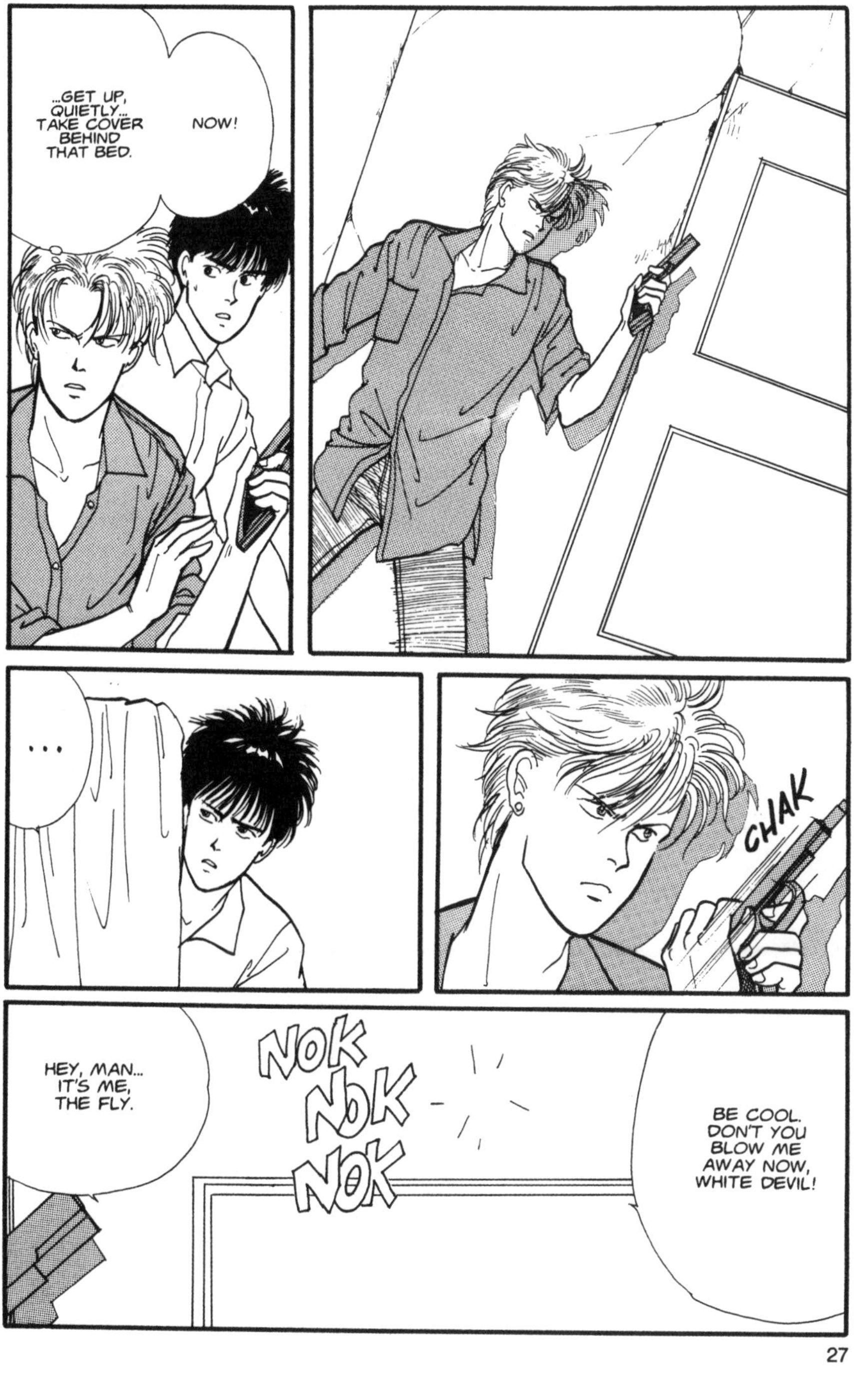

...GET UP, QUIETLY... TAKE COVER BEHIND THAT BED.
NOW!
...
CHAK
HEY, MAN... IT'S ME, THE FLY.
NOK NOK NOK
BE COOL. DON'T YOU BLOW ME AWAY NOW, WHITE DEVIL!

OH... IT'S YOU.

HEY MAN — BEEN A WHILE.

GRAPEVINE SAID YOU FINALLY BOUGHT IT...

BUT YOU LOOK PRETTY *FIRM* FOR A GHOST.

WHO CARES? YOU'D CUT A DEAL WITH SPIRITS. AS LONG AS THEY'RE PAYING CASH.

TRUE. COLD BODY STILL COL' BUSINESS, BABY. AND FO' MY PALE GHOST, RETURNED TO THIS WORLD OF PAIN...

I GOT ALL THE SHIT YO' SPIRIT CRY OUT FOR. *TOOT*-SWEET.

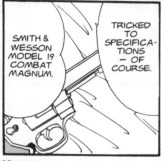

SMITH & WESSON MODEL 19 COMBAT MAGNUM.

TRICKED TO SPECIFICA-TIONS — OF COURSE.

MAN, THIS SHIT IS OLD. WHY YOU STILL GO WITH THIS SIX-GUN, COWBOY?

NOW TAKE THIS COLT GOVERNMENT .45. OLD. BUT TRUSTY NOT RUSTY. YOU-ESS-ARMY TESTED.

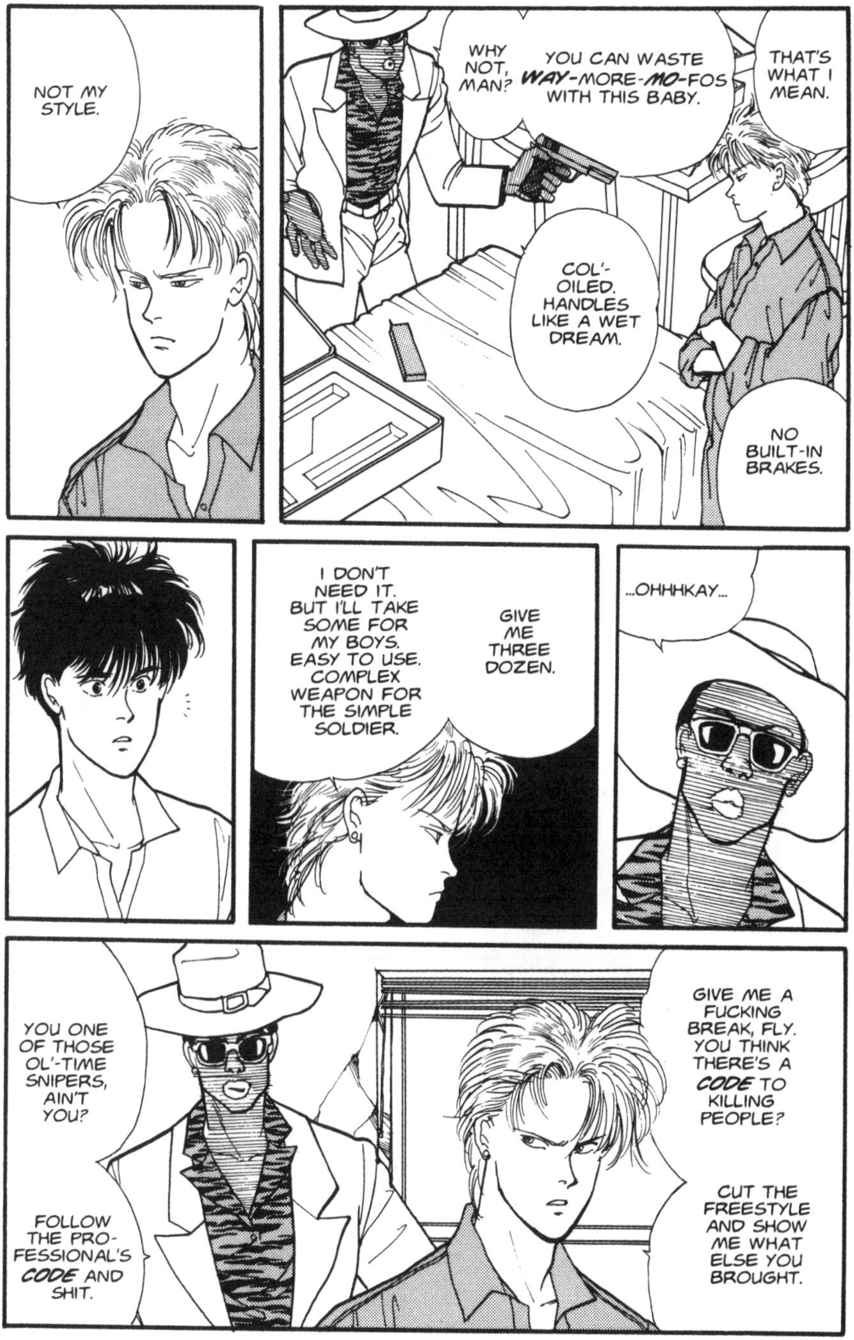
NOT MY STYLE.
WHY NOT, MAN?
YOU CAN WASTE WAY-MORE-MO-FOS WITH THIS BABY.
THAT'S WHAT I MEAN.
COL'-OILED. HANDLES LIKE A WET DREAM.
NO BUILT-IN BRAKES.
I DON'T NEED IT. BUT I'LL TAKE SOME FOR MY BOYS. EASY TO USE. COMPLEX WEAPON FOR THE SIMPLE SOLDIER.
GIVE ME THREE DOZEN.
...OHHHKAY...
YOU ONE OF THOSE OL'-TIME SNIPERS, AIN'T YOU?
FOLLOW THE PRO-FESSIONAL'S CODE AND SHIT.
GIVE ME A FUCKING BREAK, FLY. YOU THINK THERE'S A CODE TO KILLING PEOPLE?
CUT THE FREESTYLE AND SHOW ME WHAT ELSE YOU BROUGHT.

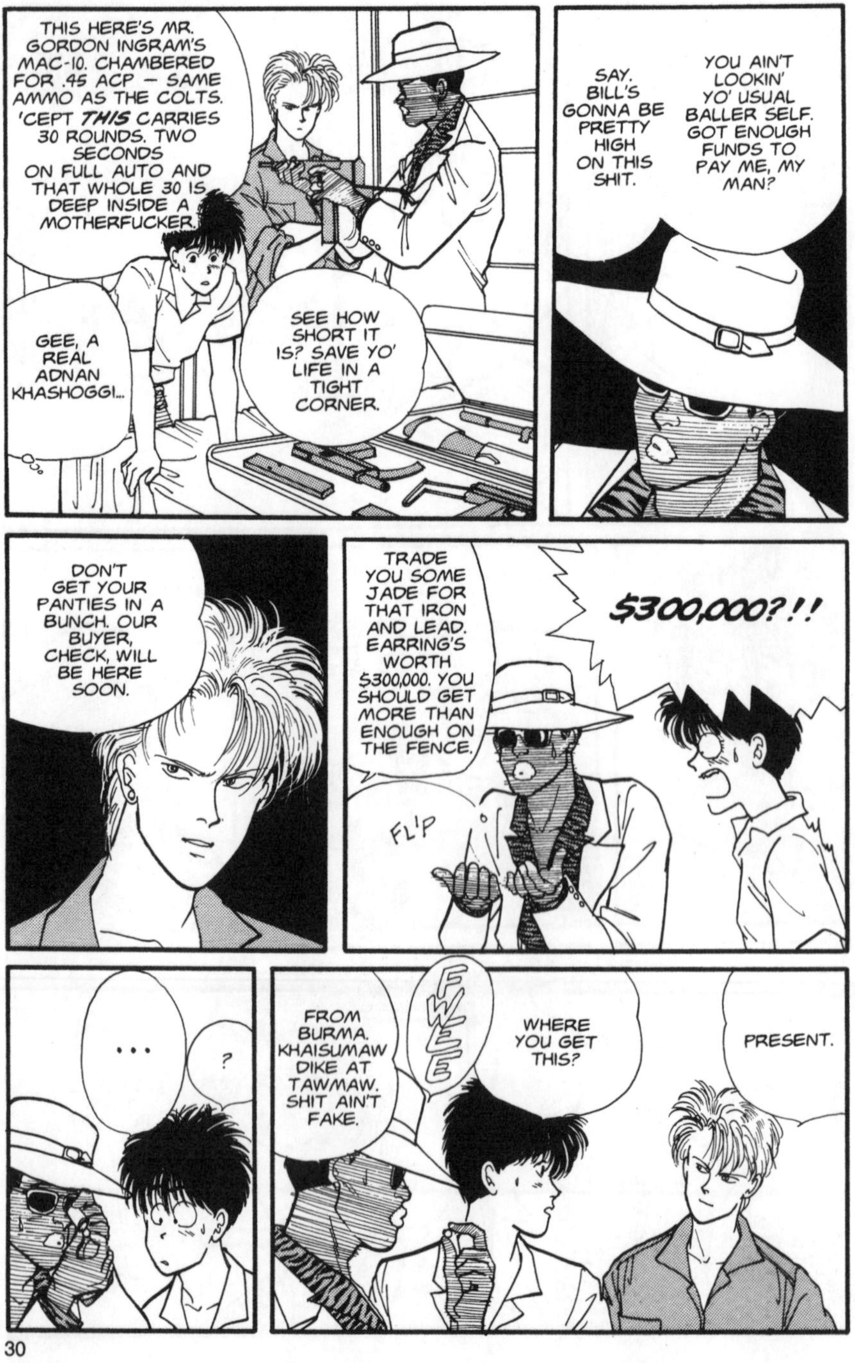
THIS HERE'S MR. GORDON INGRAM'S MAC-10. CHAMBERED FOR .45 ACP — SAME AMMO AS THE COLTS. 'CEPT *THIS* CARRIES 30 ROUNDS. TWO SECONDS ON FULL AUTO AND THAT WHOLE 30 IS DEEP INSIDE A MOTHERFUCKER.
GEE, A REAL ADNAN KHASHOGGI...
SEE HOW SHORT IT IS? SAVE YO' LIFE IN A TIGHT CORNER.
SAY. BILL'S GONNA BE PRETTY HIGH ON THIS SHIT.
YOU AIN'T LOOKIN' YO' USUAL BALLER SELF. GOT ENOUGH FUNDS TO PAY ME, MY MAN?
DON'T GET YOUR PANTIES IN A BUNCH. OUR BUYER, CHECK, WILL BE HERE SOON.
TRADE YOU SOME JADE FOR THAT IRON AND LEAD. EARRING'S WORTH $300,000. YOU SHOULD GET MORE THAN ENOUGH ON THE FENCE.
FL'P
$300,000?!!
...
?
FROM BURMA. KHAISUMAW DIKE AT TAWMAW. SHIT AIN'T FAKE.
FWEE
WHERE YOU GET THIS?
PRESENT.

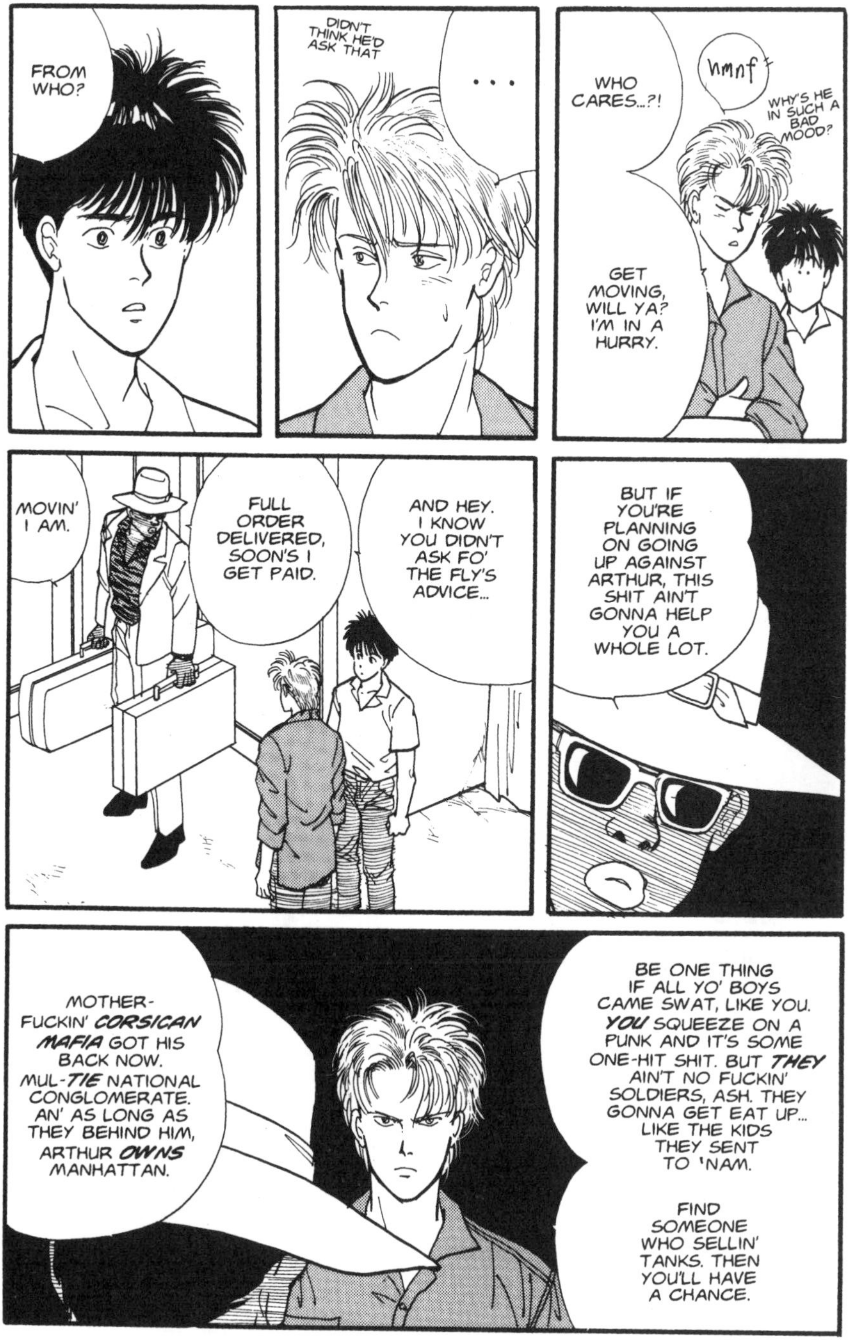
FROM WHO?
DIDN'T THINK HE'D ASK THAT
...
WHO CARES...?!
hmnf
WHY'S HE IN SUCH A BAD MOOD?
GET MOVING, WILL YA? I'M IN A HURRY.
MOVIN' I AM.
FULL ORDER DELIVERED, SOON'S I GET PAID.
AND HEY. I KNOW YOU DIDN'T ASK FO' THE FLY'S ADVICE...
BUT IF YOU'RE PLANNING ON GOING UP AGAINST ARTHUR, THIS SHIT AIN'T GONNA HELP YOU A WHOLE LOT.
MOTHER-FUCKIN' *CORSICAN MAFIA* GOT HIS BACK NOW. MUL-*TIE* NATIONAL CONGLOMERATE. AN' AS LONG AS THEY BEHIND HIM, ARTHUR *OWNS* MANHATTAN.
BE ONE THING IF ALL YO' BOYS CAME SWAT, LIKE YOU. *YOU* SQUEEZE ON A PUNK AND IT'S SOME ONE-HIT SHIT. BUT *THEY* AIN'T NO FUCKIN' SOLDIERS, ASH. THEY GONNA GET EAT UP... LIKE THE KIDS THEY SENT TO 'NAM.
FIND SOMEONE WHO SELLIN' TANKS. THEN YOU'LL HAVE A CHANCE.

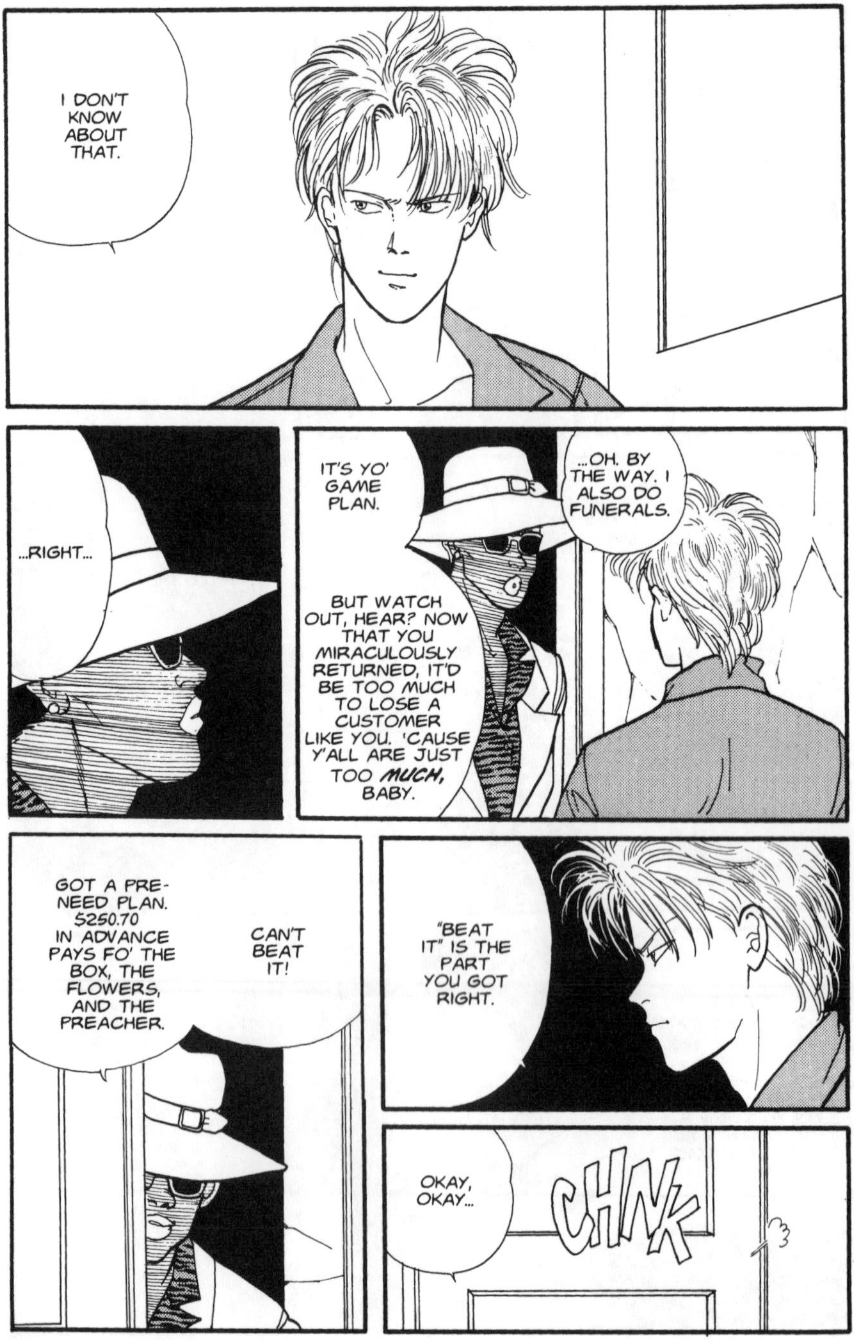
I DON'T KNOW ABOUT THAT.
...RIGHT...
IT'S YO' GAME PLAN.
BUT WATCH OUT, HEAR? NOW THAT YOU MIRACULOUSLY RETURNED, IT'D BE TOO MUCH TO LOSE A CUSTOMER LIKE YOU. 'CAUSE Y'ALL ARE JUST TOO MUCH, BABY.
...OH. BY THE WAY. I ALSO DO FUNERALS.
GOT A PRE-NEED PLAN. $250.70 IN ADVANCE PAYS FO' THE BOX, THE FLOWERS, AND THE PREACHER.
CAN'T BEAT IT!
"BEAT IT" IS THE PART YOU GOT RIGHT.
OKAY, OKAY...
CHNK

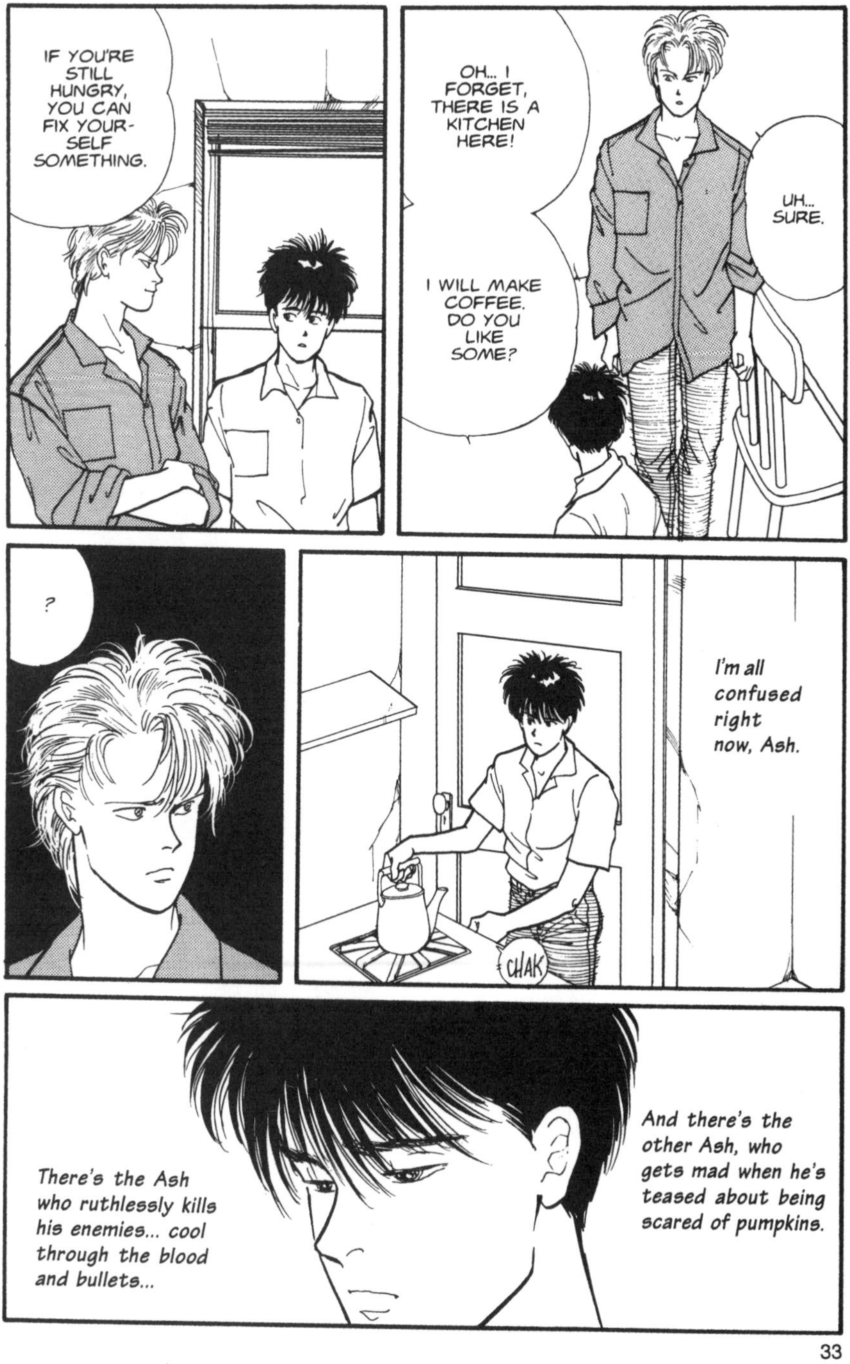

IF YOU'RE STILL HUNGRY, YOU CAN FIX YOUR-SELF SOMETHING.
OH... I FORGET, THERE IS A KITCHEN HERE!
I WILL MAKE COFFEE. DO YOU LIKE SOME?
UH... SURE.
?
I'm all confused right now, Ash.
CHAK
There's the Ash who ruthlessly kills his enemies... cool through the blood and bullets...
And there's the other Ash, who gets mad when he's teased about being scared of pumpkins.

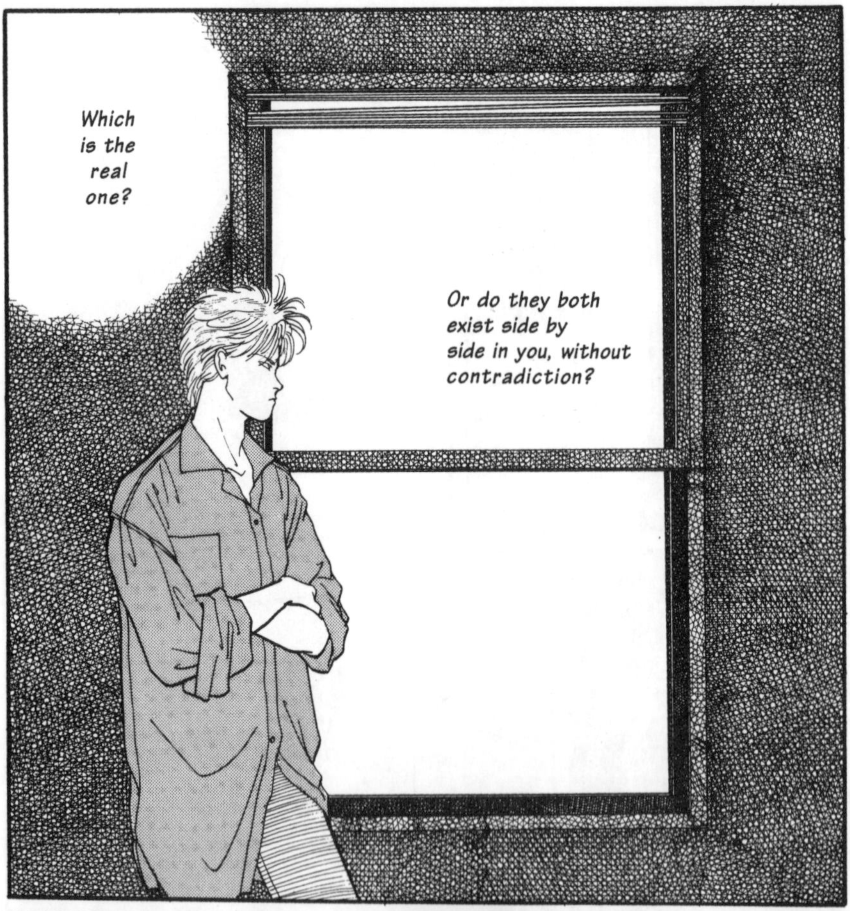
Which is the real one?
Or do they both exist side by side in you, without contradiction?

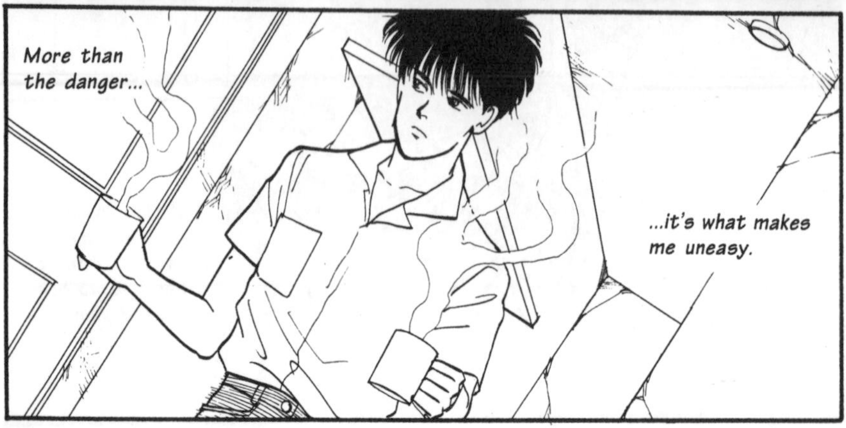
More than the danger...
...it's what makes me uneasy.

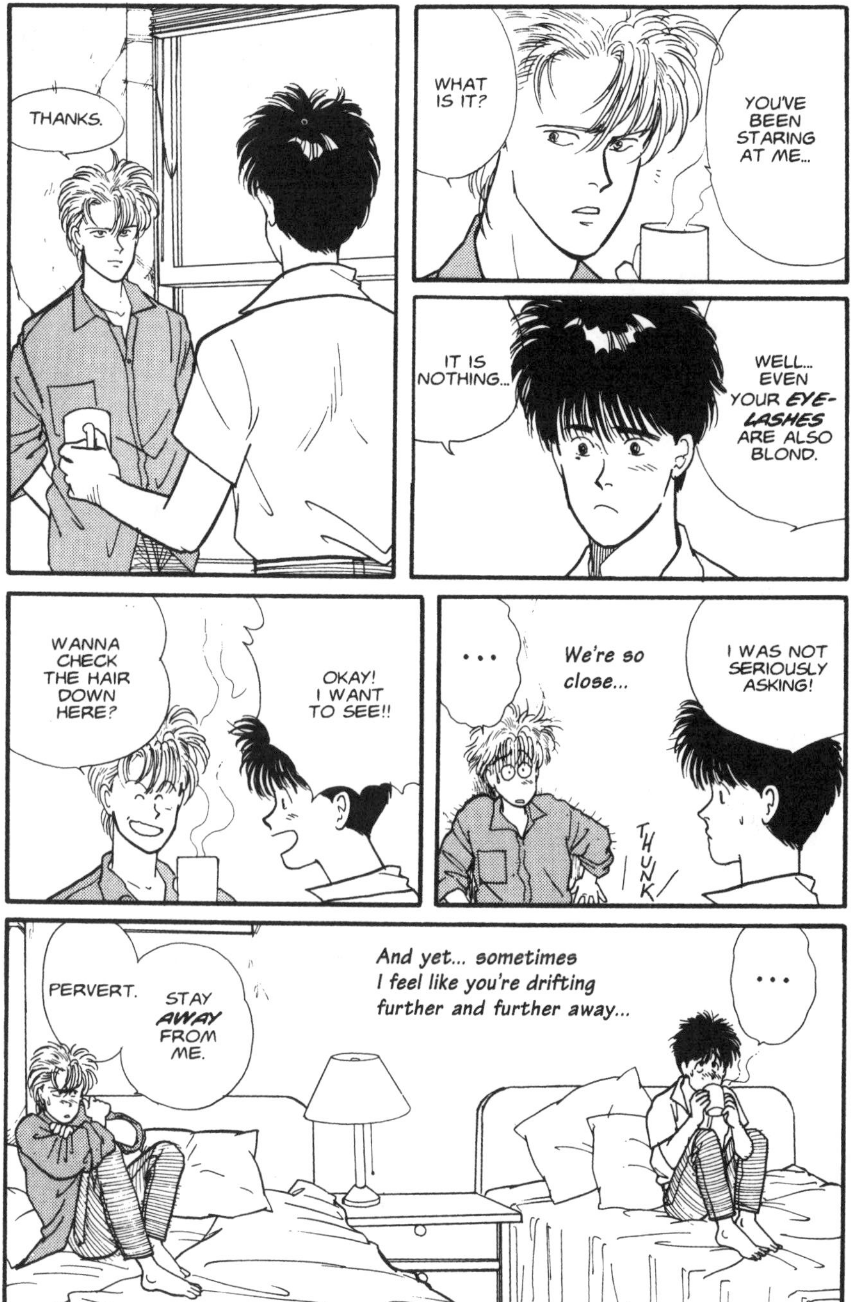
THANKS.
WHAT IS IT?
YOU'VE BEEN STARING AT ME...
IT IS NOTHING...
WELL... EVEN YOUR **EYE-LASHES** ARE ALSO BLOND.
WANNA CHECK THE HAIR DOWN HERE?
OKAY! I WANT TO SEE!!
...
We're so close...
I WAS NOT SERIOUSLY ASKING!
THUNK
PERVERT.
STAY **AWAY** FROM ME.
And yet... sometimes I feel like you're drifting further and further away...
...

New York Times
In New York, A Senator is
As a Friend, and a Hope
INITIAL INVESTIGATION
INDICATES
MURDERED BY
...
OUCH!
OOPS, SORRY.
DID THAT HURT?
"DID THAT HURT?"
LOOK, I'M VERY SENSITIVE, OKAY?
SOME KLUTZ MAN-HANDLES MY WOUND, YES, IT HURTS A LOT!
...
I CAN BANDAGE YOUR MOUTH FOR YOU TOO, ASH.

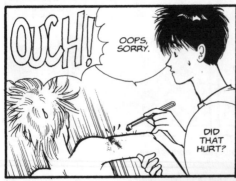

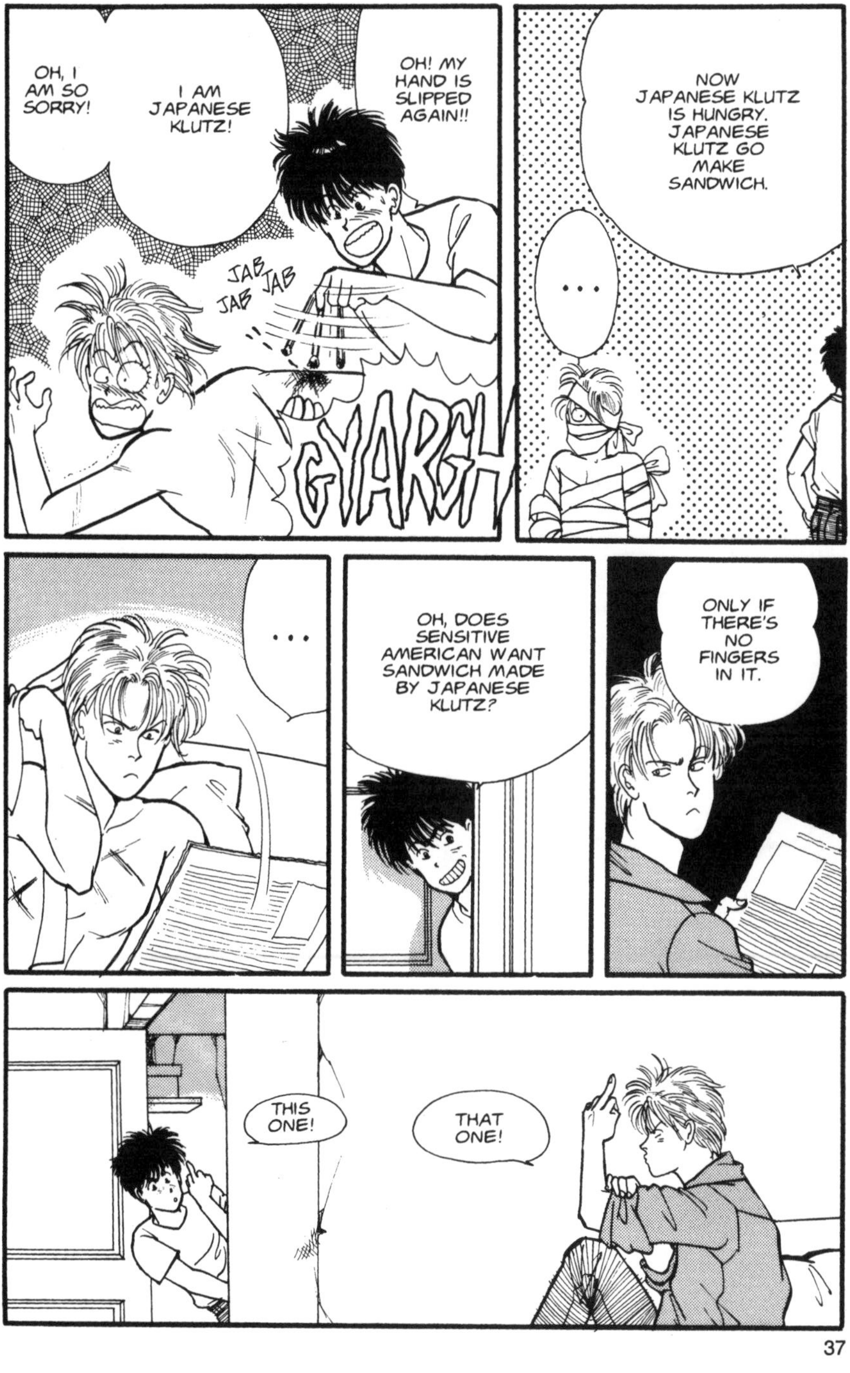
OH, I AM SO SORRY!
I AM JAPANESE KLUTZ!
OH! MY HAND IS SLIPPED AGAIN!!
JAB JAB JAB
GYARGH
NOW JAPANESE KLUTZ IS HUNGRY. JAPANESE KLUTZ GO MAKE SANDWICH.
...
...
OH, DOES SENSITIVE AMERICAN WANT SANDWICH MADE BY JAPANESE KLUTZ?
ONLY IF THERE'S NO FINGERS IN IT.
THIS ONE!
THAT ONE!

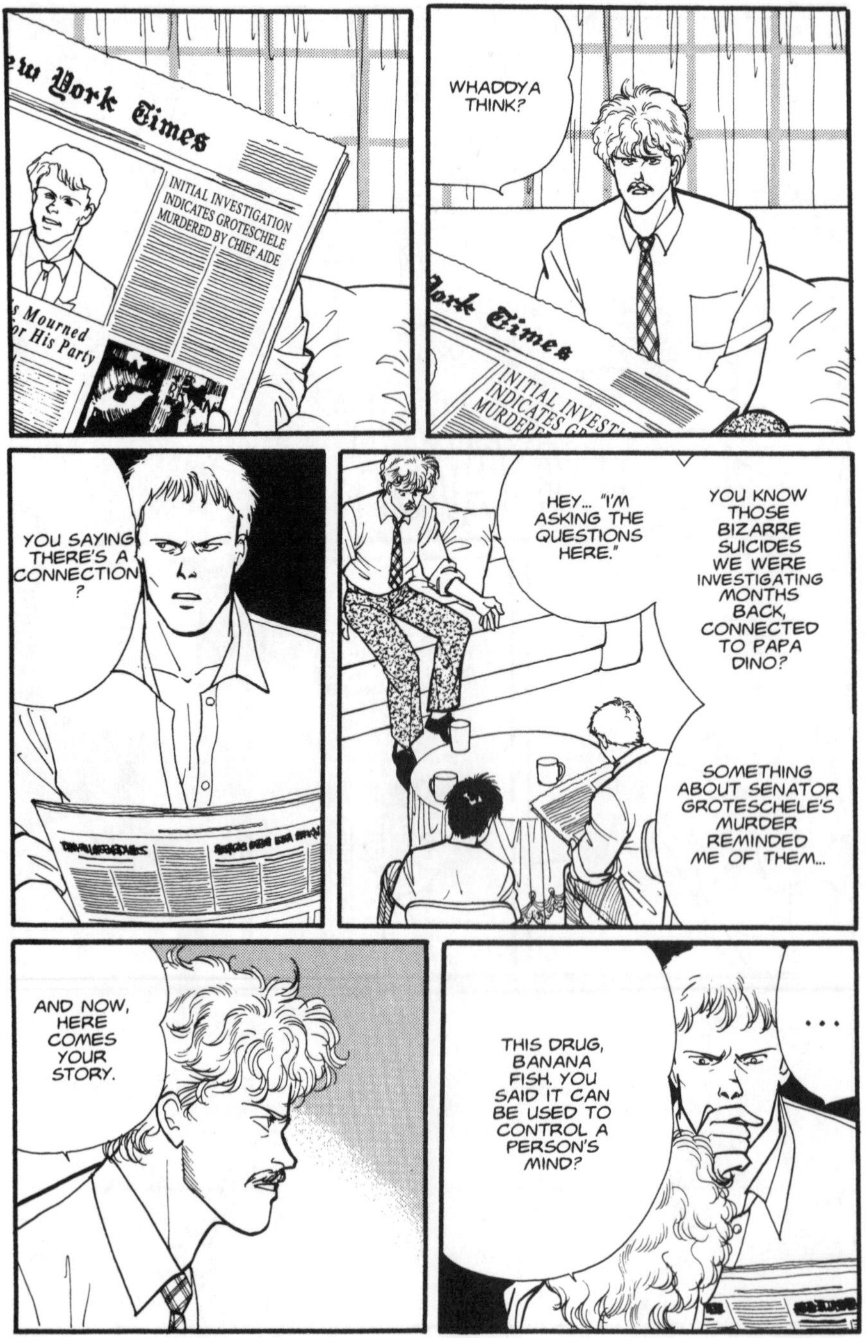

New York Times
INITIAL INVESTIGATION INDICATES GROTESCHELE MURDERED BY CHIEF AIDE
s Mourned or His Party
WHADDYA THINK?
York Times
INITIAL INVESTI INDICATES GR MURDERE
YOU SAYING THERE'S A CONNECTION ?
HEY... "I'M ASKING THE QUESTIONS HERE."
YOU KNOW THOSE BIZARRE SUICIDES WE WERE INVESTIGATING MONTHS BACK, CONNECTED TO PAPA DINO?
SOMETHING ABOUT SENATOR GROTESCHELE'S MURDER REMINDED ME OF THEM...
AND NOW, HERE COMES YOUR STORY.
THIS DRUG, BANANA FISH. YOU SAID IT CAN BE USED TO CONTROL A PERSON'S MIND?
...

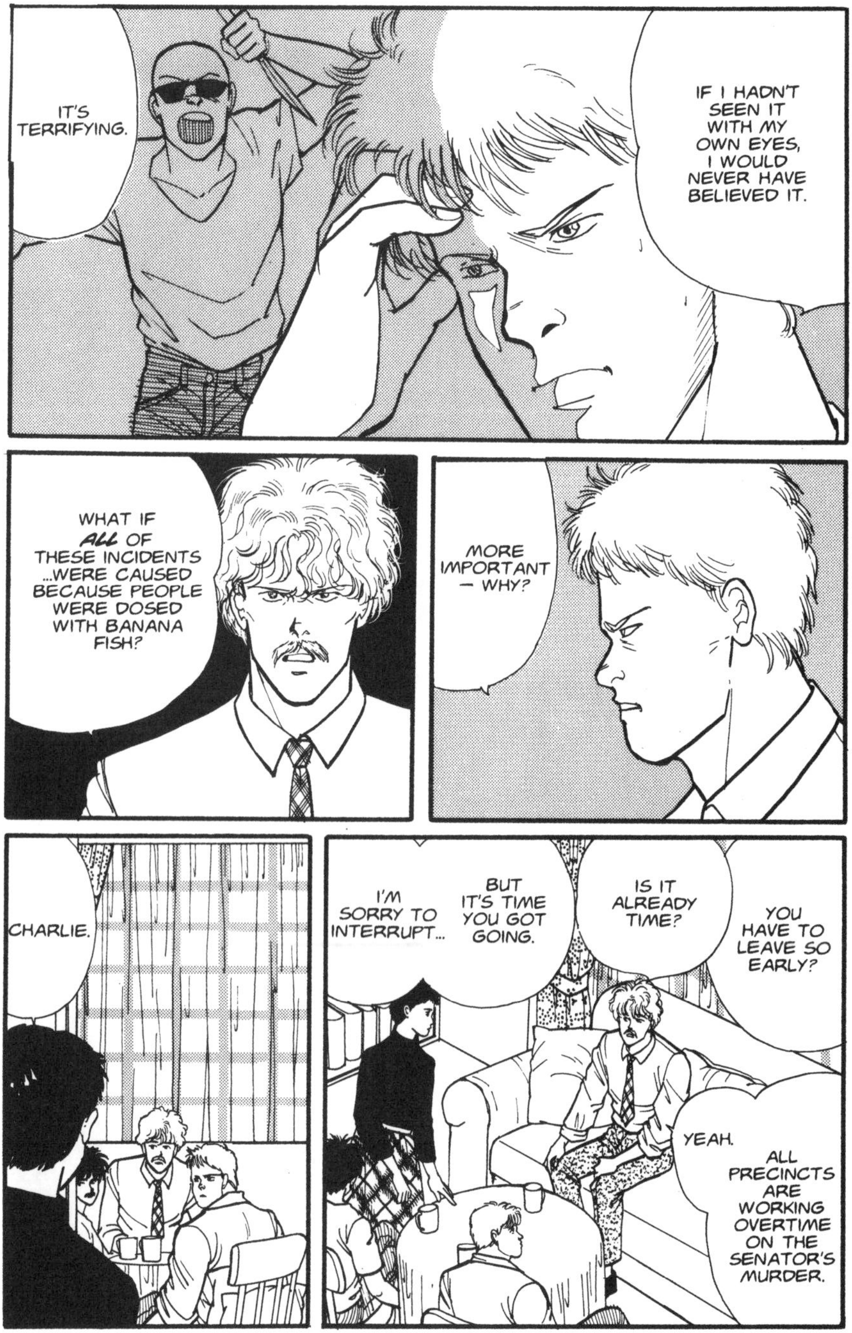
IT'S TERRIFYING.
IF I HADN'T SEEN IT WITH MY OWN EYES, I WOULD NEVER HAVE BELIEVED IT.
WHAT IF ALL OF THESE INCIDENTS ...WERE CAUSED BECAUSE PEOPLE WERE DOSED WITH BANANA FISH?
MORE IMPORTANT — WHY?
CHARLIE.
I'M SORRY TO INTERRUPT...
BUT IT'S TIME YOU GOT GOING.
IS IT ALREADY TIME?
YOU HAVE TO LEAVE SO EARLY?
YEAH.
ALL PRECINCTS ARE WORKING OVERTIME ON THE SENATOR'S MURDER.

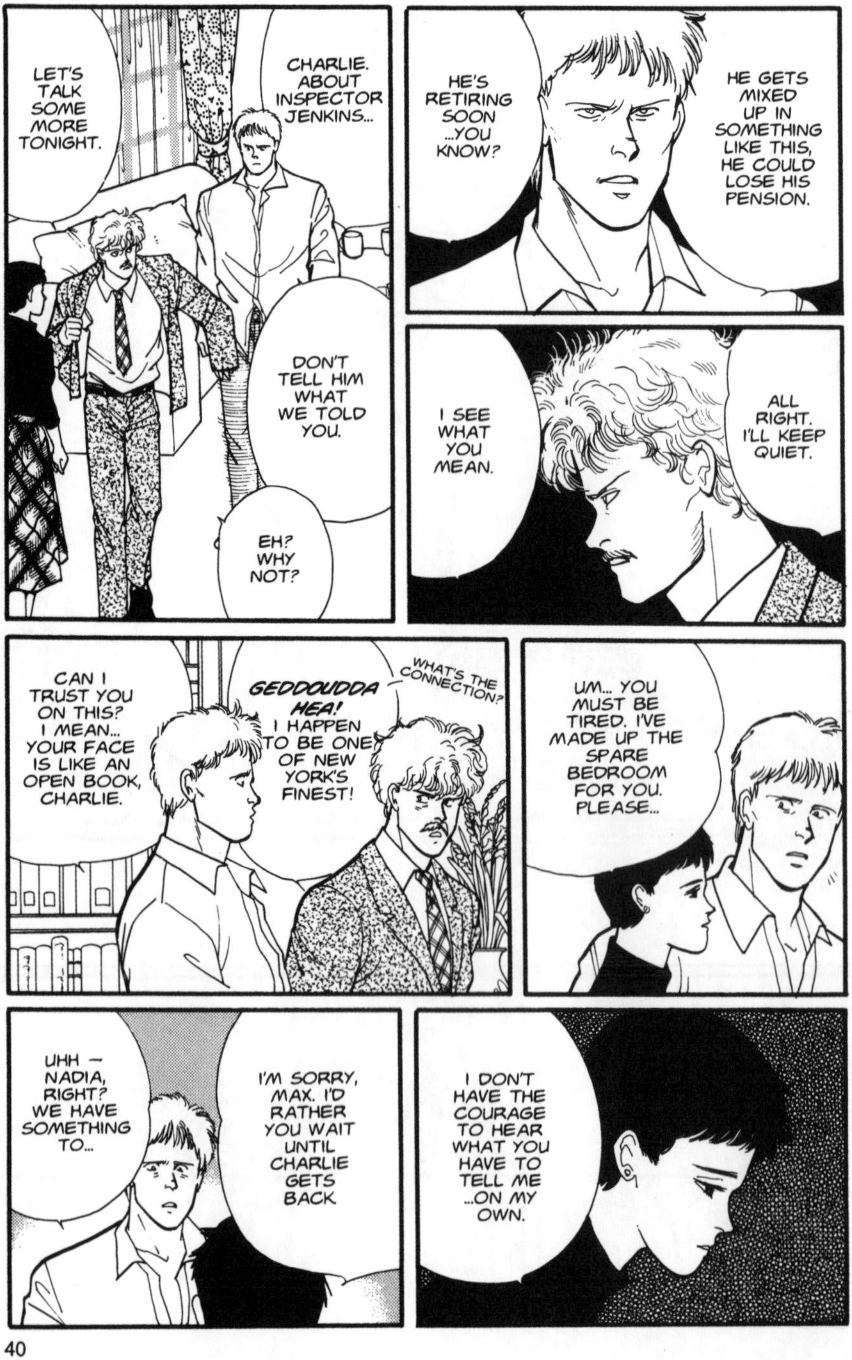
LET'S TALK SOME MORE TONIGHT.
CHARLIE. ABOUT INSPECTOR JENKINS...
DON'T TELL HIM WHAT WE TOLD YOU.
EH? WHY NOT?
HE'S RETIRING SOON ...YOU KNOW?
HE GETS MIXED UP IN SOMETHING LIKE THIS, HE COULD LOSE HIS PENSION.
I SEE WHAT YOU MEAN.
ALL RIGHT. I'LL KEEP QUIET.
CAN I TRUST YOU ON THIS? I MEAN... YOUR FACE IS LIKE AN OPEN BOOK, CHARLIE.
GEDDOUDDA HEA! I HAPPEN TO BE ONE OF NEW YORK'S FINEST!
WHAT'S THE CONNECTION?
UM... YOU MUST BE TIRED. I'VE MADE UP THE SPARE BEDROOM FOR YOU. PLEASE...
UHH — NADIA, RIGHT? WE HAVE SOMETHING TO...
I'M SORRY, MAX. I'D RATHER YOU WAIT UNTIL CHARLIE GETS BACK.
I DON'T HAVE THE COURAGE TO HEAR WHAT YOU HAVE TO TELL ME ...ON MY OWN.

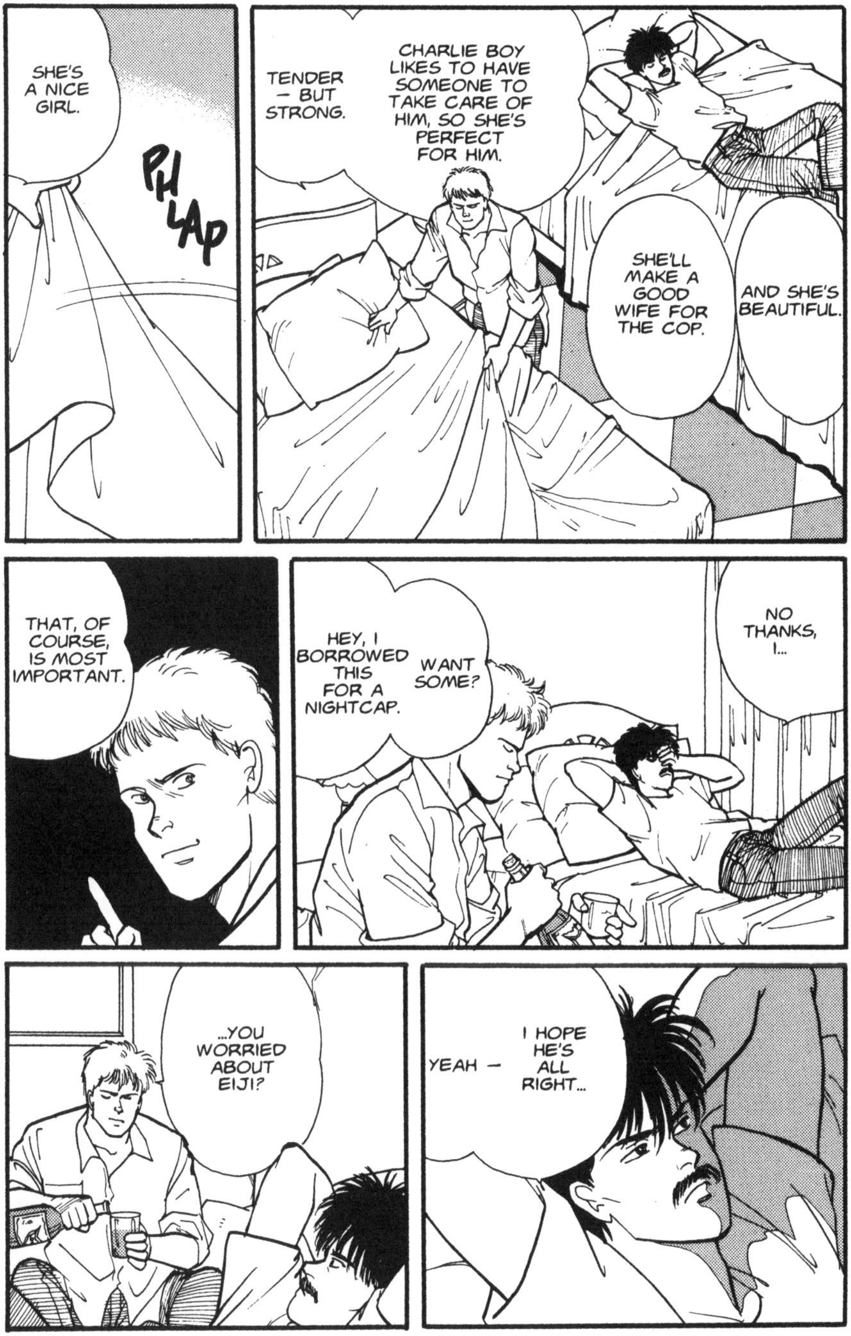
SHE'S A NICE GIRL.
PHLAP
TENDER — BUT STRONG.
CHARLIE BOY LIKES TO HAVE SOMEONE TO TAKE CARE OF HIM, SO SHE'S PERFECT FOR HIM.
SHE'LL MAKE A GOOD WIFE FOR THE COP.
AND SHE'S BEAUTIFUL.
THAT, OF COURSE, IS MOST IMPORTANT.
HEY, I BORROWED THIS FOR A NIGHTCAP.
WANT SOME?
NO THANKS, I...
...YOU WORRIED ABOUT EIJI?
YEAH —
I HOPE HE'S ALL RIGHT...

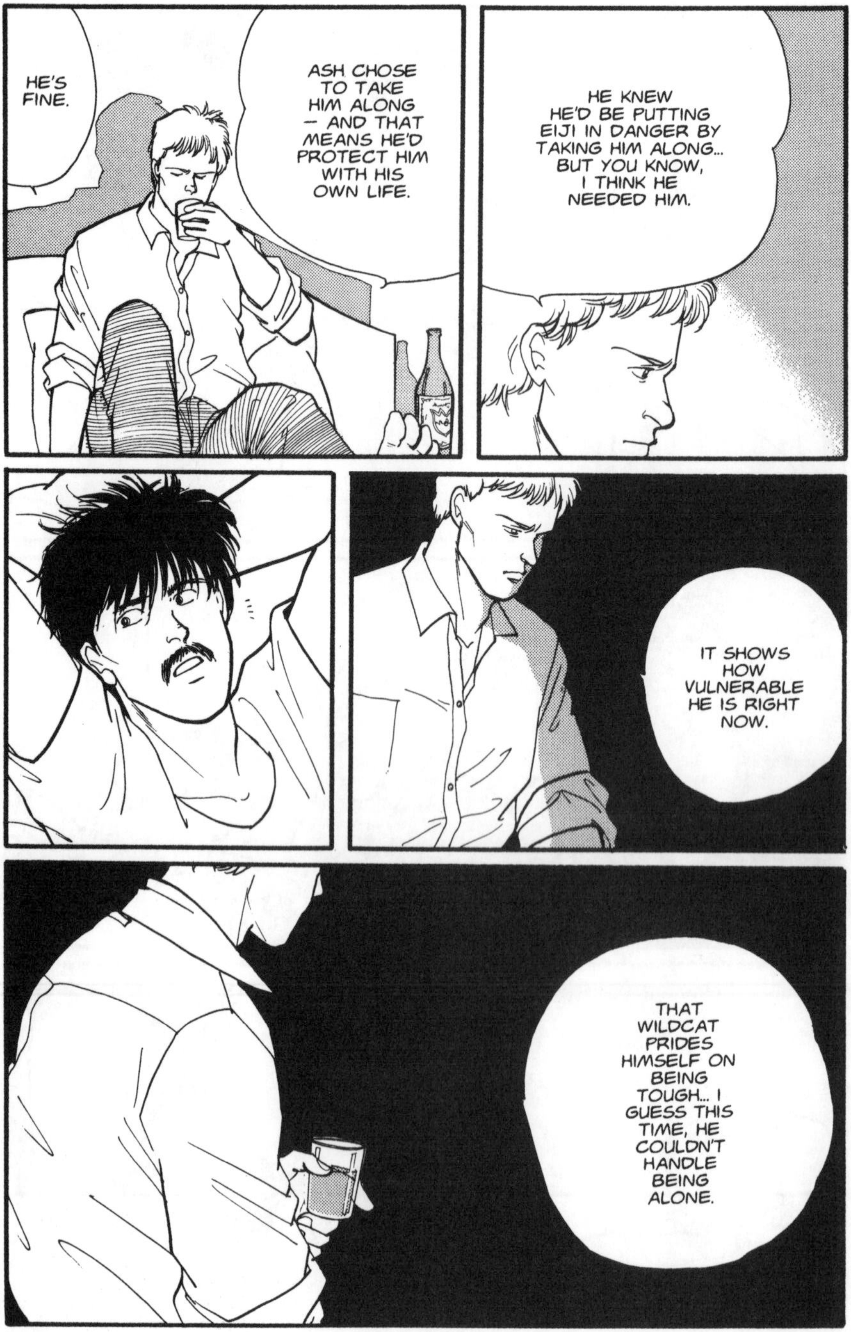
HE'S FINE.
ASH CHOSE TO TAKE HIM ALONG — AND THAT MEANS HE'D PROTECT HIM WITH HIS OWN LIFE.
HE KNEW HE'D BE PUTTING EIJI IN DANGER BY TAKING HIM ALONG... BUT YOU KNOW, I THINK HE NEEDED HIM.
IT SHOWS HOW VULNERABLE HE IS RIGHT NOW.
THAT WILDCAT PRIDES HIMSELF ON BEING TOUGH... I GUESS THIS TIME, HE COULDN'T HANDLE BEING ALONE.

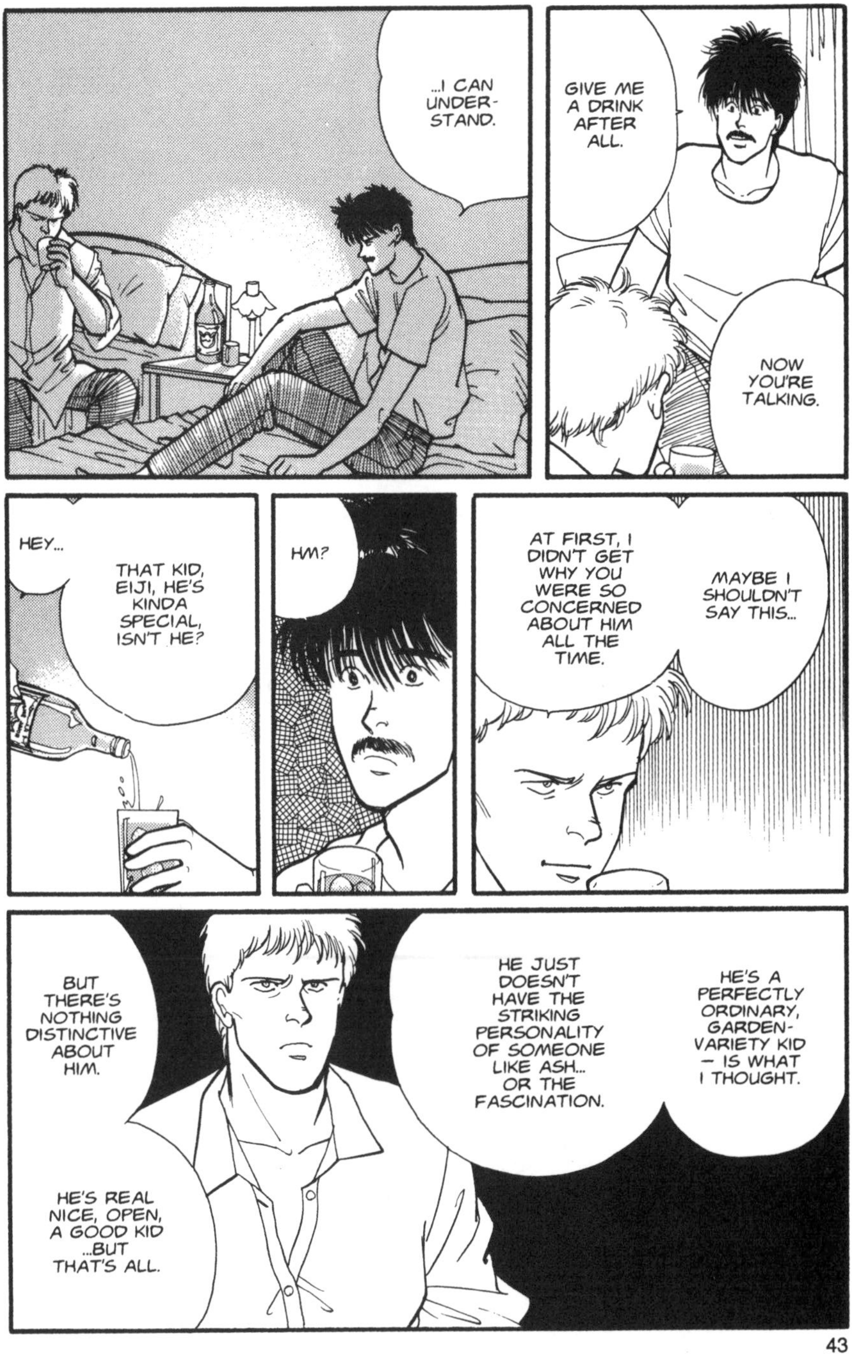
...I CAN UNDER-STAND.
GIVE ME A DRINK AFTER ALL.
NOW YOU'RE TALKING.
HEY...
THAT KID, EIJI, HE'S KINDA SPECIAL, ISN'T HE?
HM?
AT FIRST, I DIDN'T GET WHY YOU WERE SO CONCERNED ABOUT HIM ALL THE TIME.
MAYBE I SHOULDN'T SAY THIS...
BUT THERE'S NOTHING DISTINCTIVE ABOUT HIM.
HE JUST DOESN'T HAVE THE STRIKING PERSONALITY OF SOMEONE LIKE ASH... OR THE FASCINATION.
HE'S A PERFECTLY ORDINARY, GARDEN-VARIETY KID — IS WHAT I THOUGHT.
HE'S REAL NICE, OPEN, A GOOD KID ...BUT THAT'S ALL.

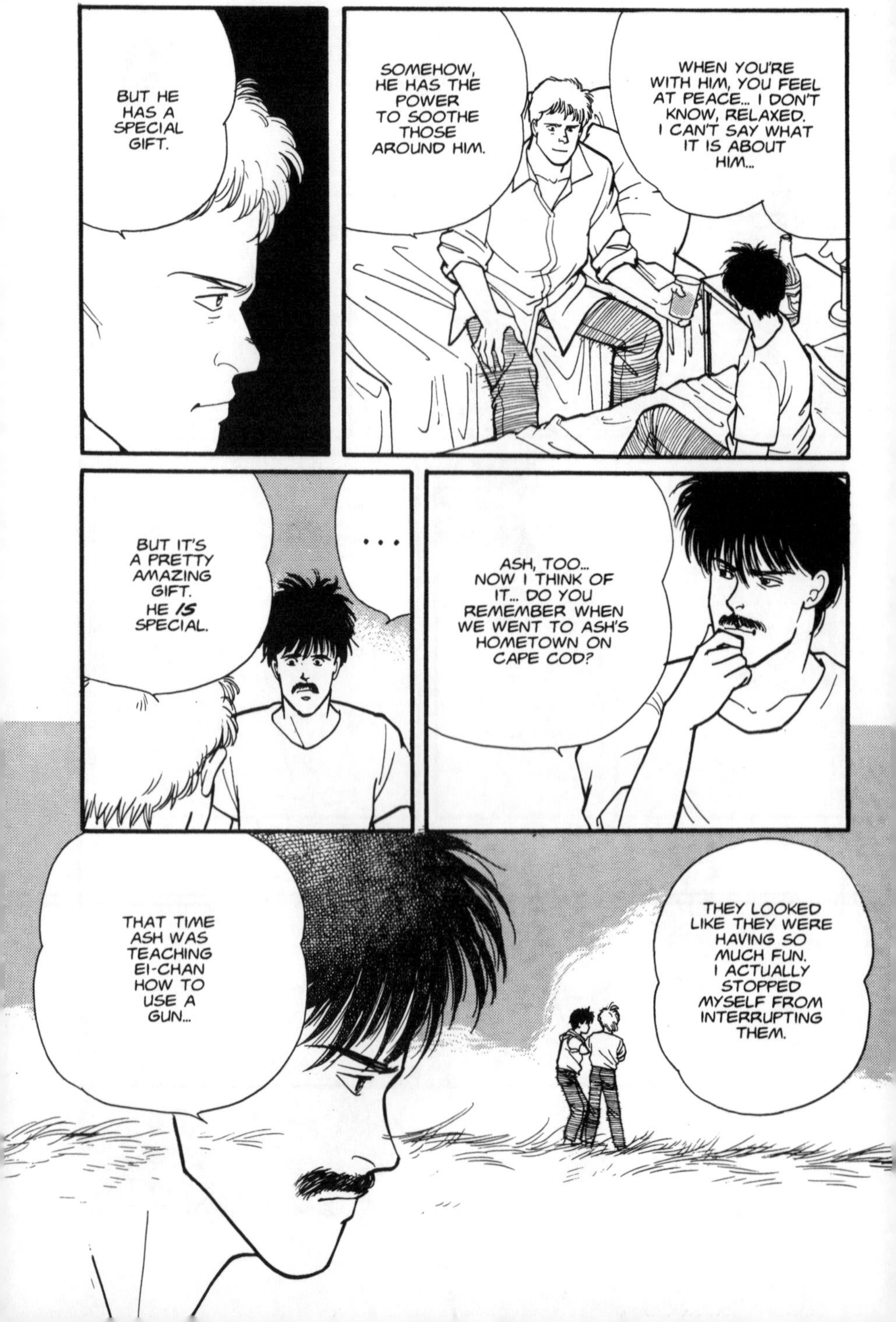
BUT HE HAS A SPECIAL GIFT.
SOMEHOW, HE HAS THE POWER TO SOOTHE THOSE AROUND HIM.
WHEN YOU'RE WITH HIM, YOU FEEL AT PEACE... I DON'T KNOW, RELAXED. I CAN'T SAY WHAT IT IS ABOUT HIM...
BUT IT'S A PRETTY AMAZING GIFT. HE *IS* SPECIAL.
...
ASH, TOO... NOW I THINK OF IT... DO YOU REMEMBER WHEN WE WENT TO ASH'S HOMETOWN ON CAPE COD?
THAT TIME ASH WAS TEACHING EI-CHAN HOW TO USE A GUN...
THEY LOOKED LIKE THEY WERE HAVING SO MUCH FUN. I ACTUALLY STOPPED MYSELF FROM INTERRUPTING THEM.

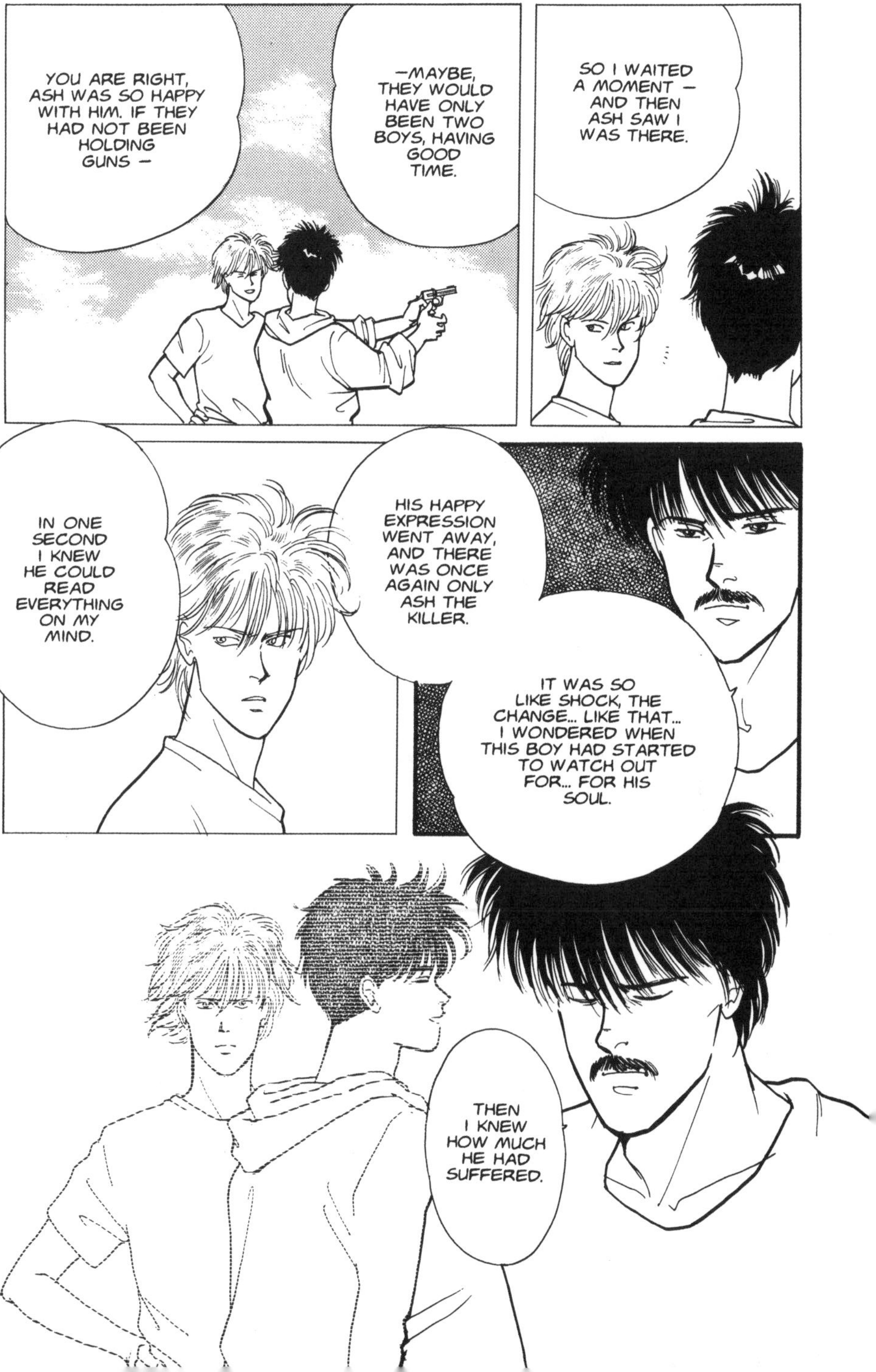
YOU ARE RIGHT, ASH WAS SO HAPPY WITH HIM. IF THEY HAD NOT BEEN HOLDING GUNS –
–MAYBE, THEY WOULD HAVE ONLY BEEN TWO BOYS, HAVING GOOD TIME.
SO I WAITED A MOMENT – AND THEN ASH SAW I WAS THERE.
IN ONE SECOND I KNEW HE COULD READ EVERYTHING ON MY MIND.
HIS HAPPY EXPRESSION WENT AWAY, AND THERE WAS ONCE AGAIN ONLY ASH THE KILLER.
IT WAS SO LIKE SHOCK, THE CHANGE... LIKE THAT... I WONDERED WHEN THIS BOY HAD STARTED TO WATCH OUT FOR... FOR HIS SOUL.
THEN I KNEW HOW MUCH HE HAD SUFFERED.

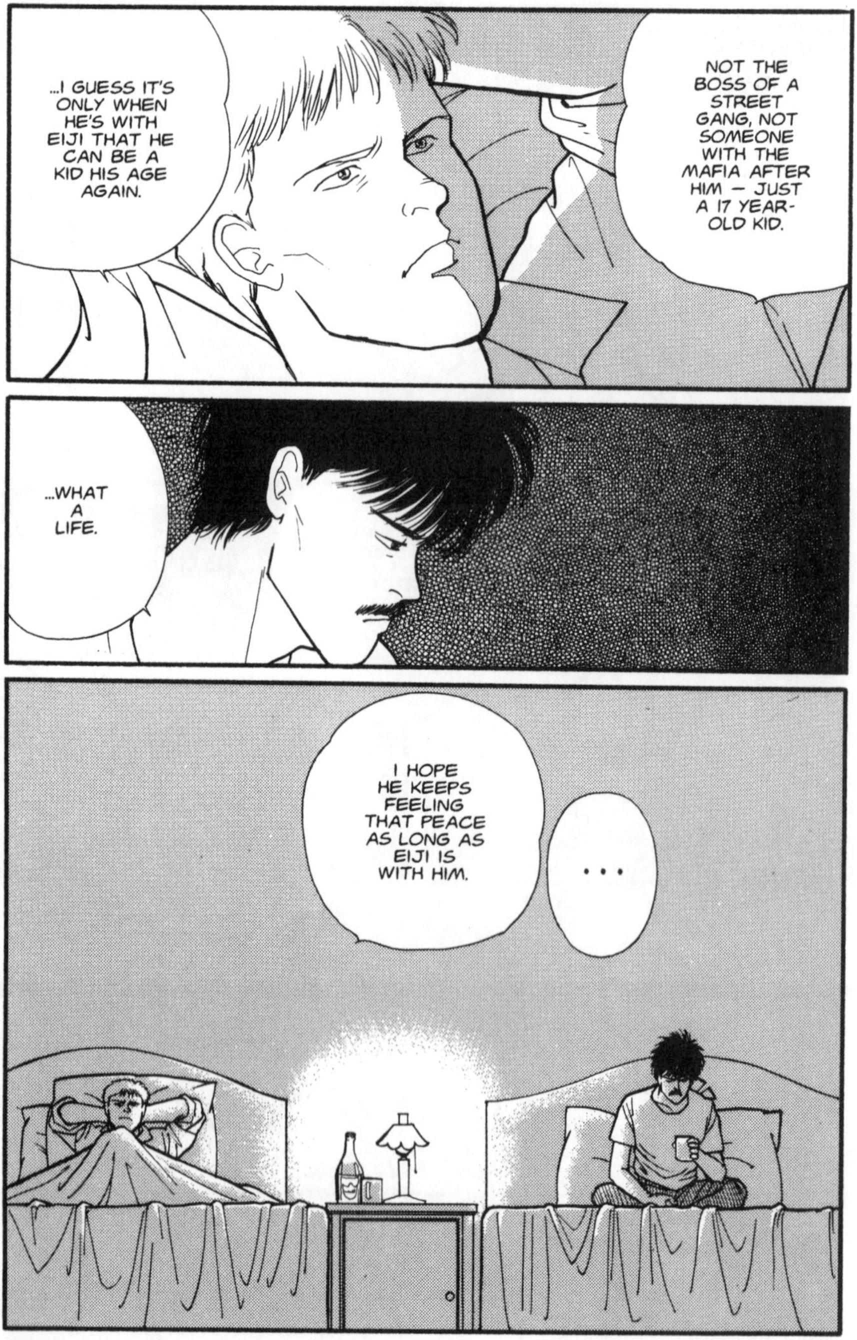
...I GUESS IT'S ONLY WHEN HE'S WITH EIJI THAT HE CAN BE A KID HIS AGE AGAIN.
NOT THE BOSS OF A STREET GANG, NOT SOMEONE WITH THE MAFIA AFTER HIM — JUST A 17 YEAR-OLD KID.
...WHAT A LIFE.
I HOPE HE KEEPS FEELING THAT PEACE AS LONG AS EIJI IS WITH HIM.
. . .

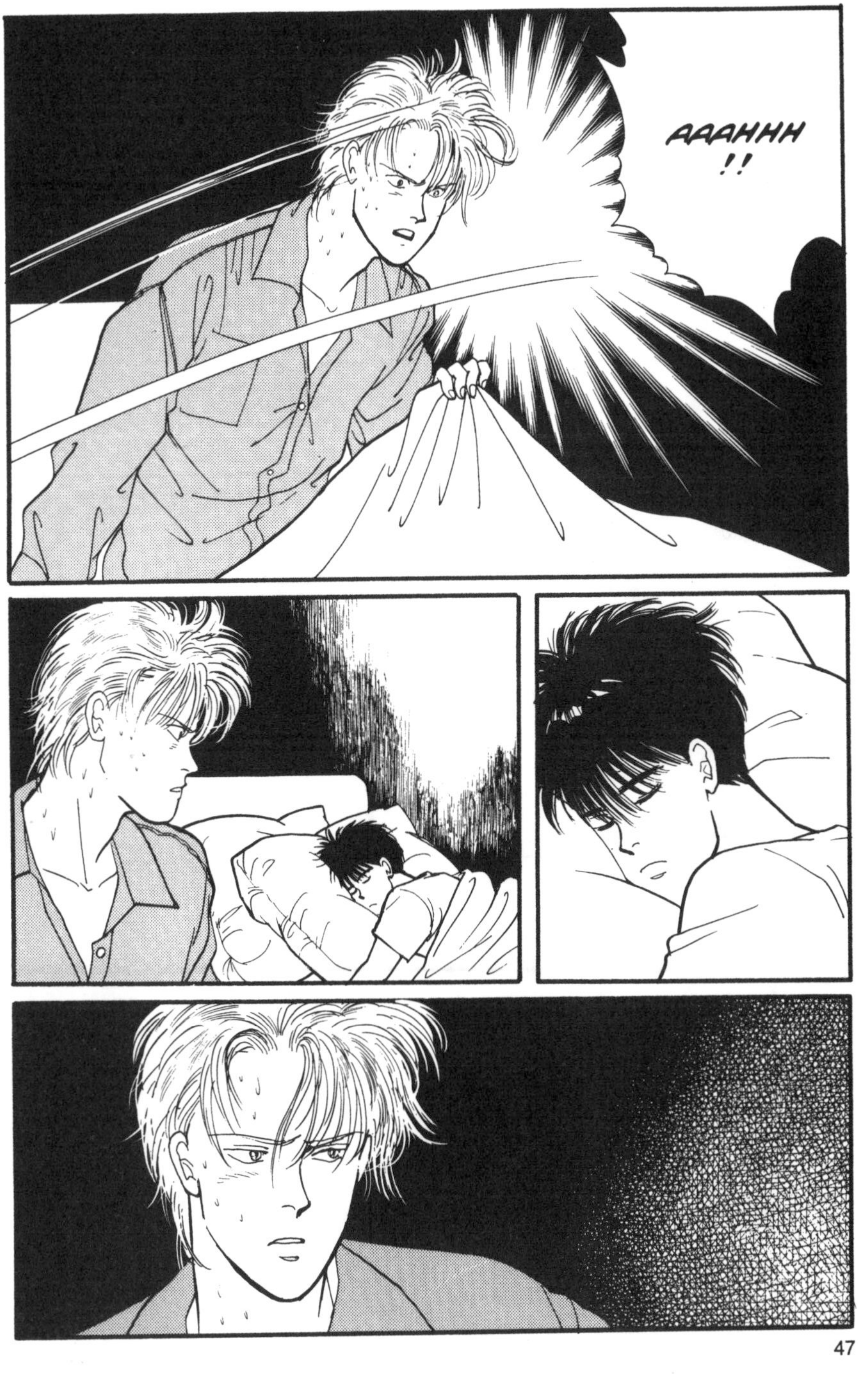
AAAHHH
!!

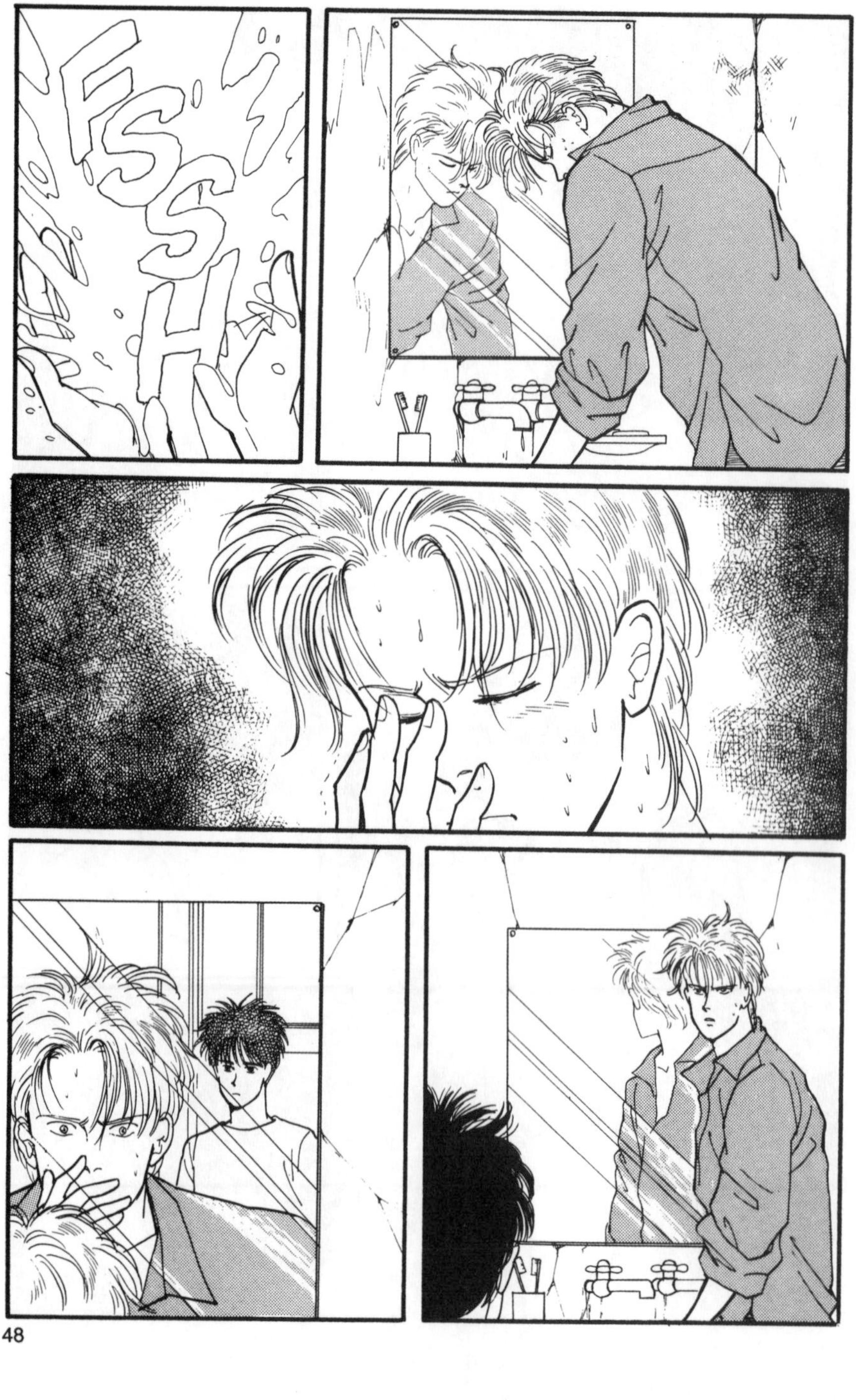
FSSH

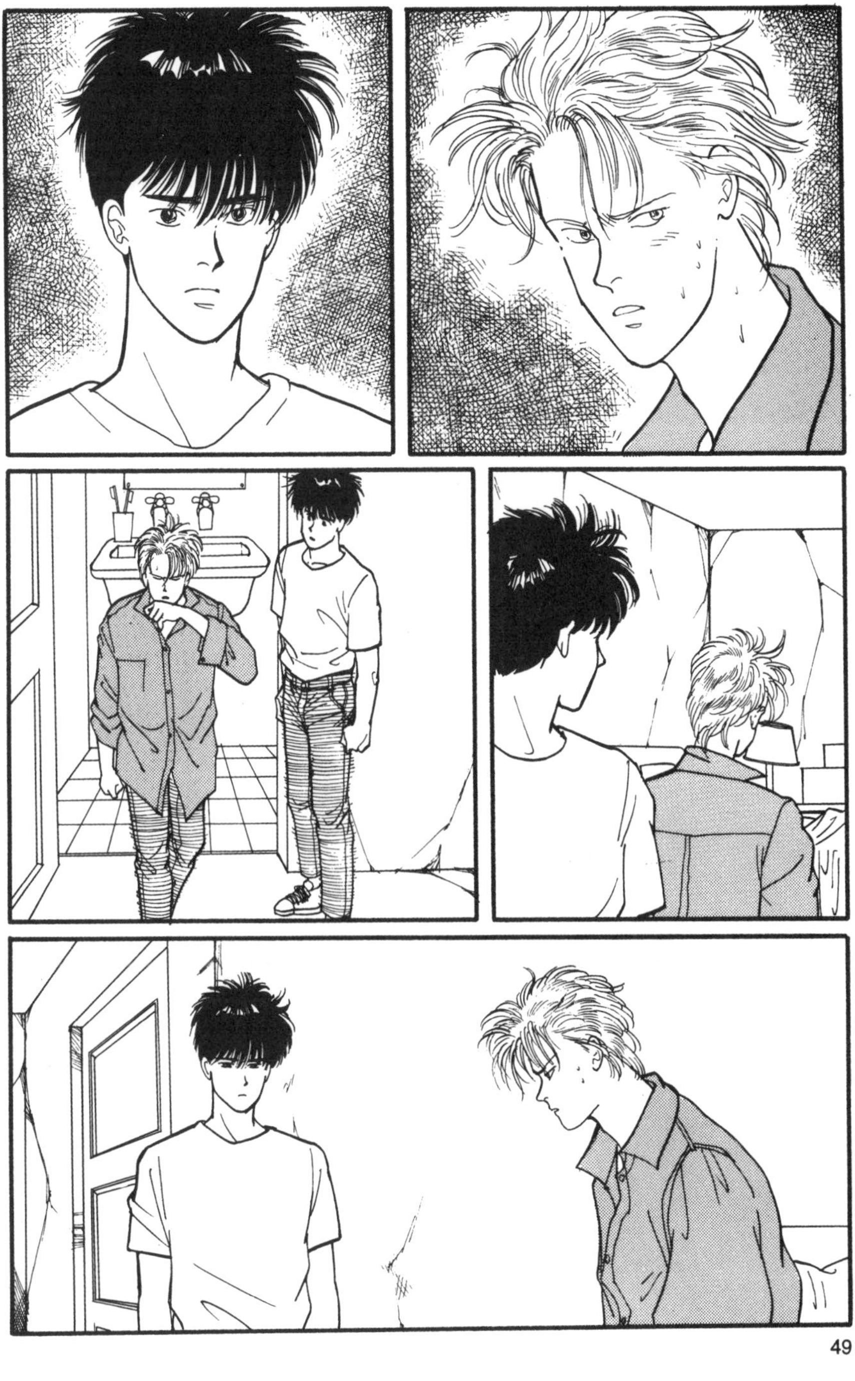

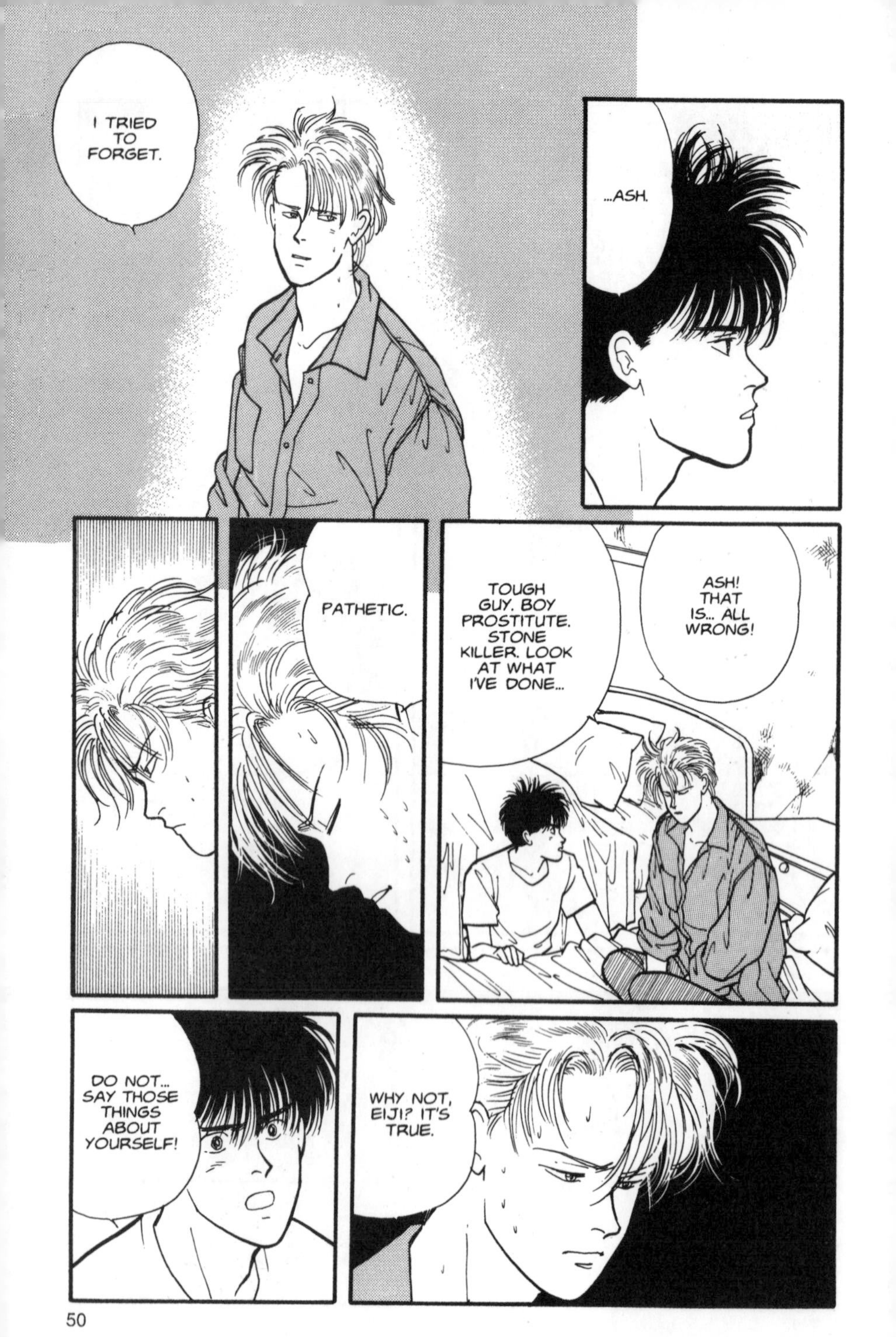
I TRIED TO FORGET.
...ASH.
PATHETIC.
TOUGH GUY. BOY PROSTITUTE. STONE KILLER. LOOK AT WHAT I'VE DONE...
ASH! THAT IS... ALL WRONG!
DO NOT... SAY THOSE THINGS ABOUT YOURSELF!
WHY NOT, EIJI? IT'S TRUE.

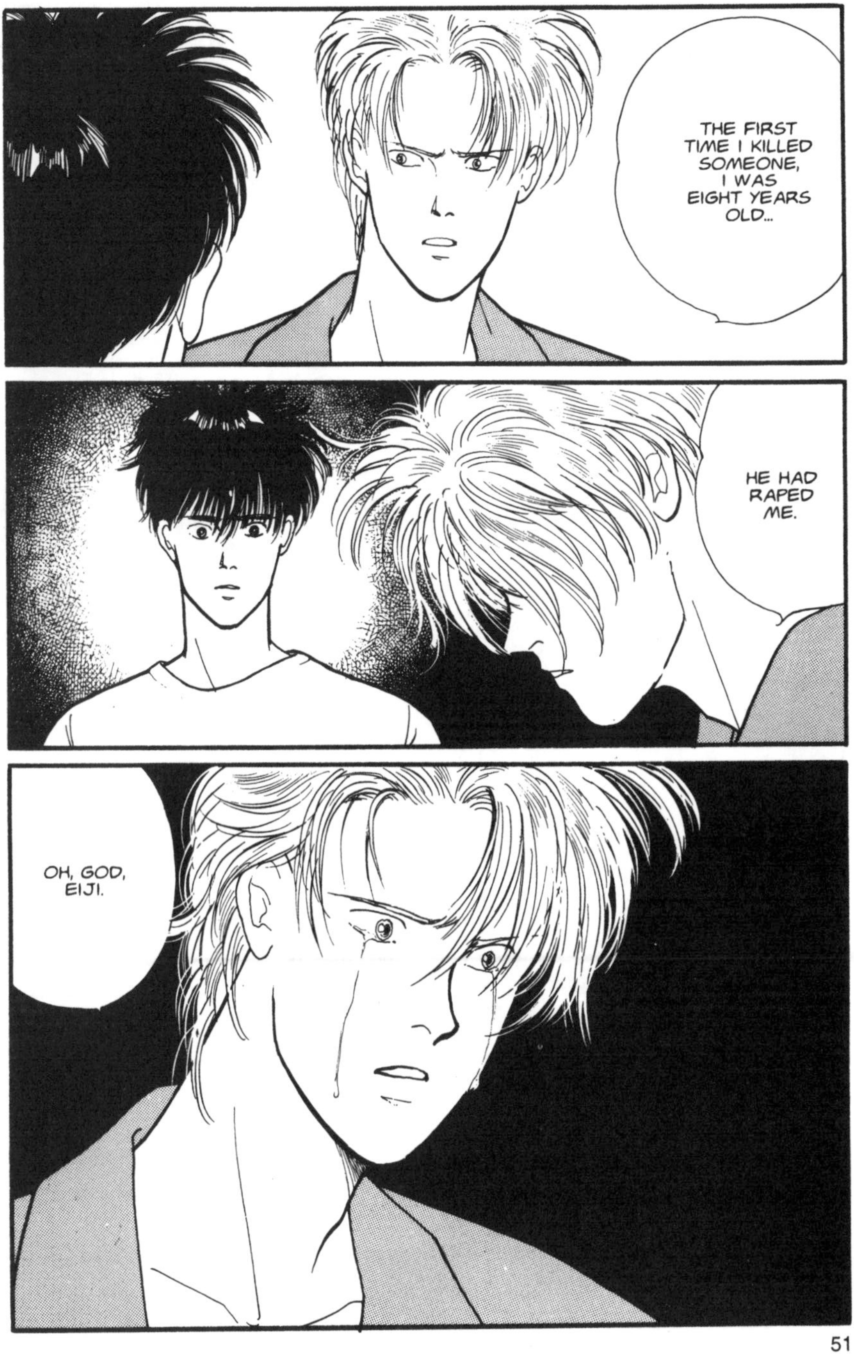
THE FIRST TIME I KILLED SOMEONE, I WAS EIGHT YEARS OLD...
HE HAD RAPED ME.
OH, GOD, EIJI.

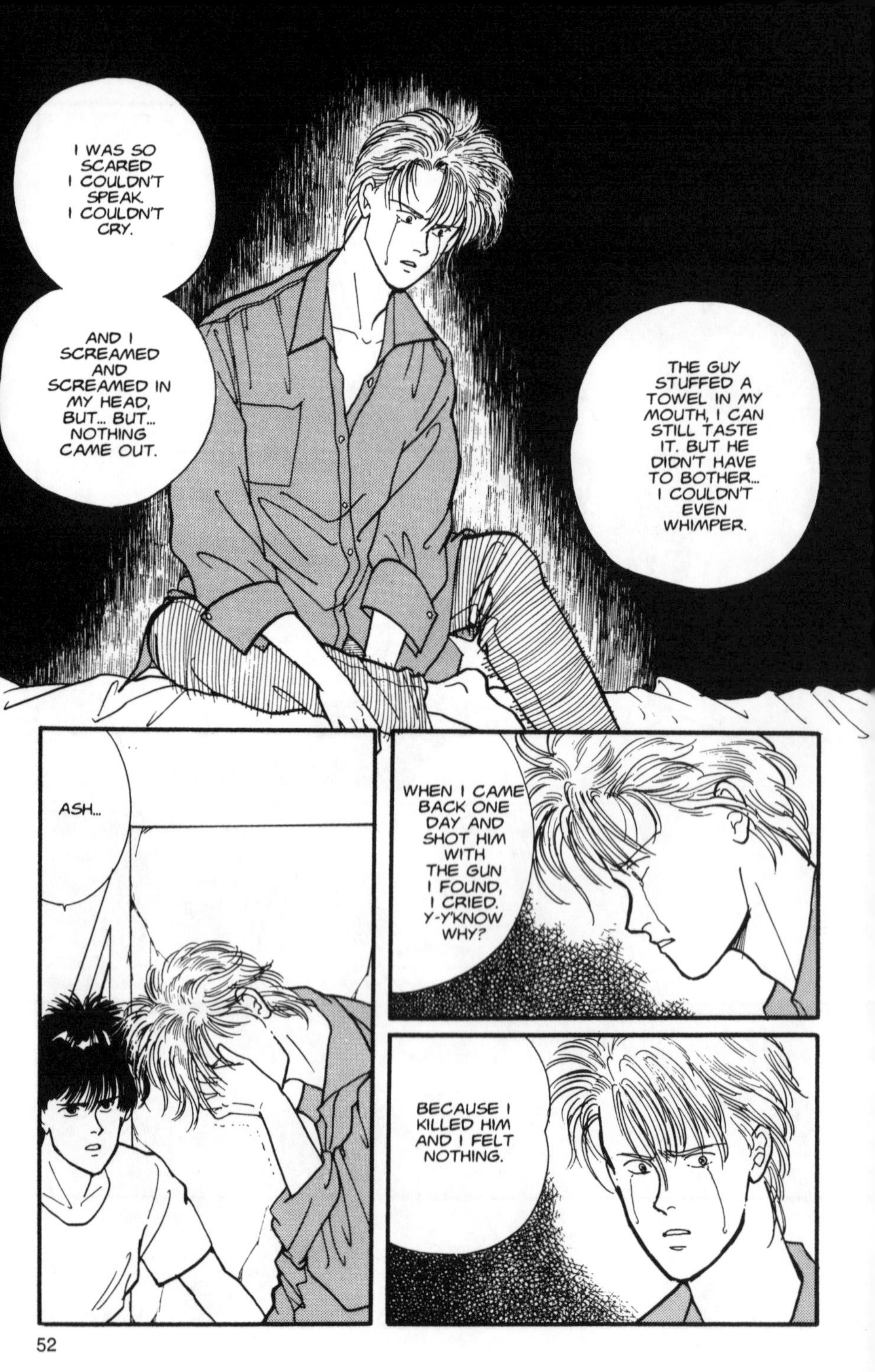
I WAS SO SCARED I COULDN'T SPEAK. I COULDN'T CRY.
AND I SCREAMED AND SCREAMED IN MY HEAD, BUT... BUT... NOTHING CAME OUT.
THE GUY STUFFED A TOWEL IN MY MOUTH, I CAN STILL TASTE IT. BUT HE DIDN'T HAVE TO BOTHER... I COULDN'T EVEN WHIMPER.
ASH...
WHEN I CAME BACK ONE DAY AND SHOT HIM WITH THE GUN I FOUND, I CRIED. Y-Y'KNOW WHY?
BECAUSE I KILLED HIM AND I FELT NOTHING.

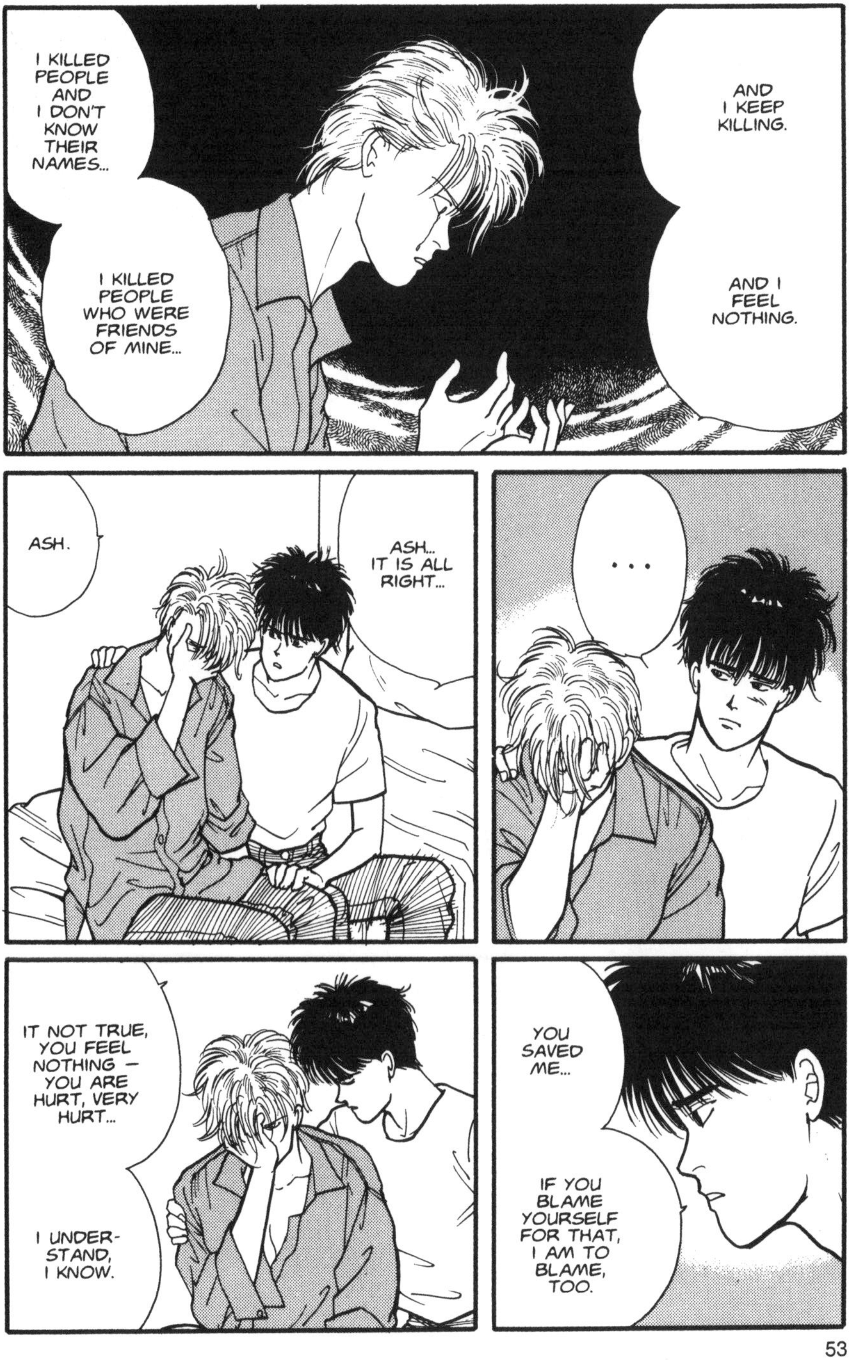
I KILLED PEOPLE AND I DON'T KNOW THEIR NAMES...
I KILLED PEOPLE WHO WERE FRIENDS OF MINE...
AND I KEEP KILLING.
AND I FEEL NOTHING.
ASH.
ASH... IT IS ALL RIGHT...
. . .
IT NOT TRUE, YOU FEEL NOTHING — YOU ARE HURT, VERY HURT...
I UNDER-STAND, I KNOW.
YOU SAVED ME...
IF YOU BLAME YOURSELF FOR THAT, I AM TO BLAME, TOO.

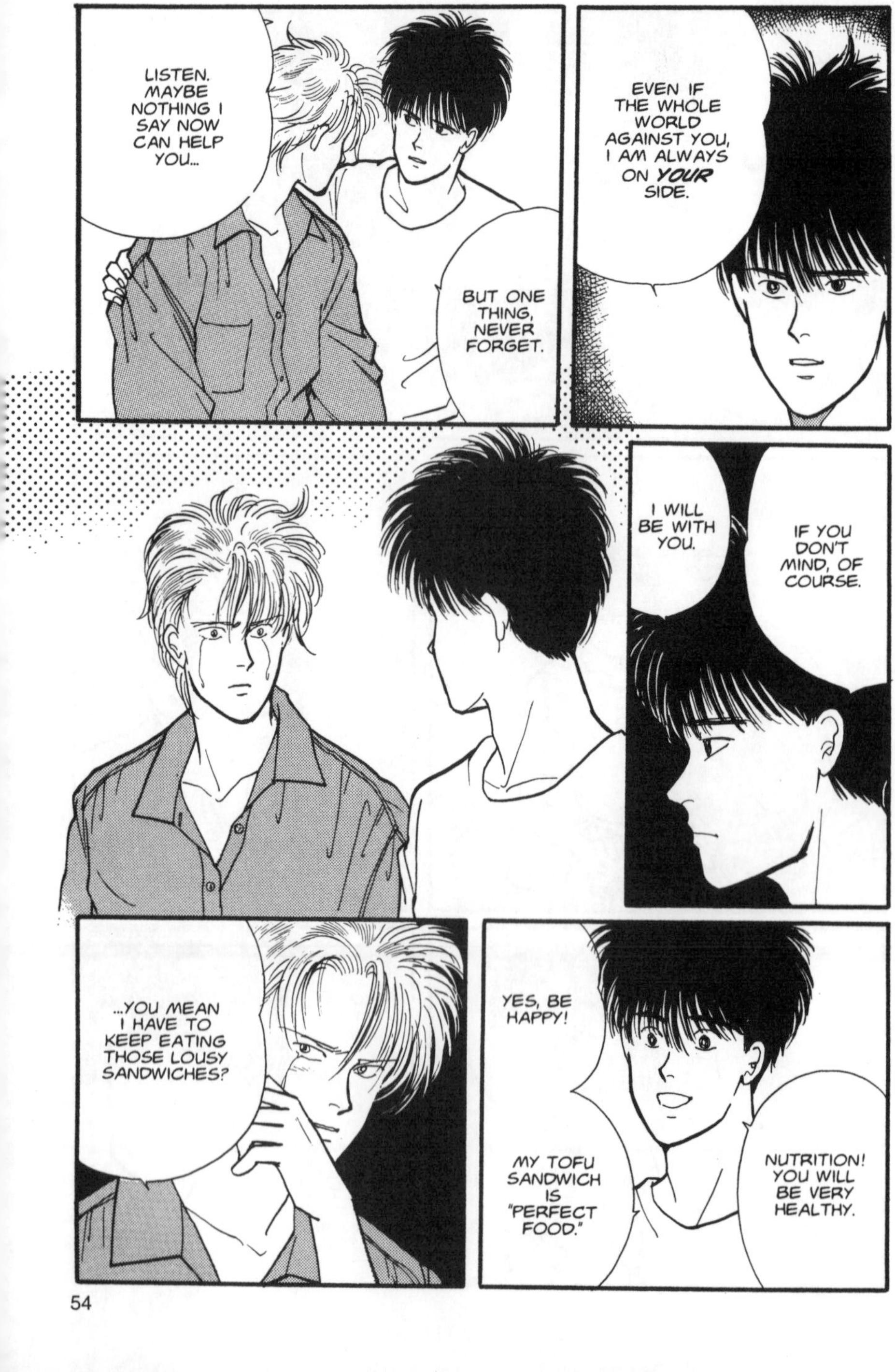
LISTEN. MAYBE NOTHING I SAY NOW CAN HELP YOU...
BUT ONE THING, NEVER FORGET.
EVEN IF THE WHOLE WORLD AGAINST YOU, I AM ALWAYS ON YOUR SIDE.
I WILL BE WITH YOU.
IF YOU DON'T MIND, OF COURSE.
...YOU MEAN I HAVE TO KEEP EATING THOSE LOUSY SANDWICHES?
YES, BE HAPPY!
MY TOFU SANDWICH IS "PERFECT FOOD."
NUTRITION! YOU WILL BE VERY HEALTHY.

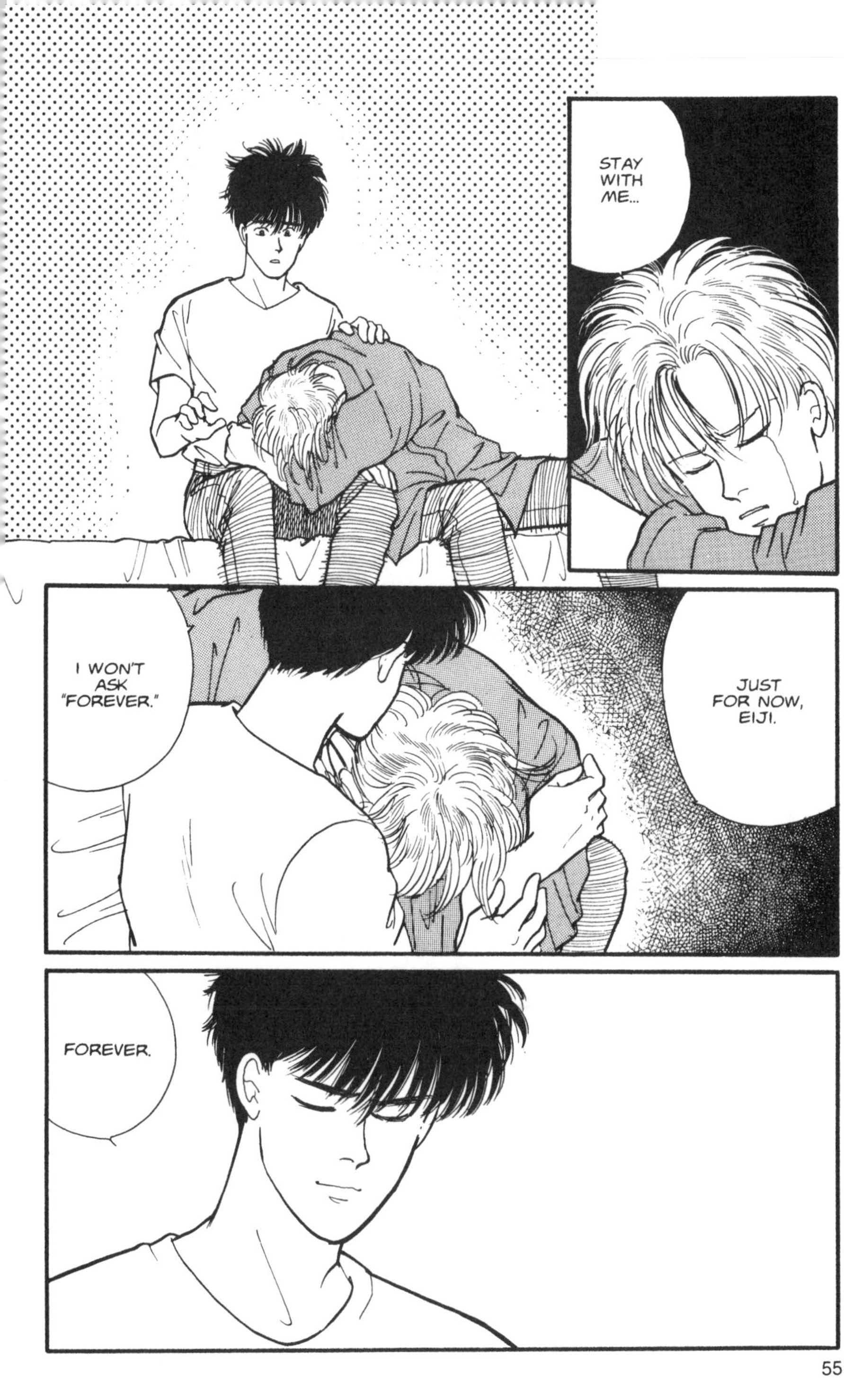
STAY WITH ME...
I WON'T ASK "FOREVER."
JUST FOR NOW, EIJI.
FOREVER.

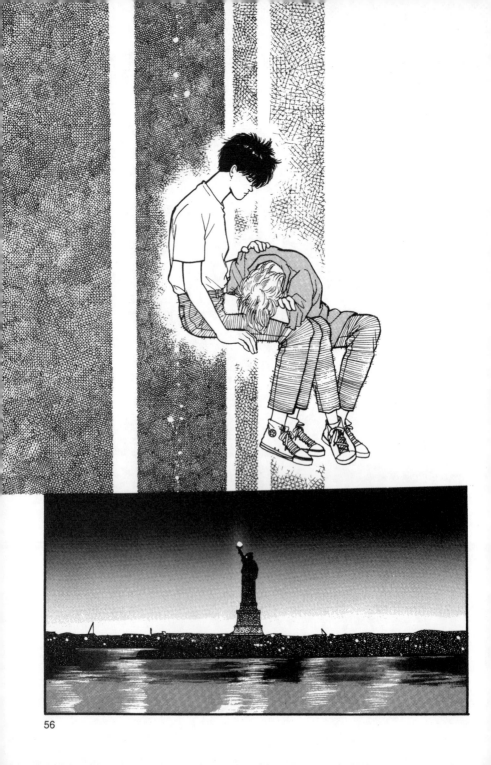

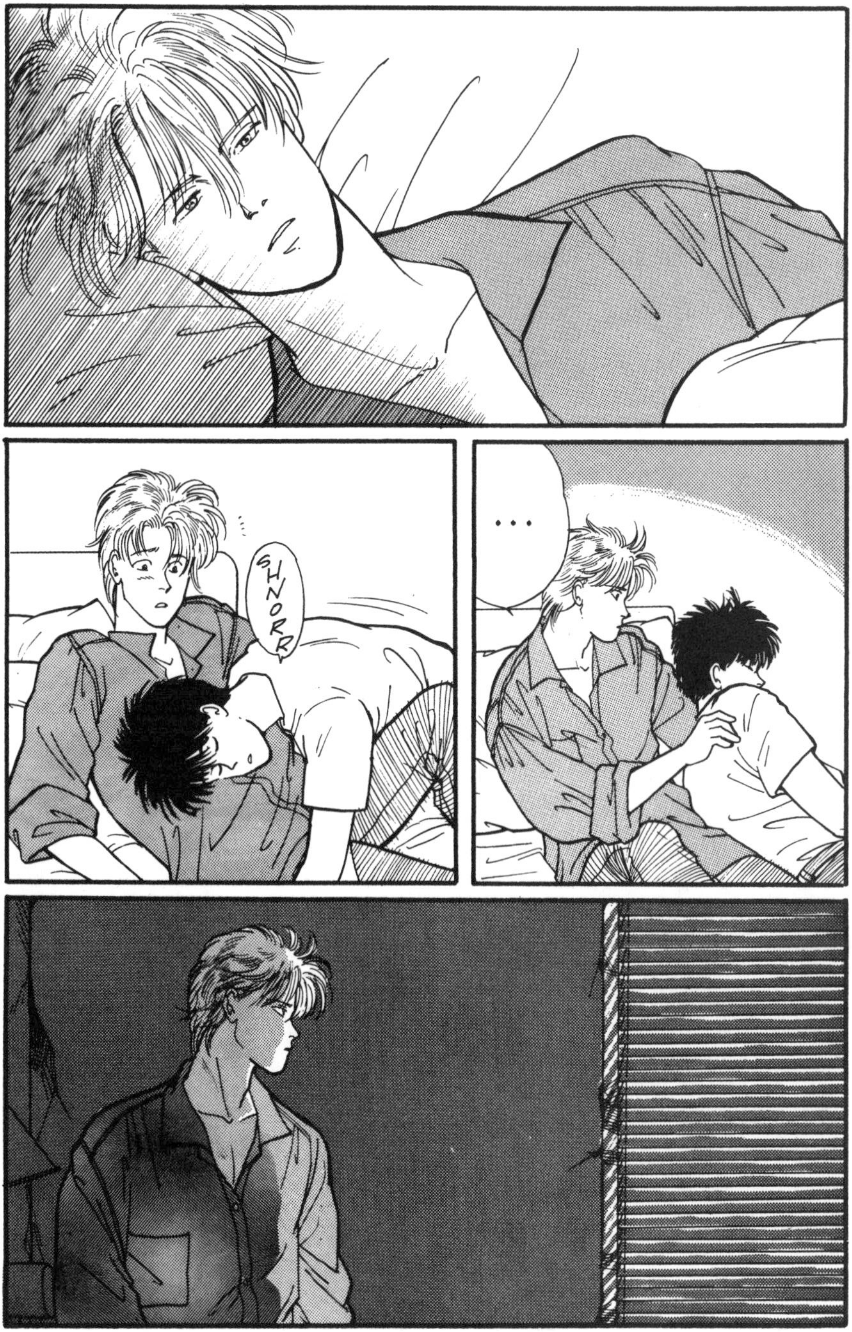

SHNORR
...

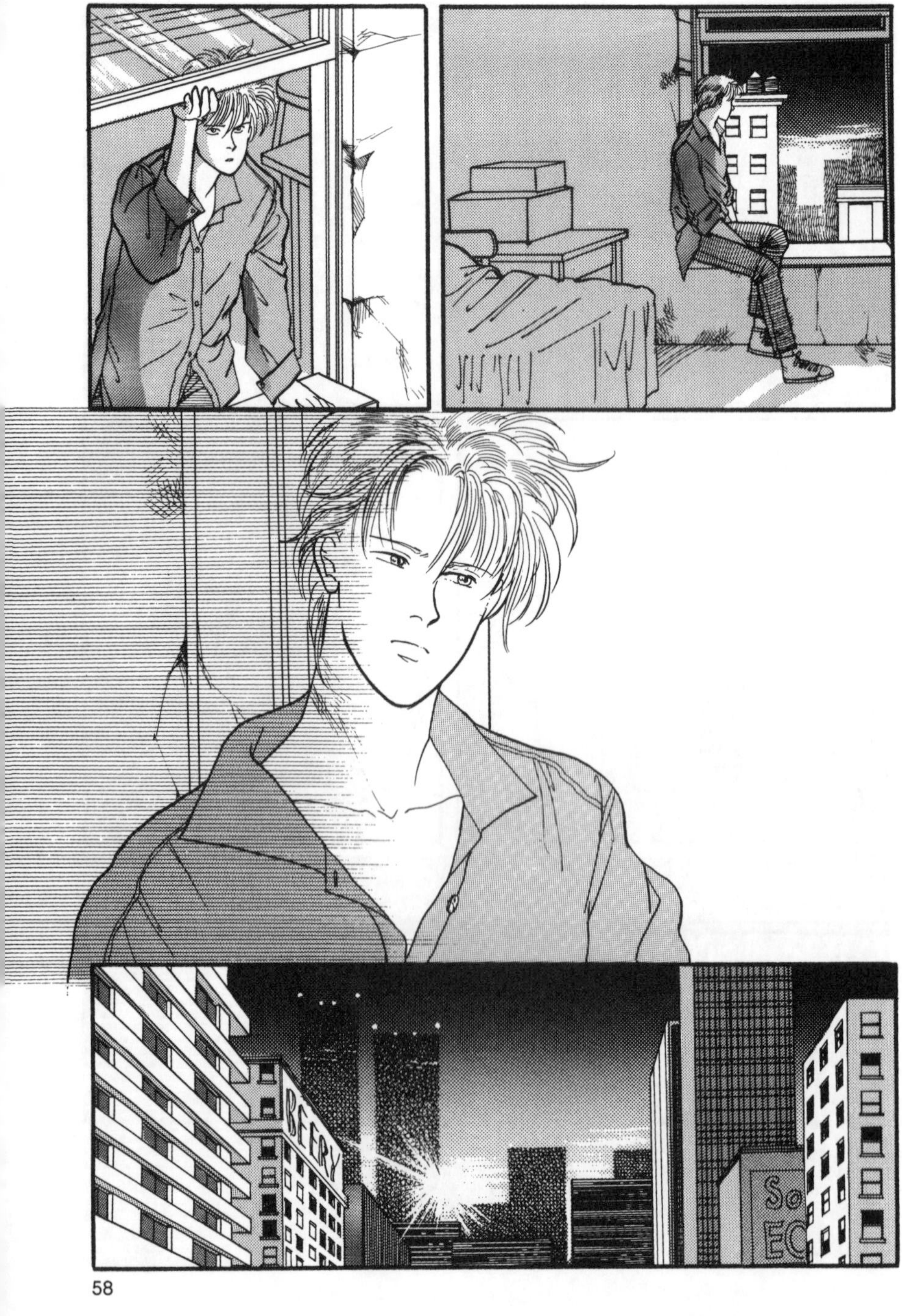
BEERY

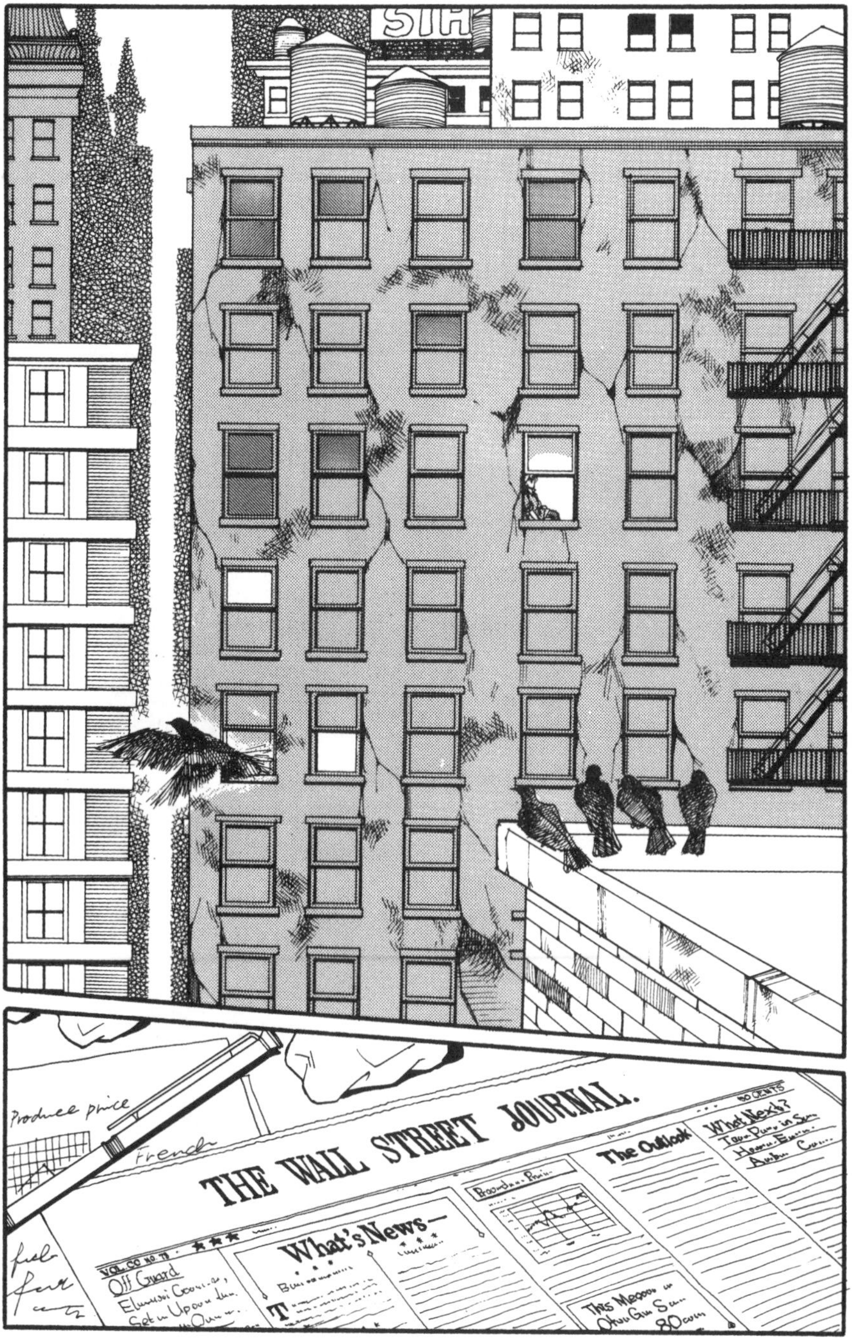
Produce price
French
THE WALL STREET JOURNAL.
80 CENTS
The Outlook
What Next?
What's News—
Off Guard

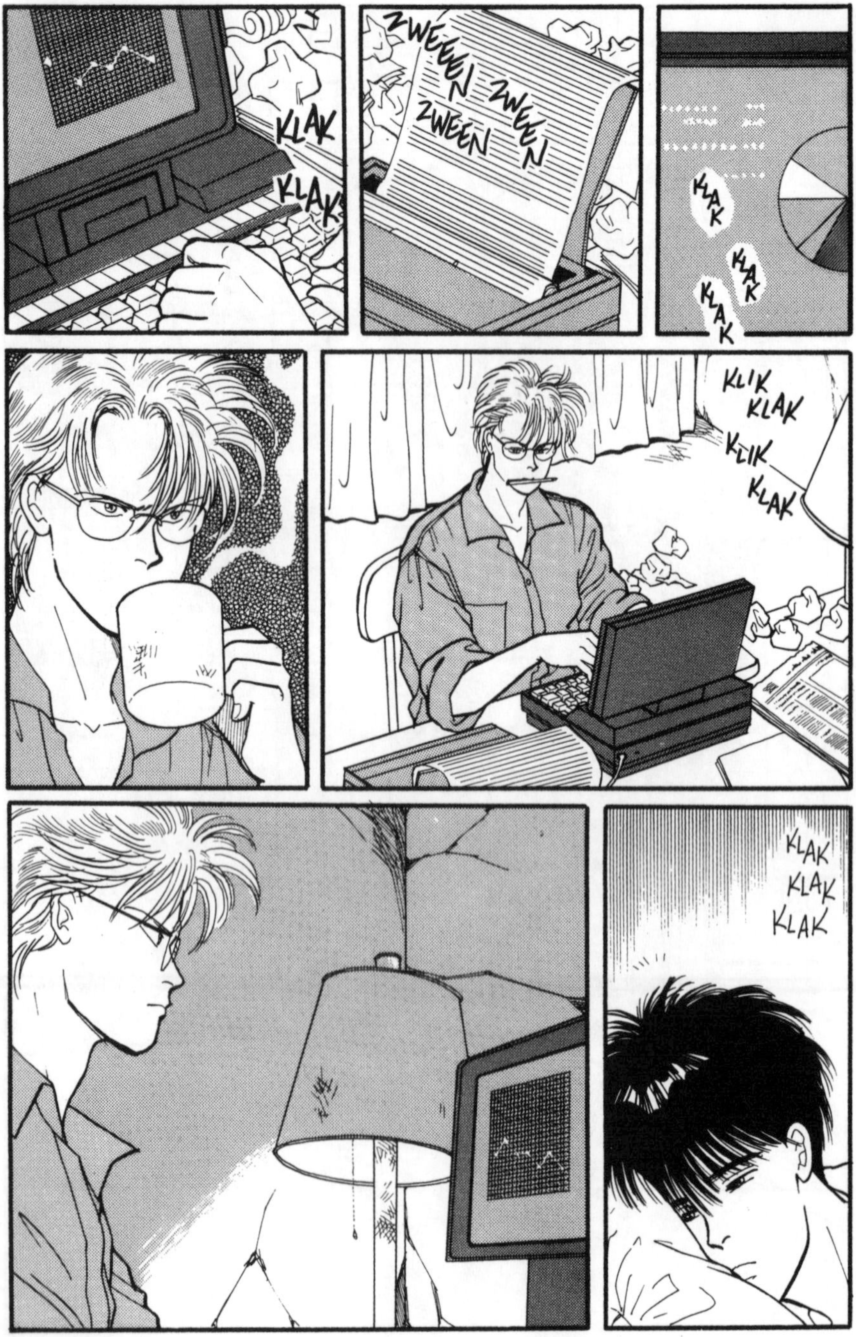
KLAK
KLAK
ZWEEEEN
ZWEEEN
ZWEEN
KLAK
KLAK
KLAK
KLIK
KLAK
KLIK
KLAK
KLAK
KLAK
KLAK

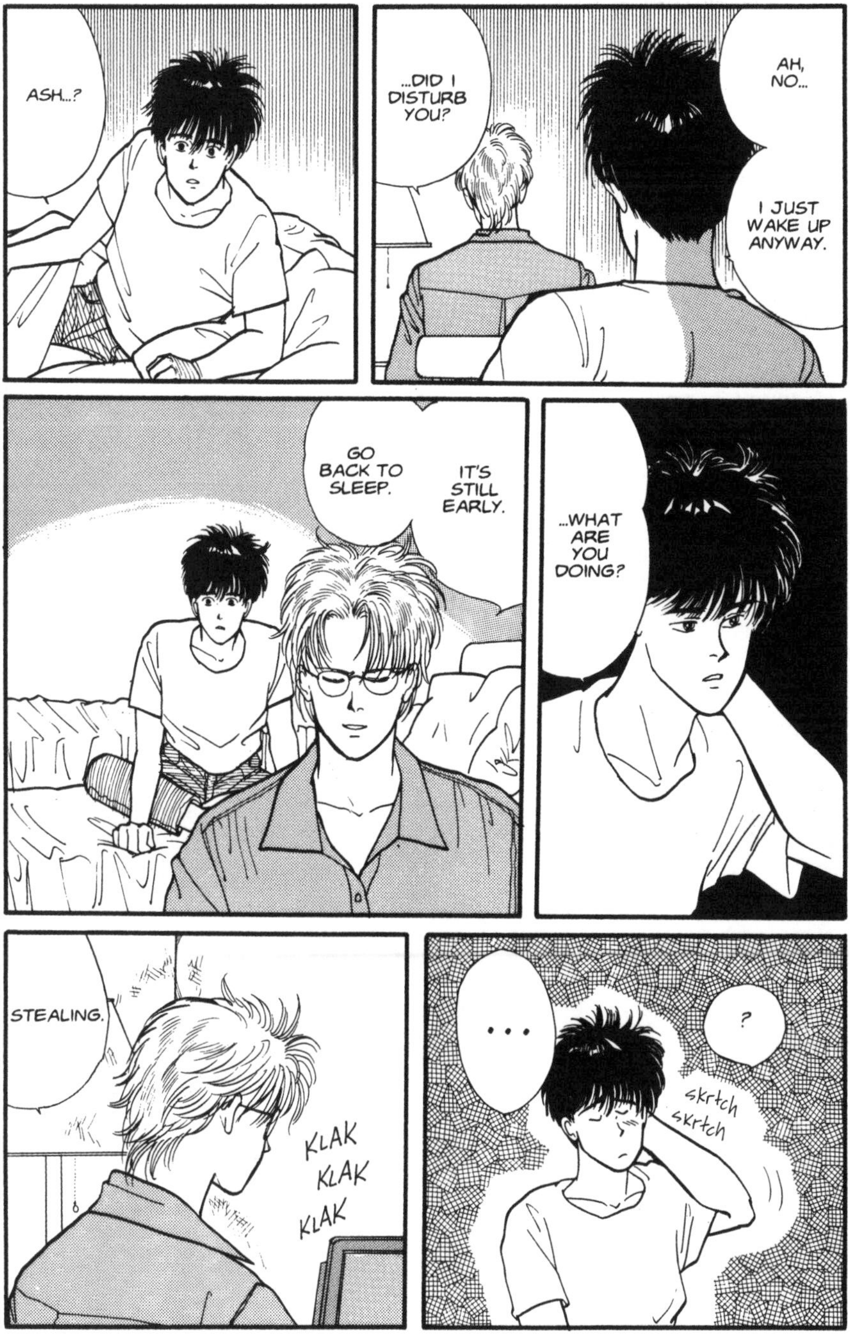
ASH...?
...DID I DISTURB YOU?
AH, NO...
I JUST WAKE UP ANYWAY.
GO BACK TO SLEEP.
IT'S STILL EARLY.
...WHAT ARE YOU DOING?
STEALING.
KLAK KLAK KLAK
...
?
skrtch skrtch

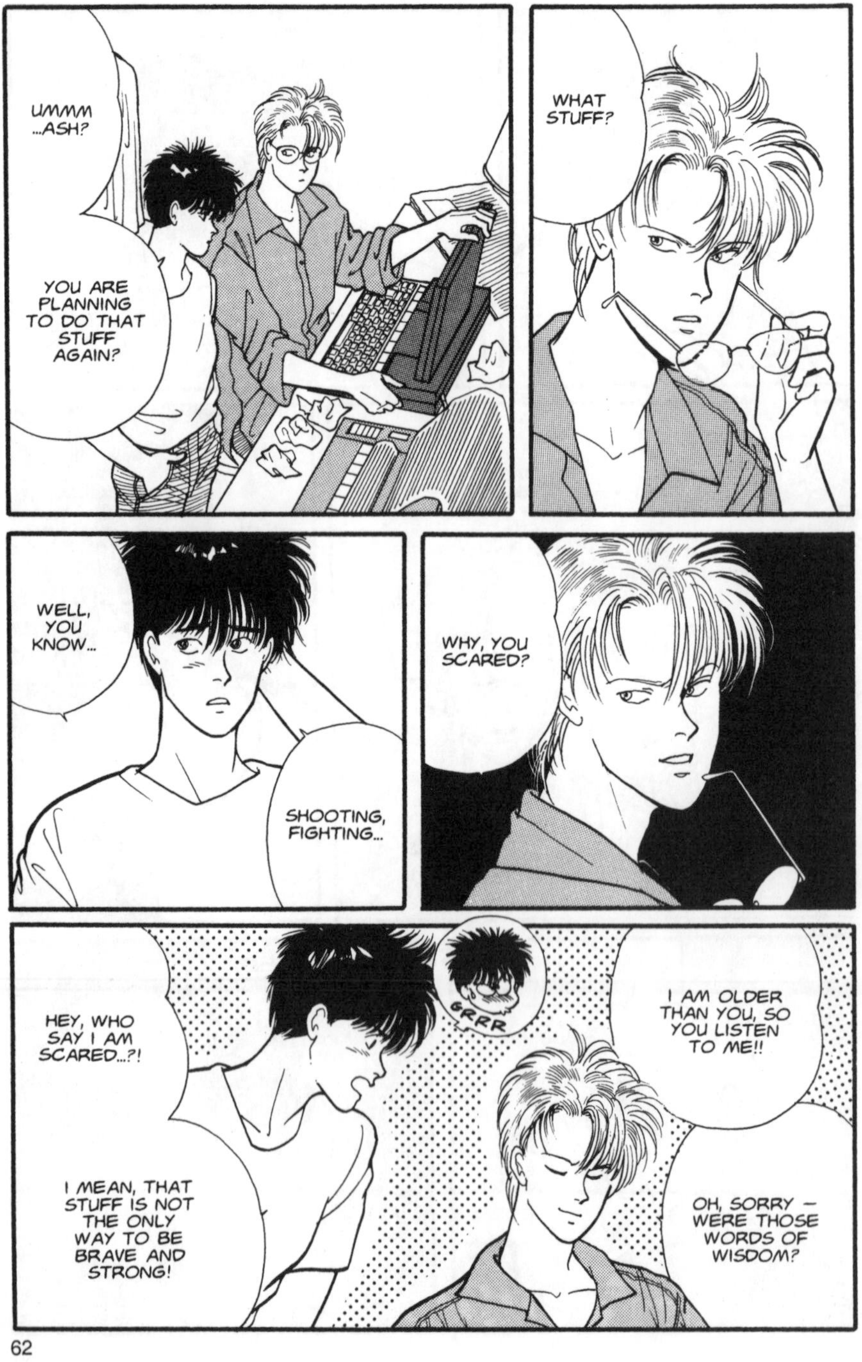
UMMM ...ASH?
YOU ARE PLANNING TO DO THAT STUFF AGAIN?
WHAT STUFF?
WELL, YOU KNOW...
SHOOTING, FIGHTING...
WHY, YOU SCARED?
HEY, WHO SAY I AM SCARED...?!
I MEAN, THAT STUFF IS NOT THE ONLY WAY TO BE BRAVE AND STRONG!
GRRR
I AM OLDER THAN YOU, SO YOU LISTEN TO ME!!
OH, SORRY — WERE THOSE WORDS OF WISDOM?

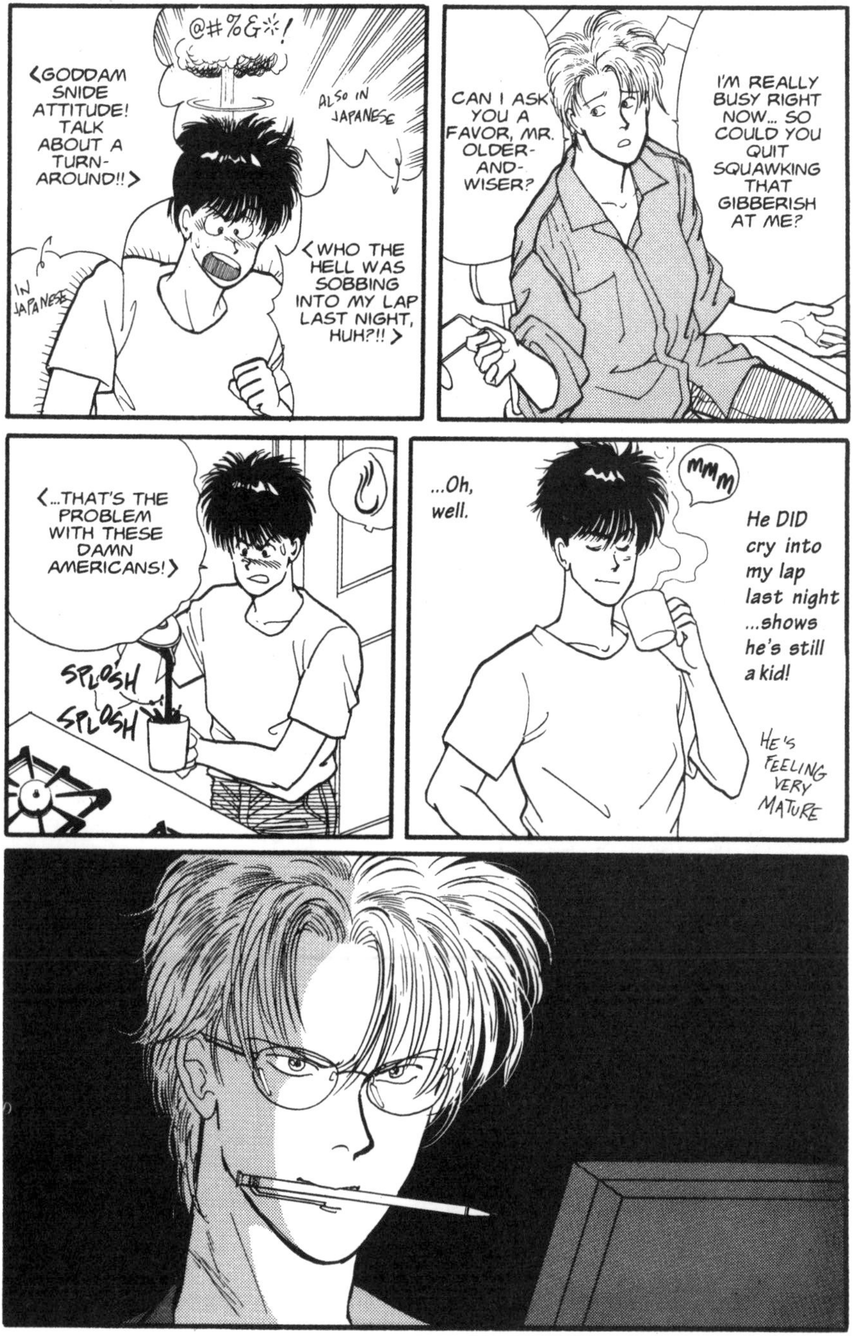
@#%&※!
〈GODDAM SNIDE ATTITUDE! TALK ABOUT A TURN-AROUND!!〉
ALSO IN JAPANESE
IN JAPANESE
〈WHO THE HELL WAS SOBBING INTO MY LAP LAST NIGHT, HUH?!!〉
CAN I ASK YOU A FAVOR, MR. OLDER-AND-WISER?
I'M REALLY BUSY RIGHT NOW... SO COULD YOU QUIT SQUAWKING THAT GIBBERISH AT ME?
〈...THAT'S THE PROBLEM WITH THESE DAMN AMERICANS!〉
SPLOSH
SPLOSH
...Oh, well.
MMM
He DID cry into my lap last night ...shows he's still a kid!
HE'S FEELING VERY MATURE

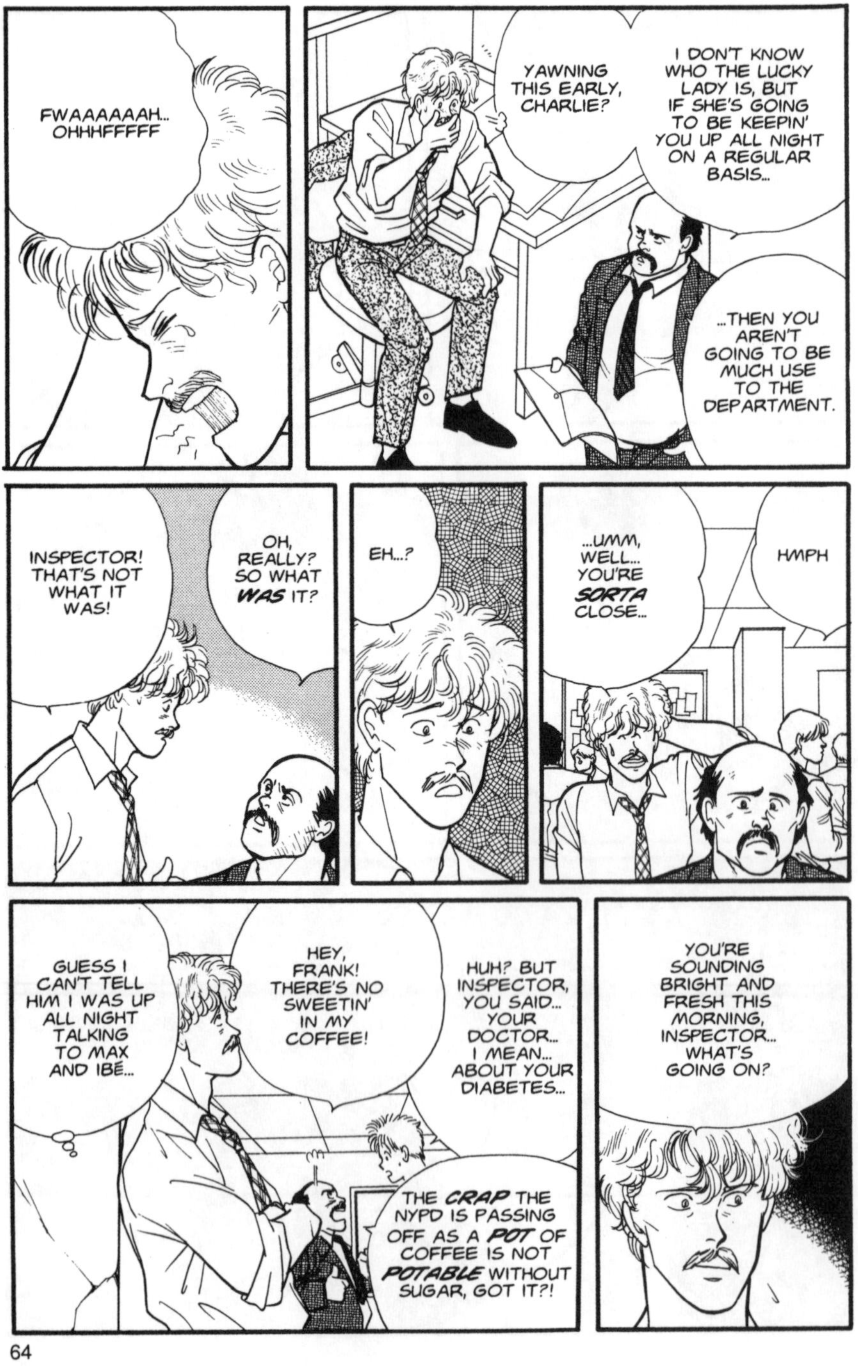
FWAAAAAAH... OHHHFFFFF
YAWNING THIS EARLY, CHARLIE?
I DON'T KNOW WHO THE LUCKY LADY IS, BUT IF SHE'S GOING TO BE KEEPIN' YOU UP ALL NIGHT ON A REGULAR BASIS...
...THEN YOU AREN'T GOING TO BE MUCH USE TO THE DEPARTMENT.
INSPECTOR! THAT'S NOT WHAT IT WAS!
OH, REALLY? SO WHAT *WAS* IT?
EH...?
...UMM, WELL... YOU'RE *SORTA* CLOSE...
HMPH
GUESS I CAN'T TELL HIM I WAS UP ALL NIGHT TALKING TO MAX AND IBÉ...
HEY, FRANK! THERE'S NO SWEETIN' IN MY COFFEE!
HUH? BUT INSPECTOR, YOU SAID... YOUR DOCTOR... I MEAN... ABOUT YOUR DIABETES...
THE *CRAP* THE NYPD IS PASSING OFF AS A *POT* OF COFFEE IS NOT *POTABLE* WITHOUT SUGAR, GOT IT?!
YOU'RE SOUNDING BRIGHT AND FRESH THIS MORNING, INSPECTOR... WHAT'S GOING ON?

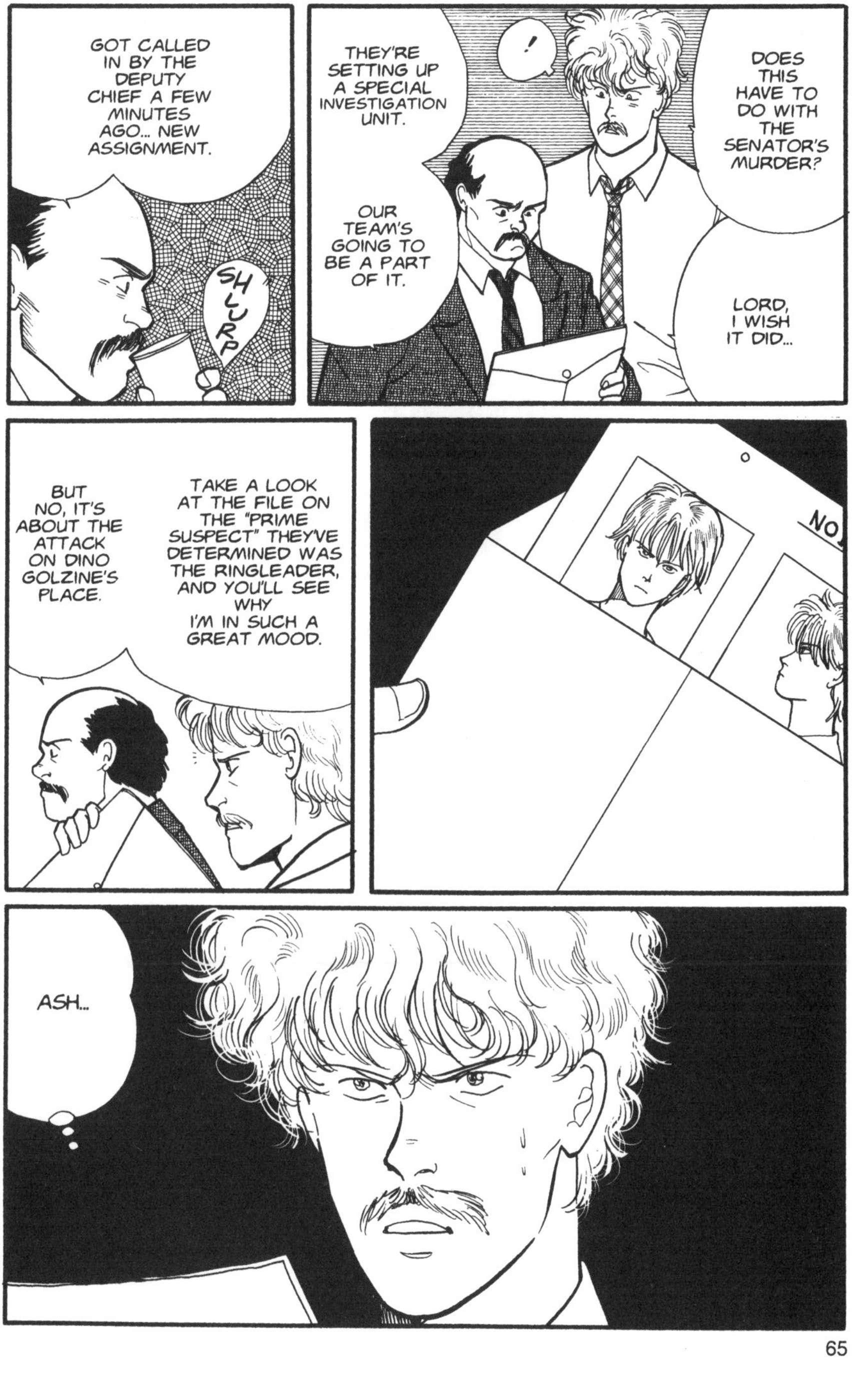
GOT CALLED IN BY THE DEPUTY CHIEF A FEW MINUTES AGO... NEW ASSIGNMENT.
SHLURP
THEY'RE SETTING UP A SPECIAL INVESTIGATION UNIT.
!
OUR TEAM'S GOING TO BE A PART OF IT.
DOES THIS HAVE TO DO WITH THE SENATOR'S MURDER?
LORD, I WISH IT DID...
BUT NO, IT'S ABOUT THE ATTACK ON DINO GOLZINE'S PLACE.
TAKE A LOOK AT THE FILE ON THE "PRIME SUSPECT" THEY'VE DETERMINED WAS THE RINGLEADER, AND YOU'LL SEE WHY I'M IN SUCH A GREAT MOOD.
ASH...

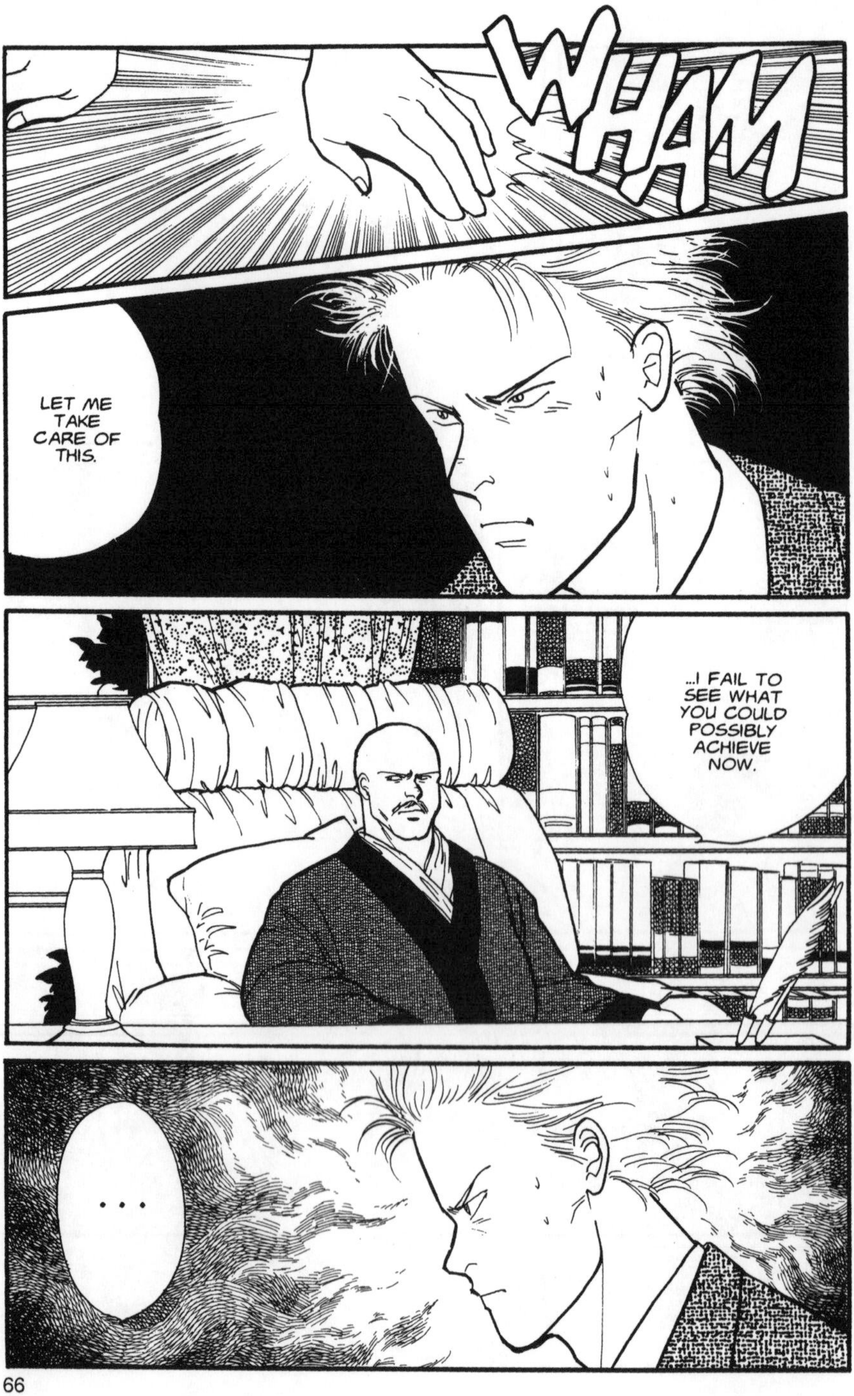
WHAM
LET ME TAKE CARE OF THIS.
...I FAIL TO SEE WHAT YOU COULD POSSIBLY ACHIEVE NOW.
...

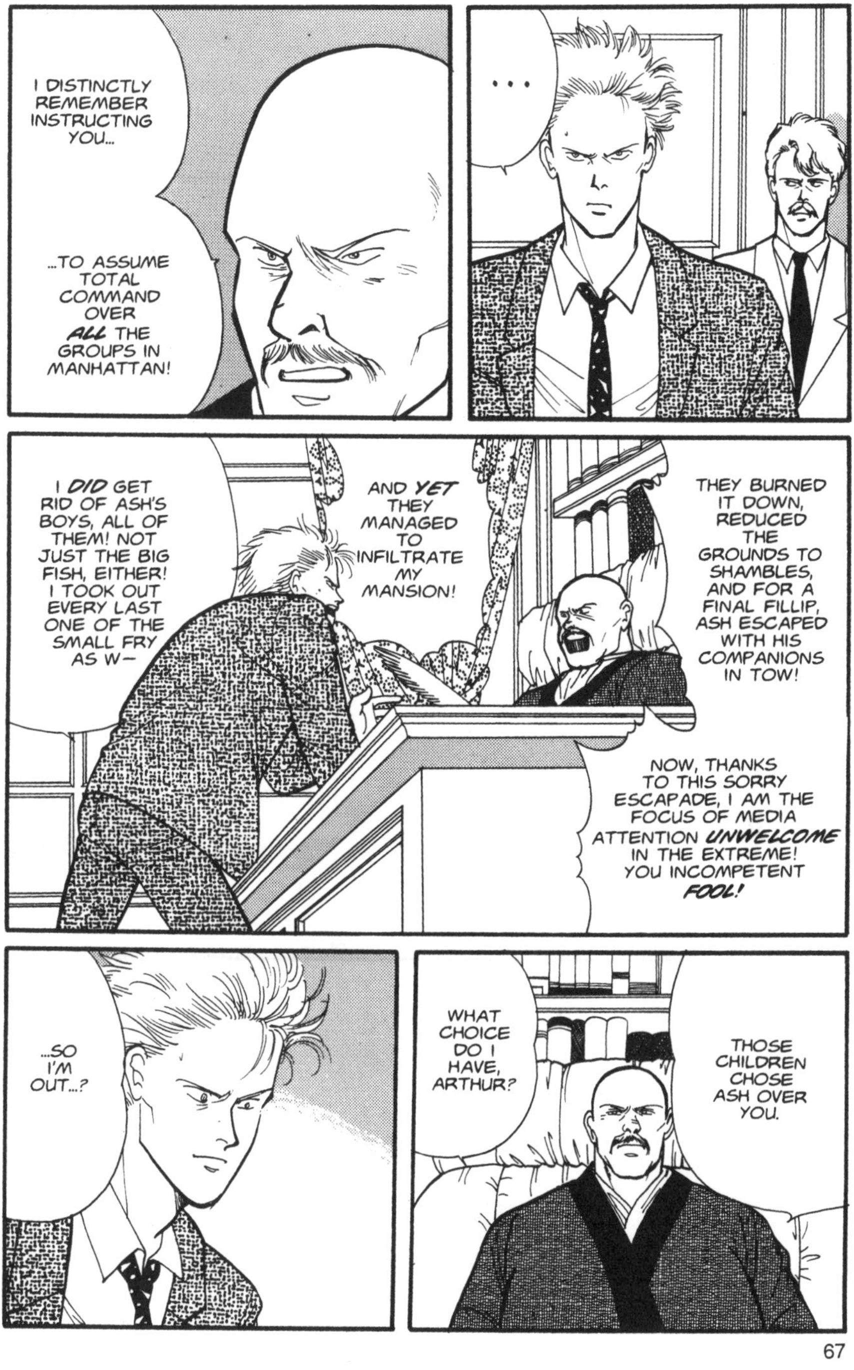

I DISTINCTLY REMEMBER INSTRUCTING YOU...
...TO ASSUME TOTAL COMMAND OVER ALL THE GROUPS IN MANHATTAN!
...
I DID GET RID OF ASH'S BOYS, ALL OF THEM! NOT JUST THE BIG FISH, EITHER! I TOOK OUT EVERY LAST ONE OF THE SMALL FRY AS W—
AND YET THEY MANAGED TO INFILTRATE MY MANSION!
THEY BURNED IT DOWN, REDUCED THE GROUNDS TO SHAMBLES, AND FOR A FINAL FILLIP, ASH ESCAPED WITH HIS COMPANIONS IN TOW!
NOW, THANKS TO THIS SORRY ESCAPADE, I AM THE FOCUS OF MEDIA ATTENTION UNWELCOME IN THE EXTREME! YOU INCOMPETENT FOOL!
...SO I'M OUT...?
WHAT CHOICE DO I HAVE, ARTHUR?
THOSE CHILDREN CHOSE ASH OVER YOU.

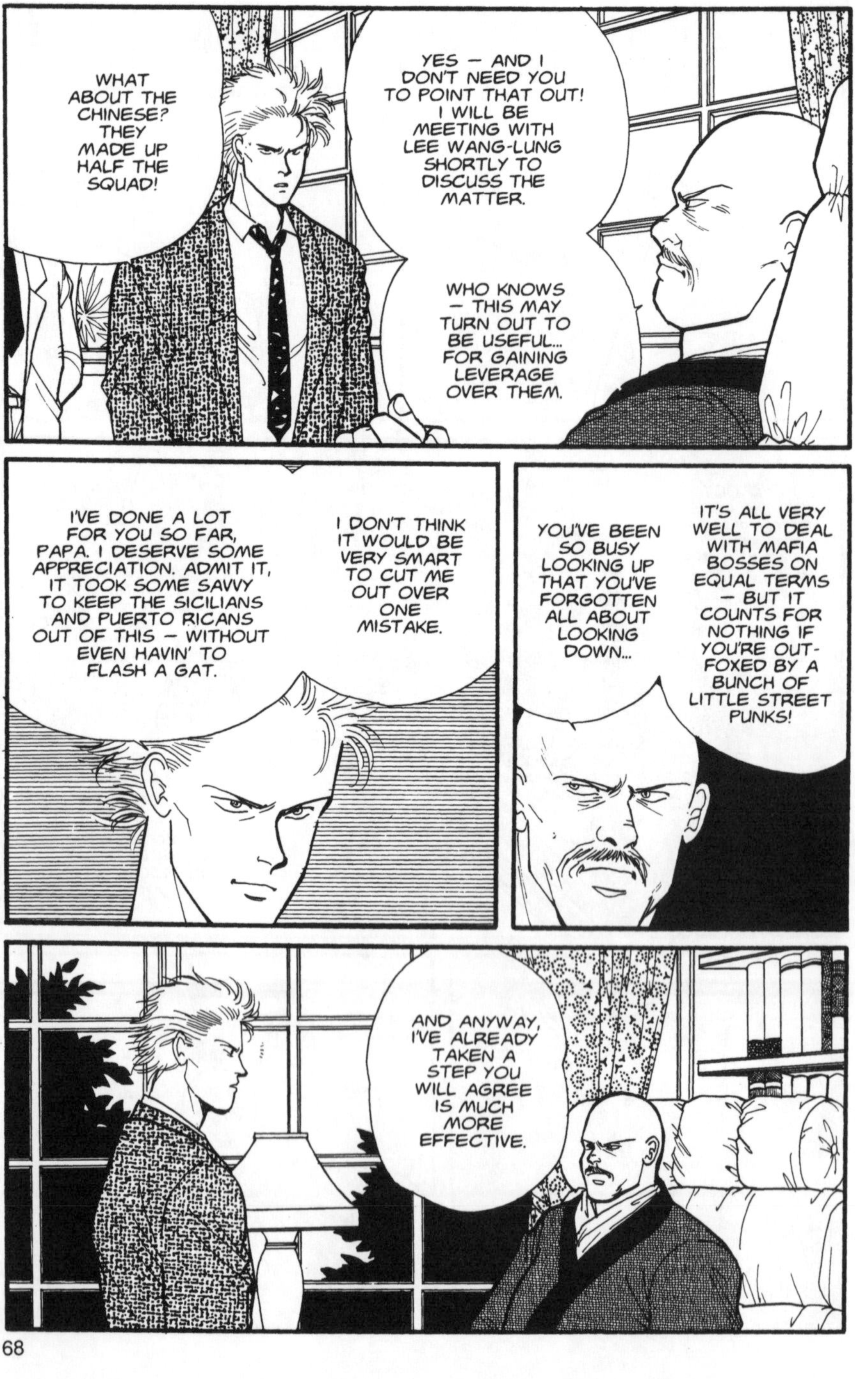
WHAT ABOUT THE CHINESE? THEY MADE UP HALF THE SQUAD!
YES — AND I DON'T NEED YOU TO POINT THAT OUT! I WILL BE MEETING WITH LEE WANG-LUNG SHORTLY TO DISCUSS THE MATTER.
WHO KNOWS — THIS MAY TURN OUT TO BE USEFUL... FOR GAINING LEVERAGE OVER THEM.
I'VE DONE A LOT FOR YOU SO FAR, PAPA. I DESERVE SOME APPRECIATION. ADMIT IT, IT TOOK SOME SAVVY TO KEEP THE SICILIANS AND PUERTO RICANS OUT OF THIS — WITHOUT EVEN HAVIN' TO FLASH A GAT.
I DON'T THINK IT WOULD BE VERY SMART TO CUT ME OUT OVER ONE MISTAKE.
YOU'VE BEEN SO BUSY LOOKING UP THAT YOU'VE FORGOTTEN ALL ABOUT LOOKING DOWN...
IT'S ALL VERY WELL TO DEAL WITH MAFIA BOSSES ON EQUAL TERMS — BUT IT COUNTS FOR NOTHING IF YOU'RE OUT-FOXED BY A BUNCH OF LITTLE STREET PUNKS!
AND ANYWAY, I'VE ALREADY TAKEN A STEP YOU WILL AGREE IS MUCH MORE EFFECTIVE.

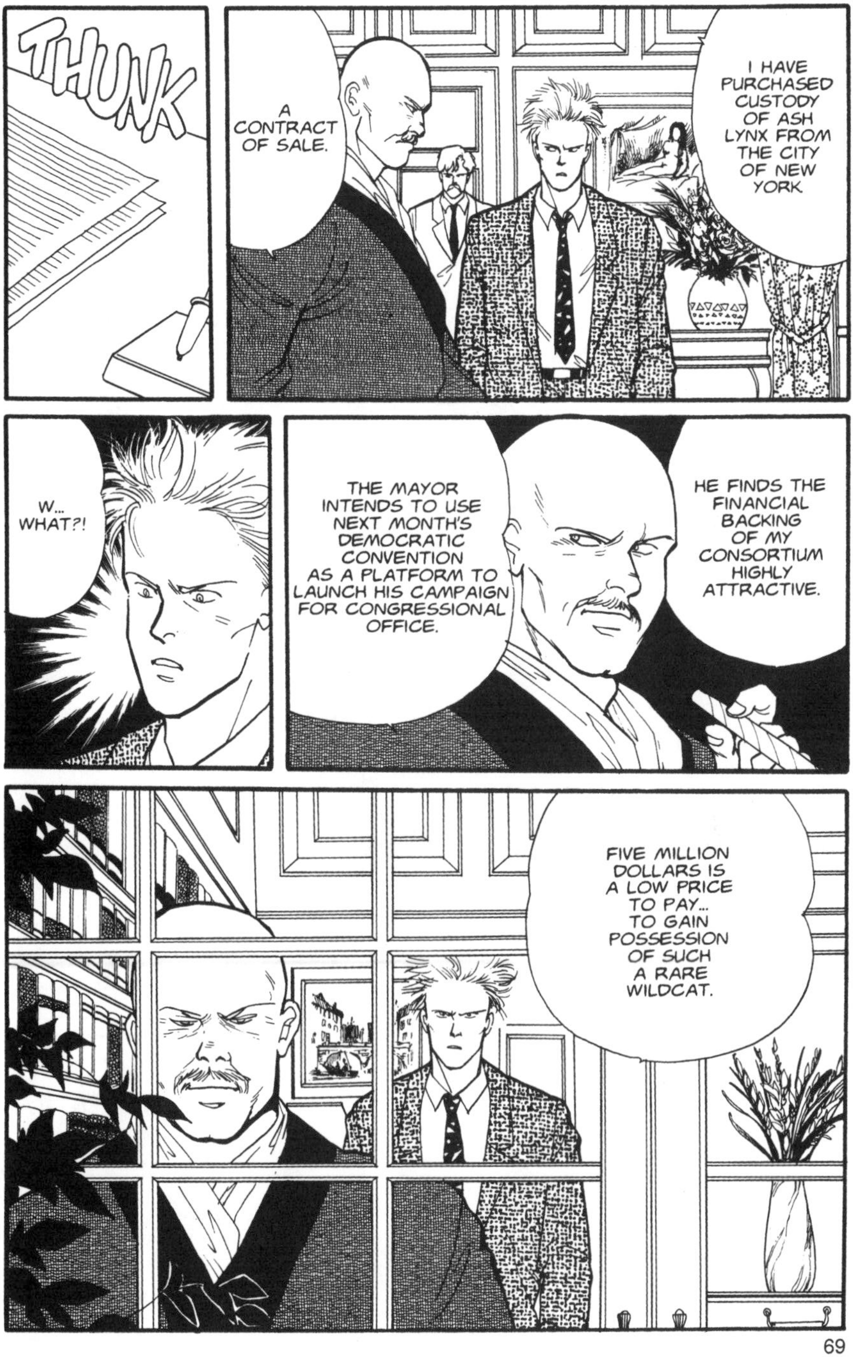
THUNK
A CONTRACT OF SALE.
I HAVE PURCHASED CUSTODY OF ASH LYNX FROM THE CITY OF NEW YORK.
W... WHAT?!
THE MAYOR INTENDS TO USE NEXT MONTH'S DEMOCRATIC CONVENTION AS A PLATFORM TO LAUNCH HIS CAMPAIGN FOR CONGRESSIONAL OFFICE.
HE FINDS THE FINANCIAL BACKING OF MY CONSORTIUM HIGHLY ATTRACTIVE.
FIVE MILLION DOLLARS IS A LOW PRICE TO PAY... TO GAIN POSSESSION OF SUCH A RARE WILDCAT.

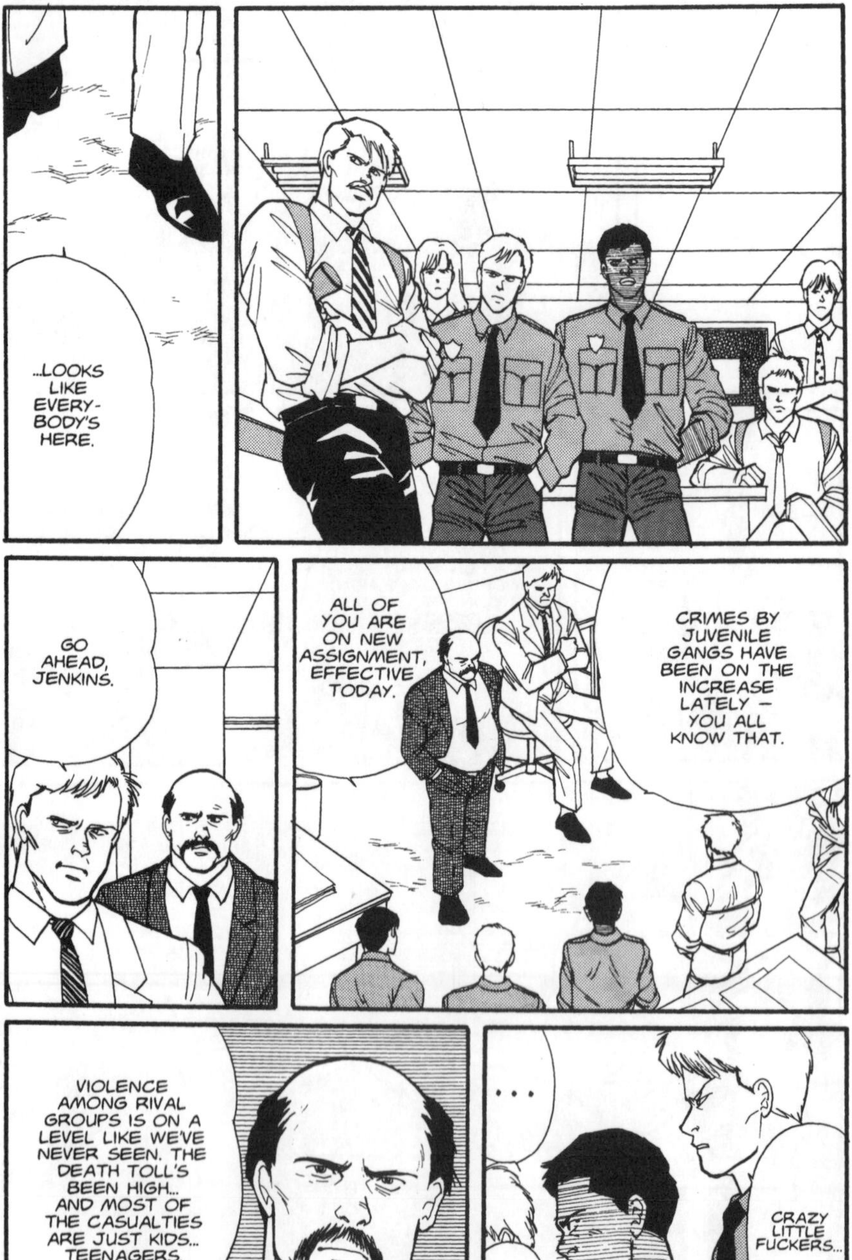
...LOOKS LIKE EVERY-BODY'S HERE.
GO AHEAD, JENKINS.
ALL OF YOU ARE ON NEW ASSIGNMENT, EFFECTIVE TODAY.
CRIMES BY JUVENILE GANGS HAVE BEEN ON THE INCREASE LATELY — YOU ALL KNOW THAT.
VIOLENCE AMONG RIVAL GROUPS IS ON A LEVEL LIKE WE'VE NEVER SEEN. THE DEATH TOLL'S BEEN HIGH... AND MOST OF THE CASUALTIES ARE JUST KIDS... TEENAGERS.
...
SHIT.
CRAZY LITTLE FUCKERS...

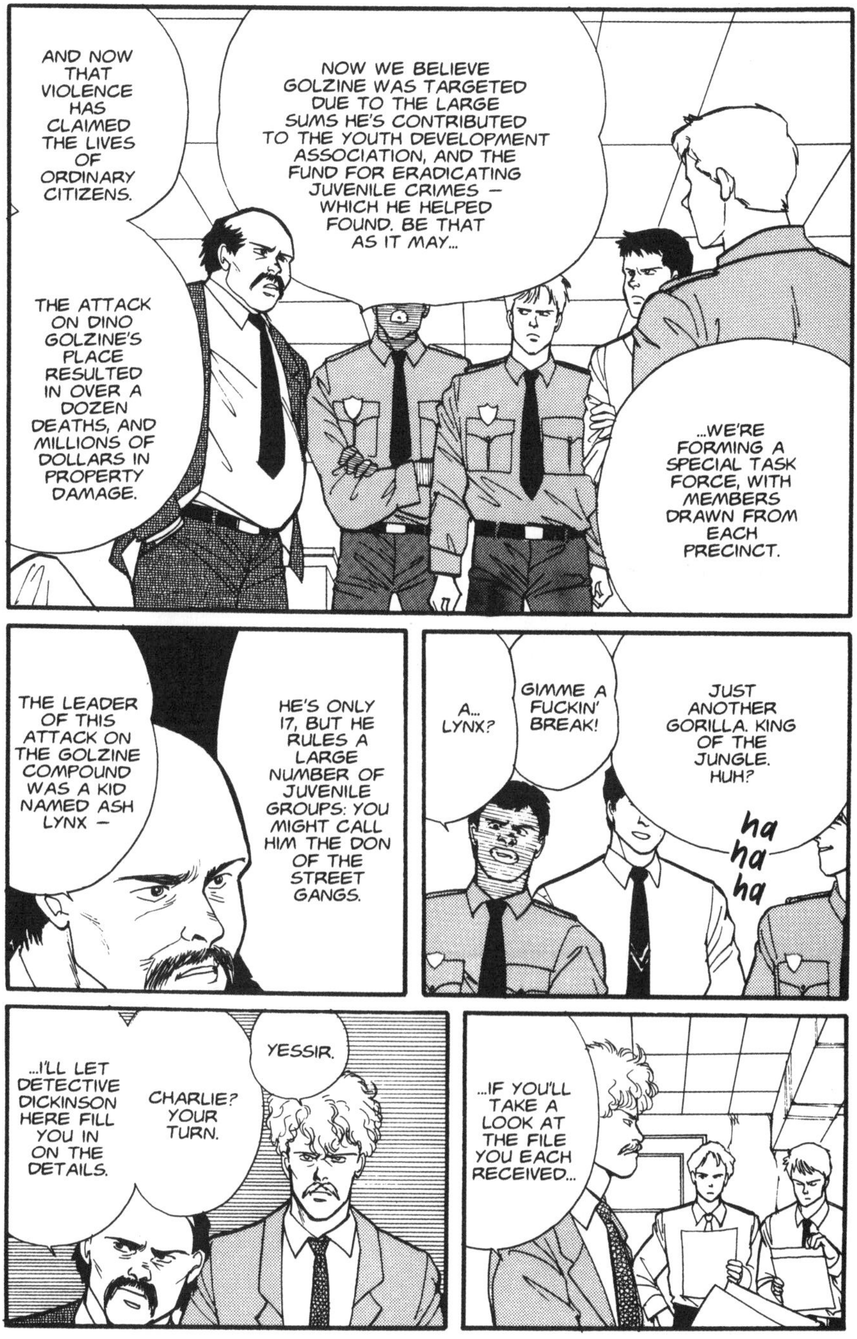
AND NOW THAT VIOLENCE HAS CLAIMED THE LIVES OF ORDINARY CITIZENS.
NOW WE BELIEVE GOLZINE WAS TARGETED DUE TO THE LARGE SUMS HE'S CONTRIBUTED TO THE YOUTH DEVELOPMENT ASSOCIATION, AND THE FUND FOR ERADICATING JUVENILE CRIMES – WHICH HE HELPED FOUND. BE THAT AS IT MAY...
THE ATTACK ON DINO GOLZINE'S PLACE RESULTED IN OVER A DOZEN DEATHS, AND MILLIONS OF DOLLARS IN PROPERTY DAMAGE.
...WE'RE FORMING A SPECIAL TASK FORCE, WITH MEMBERS DRAWN FROM EACH PRECINCT.
THE LEADER OF THIS ATTACK ON THE GOLZINE COMPOUND WAS A KID NAMED ASH LYNX –
HE'S ONLY 17, BUT HE RULES A LARGE NUMBER OF JUVENILE GROUPS: YOU MIGHT CALL HIM THE DON OF THE STREET GANGS.
A... LYNX?
GIMME A FUCKIN' BREAK!
JUST ANOTHER GORILLA. KING OF THE JUNGLE. HUH?
ha ha ha
...I'LL LET DETECTIVE DICKINSON HERE FILL YOU IN ON THE DETAILS.
CHARLIE? YOUR TURN.
YESSIR.
...IF YOU'LL TAKE A LOOK AT THE FILE YOU EACH RECEIVED...

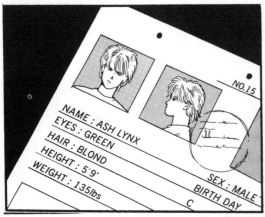

NO.15

NAME : ASH LYNX
EYES : GREEN
HAIR : BLOND
HEIGHT : 5'9"
WEIGHT : 135lbs

SEX : MALE
BIRTH DAY
C

HUH?

SOME GO-*RILLA* WE GOT HERE...

WANTED: FOR CALVIN KLEIN!

HEY, NOW... HOW'D A KID LIKE THIS *ENTICE* ALL THOSE PUNKS TO FOLLOW HIM?

PROMISED TO SUCK 'EM OFF — WHAT ELSE?

SHIT, MY DAUGHTER GOT HOLD OF THIS, SHE'D PUT IT ON HER BEDROOM WALL!

MAN, *THIS* IS A JOB FOR THE VICE SQUAD!

HOLD ON A MOMENT, GUYS.

PRETTY BOY HERE MAY LOOK LIKE A TEEN IDOL...

BUT HE'S UNDER SUSPICION FOR MULTIPLE COUNTS OF HOMICIDE, AIDING AND ABETTING HOMICIDE, ATTEMPTED MURDER, ASSAULT, AND POSSESSION OF DEADLY WEAPONS.

72

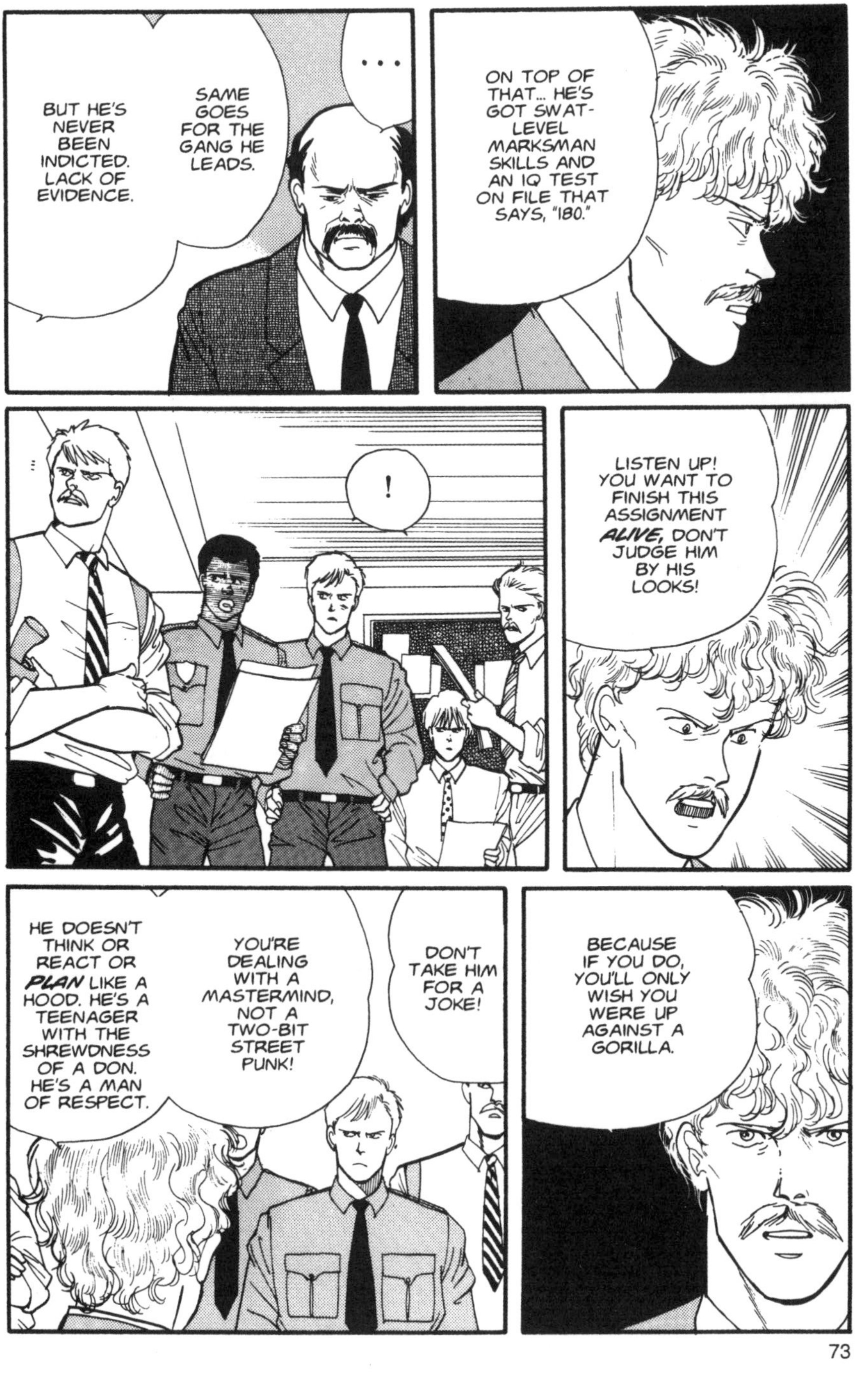

BUT HE'S NEVER BEEN INDICTED. LACK OF EVIDENCE.
SAME GOES FOR THE GANG HE LEADS.
...
ON TOP OF THAT... HE'S GOT SWAT-LEVEL MARKSMAN SKILLS AND AN IQ TEST ON FILE THAT SAYS, "180."
!
LISTEN UP! YOU WANT TO FINISH THIS ASSIGNMENT ALIVE, DON'T JUDGE HIM BY HIS LOOKS!
HE DOESN'T THINK OR REACT OR PLAN LIKE A HOOD. HE'S A TEENAGER WITH THE SHREWDNESS OF A DON. HE'S A MAN OF RESPECT.
YOU'RE DEALING WITH A MASTERMIND, NOT A TWO-BIT STREET PUNK!
DON'T TAKE HIM FOR A JOKE!
BECAUSE IF YOU DO, YOU'LL ONLY WISH YOU WERE UP AGAINST A GORILLA.

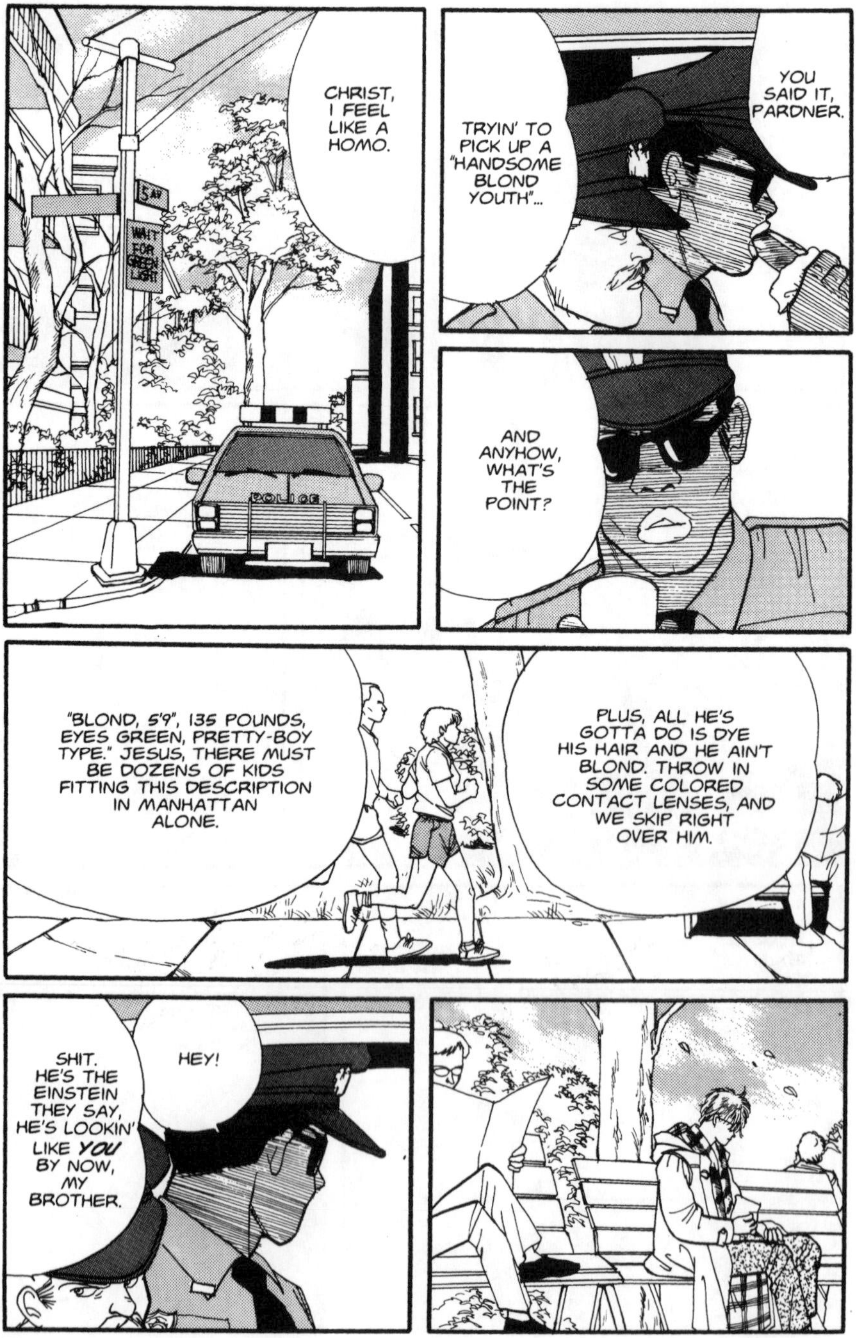
5 AV
WAIT FOR GREEN LIGHT
POLICE
CHRIST, I FEEL LIKE A HOMO.
TRYIN' TO PICK UP A "HANDSOME BLOND YOUTH"...
YOU SAID IT, PARDNER.
AND ANYHOW, WHAT'S THE POINT?
"BLOND, 5'9", 135 POUNDS, EYES GREEN, PRETTY-BOY TYPE." JESUS, THERE MUST BE DOZENS OF KIDS FITTING THIS DESCRIPTION IN MANHATTAN ALONE.
PLUS, ALL HE'S GOTTA DO IS DYE HIS HAIR AND HE AIN'T BLOND. THROW IN SOME COLORED CONTACT LENSES, AND WE SKIP RIGHT OVER HIM.
SHIT. HE'S THE EINSTEIN THEY SAY, HE'S LOOKIN' LIKE ***YOU*** BY NOW, MY BROTHER.
HEY!

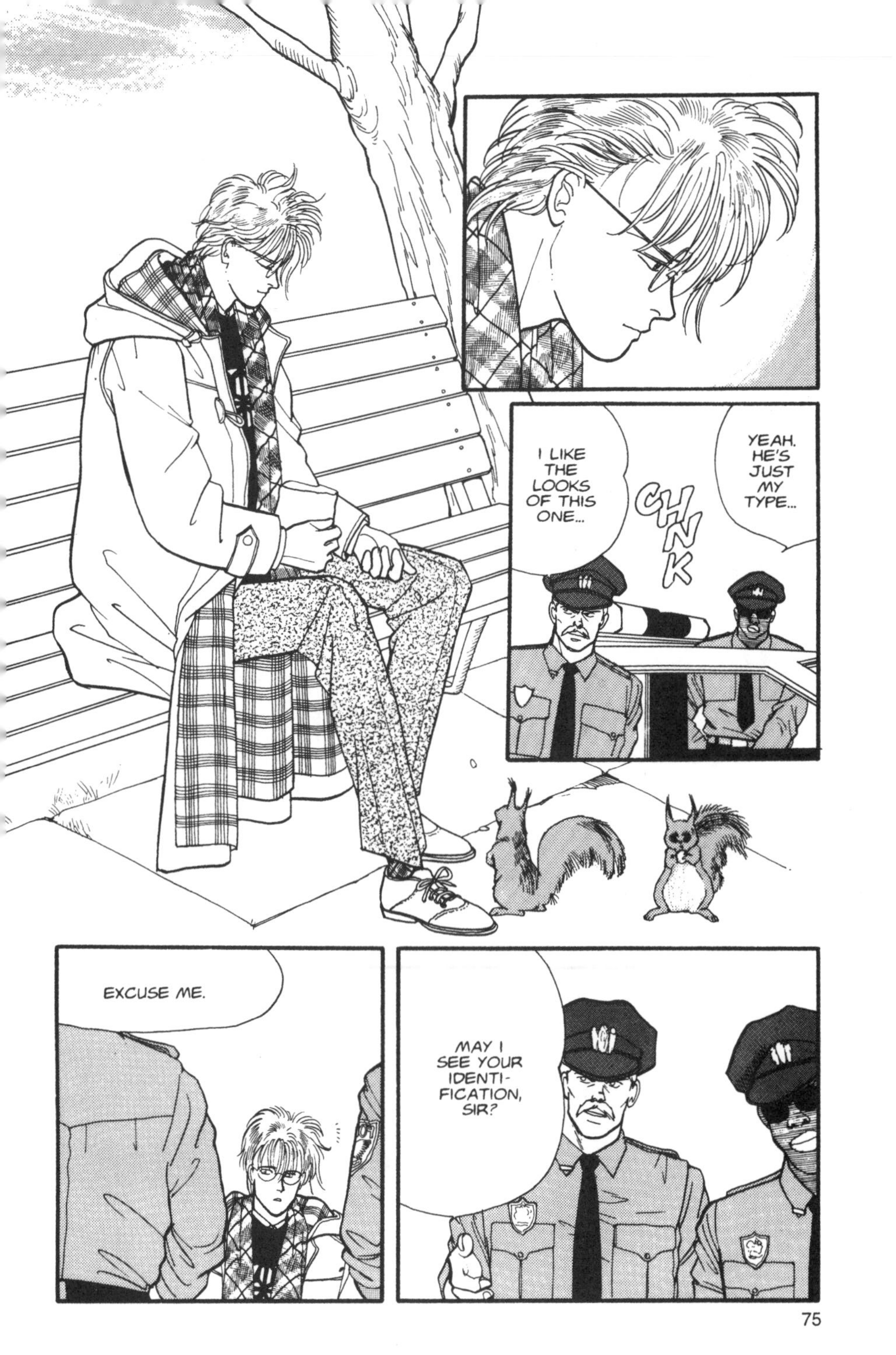
I LIKE THE LOOKS OF THIS ONE...
CHNK
YEAH. HE'S JUST MY TYPE...
EXCUSE ME.
MAY I SEE YOUR IDENTI-FICATION, SIR?

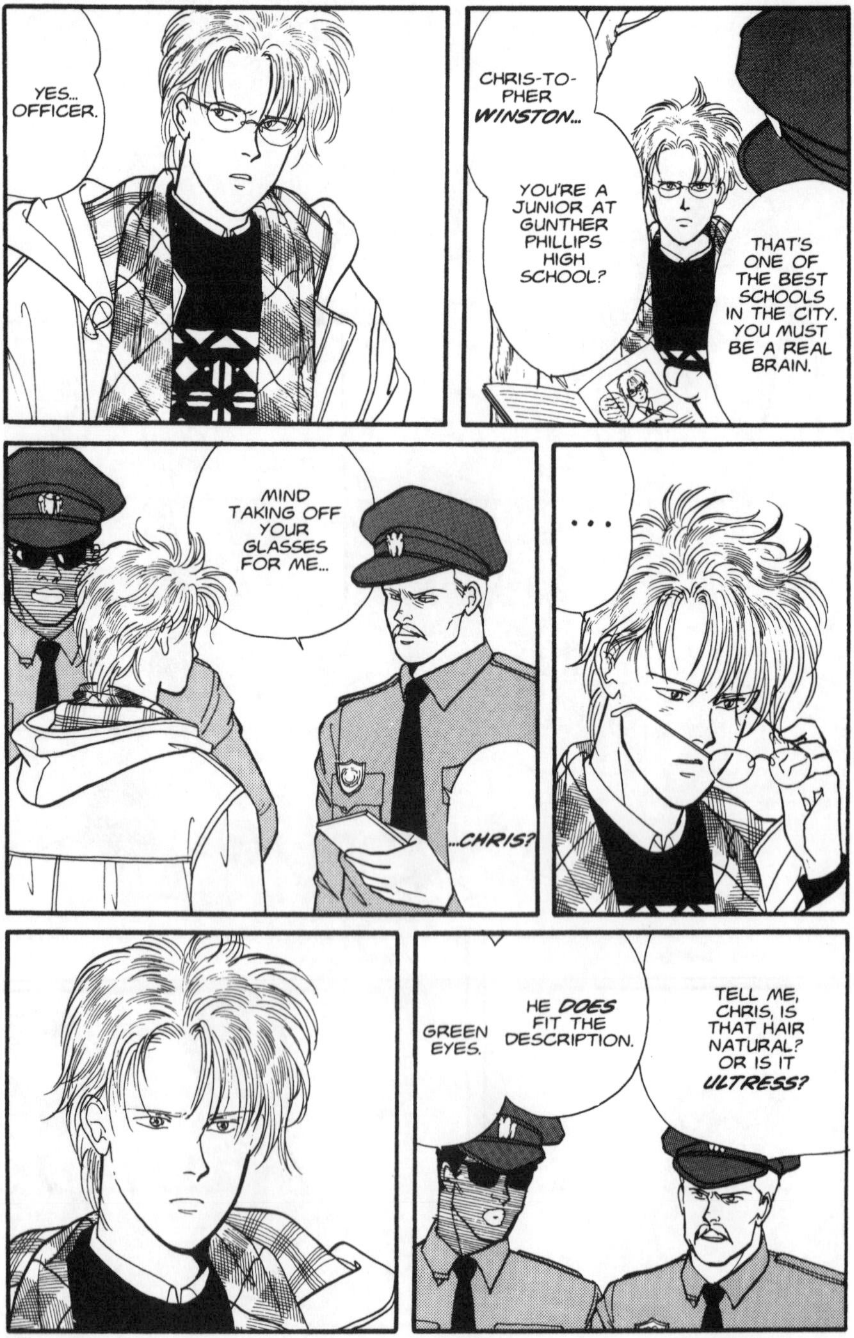
YES... OFFICER.
CHRIS-TO-PHER WINSTON...
YOU'RE A JUNIOR AT GUNTHER PHILLIPS HIGH SCHOOL?
THAT'S ONE OF THE BEST SCHOOLS IN THE CITY. YOU MUST BE A REAL BRAIN.
MIND TAKING OFF YOUR GLASSES FOR ME...
...CHRIS?
. . .
GREEN EYES.
HE DOES FIT THE DESCRIPTION.
TELL ME, CHRIS, IS THAT HAIR NATURAL? OR IS IT ULTRESS?

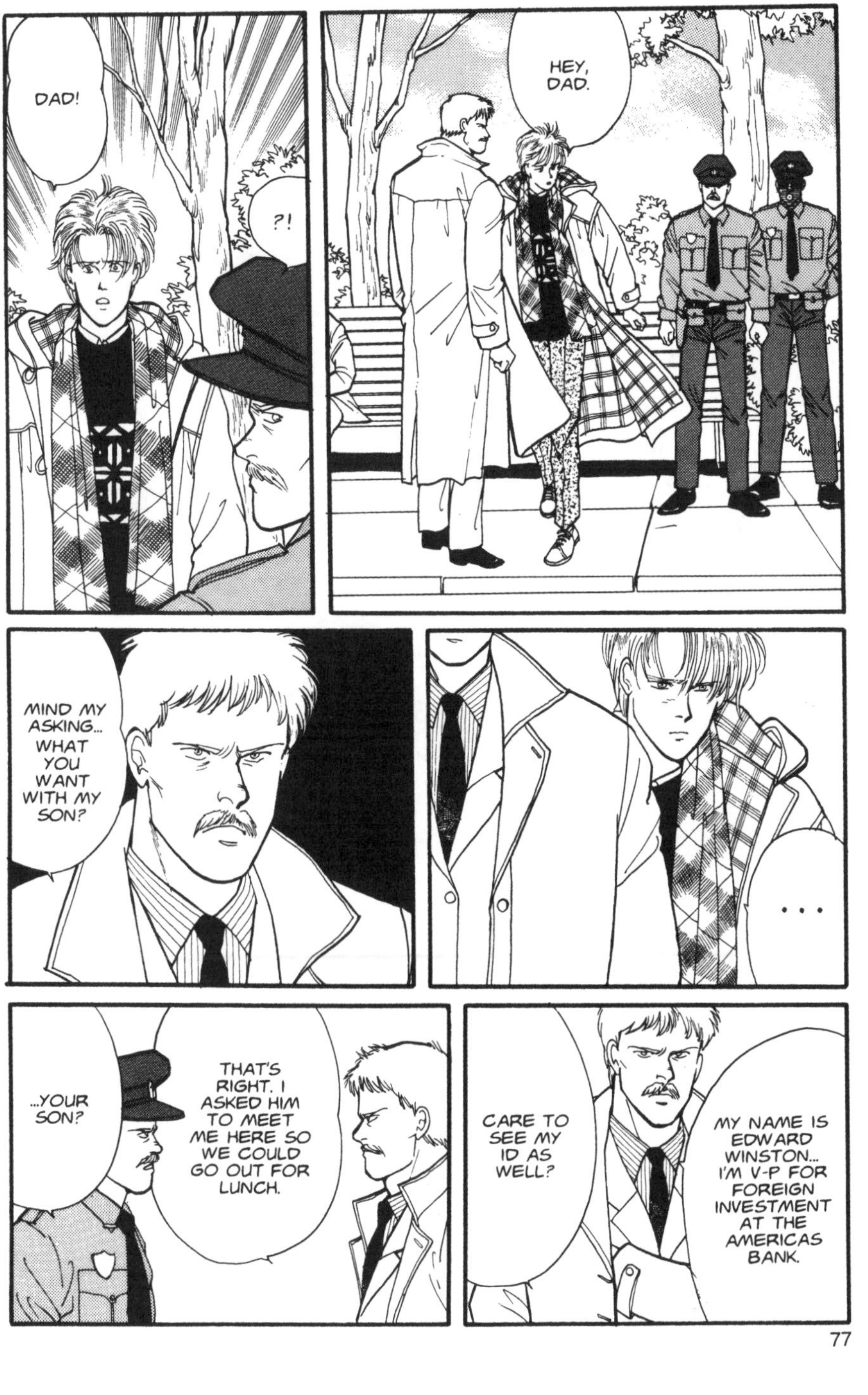
DAD!
?!
HEY, DAD.
MIND MY ASKING... WHAT YOU WANT WITH MY SON?
. . .
...YOUR SON?
THAT'S RIGHT. I ASKED HIM TO MEET ME HERE SO WE COULD GO OUT FOR LUNCH.
CARE TO SEE MY ID AS WELL?
MY NAME IS EDWARD WINSTON... I'M V-P FOR FOREIGN INVESTMENT AT THE AMERICAS BANK.

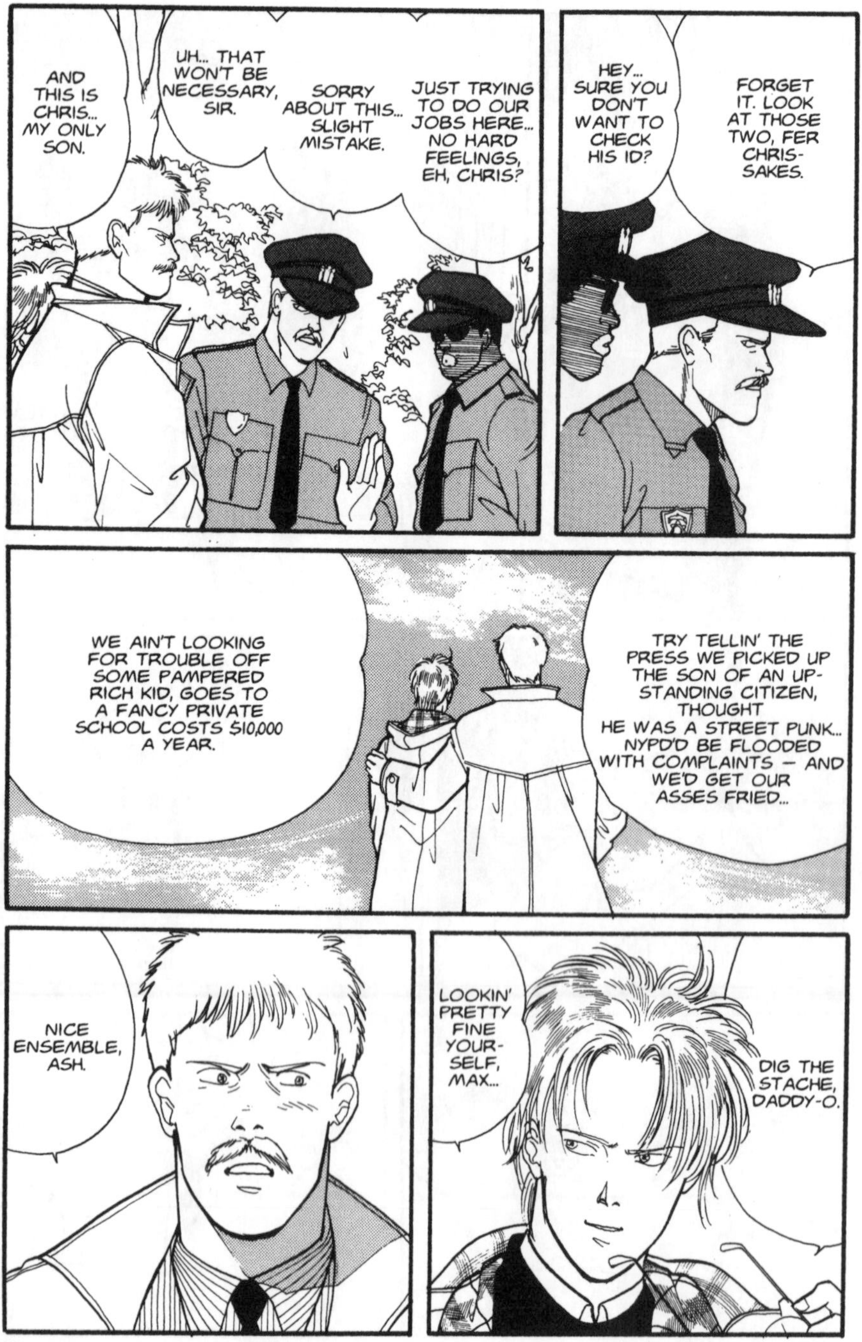
AND THIS IS CHRIS... MY ONLY SON.
UH... THAT WON'T BE NECESSARY, SIR.
SORRY ABOUT THIS... SLIGHT MISTAKE.
JUST TRYING TO DO OUR JOBS HERE... NO HARD FEELINGS, EH, CHRIS?
HEY... SURE YOU DON'T WANT TO CHECK HIS ID?
FORGET IT. LOOK AT THOSE TWO, FER CHRIS-SAKES.
WE AIN'T LOOKING FOR TROUBLE OFF SOME PAMPERED RICH KID, GOES TO A FANCY PRIVATE SCHOOL COSTS $10,000 A YEAR.
TRY TELLIN' THE PRESS WE PICKED UP THE SON OF AN UP-STANDING CITIZEN, THOUGHT HE WAS A STREET PUNK... NYPD'D BE FLOODED WITH COMPLAINTS — AND WE'D GET OUR ASSES FRIED...
NICE ENSEMBLE, ASH.
LOOKIN' PRETTY FINE YOUR-SELF, MAX...
DIG THE STACHE, DADDY-O.

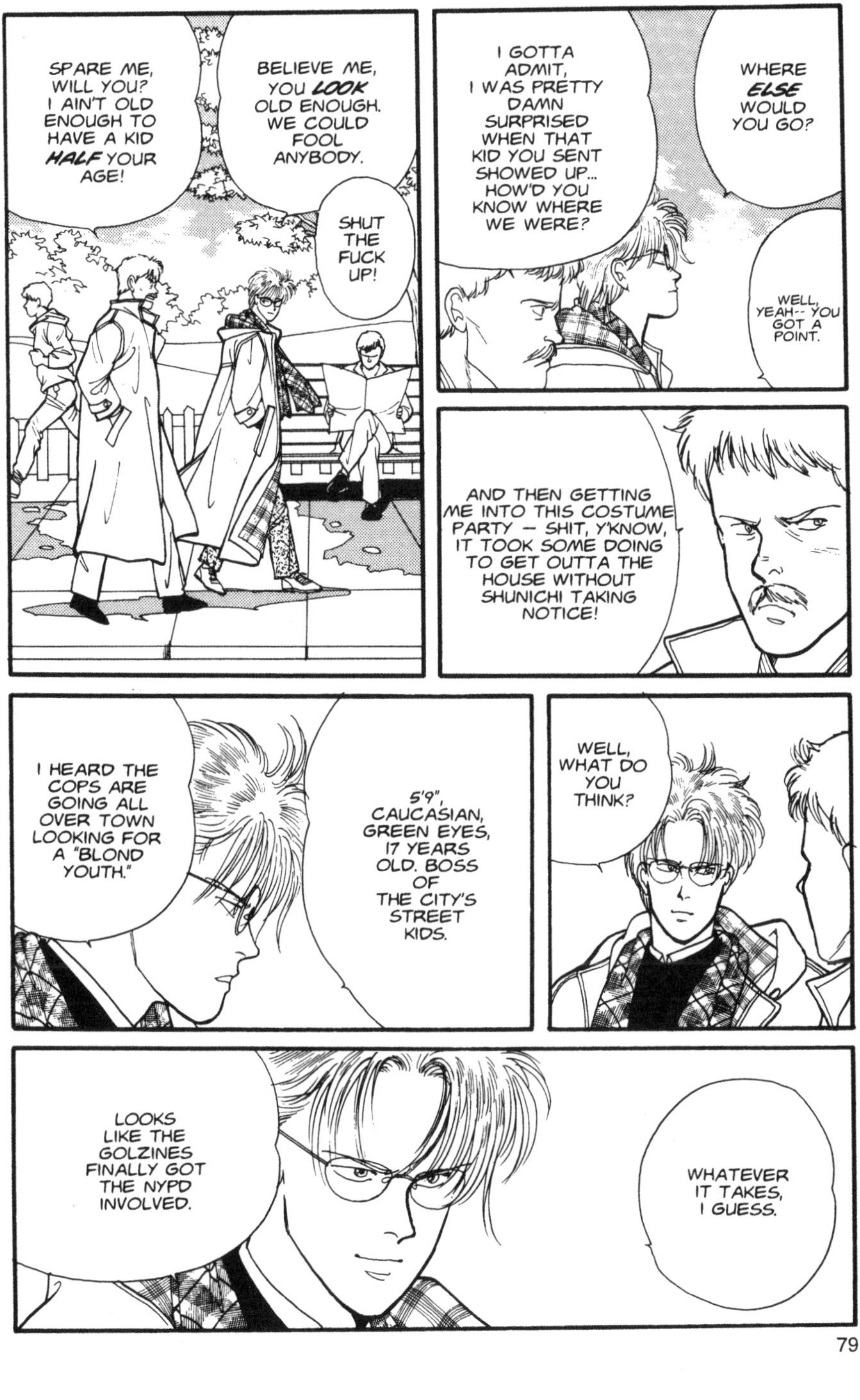
SPARE ME, WILL YOU? I AIN'T OLD ENOUGH TO HAVE A KID HALF YOUR AGE!
BELIEVE ME, YOU LOOK OLD ENOUGH. WE COULD FOOL ANYBODY.
SHUT THE FUCK UP!
I GOTTA ADMIT, I WAS PRETTY DAMN SURPRISED WHEN THAT KID YOU SENT SHOWED UP... HOW'D YOU KNOW WHERE WE WERE?
WHERE ELSE WOULD YOU GO?
WELL, YEAH-- YOU GOT A POINT.
AND THEN GETTING ME INTO THIS COSTUME PARTY — SHIT, Y'KNOW, IT TOOK SOME DOING TO GET OUTTA THE HOUSE WITHOUT SHUNICHI TAKING NOTICE!
I HEARD THE COPS ARE GOING ALL OVER TOWN LOOKING FOR A "BLOND YOUTH."
5'9", CAUCASIAN, GREEN EYES, 17 YEARS OLD. BOSS OF THE CITY'S STREET KIDS.
WELL, WHAT DO YOU THINK?
LOOKS LIKE THE GOLZINES FINALLY GOT THE NYPD INVOLVED.
WHATEVER IT TAKES, I GUESS.

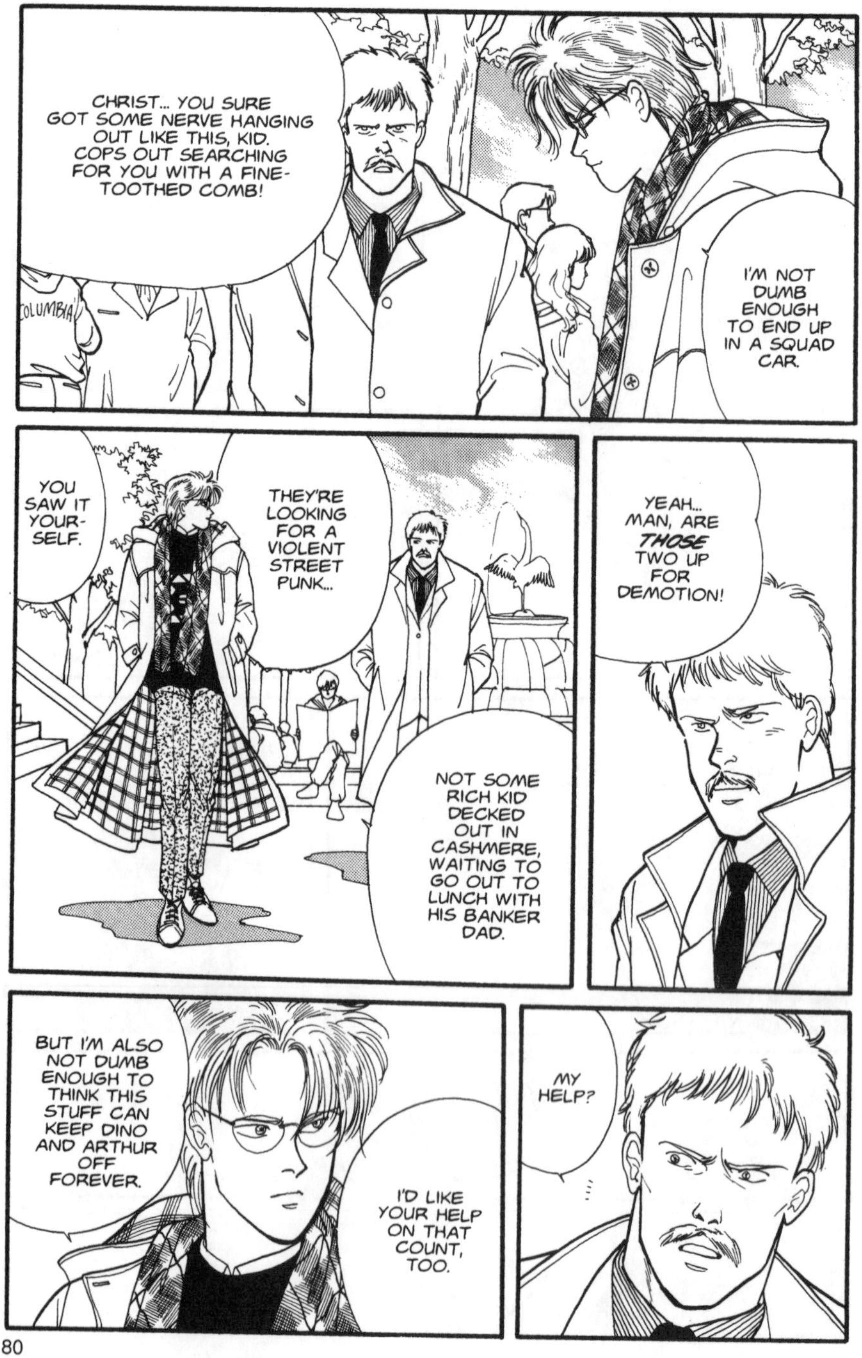
CHRIST... YOU SURE GOT SOME NERVE HANGING OUT LIKE THIS, KID. COPS OUT SEARCHING FOR YOU WITH A FINE-TOOTHED COMB!
COLUMBIA
I'M NOT DUMB ENOUGH TO END UP IN A SQUAD CAR.
YOU SAW IT YOURSELF.
THEY'RE LOOKING FOR A VIOLENT STREET PUNK...
NOT SOME RICH KID DECKED OUT IN CASHMERE, WAITING TO GO OUT TO LUNCH WITH HIS BANKER DAD.
YEAH... MAN, ARE *THOSE* TWO UP FOR DEMOTION!
BUT I'M ALSO NOT DUMB ENOUGH TO THINK THIS STUFF CAN KEEP DINO AND ARTHUR OFF FOREVER.
I'D LIKE YOUR HELP ON THAT COUNT, TOO.
MY HELP?

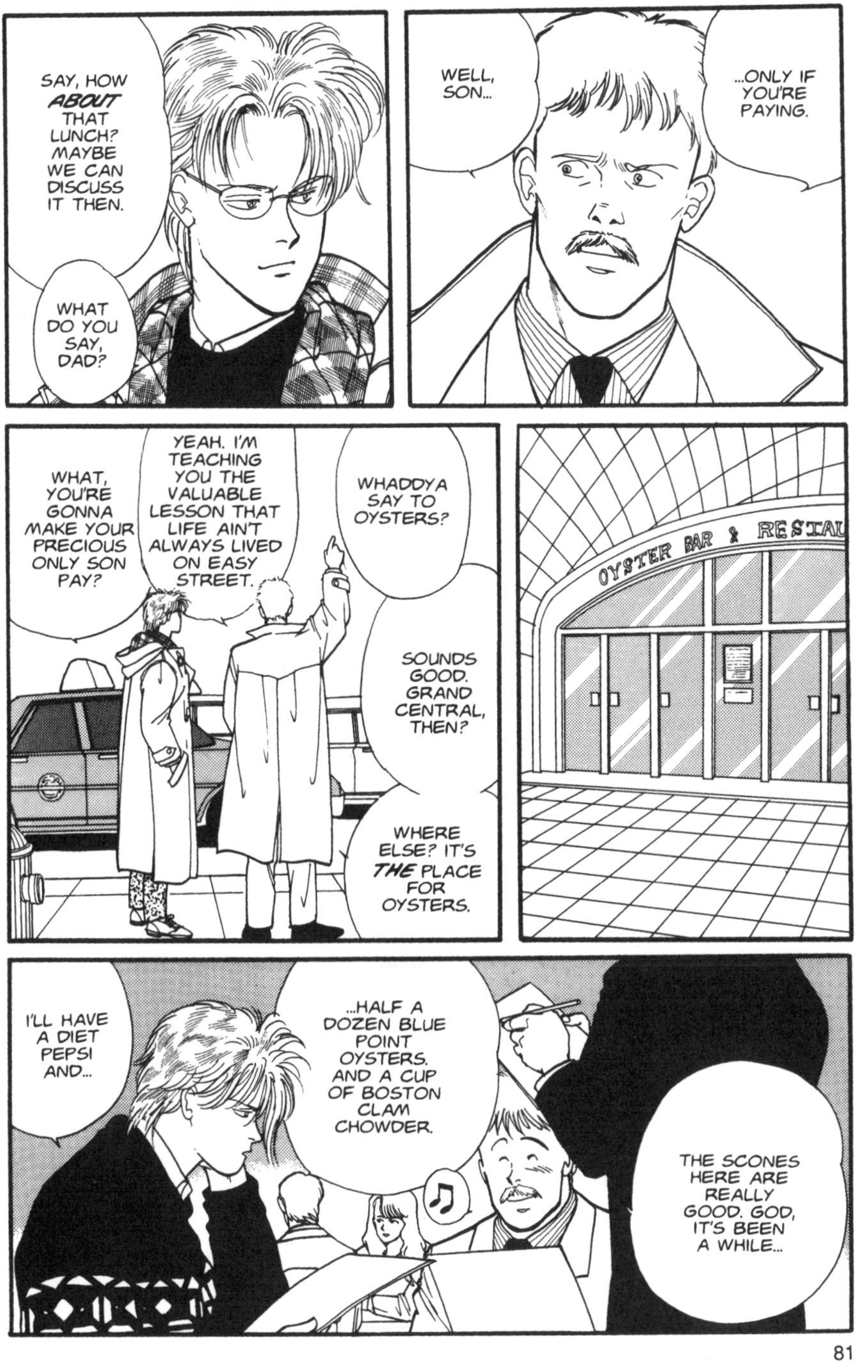
SAY, HOW *ABOUT* THAT LUNCH? MAYBE WE CAN DISCUSS IT THEN.
WHAT DO YOU SAY, DAD?
WELL, SON...
...ONLY IF YOU'RE PAYING.
WHAT, YOU'RE GONNA MAKE YOUR PRECIOUS ONLY SON PAY?
YEAH. I'M TEACHING YOU THE VALUABLE LESSON THAT LIFE AIN'T ALWAYS LIVED ON EASY STREET.
WHADDYA SAY TO OYSTERS?
SOUNDS GOOD. GRAND CENTRAL, THEN?
WHERE ELSE? IT'S *THE* PLACE FOR OYSTERS.
OYSTER BAR & RESTAU
I'LL HAVE A DIET PEPSI AND...
...HALF A DOZEN BLUE POINT OYSTERS. AND A CUP OF BOSTON CLAM CHOWDER.
THE SCONES HERE ARE REALLY GOOD. GOD, IT'S BEEN A WHILE...

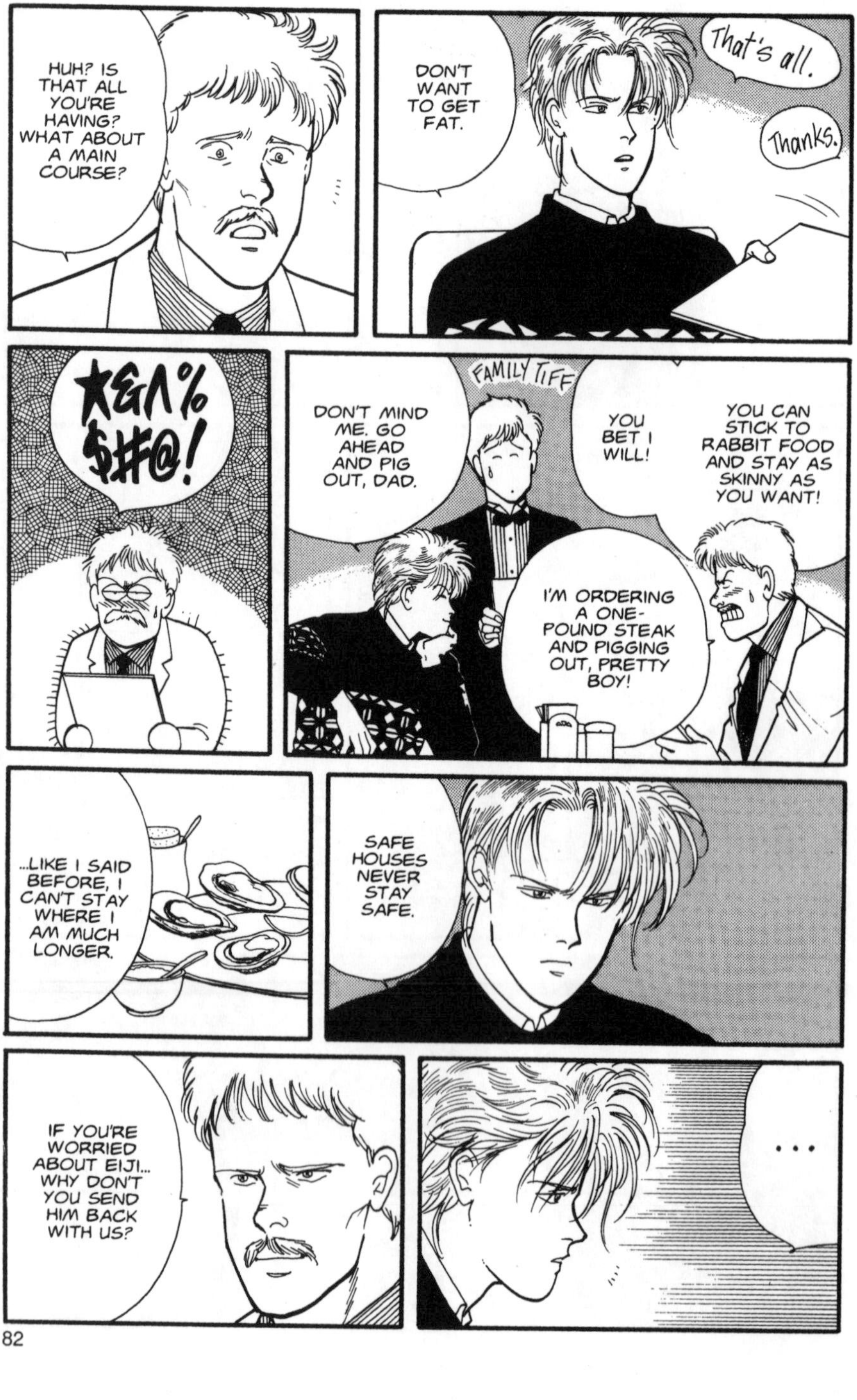
HUH? IS THAT ALL YOU'RE HAVING? WHAT ABOUT A MAIN COURSE?
DON'T WANT TO GET FAT.
That's all.
Thanks.
★€∧%$#@!
FAMILY TIFF
DON'T MIND ME. GO AHEAD AND PIG OUT, DAD.
YOU BET I WILL!
YOU CAN STICK TO RABBIT FOOD AND STAY AS SKINNY AS YOU WANT!
I'M ORDERING A ONE-POUND STEAK AND PIGGING OUT, PRETTY BOY!
...LIKE I SAID BEFORE, I CAN'T STAY WHERE I AM MUCH LONGER.
SAFE HOUSES NEVER STAY SAFE.
IF YOU'RE WORRIED ABOUT EIJI... WHY DON'T YOU SEND HIM BACK WITH US?
...

...HE'S STILL SAFER WITH ME.

IF THE SHIT COMES DOWN, I DON'T THINK YOU GUYS COULD TAKE CARE OF HIM.

WELL, LET'S JUST LEAVE IT AT THAT, FOR NOW.

SO... YOU SAID YOU WANTED MY HELP?

YEAH, I BOUGHT AN APARTMENT ON 59TH, AND I WANT YOU TO GO SIGN THE CONTRACT FOR ME.

YOU *BOUGHT* AN APART-MENT?

YEAH.

ANYWAY, I CAN'T SIGN OFF ON IT MYSELF... I'M A MINOR, REMEMBER?

WHADDYA MEAN, YOU *BOUGHT* AN APART-MENT?

NO BIG DEAL. JUST HACKED INTO THE BROKER'S CHEAP-ASS COMPUTER.

WHAT?! YOU MEAN YOU—

AND THAT'S NOT ALL I'VE BEEN UP TO...

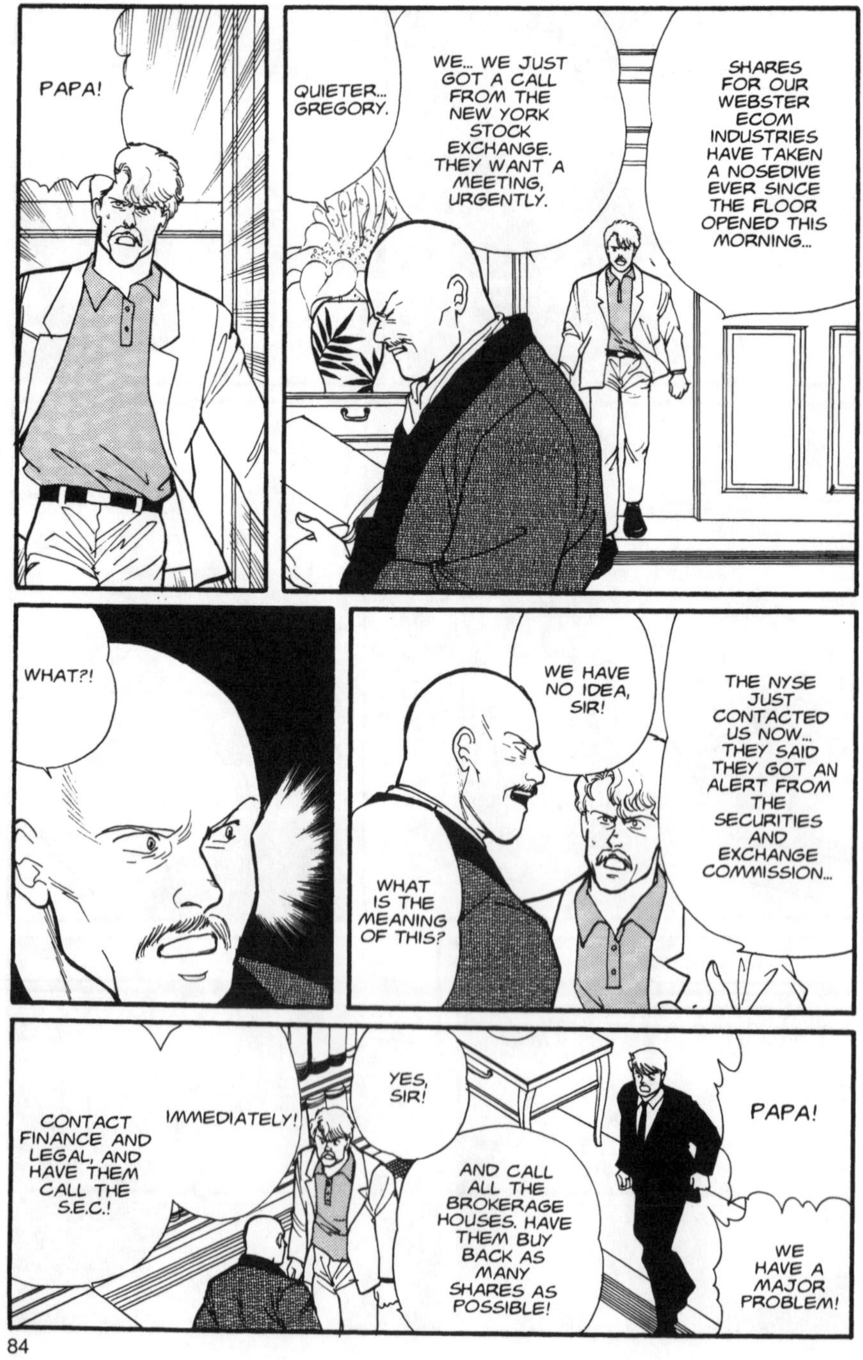
PAPA!
QUIETER... GREGORY.
WE... WE JUST GOT A CALL FROM THE NEW YORK STOCK EXCHANGE. THEY WANT A MEETING, URGENTLY.
SHARES FOR OUR WEBSTER ECOM INDUSTRIES HAVE TAKEN A NOSEDIVE EVER SINCE THE FLOOR OPENED THIS MORNING...
WHAT?!
WHAT IS THE MEANING OF THIS?
WE HAVE NO IDEA, SIR!
THE NYSE JUST CONTACTED US NOW... THEY SAID THEY GOT AN ALERT FROM THE SECURITIES AND EXCHANGE COMMISSION...
CONTACT FINANCE AND LEGAL, AND HAVE THEM CALL THE S.E.C.!
IMMEDIATELY!
YES, SIR!
AND CALL ALL THE BROKERAGE HOUSES. HAVE THEM BUY BACK AS MANY SHARES AS POSSIBLE!
PAPA!
WE HAVE A MAJOR PROBLEM!

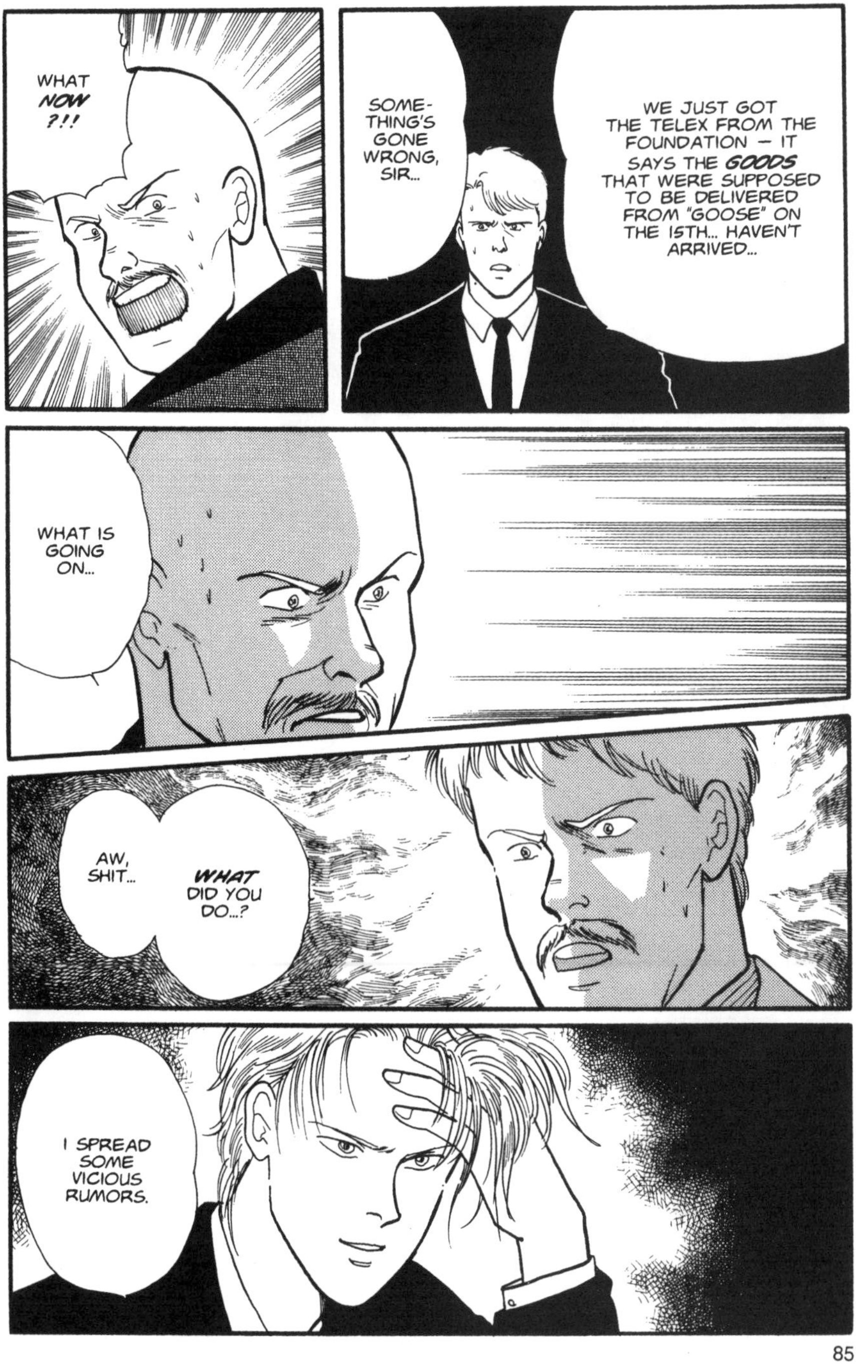
WHAT *NOW* ?!!
SOME-THING'S GONE WRONG, SIR...
WE JUST GOT THE TELEX FROM THE FOUNDATION — IT SAYS THE *GOODS* THAT WERE SUPPOSED TO BE DELIVERED FROM "GOOSE" ON THE 15TH... HAVEN'T ARRIVED...
WHAT IS GOING ON...
AW, SHIT...
WHAT DID YOU DO...?
I SPREAD SOME VICIOUS RUMORS.

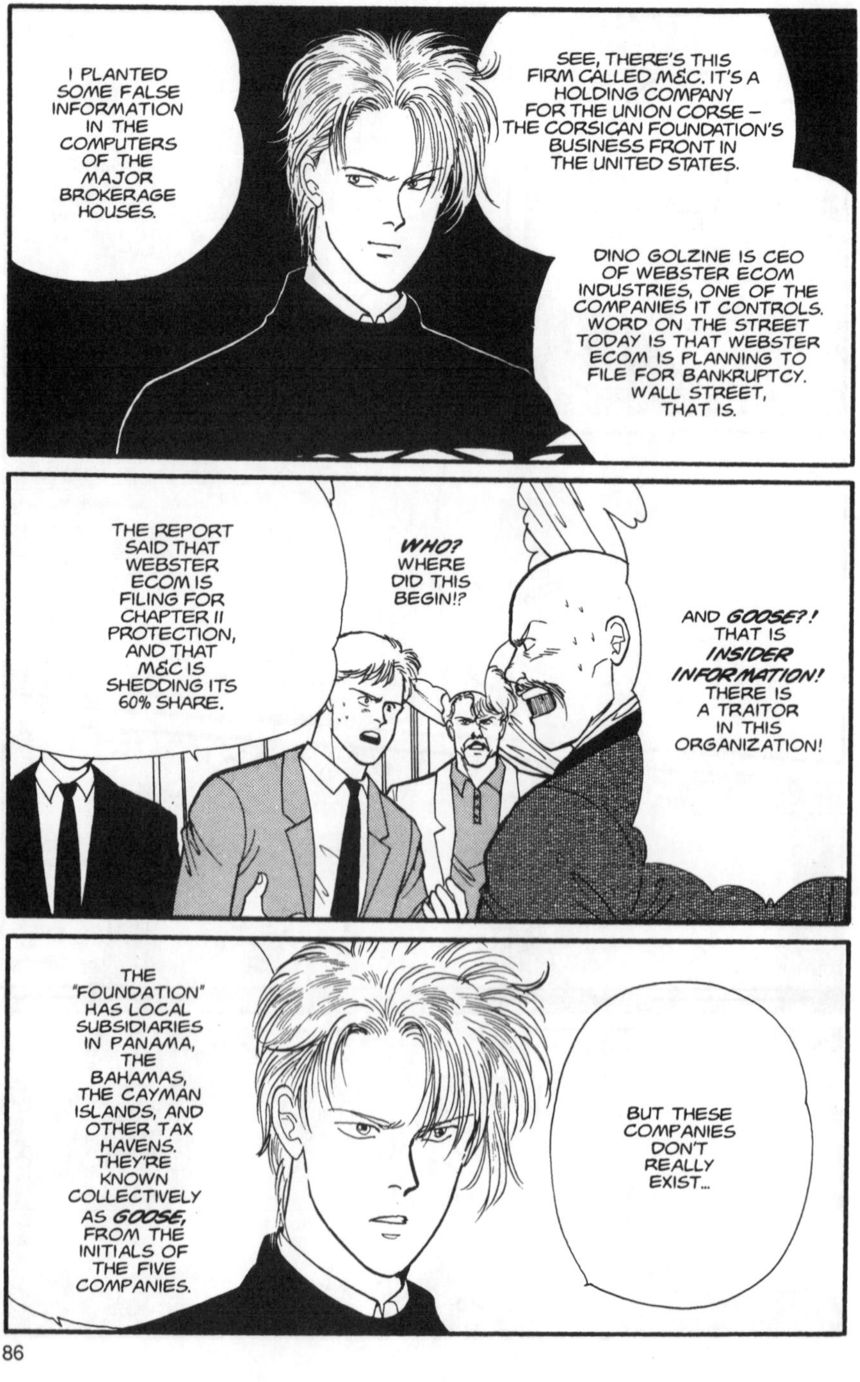
I PLANTED SOME FALSE INFORMATION IN THE COMPUTERS OF THE MAJOR BROKERAGE HOUSES.
SEE, THERE'S THIS FIRM CALLED M&C. IT'S A HOLDING COMPANY FOR THE UNION CORSE – THE CORSICAN FOUNDATION'S BUSINESS FRONT IN THE UNITED STATES.
DINO GOLZINE IS CEO OF WEBSTER ECOM INDUSTRIES, ONE OF THE COMPANIES IT CONTROLS. WORD ON THE STREET TODAY IS THAT WEBSTER ECOM IS PLANNING TO FILE FOR BANKRUPTCY. WALL STREET, THAT IS.
THE REPORT SAID THAT WEBSTER ECOM IS FILING FOR CHAPTER II PROTECTION, AND THAT M&C IS SHEDDING ITS 60% SHARE.
WHO? WHERE DID THIS BEGIN!?
AND GOOSE?! THAT IS INSIDER INFORMATION! THERE IS A TRAITOR IN THIS ORGANIZATION!
THE "FOUNDATION" HAS LOCAL SUBSIDIARIES IN PANAMA, THE BAHAMAS, THE CAYMAN ISLANDS, AND OTHER TAX HAVENS. THEY'RE KNOWN COLLECTIVELY AS GOOSE, FROM THE INITIALS OF THE FIVE COMPANIES.
BUT THESE COMPANIES DON'T REALLY EXIST...

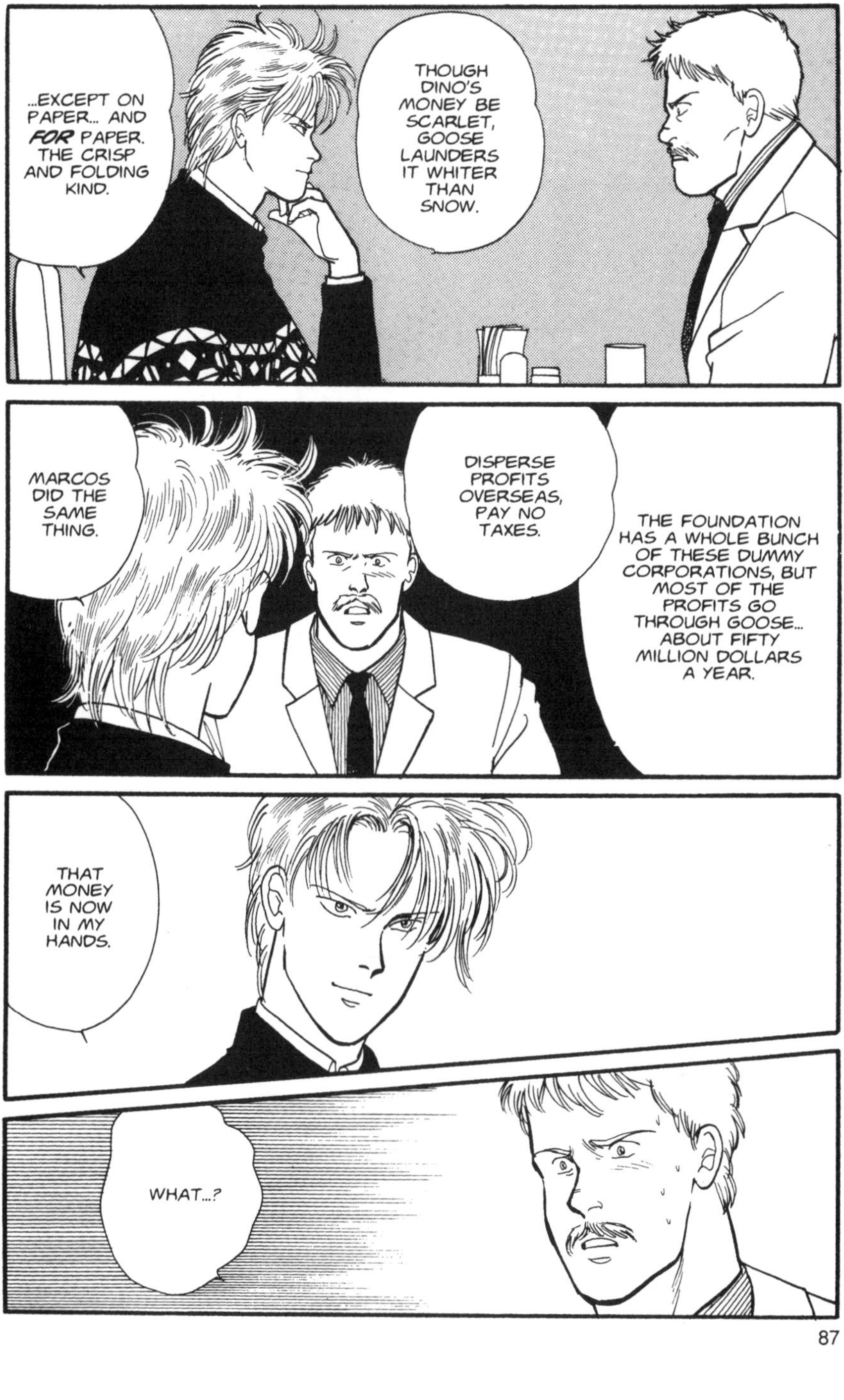
...EXCEPT ON PAPER... AND *FOR* PAPER. THE CRISP AND FOLDING KIND.
THOUGH DINO'S MONEY BE SCARLET, GOOSE LAUNDERS IT WHITER THAN SNOW.
MARCOS DID THE SAME THING.
DISPERSE PROFITS OVERSEAS, PAY NO TAXES.
THE FOUNDATION HAS A WHOLE BUNCH OF THESE DUMMY CORPORATIONS, BUT MOST OF THE PROFITS GO THROUGH GOOSE... ABOUT FIFTY MILLION DOLLARS A YEAR.
THAT MONEY IS NOW IN MY HANDS.
WHAT...?

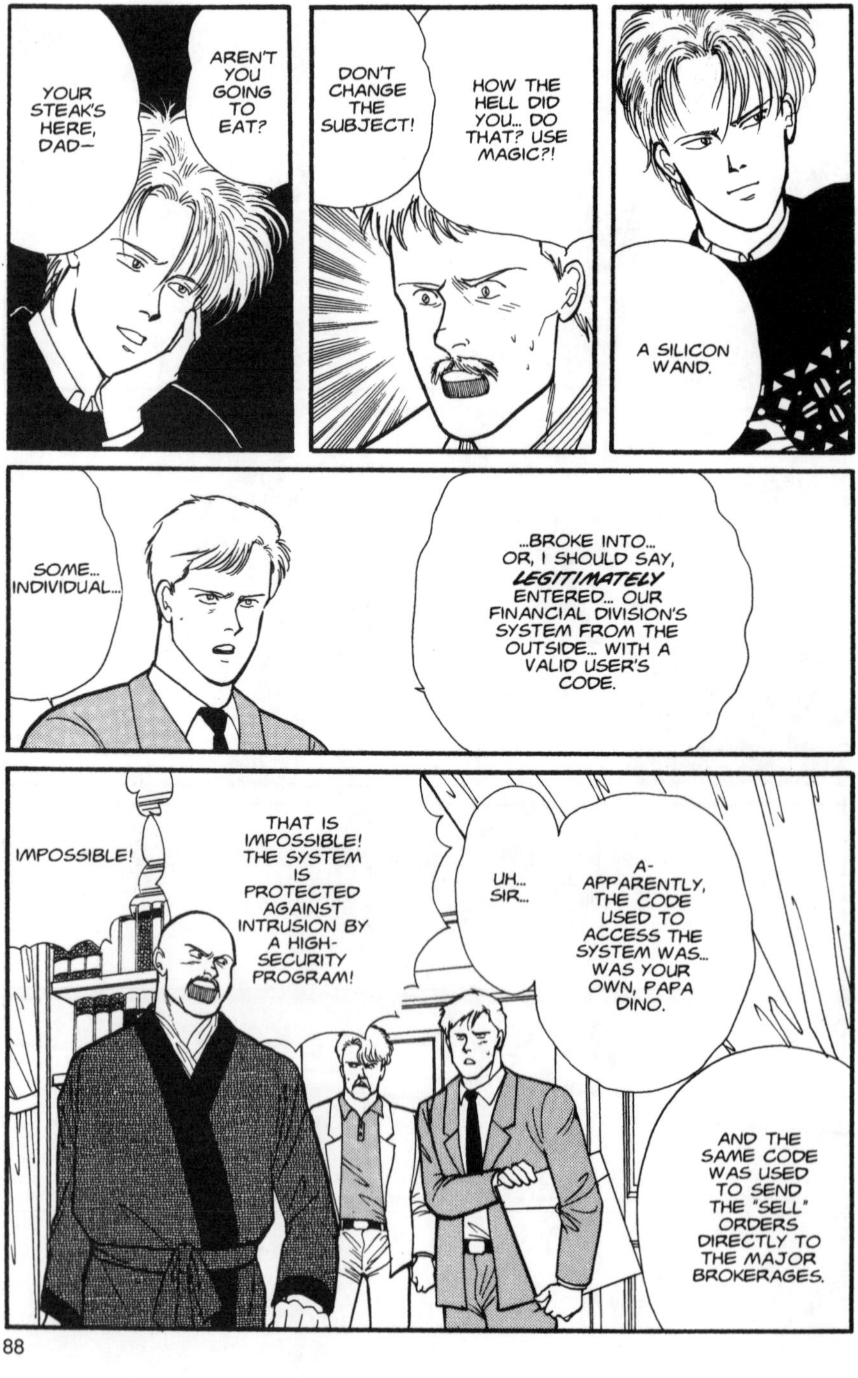

YOUR STEAK'S HERE, DAD—
AREN'T YOU GOING TO EAT?
DON'T CHANGE THE SUBJECT!
HOW THE HELL DID YOU... DO THAT? USE MAGIC?!
A SILICON WAND.
SOME... INDIVIDUAL...
...BROKE INTO... OR, I SHOULD SAY, LEGITIMATELY ENTERED... OUR FINANCIAL DIVISION'S SYSTEM FROM THE OUTSIDE... WITH A VALID USER'S CODE.
IMPOSSIBLE!
THAT IS IMPOSSIBLE! THE SYSTEM IS PROTECTED AGAINST INTRUSION BY A HIGH-SECURITY PROGRAM!
UH... SIR...
A-APPARENTLY, THE CODE USED TO ACCESS THE SYSTEM WAS... WAS YOUR OWN, PAPA DINO.
AND THE SAME CODE WAS USED TO SEND THE "SELL" ORDERS DIRECTLY TO THE MAJOR BROKERAGES.

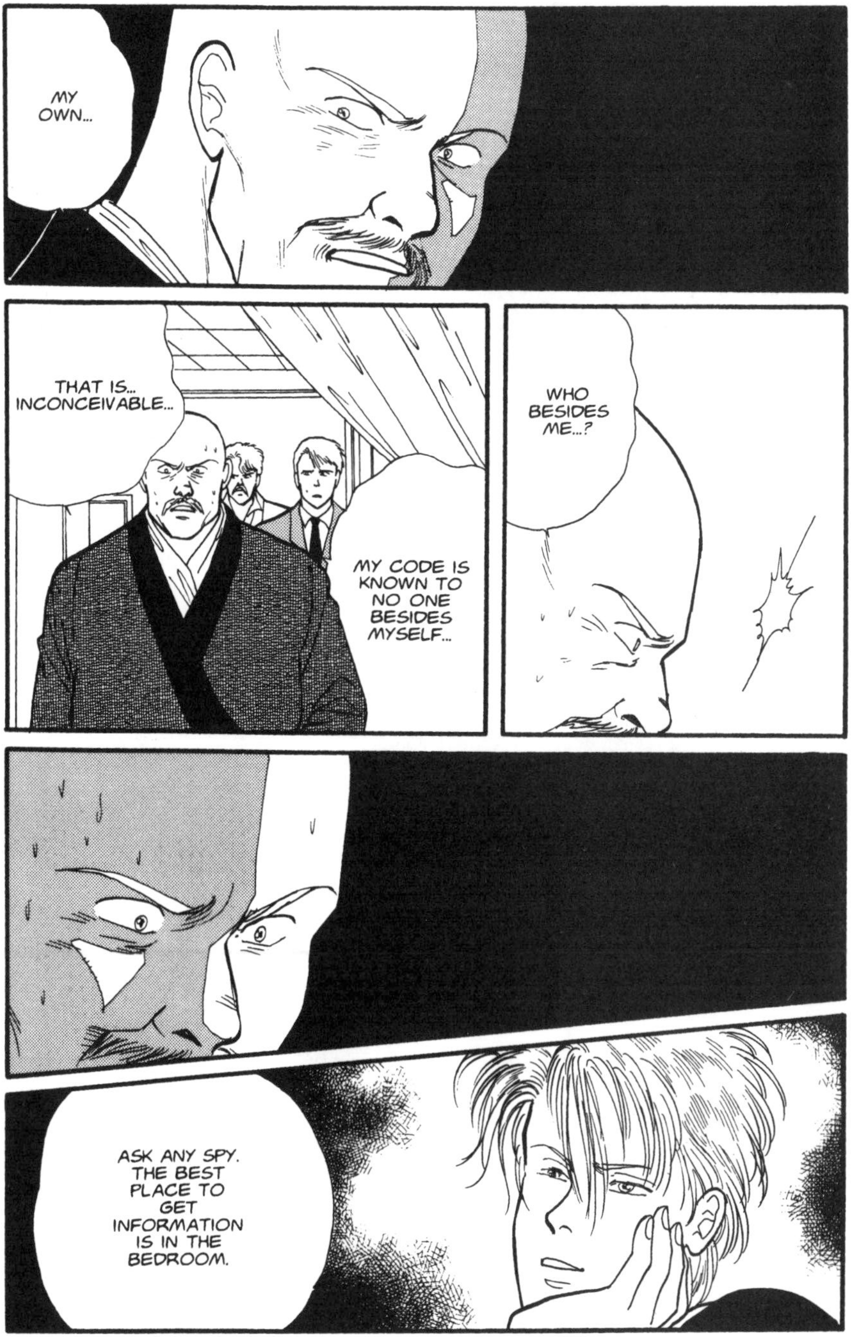
MY OWN...
THAT IS... INCONCEIVABLE...
MY CODE IS KNOWN TO NO ONE BESIDES MYSELF...
WHO BESIDES ME...?
ASK ANY SPY. THE BEST PLACE TO GET INFORMATION IS IN THE BEDROOM.

AND THE ONLY PEOPLE WHO HAVE FREE ACCESS TO GOLZINE'S... ARE HIS YOUNG FRIENDS...

WHILE THE OLD PERVERT INDULGED HIS TWISTED TASTES, MY MIND WAS ELSEWHERE, THANK GOD. YOU MIGHT SAY I JUST LAID BACK, AND THOUGHT OF THE BANK OF ENGLAND.

SEE, HE'S A SHARP THINKER. SUMS UP EVERY MAN AS A THREAT OR BENEFACTOR. BUT THE ONE SORT OF PERSON HE *NEVER* THINKS ABOUT ARE THE BOYS.

BECAUSE THEY'RE NOT PEOPLE TO HIM. THEY'RE JUST TALKING SEX TOYS — TO BE USED, BROKEN, AND THROWN AWAY. ME TOO, AT FIRST. IT PROBABLY NEVER OCCURRED TO HIM IN THE BEGINNING THAT I HAD A BRAIN IN MY PRETTY LITTLE HEAD.

WELL, HE'S PAYING FOR IT NOW. M&C IS GOING TO BE HIT BY THIS, AND ALL THE COMPANIES IT CON-TROLS TOO.

GOLZINE WILL BE DESPERATE, TRYING TO BUY BACK SHARES AND SHORE UP HIS STOCK VALUE.

WEBSTER ECOM SHARES MIGHT RALLY FOR A WHILE...

BUT ONCE A COMPANY STARTS TO LOOK SHAKY —

IT ATTRACTS THE ATTENTION OF CORPORATE RAIDERS.

OR... CAPITAL FROM ANOTHER "ORGANIZA-TION" COMES FLOWING IN.

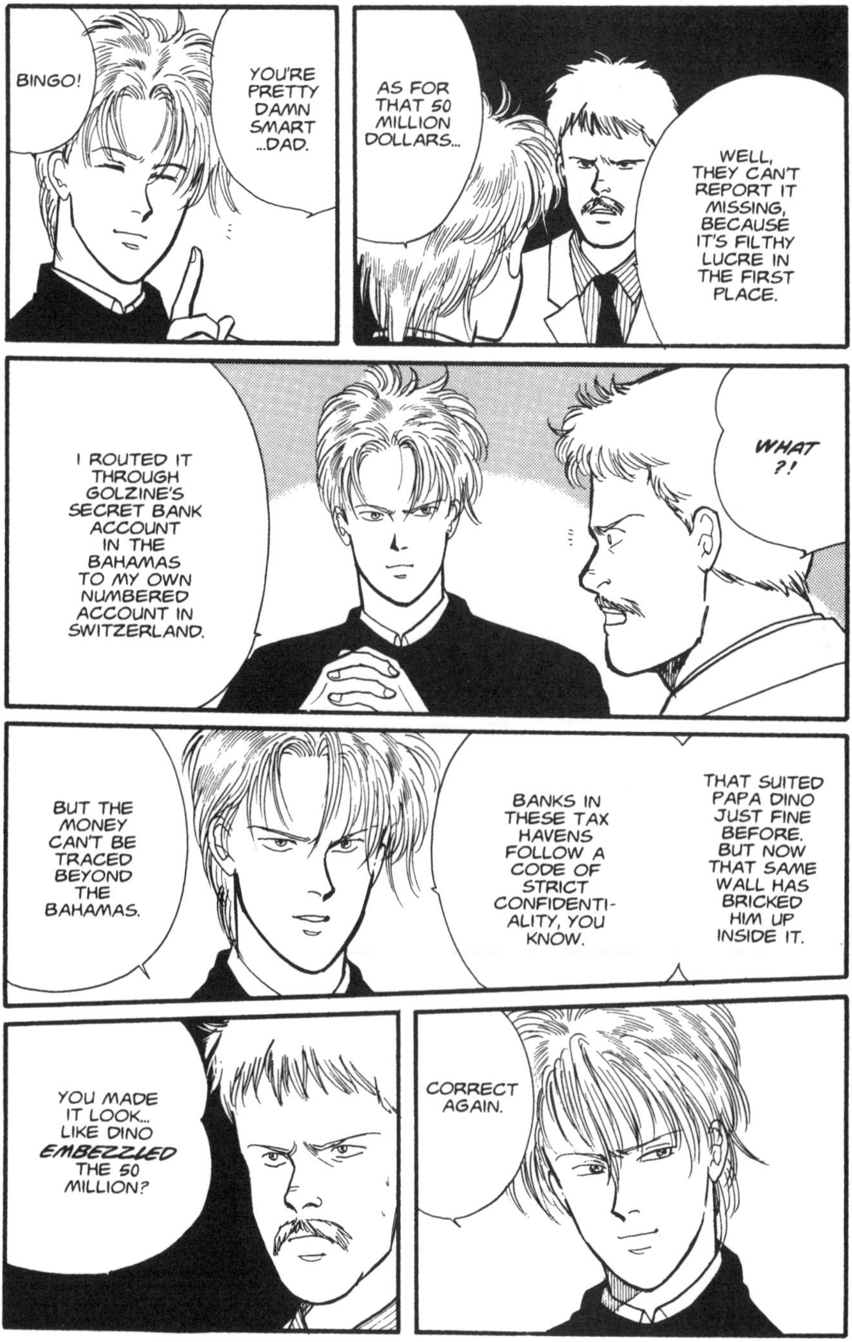
BINGO!
YOU'RE PRETTY DAMN SMART ...DAD.
AS FOR THAT 50 MILLION DOLLARS...
WELL, THEY CAN'T REPORT IT MISSING, BECAUSE IT'S FILTHY LUCRE IN THE FIRST PLACE.
I ROUTED IT THROUGH GOLZINE'S SECRET BANK ACCOUNT IN THE BAHAMAS TO MY OWN NUMBERED ACCOUNT IN SWITZERLAND.
WHAT ?!
BUT THE MONEY CAN'T BE TRACED BEYOND THE BAHAMAS.
BANKS IN THESE TAX HAVENS FOLLOW A CODE OF STRICT CONFIDENTI-ALITY, YOU KNOW.
THAT SUITED PAPA DINO JUST FINE BEFORE. BUT NOW THAT SAME WALL HAS BRICKED HIM UP INSIDE IT.
YOU MADE IT LOOK... LIKE DINO EMBEZZLED THE 50 MILLION?
CORRECT AGAIN.

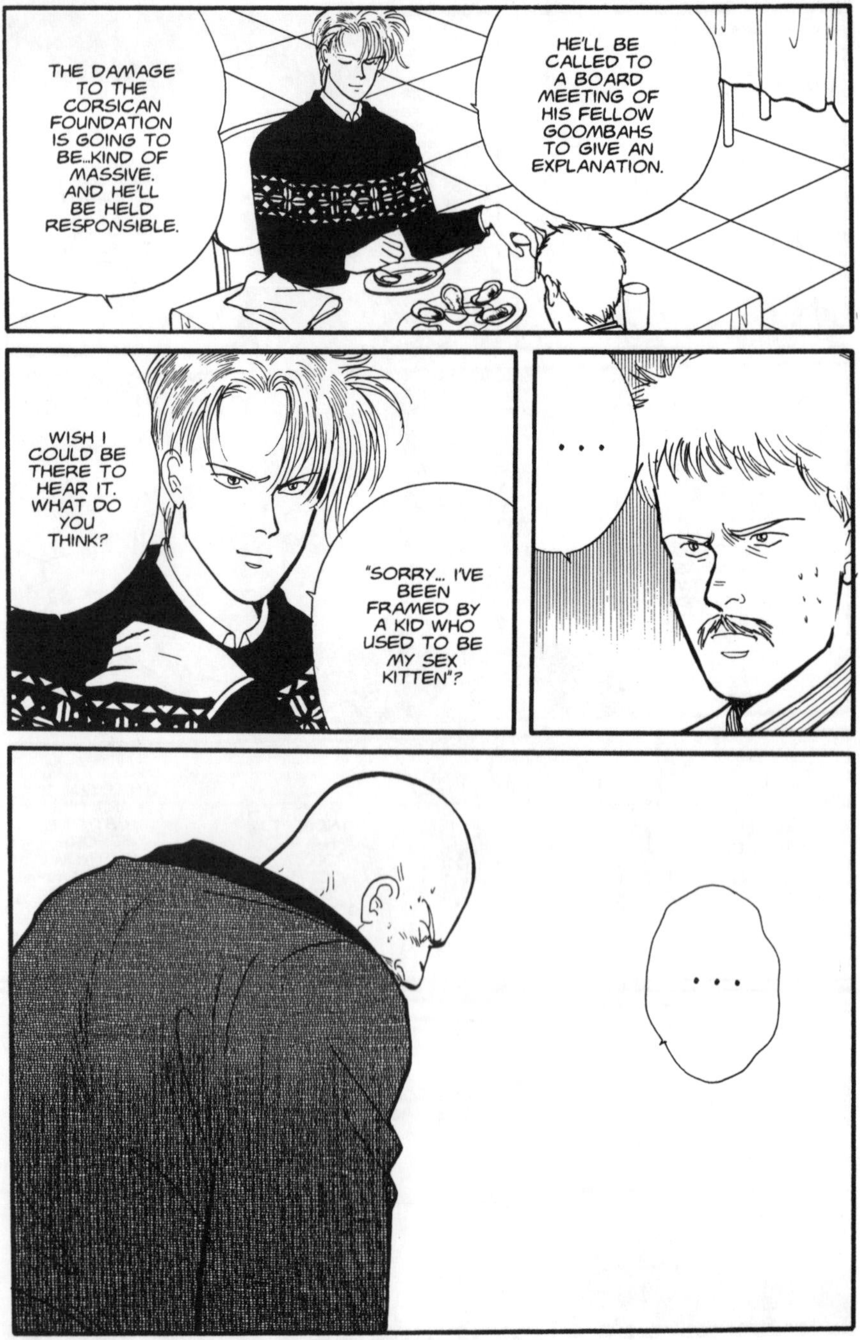
THE DAMAGE TO THE CORSICAN FOUNDATION IS GOING TO BE...KIND OF MASSIVE. AND HE'LL BE HELD RESPONSIBLE.
HE'LL BE CALLED TO A BOARD MEETING OF HIS FELLOW GOOMBAHS TO GIVE AN EXPLANATION.
WISH I COULD BE THERE TO HEAR IT. WHAT DO YOU THINK?
"SORRY... I'VE BEEN FRAMED BY A KID WHO USED TO BE MY SEX KITTEN"?
...
...

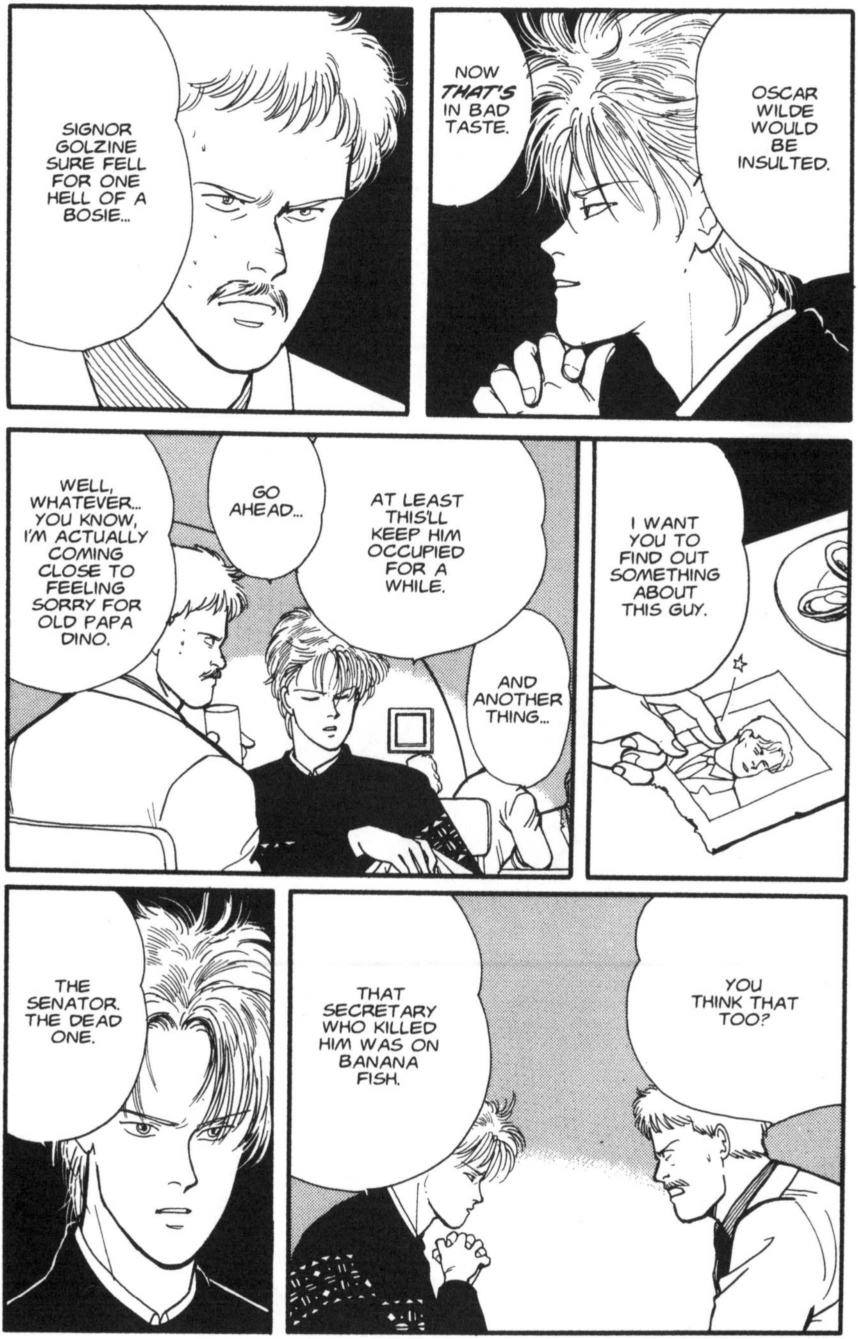
SIGNOR GOLZINE SURE FELL FOR ONE HELL OF A BOSIE...
NOW *THAT'S* IN BAD TASTE.
OSCAR WILDE WOULD BE INSULTED.
WELL, WHATEVER... YOU KNOW, I'M ACTUALLY COMING CLOSE TO FEELING SORRY FOR OLD PAPA DINO.
GO AHEAD...
AT LEAST THIS'LL KEEP HIM OCCUPIED FOR A WHILE.
AND ANOTHER THING...
I WANT YOU TO FIND OUT SOMETHING ABOUT THIS GUY.
THE SENATOR. THE DEAD ONE.
THAT SECRETARY WHO KILLED HIM WAS ON BANANA FISH.
YOU THINK THAT TOO?

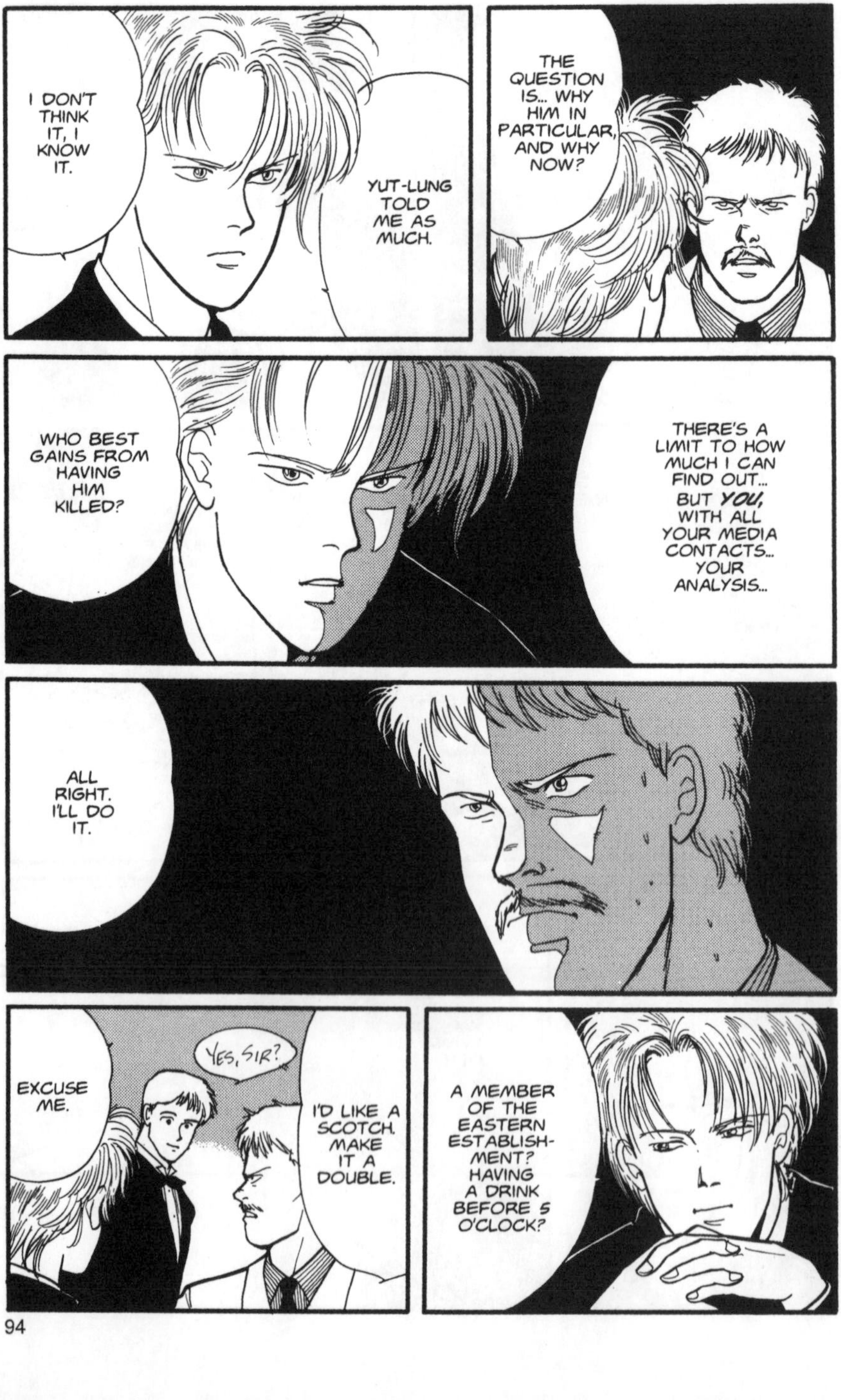
I DON'T THINK IT, I KNOW IT.
YUT-LUNG TOLD ME AS MUCH.
THE QUESTION IS... WHY HIM IN PARTICULAR, AND WHY NOW?
WHO BEST GAINS FROM HAVING HIM KILLED?
THERE'S A LIMIT TO HOW MUCH I CAN FIND OUT... BUT YOU, WITH ALL YOUR MEDIA CONTACTS... YOUR ANALYSIS...
ALL RIGHT. I'LL DO IT.
EXCUSE ME.
YES, SIR?
I'D LIKE A SCOTCH. MAKE IT A DOUBLE.
A MEMBER OF THE EASTERN ESTABLISHMENT? HAVING A DRINK BEFORE 5 O'CLOCK?

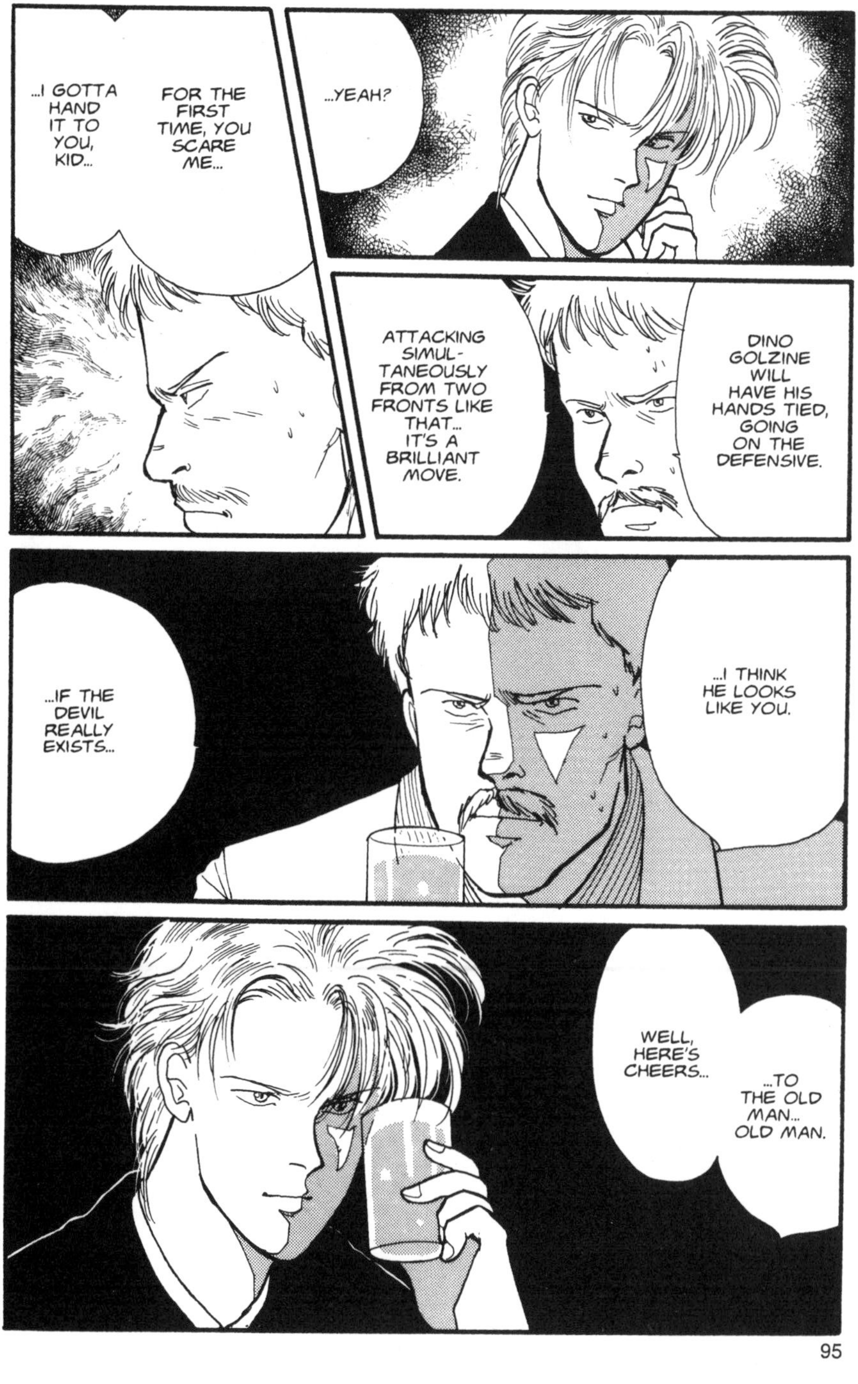
...I GOTTA HAND IT TO YOU, KID...
FOR THE FIRST TIME, YOU SCARE ME...
...YEAH?
ATTACKING SIMUL-TANEOUSLY FROM TWO FRONTS LIKE THAT... IT'S A BRILLIANT MOVE.
DINO GOLZINE WILL HAVE HIS HANDS TIED, GOING ON THE DEFENSIVE.
...IF THE DEVIL REALLY EXISTS...
...I THINK HE LOOKS LIKE YOU.
WELL, HERE'S CHEERS...
...TO THE OLD MAN... OLD MAN.

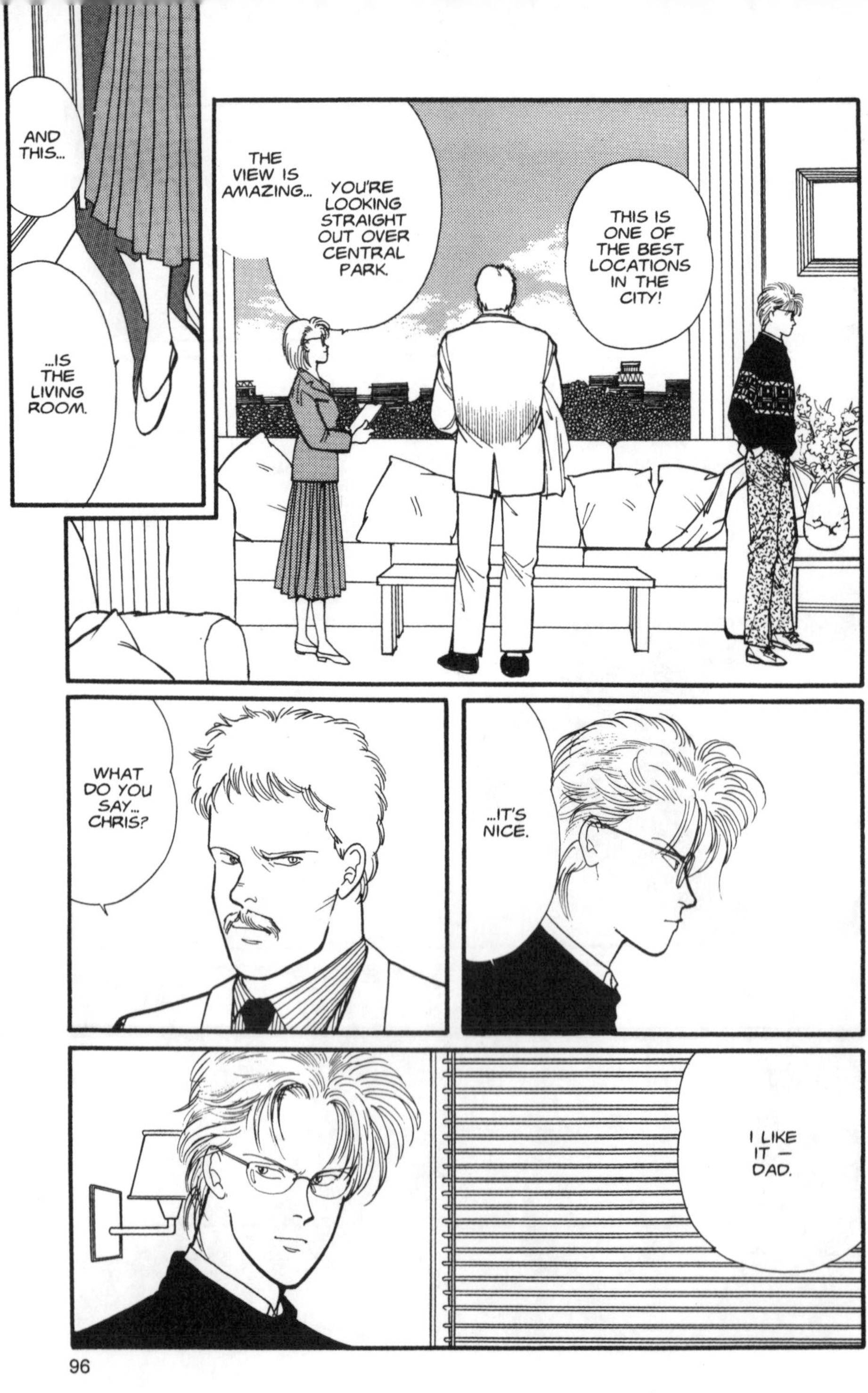
AND THIS...
...IS THE LIVING ROOM.
THE VIEW IS AMAZING...
YOU'RE LOOKING STRAIGHT OUT OVER CENTRAL PARK.
THIS IS ONE OF THE BEST LOCATIONS IN THE CITY!
WHAT DO YOU SAY... CHRIS?
...IT'S NICE.
I LIKE IT — DAD.

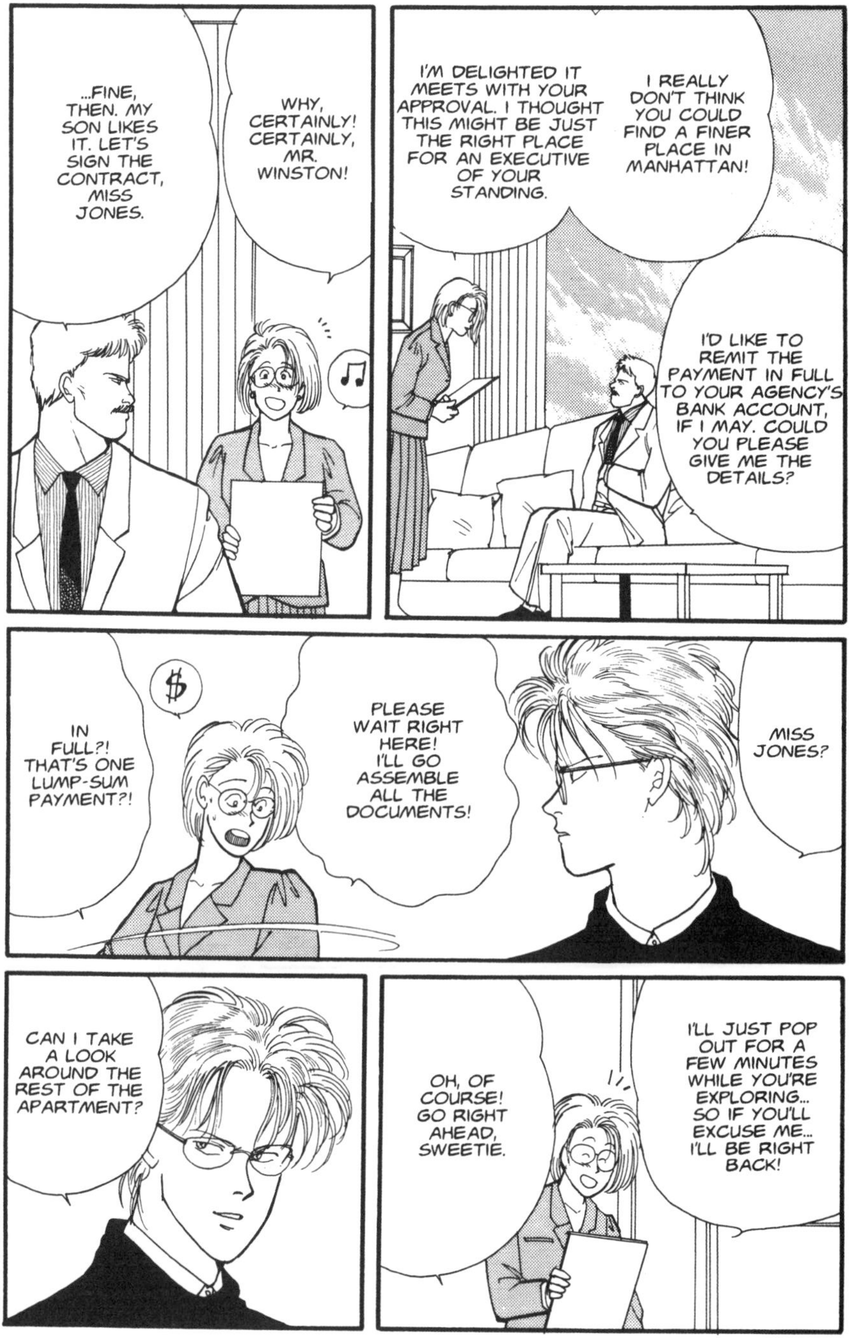
...FINE, THEN. MY SON LIKES IT. LET'S SIGN THE CONTRACT, MISS JONES.
WHY, CERTAINLY! CERTAINLY, MR. WINSTON!
I'M DELIGHTED IT MEETS WITH YOUR APPROVAL. I THOUGHT THIS MIGHT BE JUST THE RIGHT PLACE FOR AN EXECUTIVE OF YOUR STANDING.
I REALLY DON'T THINK YOU COULD FIND A FINER PLACE IN MANHATTAN!
I'D LIKE TO REMIT THE PAYMENT IN FULL TO YOUR AGENCY'S BANK ACCOUNT, IF I MAY. COULD YOU PLEASE GIVE ME THE DETAILS?
IN FULL?! THAT'S ONE LUMP-SUM PAYMENT?!
$
PLEASE WAIT RIGHT HERE! I'LL GO ASSEMBLE ALL THE DOCUMENTS!
MISS JONES?
CAN I TAKE A LOOK AROUND THE REST OF THE APARTMENT?
OH, OF COURSE! GO RIGHT AHEAD, SWEETIE.
I'LL JUST POP OUT FOR A FEW MINUTES WHILE YOU'RE EXPLORING... SO IF YOU'LL EXCUSE ME... I'LL BE RIGHT BACK!

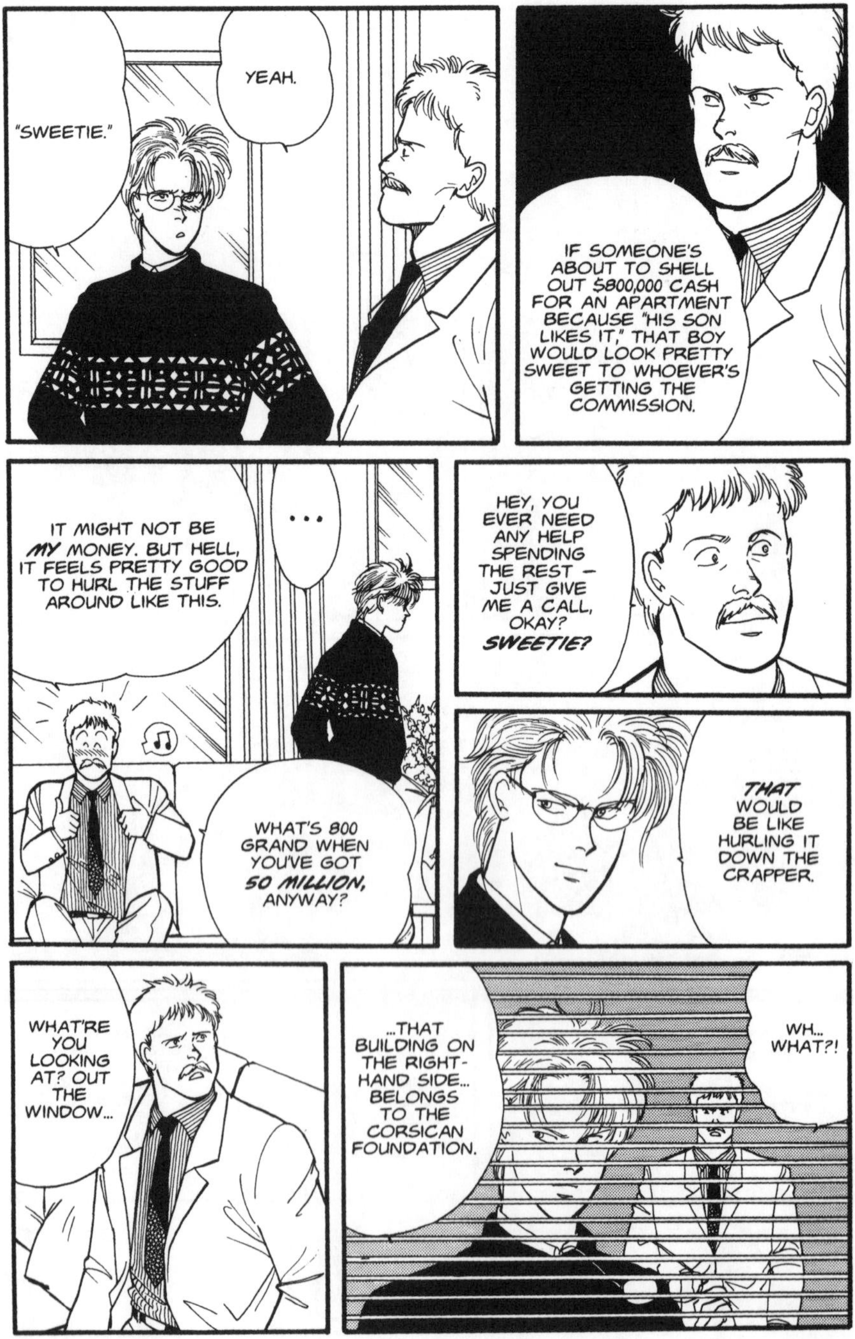
"SWEETIE."
YEAH.
IF SOMEONE'S ABOUT TO SHELL OUT $800,000 CASH FOR AN APARTMENT BECAUSE "HIS SON LIKES IT," THAT BOY WOULD LOOK PRETTY SWEET TO WHOEVER'S GETTING THE COMMISSION.
IT MIGHT NOT BE *MY* MONEY. BUT HELL, IT FEELS PRETTY GOOD TO HURL THE STUFF AROUND LIKE THIS.
...
WHAT'S 800 GRAND WHEN YOU'VE GOT *50 MILLION,* ANYWAY?
HEY, YOU EVER NEED ANY HELP SPENDING THE REST – JUST GIVE ME A CALL, OKAY? *SWEETIE?*
THAT WOULD BE LIKE HURLING IT DOWN THE CRAPPER.
WHAT'RE YOU LOOKING AT? OUT THE WINDOW...
...THAT BUILDING ON THE RIGHT-HAND SIDE... BELONGS TO THE CORSICAN FOUNDATION.
WH... WHAT?!

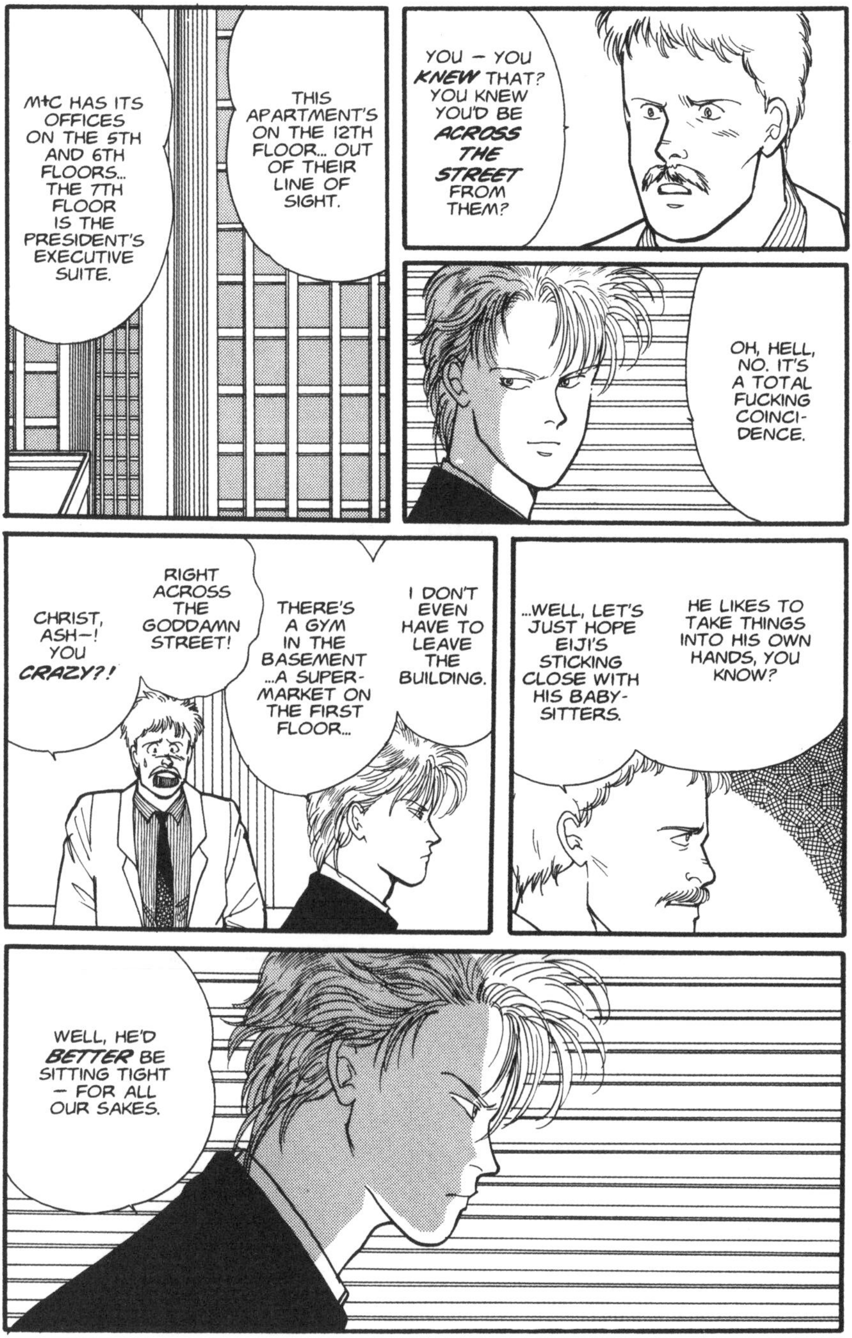
M+C HAS ITS OFFICES ON THE 5TH AND 6TH FLOORS... THE 7TH FLOOR IS THE PRESIDENT'S EXECUTIVE SUITE.
THIS APARTMENT'S ON THE 12TH FLOOR... OUT OF THEIR LINE OF SIGHT.
YOU - YOU KNEW THAT? YOU KNEW YOU'D BE ACROSS THE STREET FROM THEM?
OH, HELL, NO. IT'S A TOTAL FUCKING COINCI-DENCE.
CHRIST, ASH-! YOU CRAZY?!
RIGHT ACROSS THE GODDAMN STREET!
THERE'S A GYM IN THE BASEMENT ...A SUPER-MARKET ON THE FIRST FLOOR...
I DON'T EVEN HAVE TO LEAVE THE BUILDING.
...WELL, LET'S JUST HOPE EIJI'S STICKING CLOSE WITH HIS BABY-SITTERS.
HE LIKES TO TAKE THINGS INTO HIS OWN HANDS, YOU KNOW?
WELL, HE'D BETTER BE SITTING TIGHT - FOR ALL OUR SAKES.

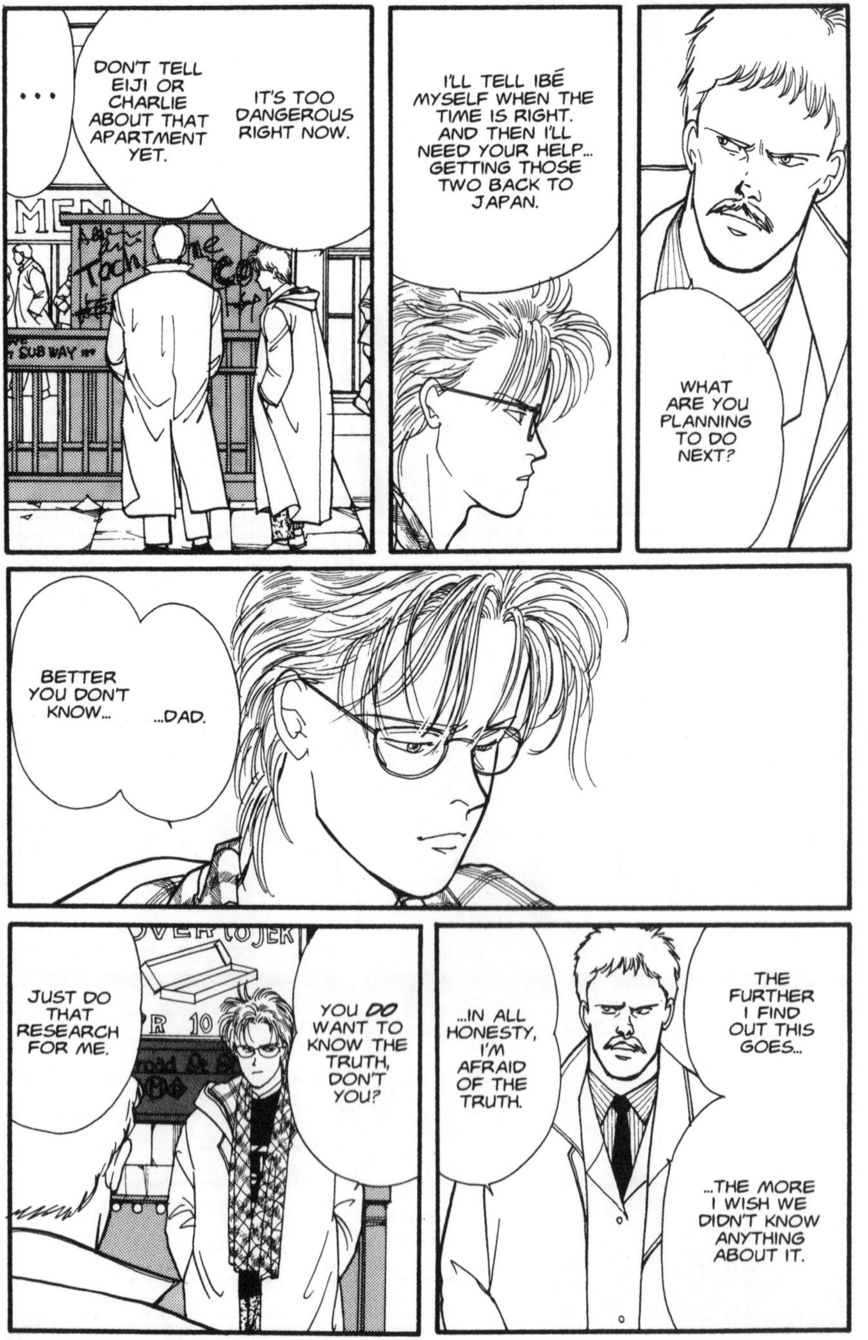
...
DON'T TELL EIJI OR CHARLIE ABOUT THAT APARTMENT YET.
IT'S TOO DANGEROUS RIGHT NOW.
MEN
SUBWAY
I'LL TELL IBÉ MYSELF WHEN THE TIME IS RIGHT. AND THEN I'LL NEED YOUR HELP... GETTING THOSE TWO BACK TO JAPAN.
WHAT ARE YOU PLANNING TO DO NEXT?
BETTER YOU DON'T KNOW...
...DAD.
JUST DO THAT RESEARCH FOR ME.
YOU ***DO*** WANT TO KNOW THE TRUTH, DON'T YOU?
...IN ALL HONESTY, I'M AFRAID OF THE TRUTH.
THE FURTHER I FIND OUT THIS GOES...
...THE MORE I WISH WE DIDN'T KNOW ANYTHING ABOUT IT.

MAX...

YOU CAN'T MAKE THAT WISH ANYMORE.

...YOU'RE RIGHT.

IT'S TOO LATE.

CAN YOU FORGET WHAT I JUST SAID, INSTEAD?

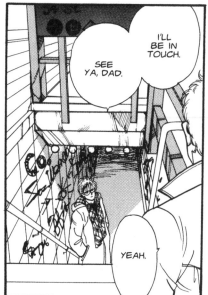

SEE YA, DAD.

I'LL BE IN TOUCH.

YEAH.

BE CARE-FUL.

WOULDN'T DREAM OTHER-WISE.

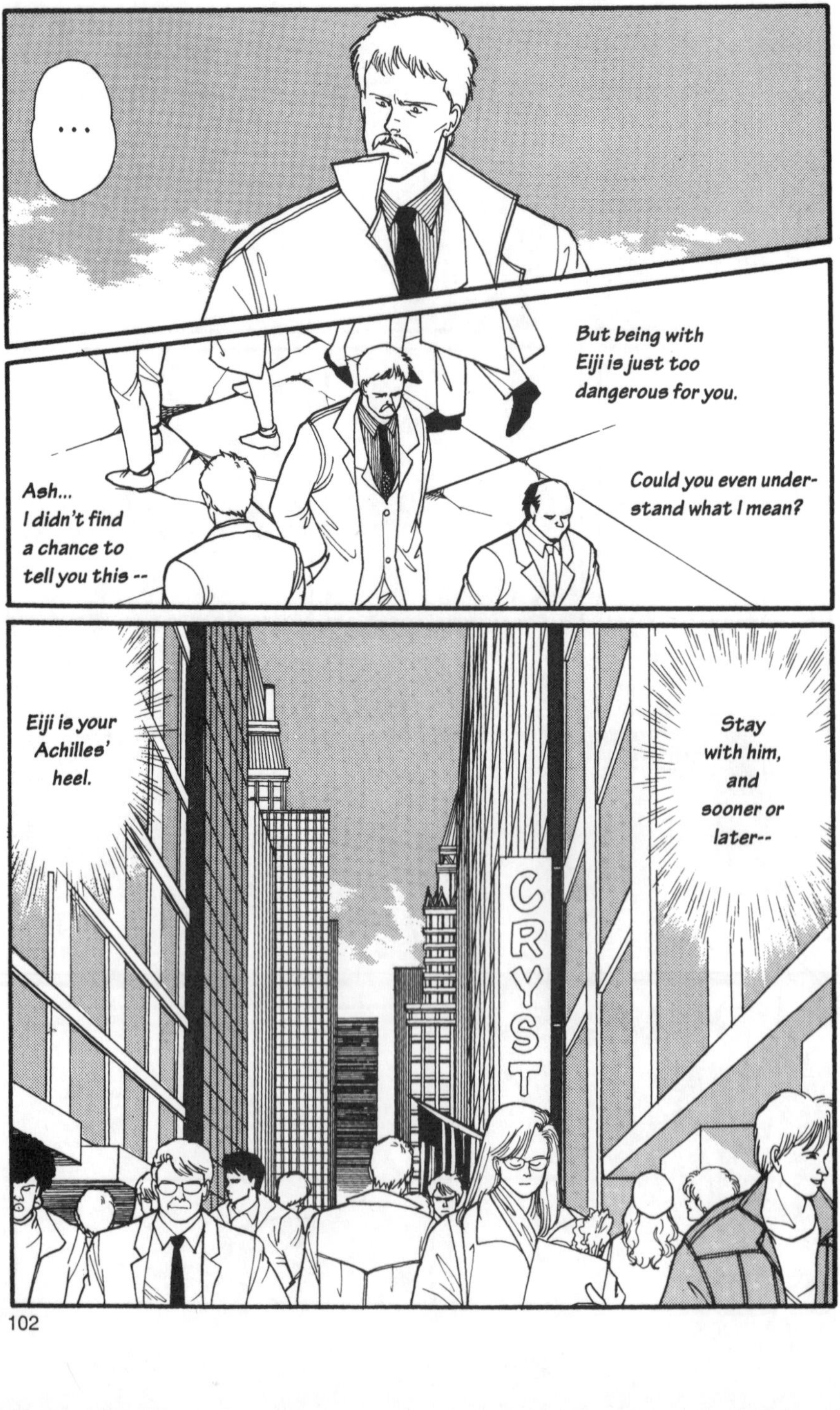
...
Ash...
I didn't find
a chance to
tell you this --
But being with
Eiji is just too
dangerous for you.
Could you even under-
stand what I mean?
Eiji is your
Achilles'
heel.
CRYST
Stay
with him,
and
sooner or
later--

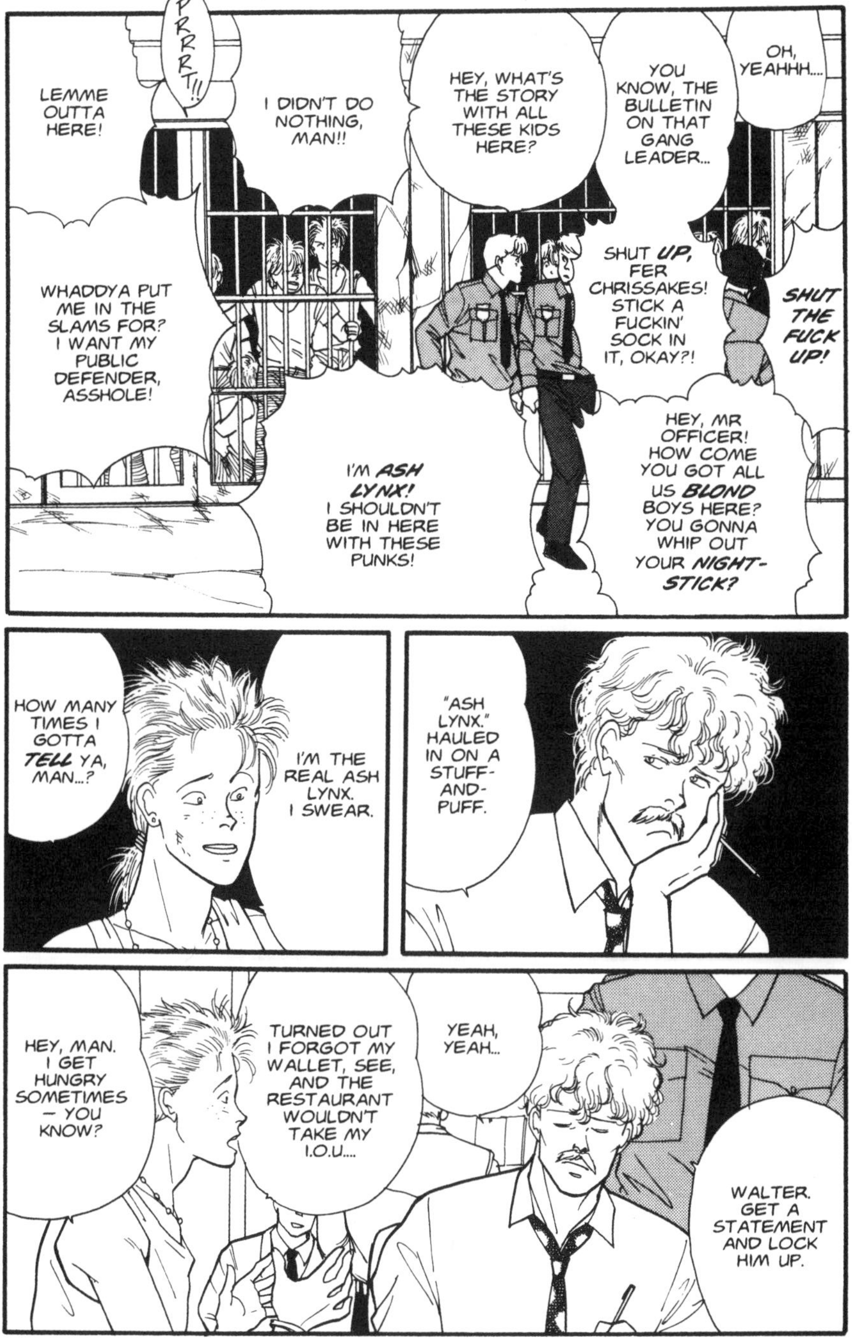
PRRRT!!
LEMME OUTTA HERE!
I DIDN'T DO NOTHING, MAN!!
HEY, WHAT'S THE STORY WITH ALL THESE KIDS HERE?
YOU KNOW, THE BULLETIN ON THAT GANG LEADER...
OH, YEAHHH....
WHADDYA PUT ME IN THE SLAMS FOR? I WANT MY PUBLIC DEFENDER, ASSHOLE!
SHUT *UP,* FER CHRISSAKES! STICK A FUCKIN' SOCK IN IT, OKAY?!
SHUT THE FUCK UP!
I'M *ASH LYNX!* I SHOULDN'T BE IN HERE WITH THESE PUNKS!
HEY, MR OFFICER! HOW COME YOU GOT ALL US *BLOND* BOYS HERE? YOU GONNA WHIP OUT YOUR *NIGHT-STICK?*
HOW MANY TIMES I GOTTA *TELL* YA, MAN...?
I'M THE REAL ASH LYNX. I SWEAR.
"ASH LYNX." HAULED IN ON A STUFF-AND-PUFF.
HEY, MAN. I GET HUNGRY SOMETIMES — YOU KNOW?
TURNED OUT I FORGOT MY WALLET, SEE, AND THE RESTAURANT WOULDN'T TAKE MY I.O.U....
YEAH, YEAH...
WALTER. GET A STATEMENT AND LOCK HIM UP.

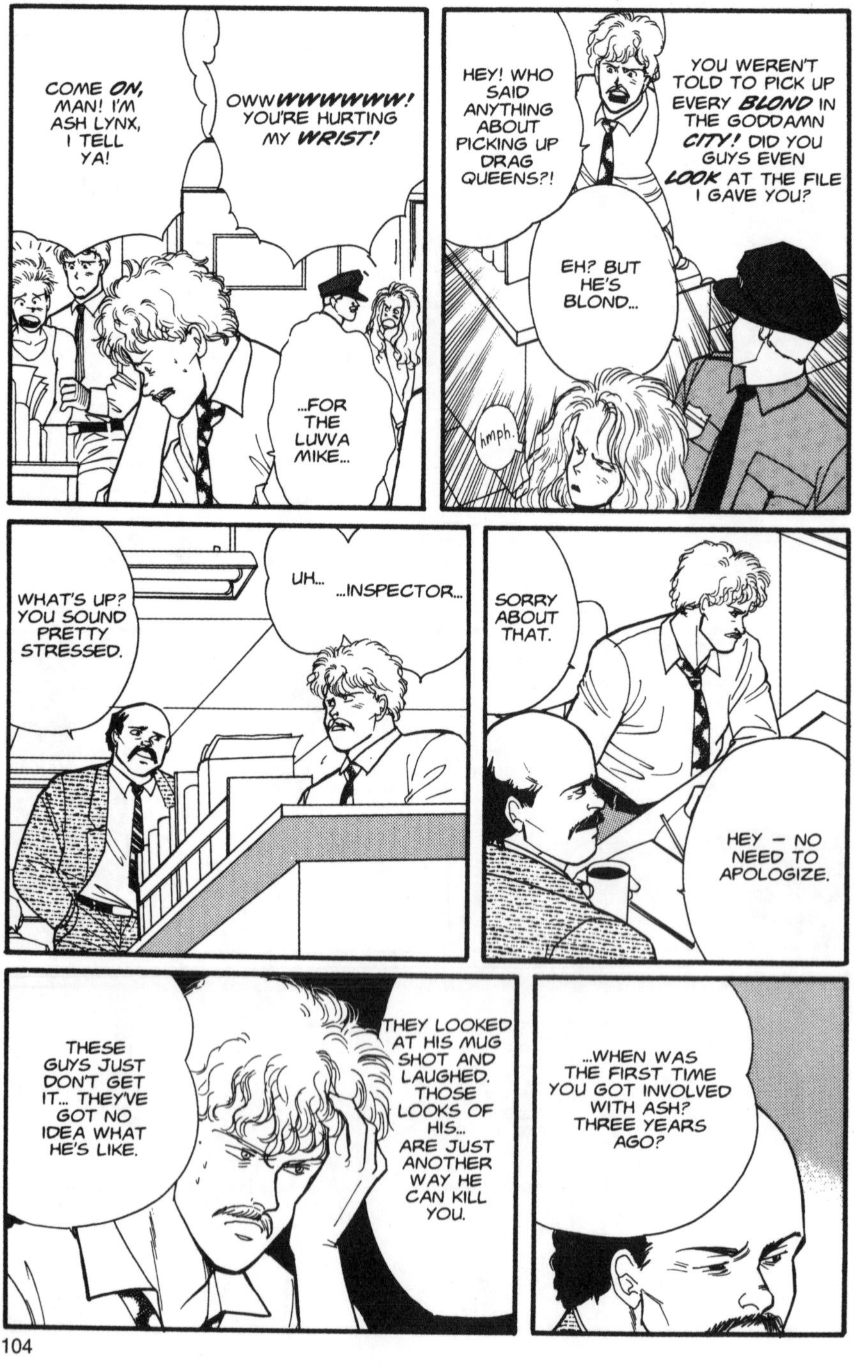

COME ON, MAN! I'M ASH LYNX, I TELL YA!
OWWWWWWWW! YOU'RE HURTING MY WRIST!
...FOR THE LUVVA MIKE...
HEY! WHO SAID ANYTHING ABOUT PICKING UP DRAG QUEENS?!
YOU WEREN'T TOLD TO PICK UP EVERY BLOND IN THE GODDAMN CITY! DID YOU GUYS EVEN LOOK AT THE FILE I GAVE YOU?
EH? BUT HE'S BLOND...
hmph.
WHAT'S UP? YOU SOUND PRETTY STRESSED.
UH...
...INSPECTOR...
SORRY ABOUT THAT.
HEY – NO NEED TO APOLOGIZE.
THESE GUYS JUST DON'T GET IT... THEY'VE GOT NO IDEA WHAT HE'S LIKE.
THEY LOOKED AT HIS MUG SHOT AND LAUGHED. THOSE LOOKS OF HIS... ARE JUST ANOTHER WAY HE CAN KILL YOU.
...WHEN WAS THE FIRST TIME YOU GOT INVOLVED WITH ASH? THREE YEARS AGO?

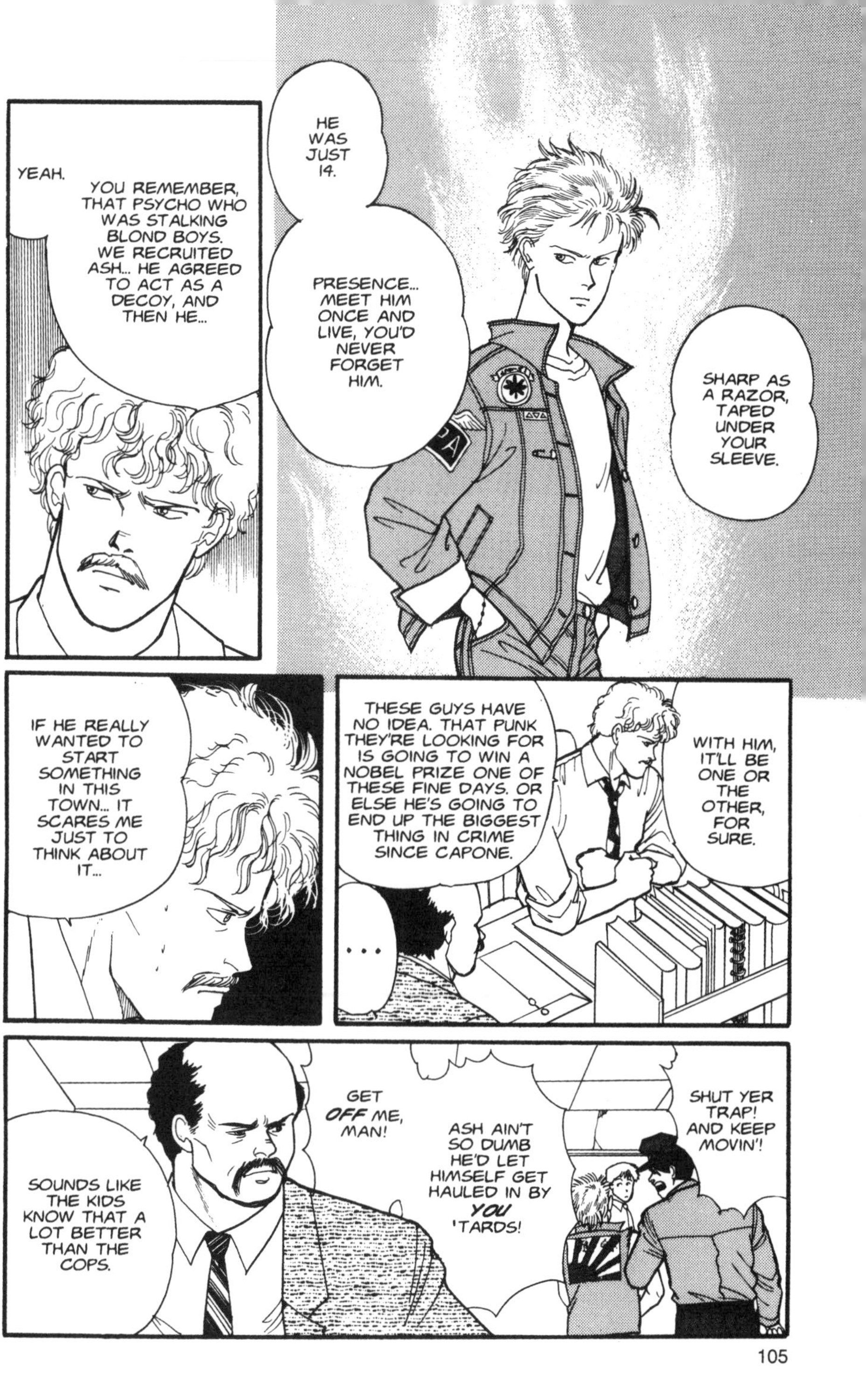
YEAH.
YOU REMEMBER, THAT PSYCHO WHO WAS STALKING BLOND BOYS. WE RECRUITED ASH... HE AGREED TO ACT AS A DECOY, AND THEN HE...
HE WAS JUST 14.
PRESENCE... MEET HIM ONCE AND LIVE, YOU'D NEVER FORGET HIM.
SHARP AS A RAZOR, TAPED UNDER YOUR SLEEVE.
IF HE REALLY WANTED TO START SOMETHING IN THIS TOWN... IT SCARES ME JUST TO THINK ABOUT IT...
THESE GUYS HAVE NO IDEA. THAT PUNK THEY'RE LOOKING FOR IS GOING TO WIN A NOBEL PRIZE ONE OF THESE FINE DAYS. OR ELSE HE'S GOING TO END UP THE BIGGEST THING IN CRIME SINCE CAPONE.
WITH HIM, IT'LL BE ONE OR THE OTHER, FOR SURE.
...
SOUNDS LIKE THE KIDS KNOW THAT A LOT BETTER THAN THE COPS.
GET *OFF* ME, MAN!
ASH AIN'T SO DUMB HE'D LET HIMSELF GET HAULED IN BY *YOU* 'TARDS!
SHUT YER TRAP! AND KEEP MOVIN'!

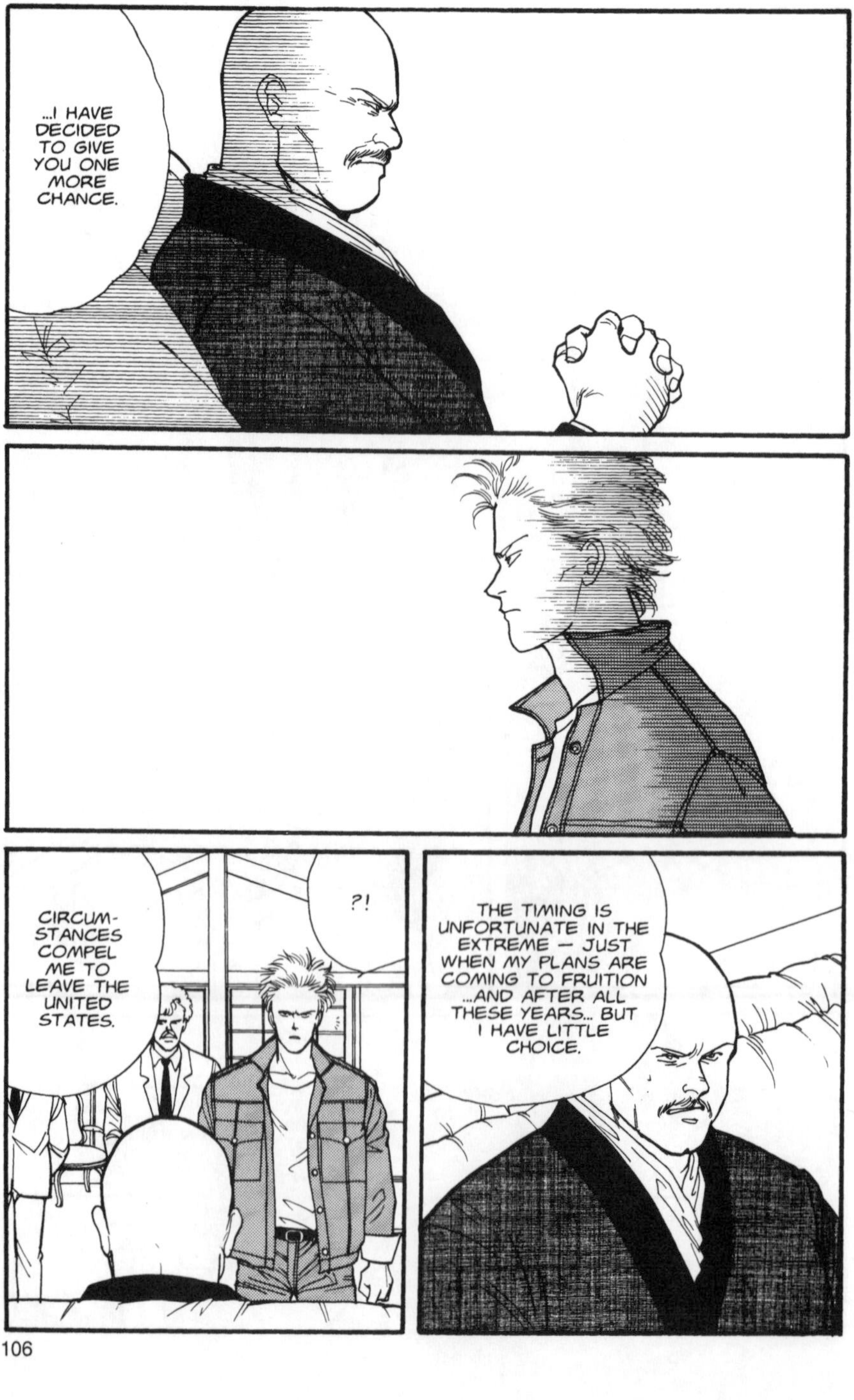
...I HAVE DECIDED TO GIVE YOU ONE MORE CHANCE.
CIRCUM-STANCES COMPEL ME TO LEAVE THE UNITED STATES.
?!
THE TIMING IS UNFORTUNATE IN THE EXTREME — JUST WHEN MY PLANS ARE COMING TO FRUITION ...AND AFTER ALL THESE YEARS... BUT I HAVE LITTLE CHOICE.

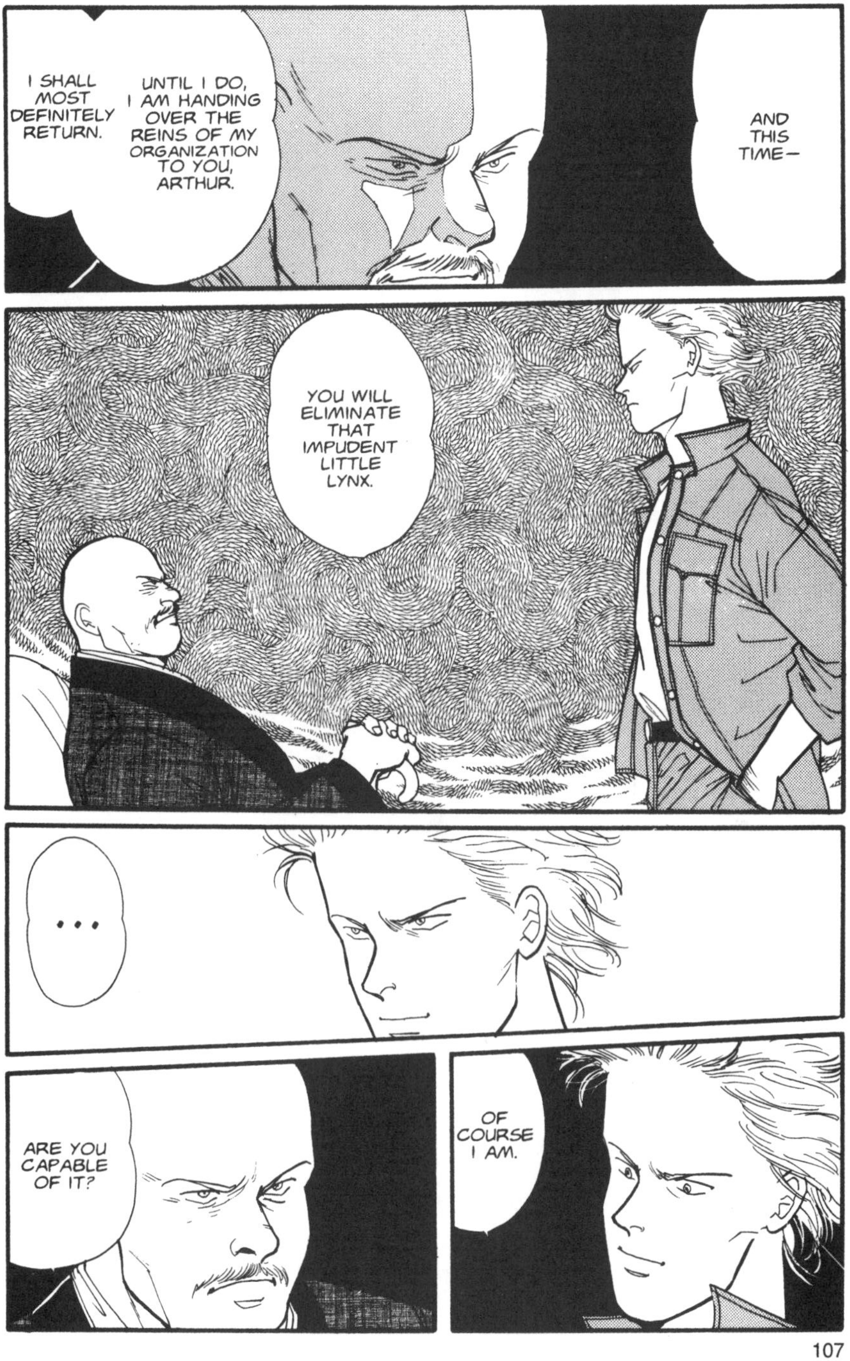
I SHALL MOST DEFINITELY RETURN.
UNTIL I DO, I AM HANDING OVER THE REINS OF MY ORGANIZATION TO YOU, ARTHUR.
AND THIS TIME—
YOU WILL ELIMINATE THAT IMPUDENT LITTLE LYNX.
...
ARE YOU CAPABLE OF IT?
OF COURSE I AM.

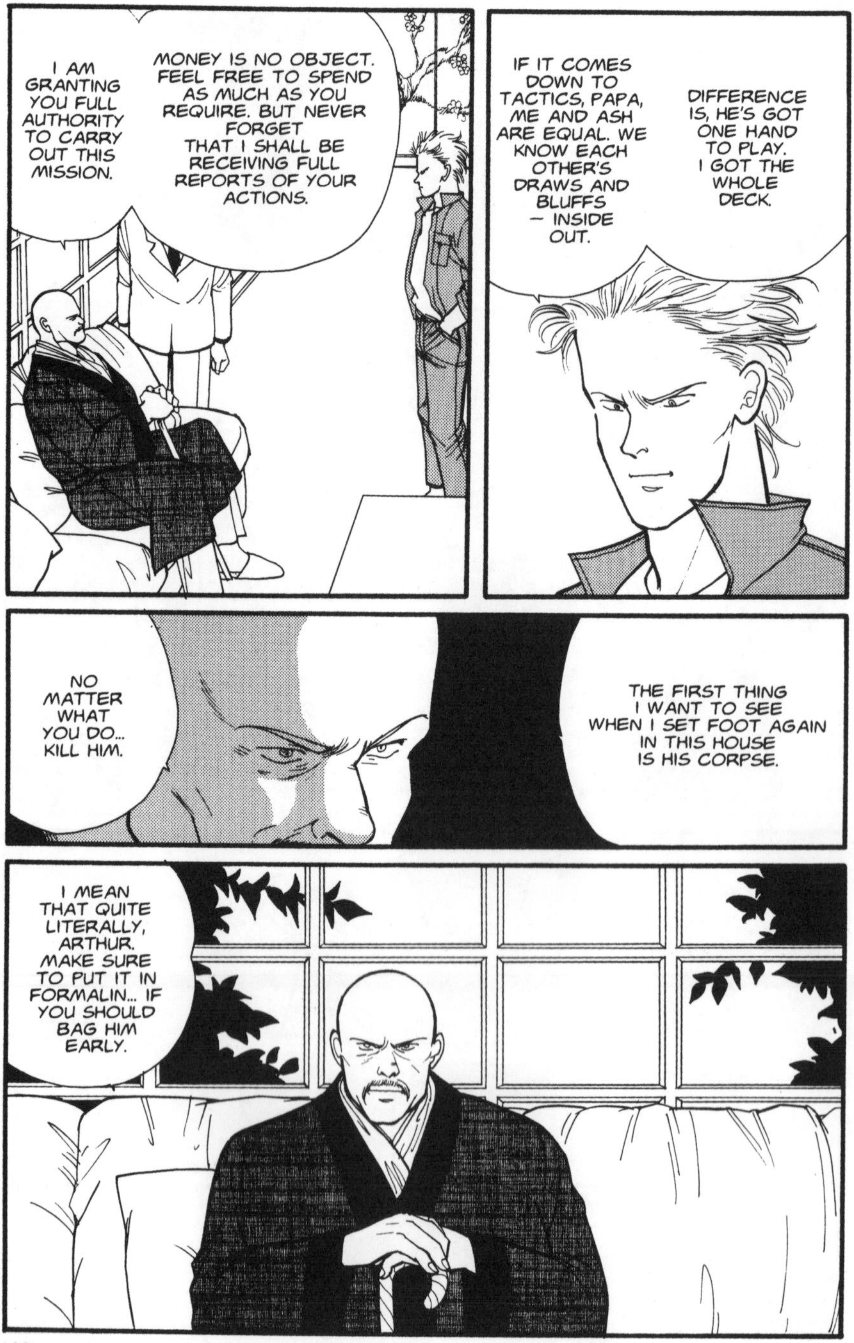
I AM GRANTING YOU FULL AUTHORITY TO CARRY OUT THIS MISSION.
MONEY IS NO OBJECT. FEEL FREE TO SPEND AS MUCH AS YOU REQUIRE. BUT NEVER FORGET THAT I SHALL BE RECEIVING FULL REPORTS OF YOUR ACTIONS.
IF IT COMES DOWN TO TACTICS, PAPA, ME AND ASH ARE EQUAL. WE KNOW EACH OTHER'S DRAWS AND BLUFFS — INSIDE OUT.
DIFFERENCE IS, HE'S GOT ONE HAND TO PLAY. I GOT THE WHOLE DECK.
NO MATTER WHAT YOU DO... KILL HIM.
THE FIRST THING I WANT TO SEE WHEN I SET FOOT AGAIN IN THIS HOUSE IS HIS CORPSE.
I MEAN THAT QUITE LITERALLY, ARTHUR. MAKE SURE TO PUT IT IN FORMALIN... IF YOU SHOULD BAG HIM EARLY.

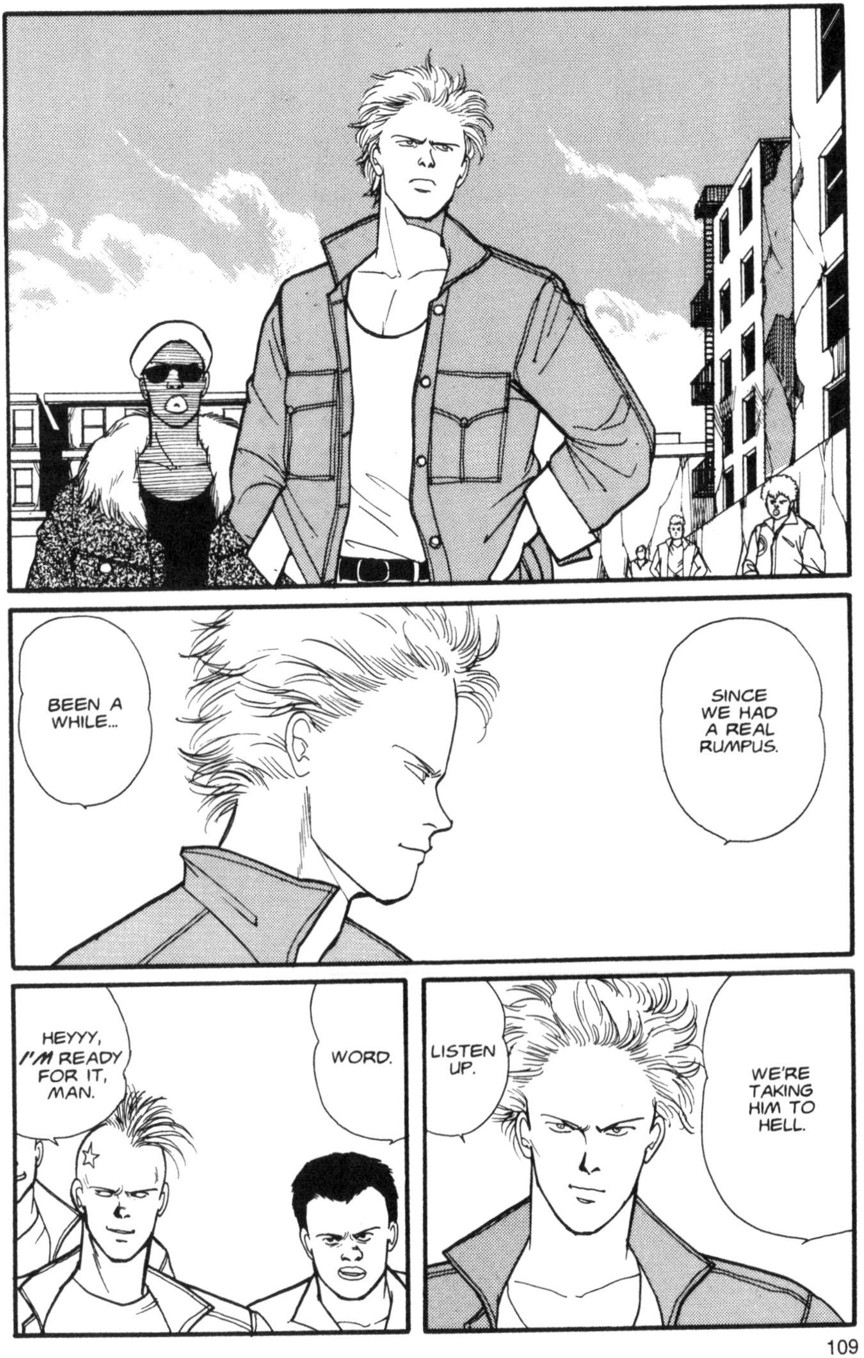
BEEN A WHILE...
SINCE WE HAD A REAL RUMPUS.
HEYYY, I'M READY FOR IT, MAN.
WORD.
LISTEN UP.
WE'RE TAKING HIM TO HELL.

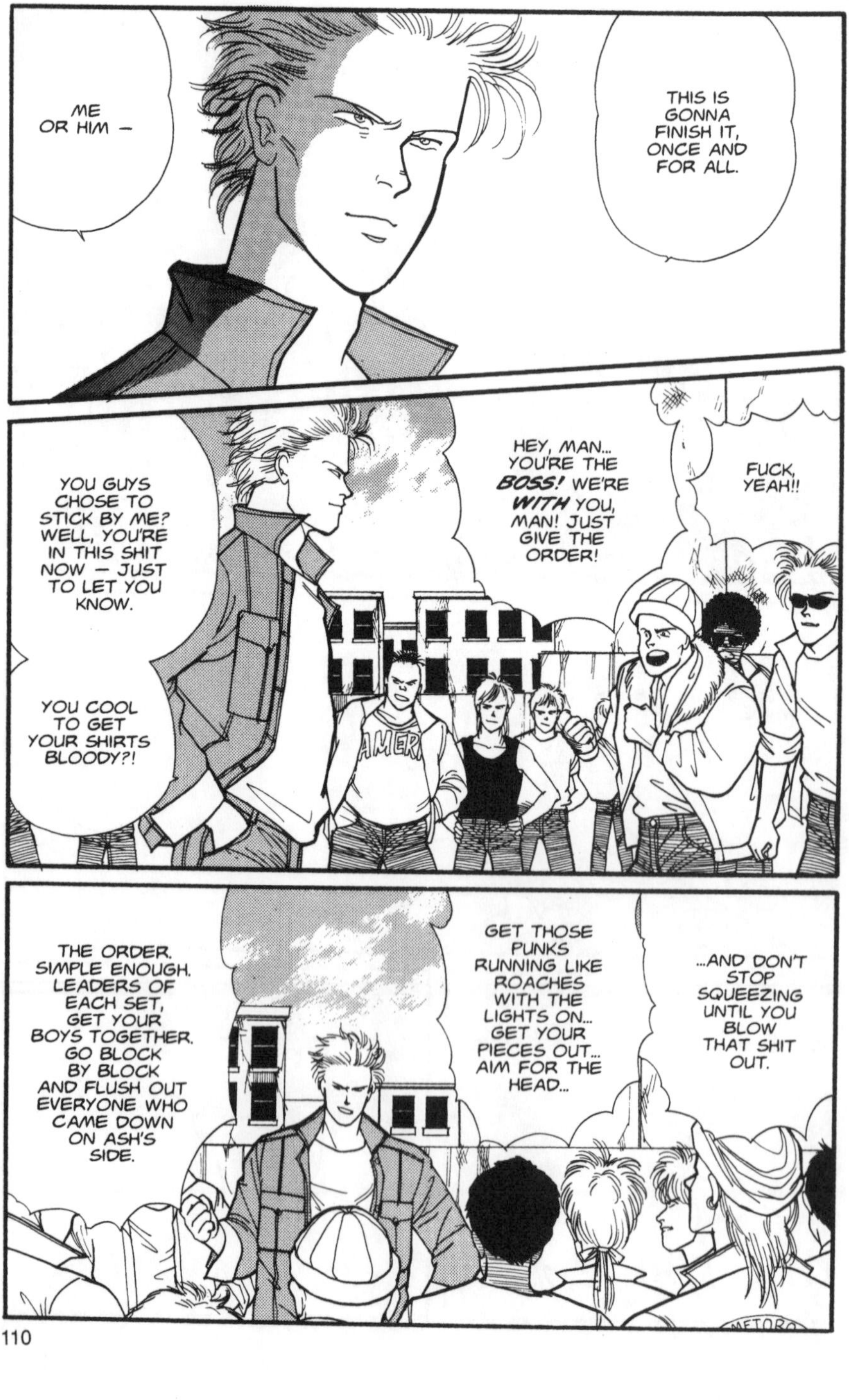
ME OR HIM –
THIS IS GONNA FINISH IT, ONCE AND FOR ALL.
YOU GUYS CHOSE TO STICK BY ME? WELL, YOU'RE IN THIS SHIT NOW – JUST TO LET YOU KNOW.
YOU COOL TO GET YOUR SHIRTS BLOODY?!
HEY, MAN... YOU'RE THE BOSS! WE'RE WITH YOU, MAN! JUST GIVE THE ORDER!
FUCK, YEAH!!
THE ORDER. SIMPLE ENOUGH. LEADERS OF EACH SET, GET YOUR BOYS TOGETHER. GO BLOCK BY BLOCK AND FLUSH OUT EVERYONE WHO CAME DOWN ON ASH'S SIDE.
GET THOSE PUNKS RUNNING LIKE ROACHES WITH THE LIGHTS ON... GET YOUR PIECES OUT... AIM FOR THE HEAD...
...AND DON'T STOP SQUEEZING UNTIL YOU BLOW THAT SHIT OUT.
AMERI
METORO

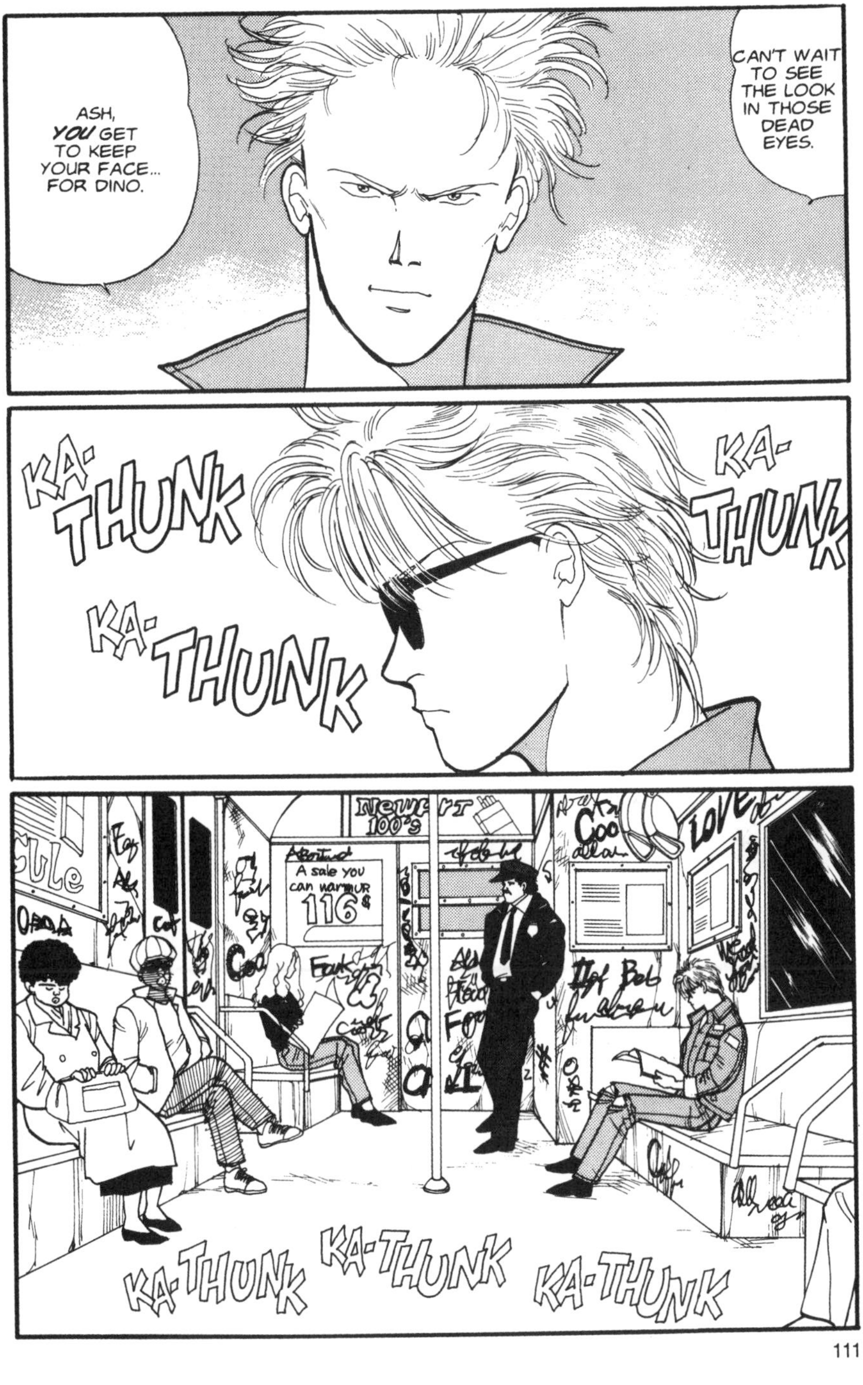
ASH, *YOU* GET TO KEEP YOUR FACE... FOR DINO.
CAN'T WAIT TO SEE THE LOOK IN THOSE DEAD EYES.
KA-THUNK
KA-THUNK
KA-THUNK
KA-THUNK
KA-THUNK
KA-THUNK

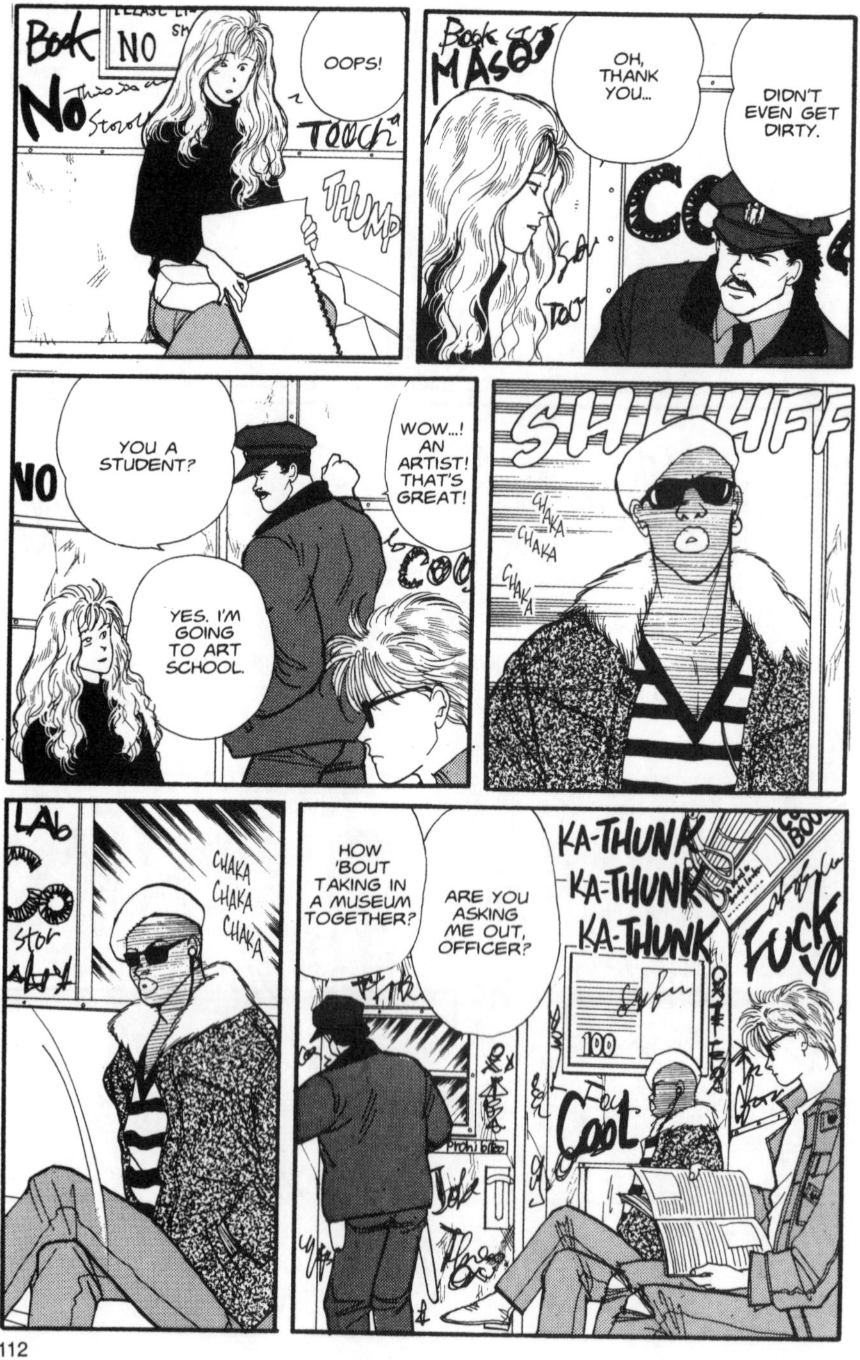
OOPS!
THUMP
OH, THANK YOU...
DIDN'T EVEN GET DIRTY.
YOU A STUDENT?
WOW...! AN ARTIST! THAT'S GREAT!
YES. I'M GOING TO ART SCHOOL.
CHAKA CHAKA CHAKA
CHAKA CHAKA CHAKA
HOW 'BOUT TAKING IN A MUSEUM TOGETHER?
ARE YOU ASKING ME OUT, OFFICER?
KA-THUNK KA-THUNK KA-THUNK

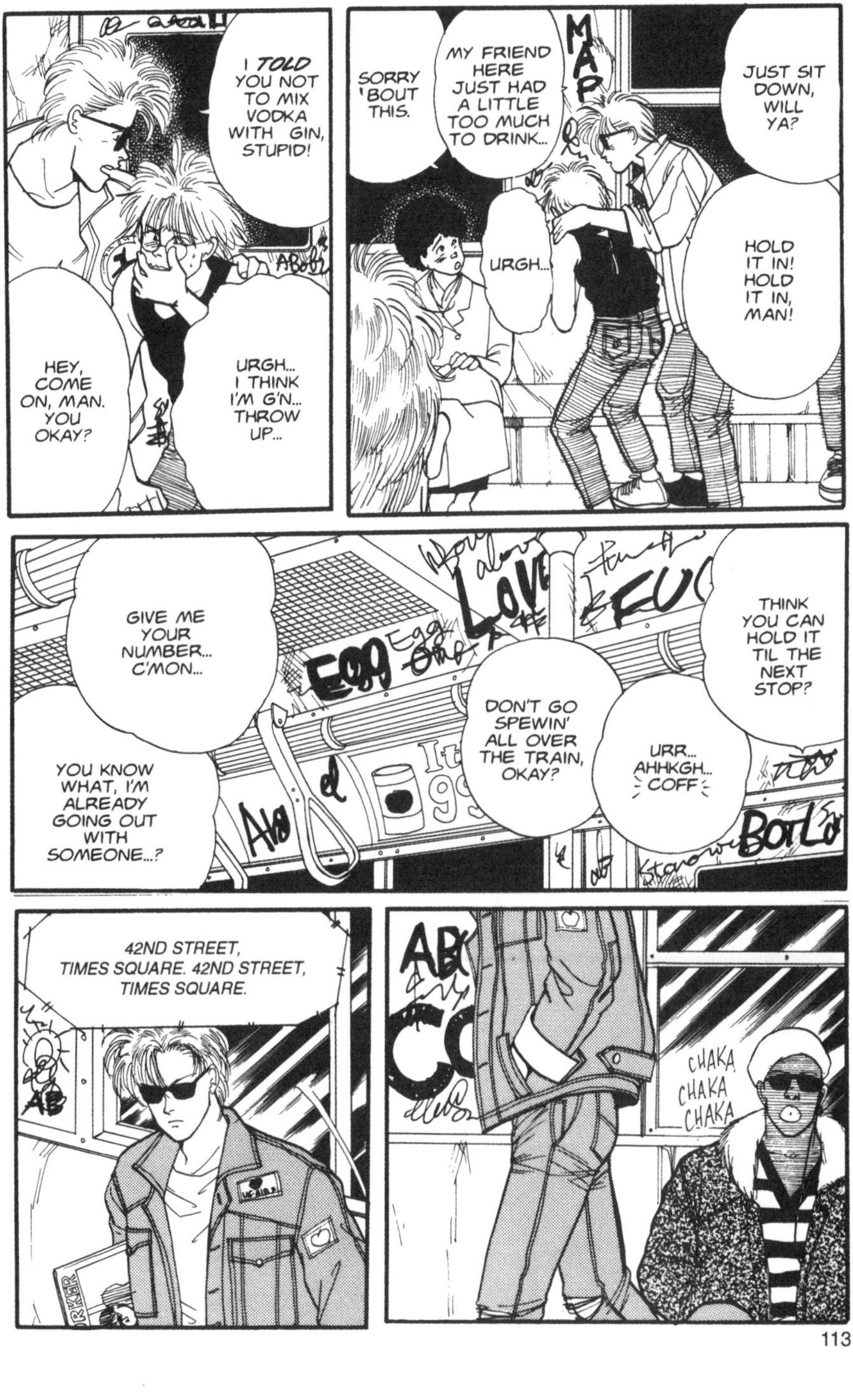
I TOLD YOU NOT TO MIX VODKA WITH GIN, STUPID!
HEY, COME ON, MAN. YOU OKAY?
URGH... I THINK I'M G'N... THROW UP...
SORRY 'BOUT THIS.
MY FRIEND HERE JUST HAD A LITTLE TOO MUCH TO DRINK...
JUST SIT DOWN, WILL YA?
URGH...
HOLD IT IN! HOLD IT IN, MAN!
GIVE ME YOUR NUMBER... C'MON...
YOU KNOW WHAT, I'M ALREADY GOING OUT WITH SOMEONE...?
DON'T GO SPEWIN' ALL OVER THE TRAIN, OKAY?
URR... AHHKGH... COFF
THINK YOU CAN HOLD IT TIL THE NEXT STOP?
42ND STREET, TIMES SQUARE. 42ND STREET, TIMES SQUARE.
CHAKA CHAKA CHAKA

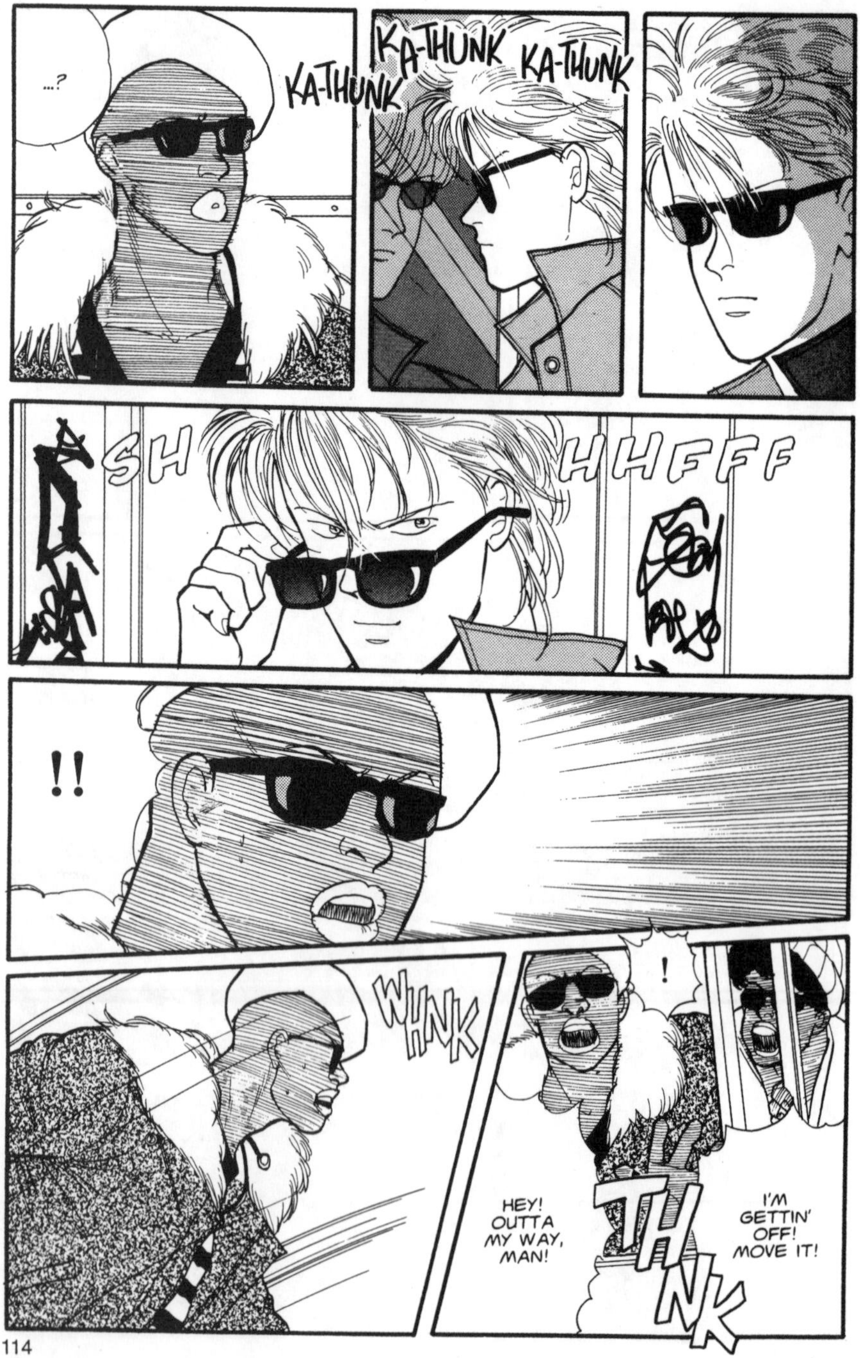
...?
KA-THUNK
KA-THUNK
KA-THUNK
SH
HHFFF
!!
WHNK
!
HEY! OUTTA MY WAY, MAN!
THNK
I'M GETTIN' OFF! MOVE IT!

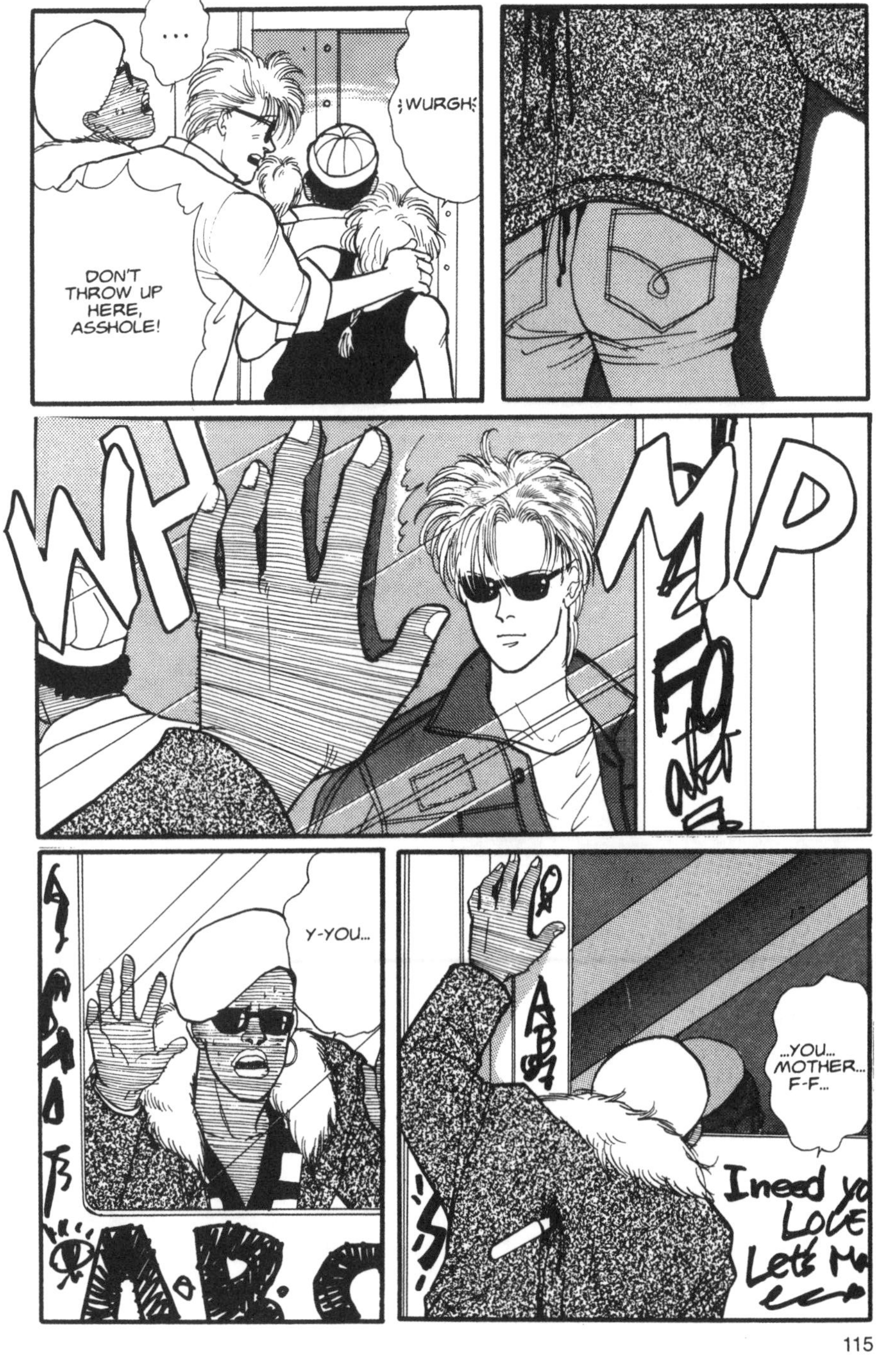
...
WURGH
DON'T THROW UP HERE, ASSHOLE!
WHUMP
Y-YOU...
...YOU... MOTHER... F-F...

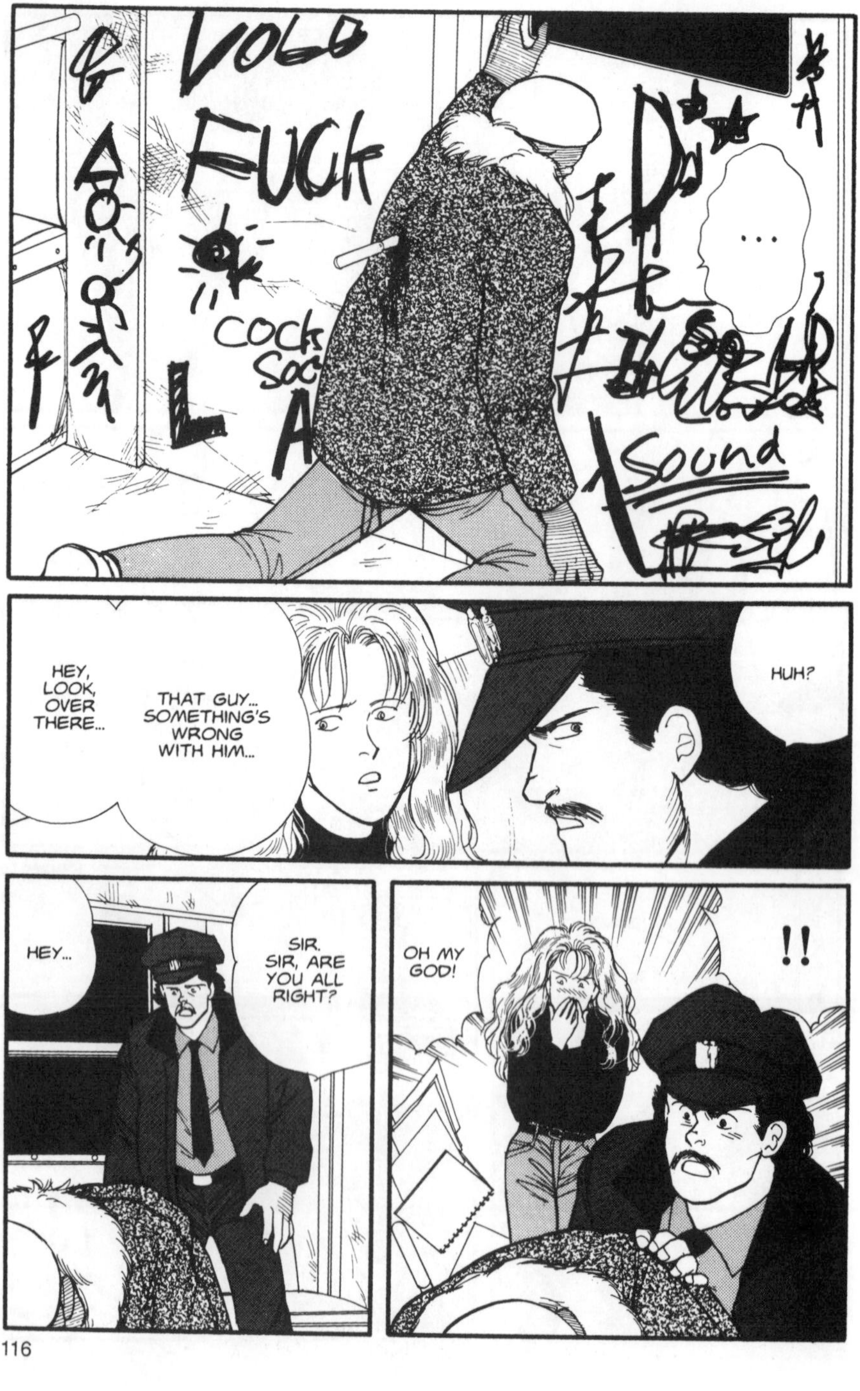
FUCK
COCK
Sound
...
HEY, LOOK, OVER THERE...
THAT GUY... SOMETHING'S WRONG WITH HIM...
HUH?
HEY...
SIR. SIR, ARE YOU ALL RIGHT?
OH MY GOD!
!!

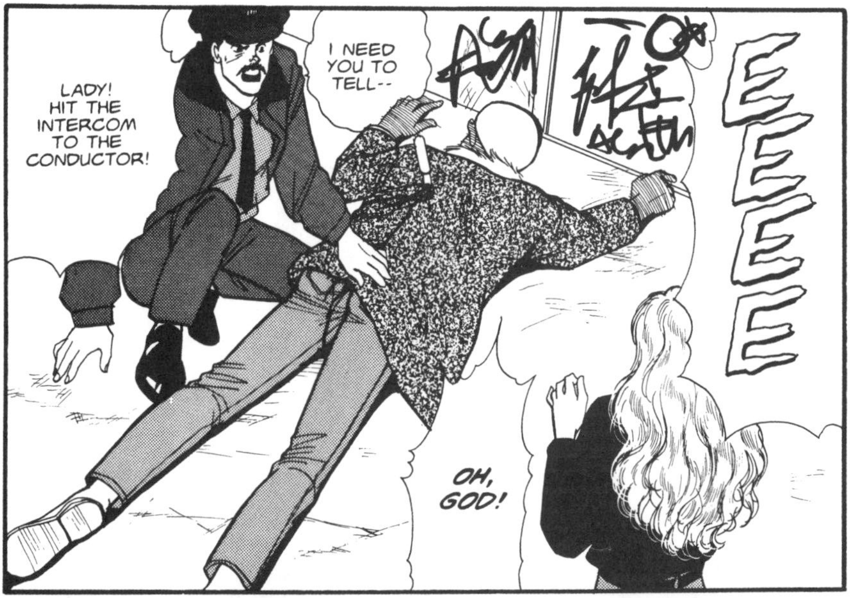
LADY! HIT THE INTERCOM TO THE CONDUCTOR!
I NEED YOU TO TELL--
EEEEE
OH, GOD!

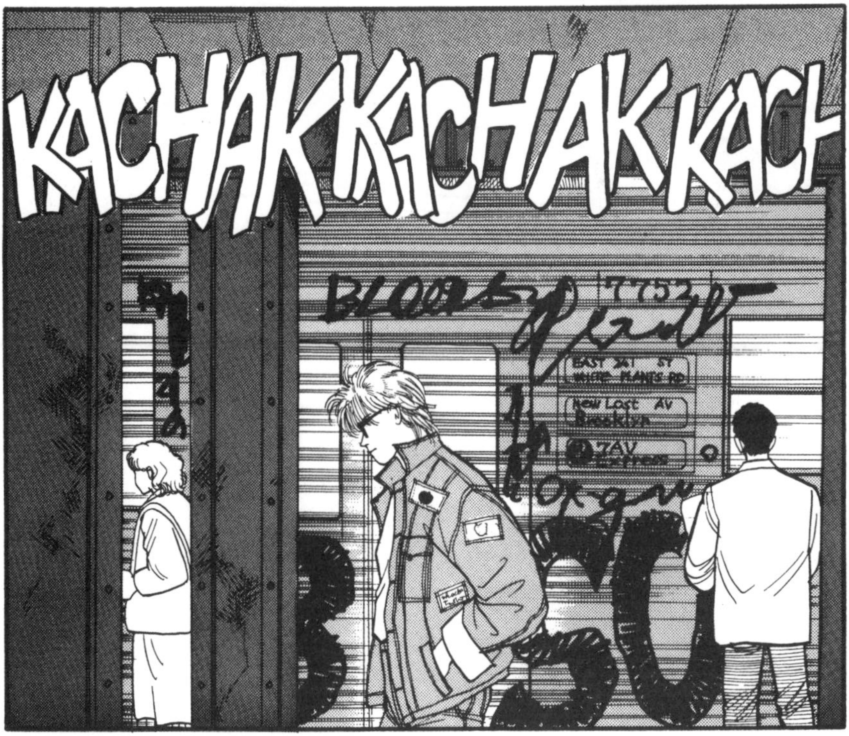
KACHAKKACHAKKACH

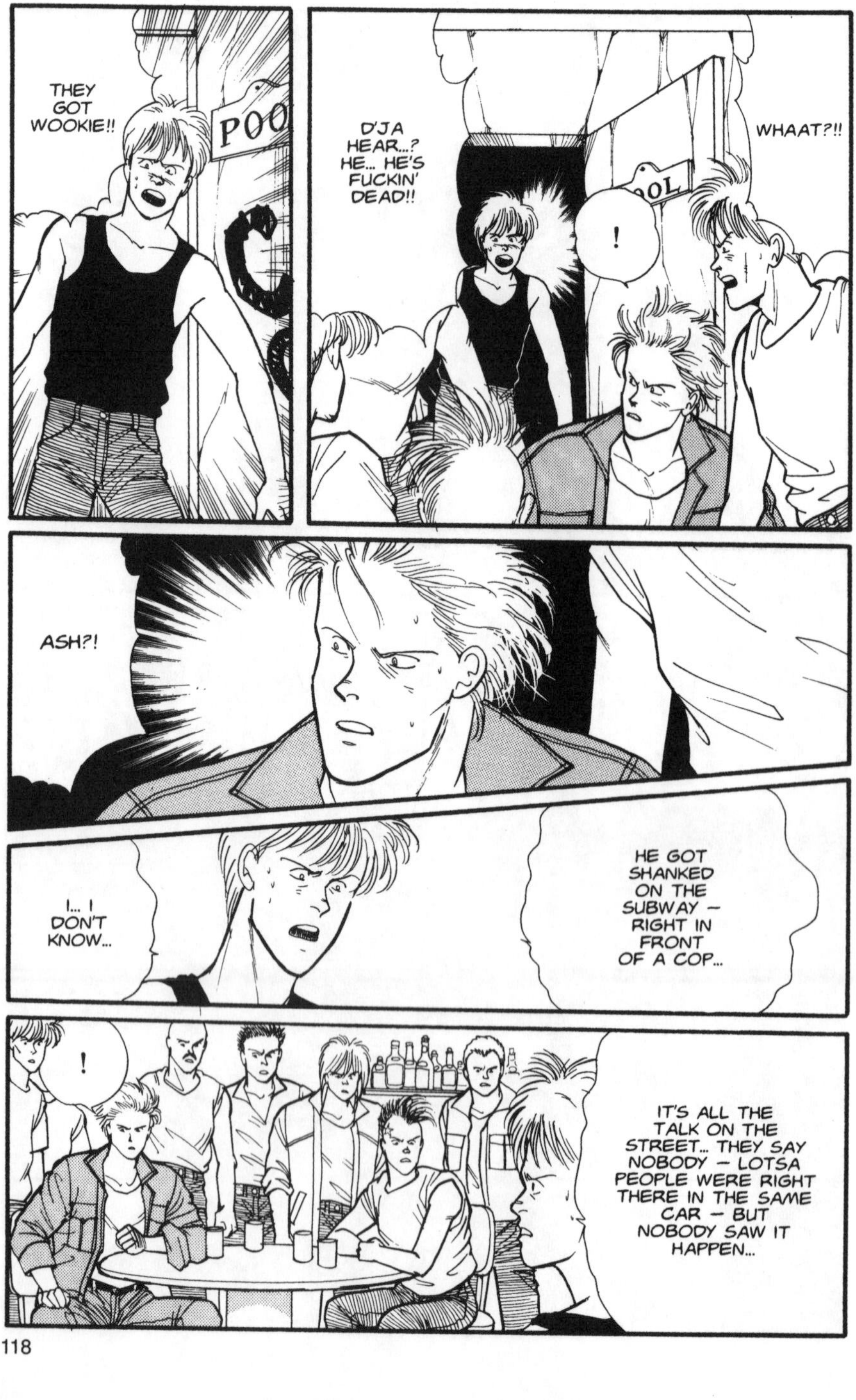
THEY GOT WOOKIE!!
POO
D'JA HEAR...? HE... HE'S FUCKIN' DEAD!!
!
OOL
WHAAT?!!
ASH?!
I... I DON'T KNOW...
HE GOT SHANKED ON THE SUBWAY – RIGHT IN FRONT OF A COP...
!
IT'S ALL THE TALK ON THE STREET... THEY SAY NOBODY – LOTSA PEOPLE WERE RIGHT THERE IN THE SAME CAR – BUT NOBODY SAW IT HAPPEN...

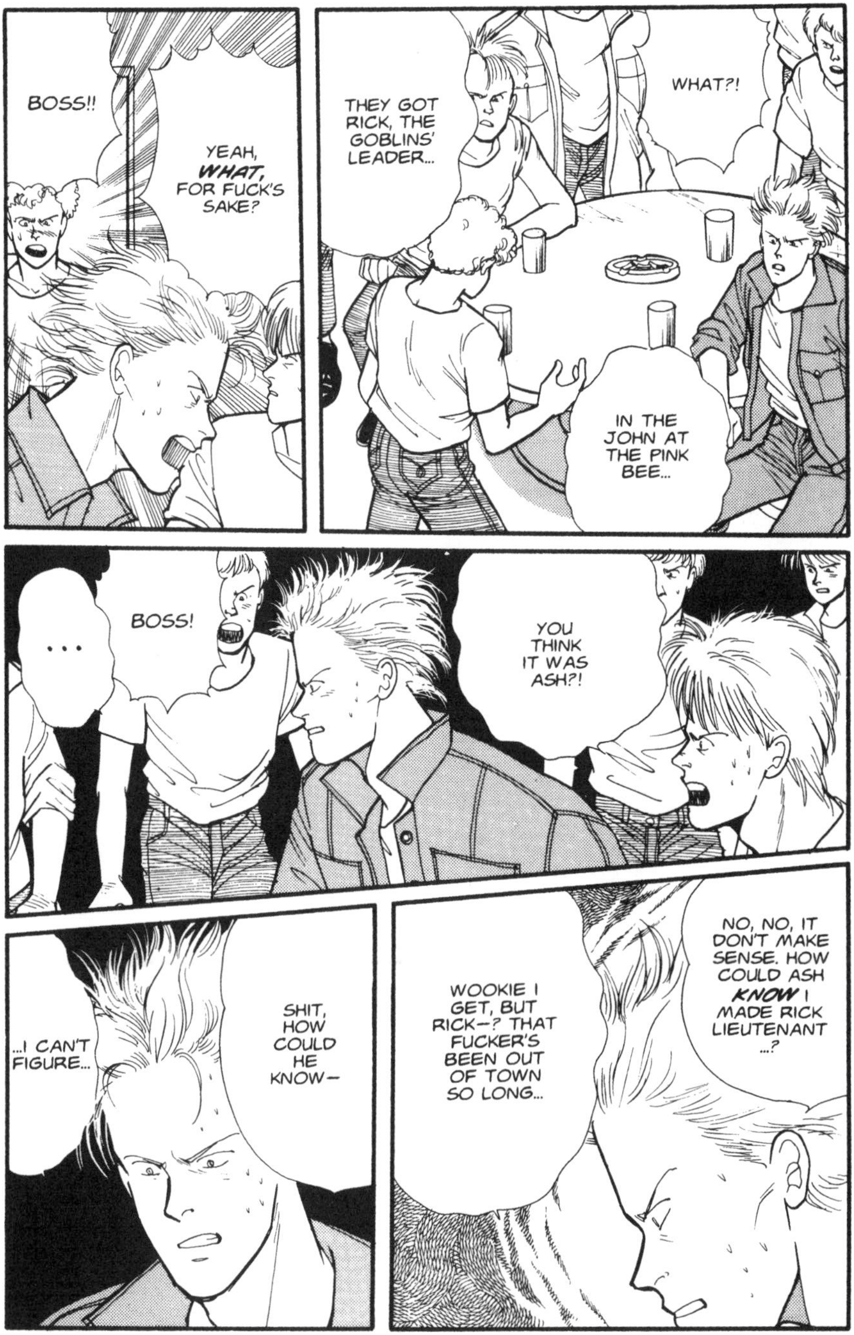
BOSS!!
YEAH, WHAT, FOR FUCK'S SAKE?
THEY GOT RICK, THE GOBLINS' LEADER...
WHAT?!
IN THE JOHN AT THE PINK BEE...
...
BOSS!
YOU THINK IT WAS ASH?!
...I CAN'T FIGURE...
SHIT, HOW COULD HE KNOW—
WOOKIE I GET, BUT RICK—? THAT FUCKER'S BEEN OUT OF TOWN SO LONG...
NO, NO, IT DON'T MAKE SENSE. HOW COULD ASH KNOW I MADE RICK LIEUTENANT ...?

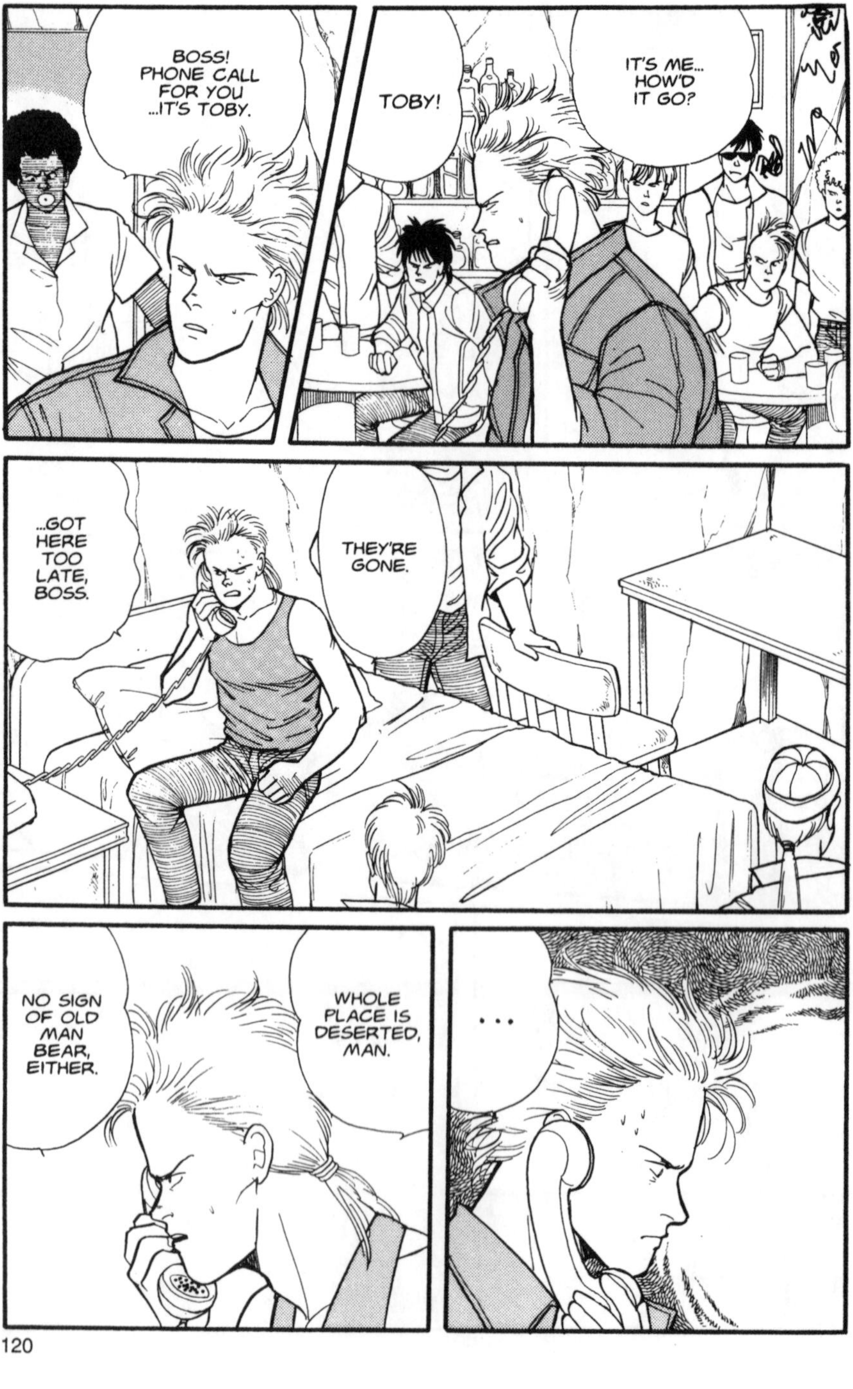
BOSS! PHONE CALL FOR YOU ...IT'S TOBY.
TOBY!
IT'S ME... HOW'D IT GO?
...GOT HERE TOO LATE, BOSS.
THEY'RE GONE.
NO SIGN OF OLD MAN BEAR, EITHER.
WHOLE PLACE IS DESERTED, MAN.
...

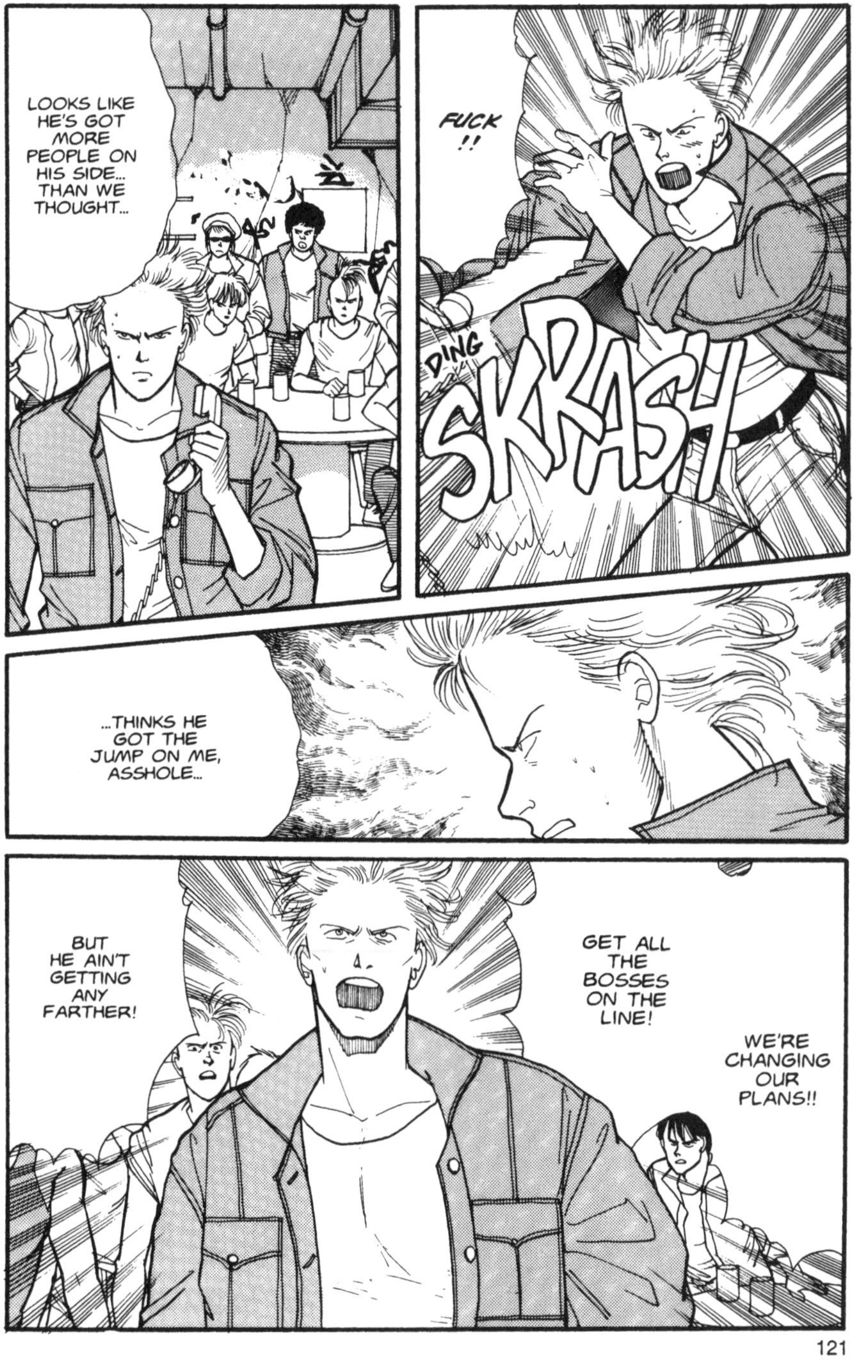
LOOKS LIKE HE'S GOT MORE PEOPLE ON HIS SIDE... THAN WE THOUGHT...
FUCK !!
DING
SKRASH
...THINKS HE GOT THE JUMP ON ME, ASSHOLE...
BUT HE AIN'T GETTING ANY FARTHER!
GET ALL THE BOSSES ON THE LINE!
WE'RE CHANGING OUR PLANS!!

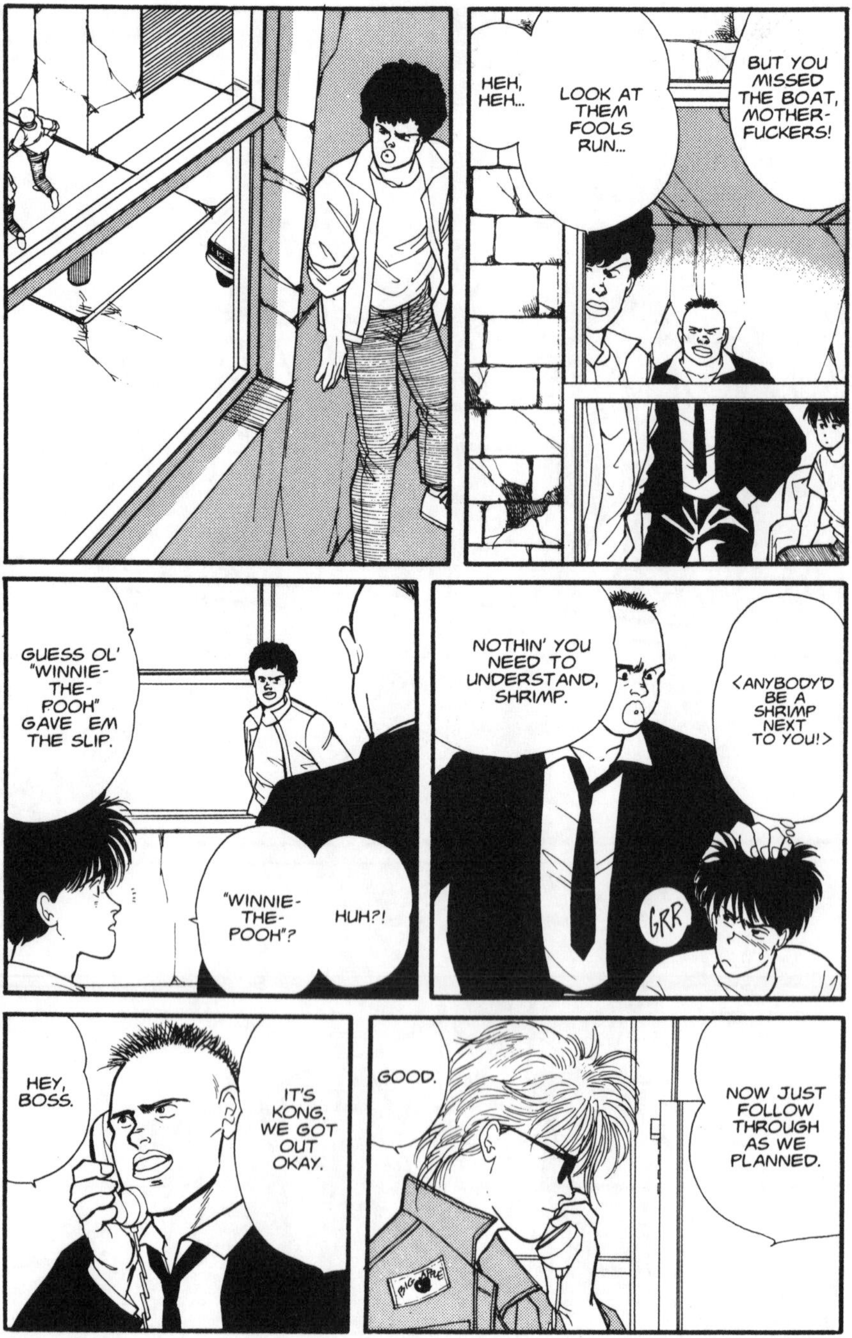
HEH, HEH...
LOOK AT THEM FOOLS RUN...
BUT YOU MISSED THE BOAT, MOTHER-FUCKERS!
GUESS OL' "WINNIE-THE-POOH" GAVE EM THE SLIP.
"WINNIE-THE-POOH"?
HUH?!
NOTHIN' YOU NEED TO UNDERSTAND, SHRIMP.
<ANYBODY'D BE A SHRIMP NEXT TO YOU!>
GRR
HEY, BOSS.
IT'S KONG. WE GOT OUT OKAY.
GOOD.
NOW JUST FOLLOW THROUGH AS WE PLANNED.
BIG APPLE

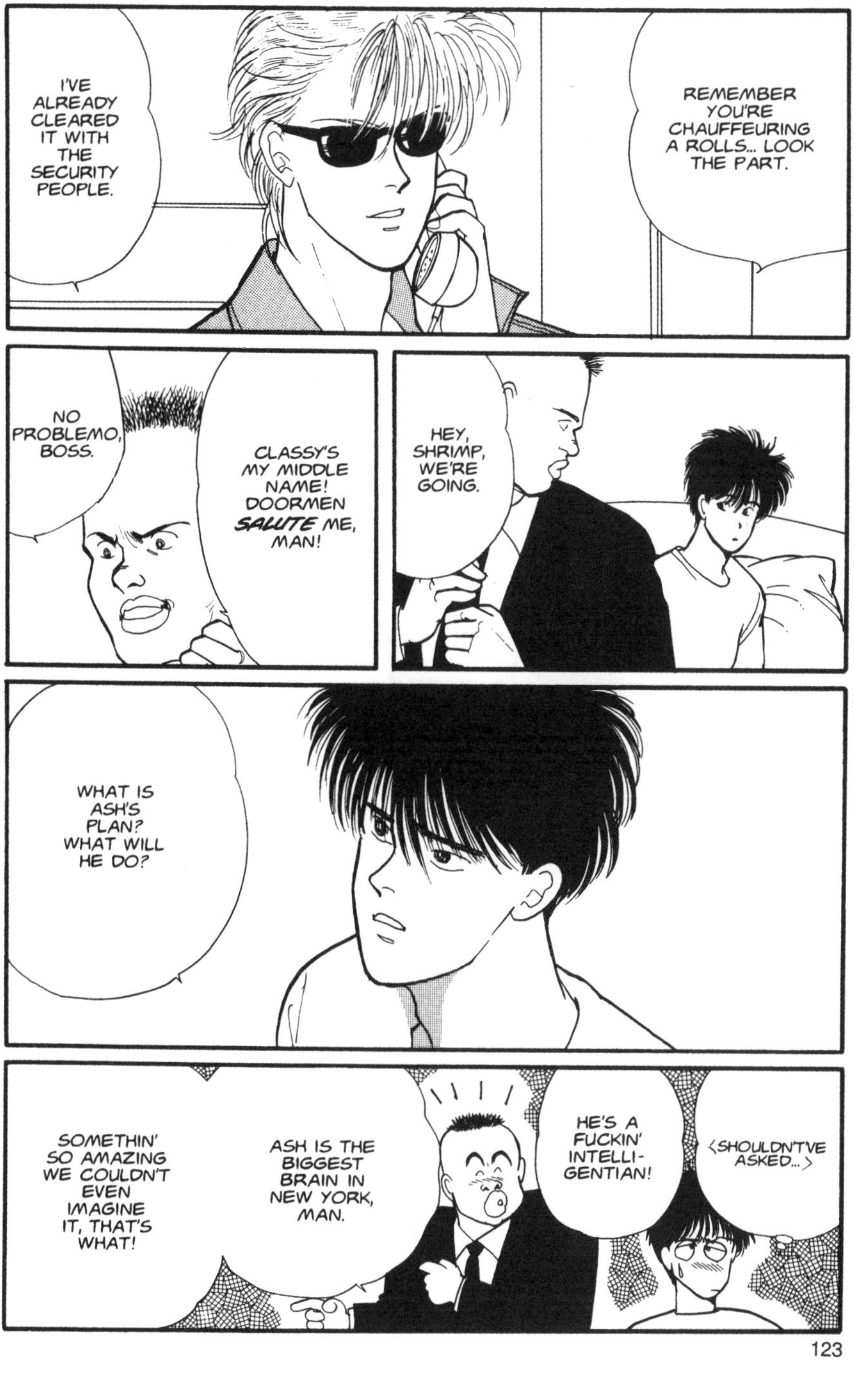
I'VE ALREADY CLEARED IT WITH THE SECURITY PEOPLE.
REMEMBER YOU'RE CHAUFFEURING A ROLLS... LOOK THE PART.
NO PROBLEMO, BOSS.
CLASSY'S MY MIDDLE NAME! DOORMEN *SALUTE* ME, MAN!
HEY, SHRIMP, WE'RE GOING.
WHAT IS ASH'S PLAN? WHAT WILL HE DO?
SOMETHIN' SO AMAZING WE COULDN'T EVEN IMAGINE IT, THAT'S WHAT!
ASH IS THE BIGGEST BRAIN IN NEW YORK, MAN.
HE'S A FUCKIN' INTELLI-GENTIAN!
〈SHOULDN'T'VE ASKED...〉

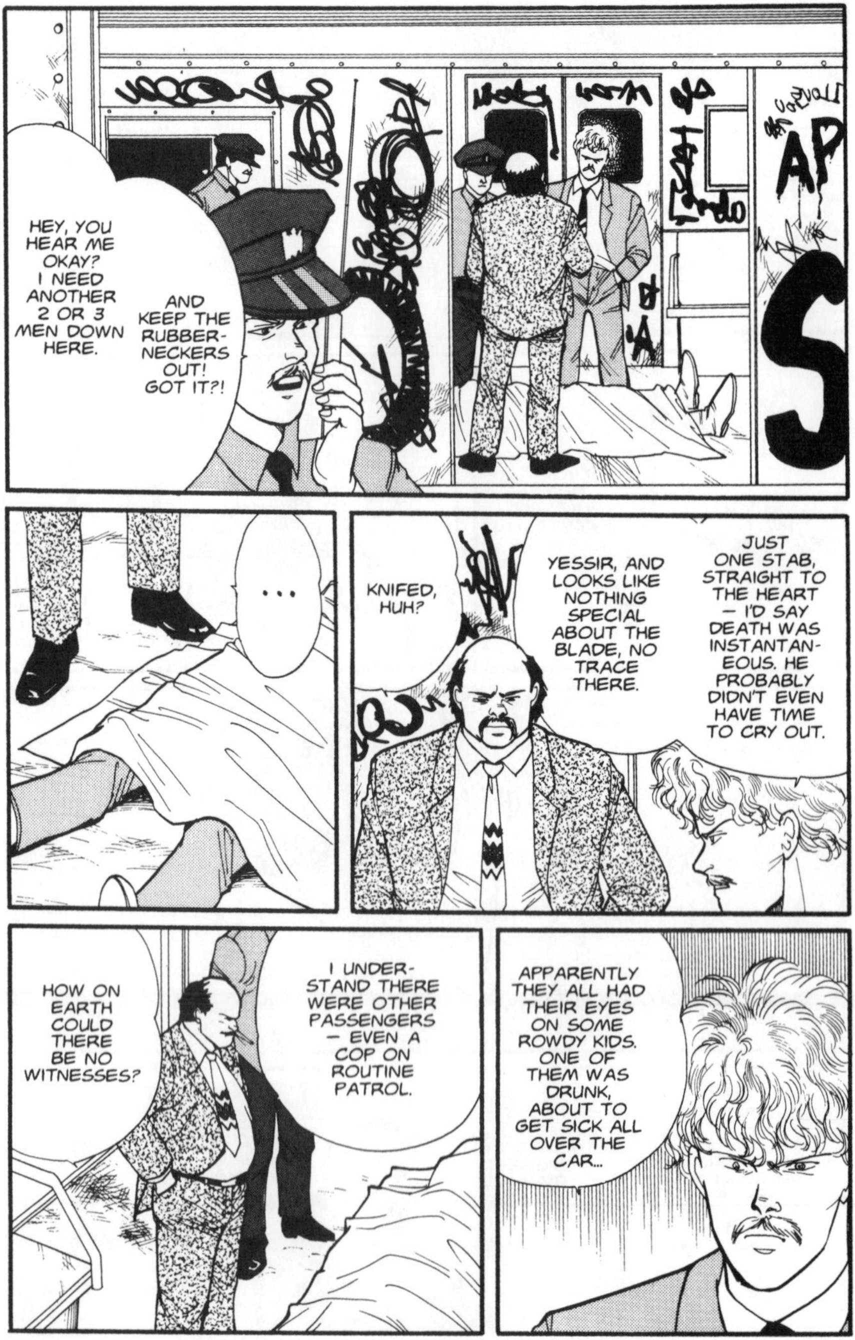
HEY, YOU HEAR ME OKAY? I NEED ANOTHER 2 OR 3 MEN DOWN HERE.
AND KEEP THE RUBBER-NECKERS OUT! GOT IT?!
...
KNIFED, HUH?
YESSIR, AND LOOKS LIKE NOTHING SPECIAL ABOUT THE BLADE, NO TRACE THERE.
JUST ONE STAB, STRAIGHT TO THE HEART — I'D SAY DEATH WAS INSTANTAN-EOUS. HE PROBABLY DIDN'T EVEN HAVE TIME TO CRY OUT.
HOW ON EARTH COULD THERE BE NO WITNESSES?
I UNDER-STAND THERE WERE OTHER PASSENGERS — EVEN A COP ON ROUTINE PATROL.
APPARENTLY THEY ALL HAD THEIR EYES ON SOME ROWDY KIDS. ONE OF THEM WAS DRUNK, ABOUT TO GET SICK ALL OVER THE CAR...

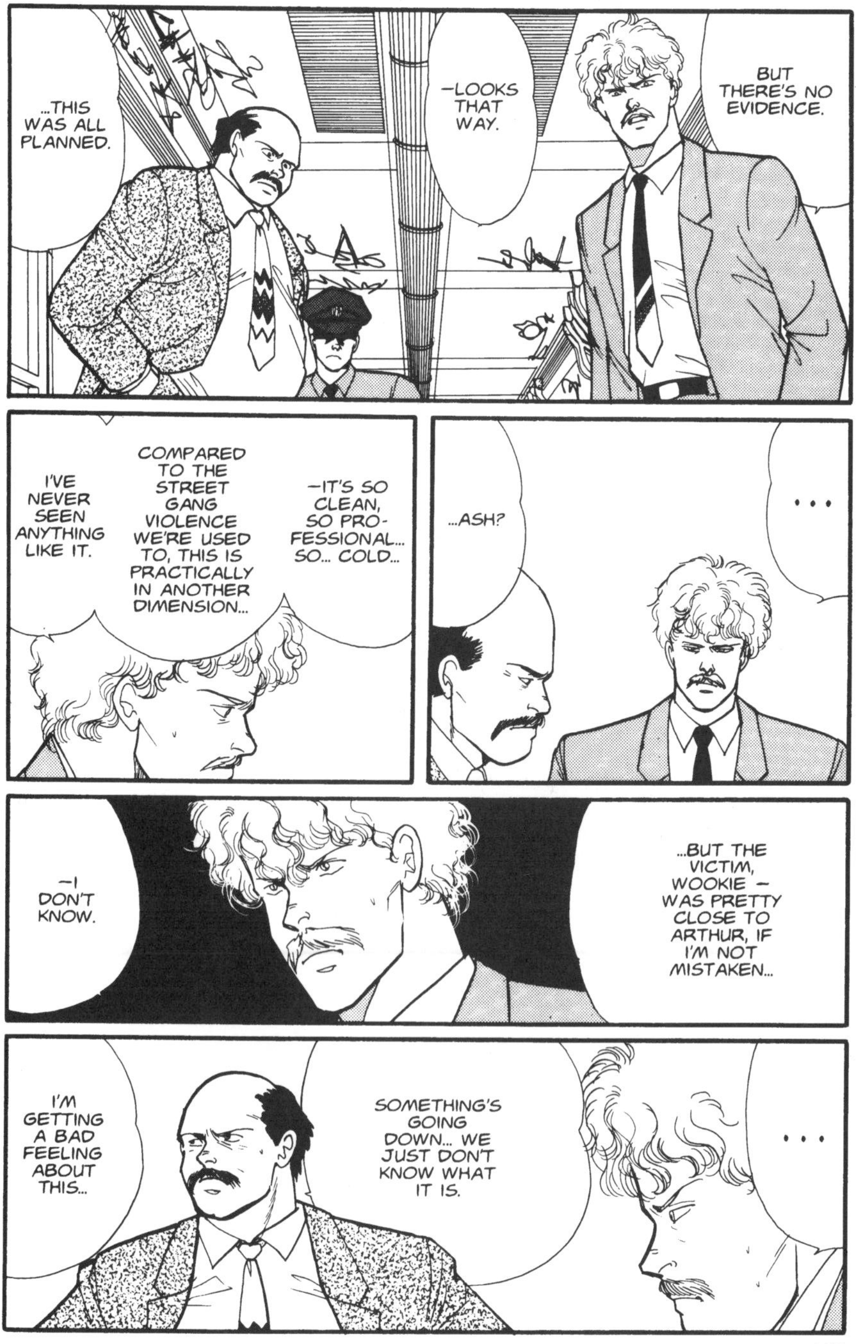
...THIS WAS ALL PLANNED.
—LOOKS THAT WAY.
BUT THERE'S NO EVIDENCE.
I'VE NEVER SEEN ANYTHING LIKE IT.
COMPARED TO THE STREET GANG VIOLENCE WE'RE USED TO, THIS IS PRACTICALLY IN ANOTHER DIMENSION...
—IT'S SO CLEAN, SO PRO-FESSIONAL... SO... COLD...
...ASH?
• • •
—I DON'T KNOW.
...BUT THE VICTIM, WOOKIE — WAS PRETTY CLOSE TO ARTHUR, IF I'M NOT MISTAKEN...
I'M GETTING A BAD FEELING ABOUT THIS...
SOMETHING'S GOING DOWN... WE JUST DON'T KNOW WHAT IT IS.
• • •

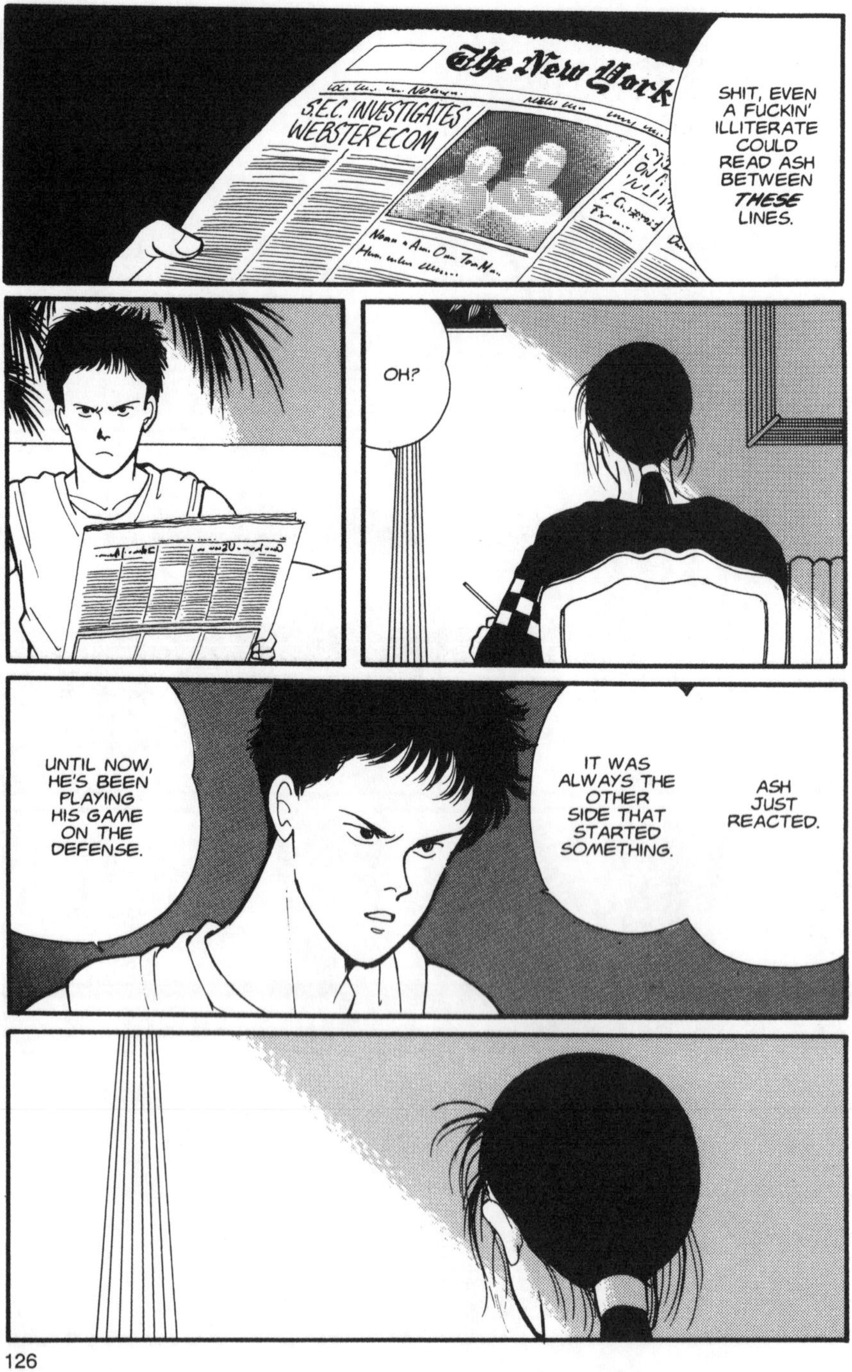
The New York
S.E.C. INVESTIGATES WEBSTER ECOM
SHIT, EVEN A FUCKIN' ILLITERATE COULD READ ASH BETWEEN *THESE* LINES.
OH?
UNTIL NOW, HE'S BEEN PLAYING HIS GAME ON THE DEFENSE.
IT WAS ALWAYS THE OTHER SIDE THAT STARTED SOMETHING.
ASH JUST REACTED.

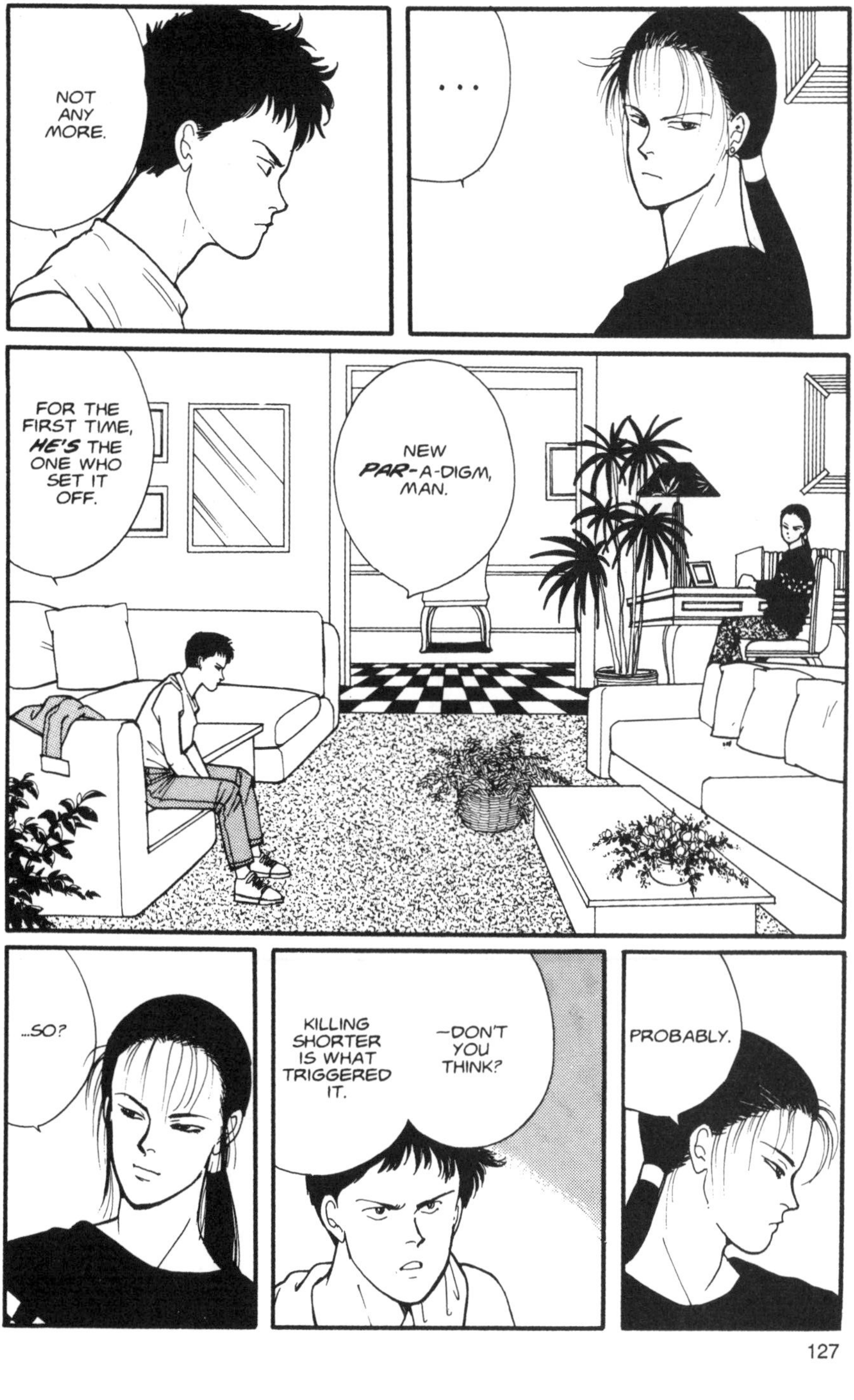
NOT ANY MORE.
...
FOR THE FIRST TIME, ***HE'S*** THE ONE WHO SET IT OFF.
NEW ***PAR***-A-DIGM, MAN.
...SO?
KILLING SHORTER IS WHAT TRIGGERED IT.
–DON'T YOU THINK?
PROBABLY.

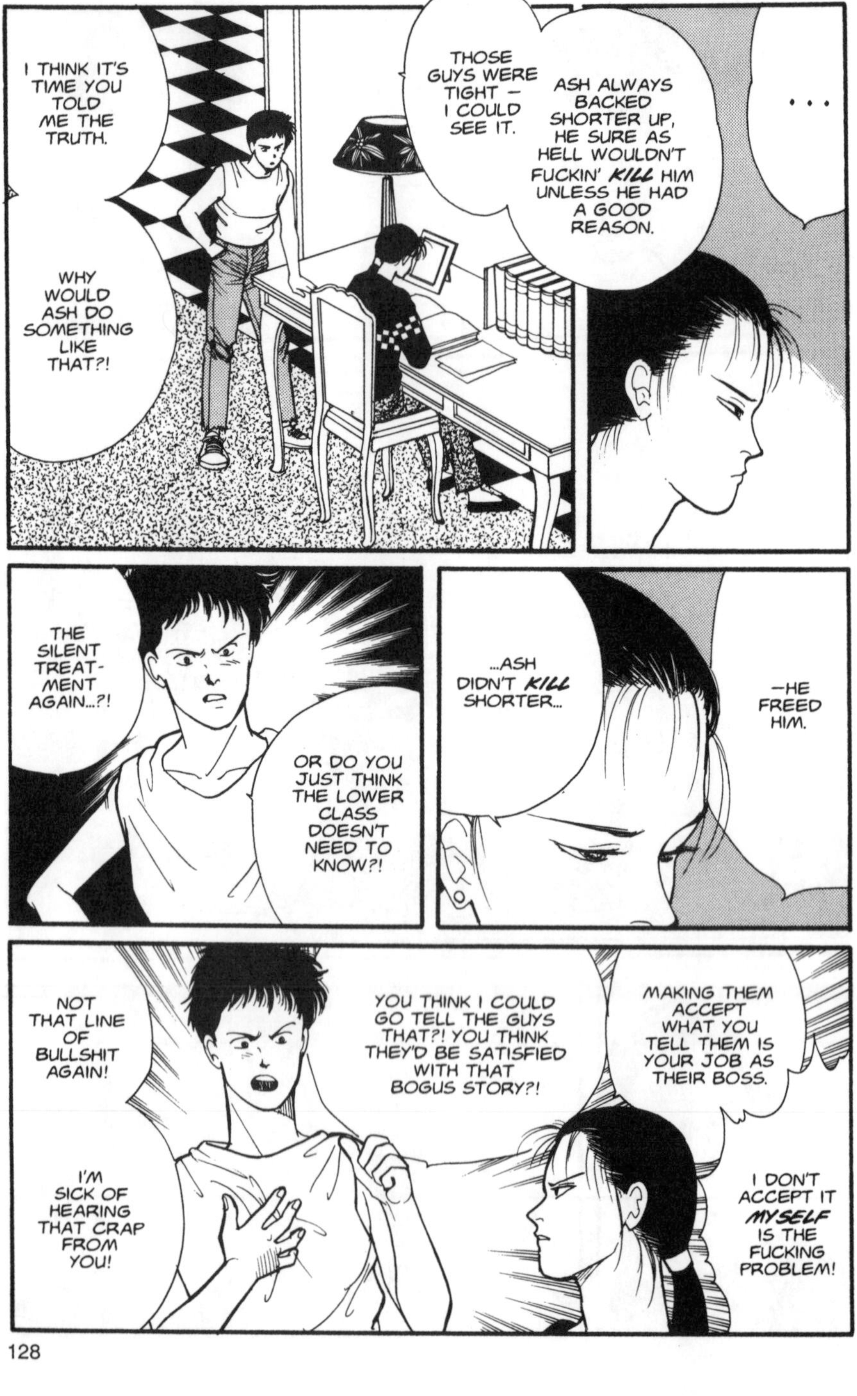
I THINK IT'S TIME YOU TOLD ME THE TRUTH.
WHY WOULD ASH DO SOMETHING LIKE THAT?!
THOSE GUYS WERE TIGHT — I COULD SEE IT.
ASH ALWAYS BACKED SHORTER UP, HE SURE AS HELL WOULDN'T FUCKIN' KILL HIM UNLESS HE HAD A GOOD REASON.
. . .
THE SILENT TREAT-MENT AGAIN...?!
OR DO YOU JUST THINK THE LOWER CLASS DOESN'T NEED TO KNOW?!
...ASH DIDN'T KILL SHORTER...
—HE FREED HIM.
NOT THAT LINE OF BULLSHIT AGAIN!
I'M SICK OF HEARING THAT CRAP FROM YOU!
YOU THINK I COULD GO TELL THE GUYS THAT?! YOU THINK THEY'D BE SATISFIED WITH THAT BOGUS STORY?!
MAKING THEM ACCEPT WHAT YOU TELL THEM IS YOUR JOB AS THEIR BOSS.
I DON'T ACCEPT IT MYSELF IS THE FUCKING PROBLEM!

THE REASON I WON'T TELL YOU... IS THAT I DON'T WANT TO DRAG YOU INTO THE HELL I NOW INHABIT.

?!

I AM LIVING IN WHAT I CAN ONLY DESCRIBE AS MENTAL, EMOTIONAL HELL...

AND — SO IS ASH.

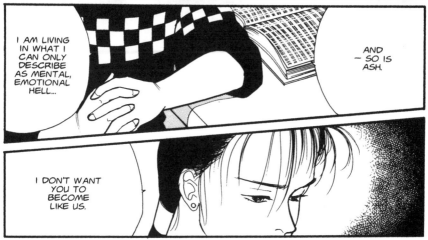

I DON'T WANT YOU TO BECOME LIKE US.

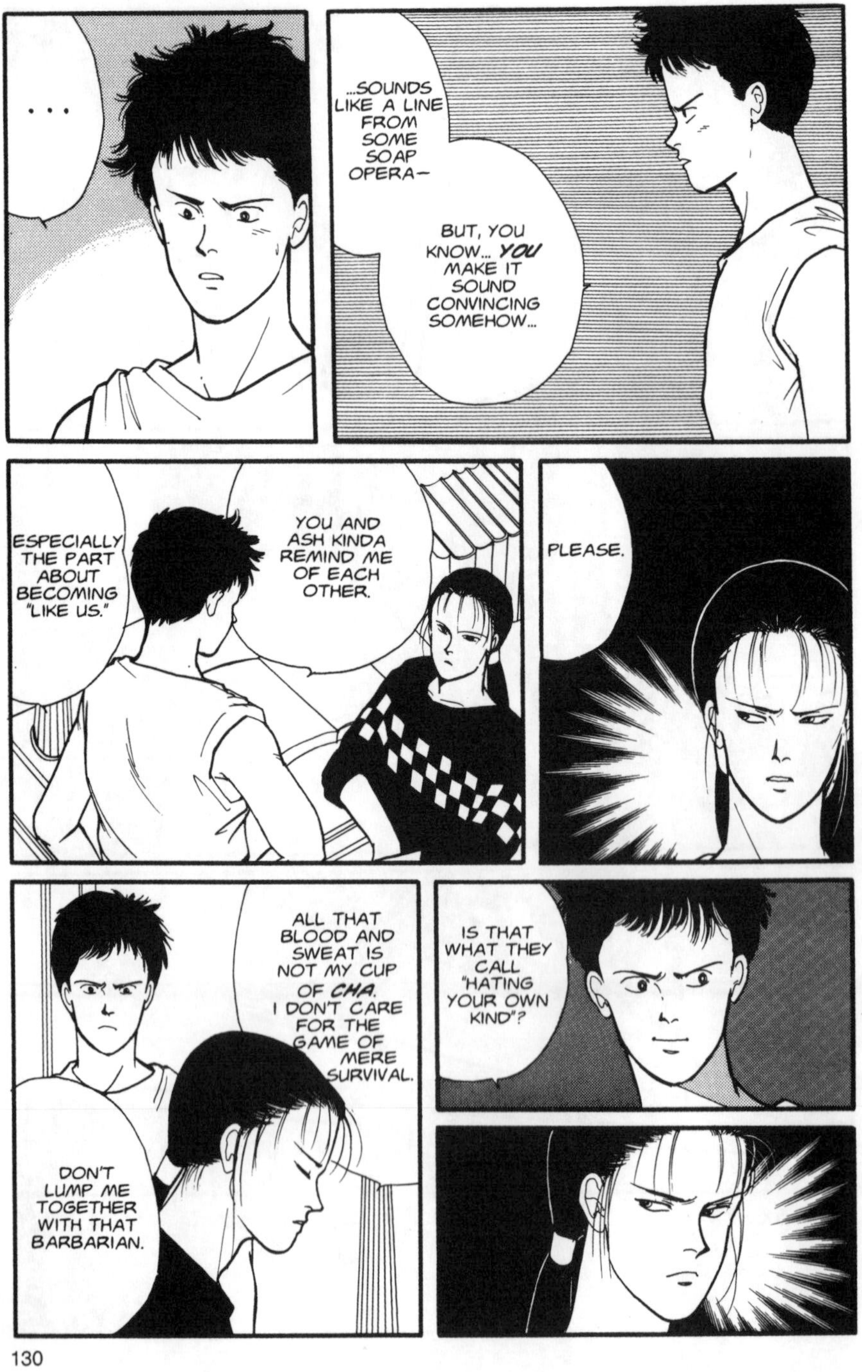
. . .
...SOUNDS LIKE A LINE FROM SOME SOAP OPERA—
BUT, YOU KNOW... *YOU* MAKE IT SOUND CONVINCING SOMEHOW...
ESPECIALLY THE PART ABOUT BECOMING "LIKE US."
YOU AND ASH KINDA REMIND ME OF EACH OTHER.
PLEASE.
ALL THAT BLOOD AND SWEAT IS NOT MY CUP OF *CHA*. I DON'T CARE FOR THE GAME OF MERE SURVIVAL.
DON'T LUMP ME TOGETHER WITH THAT BARBARIAN.
IS THAT WHAT THEY CALL "HATING YOUR OWN KIND"?

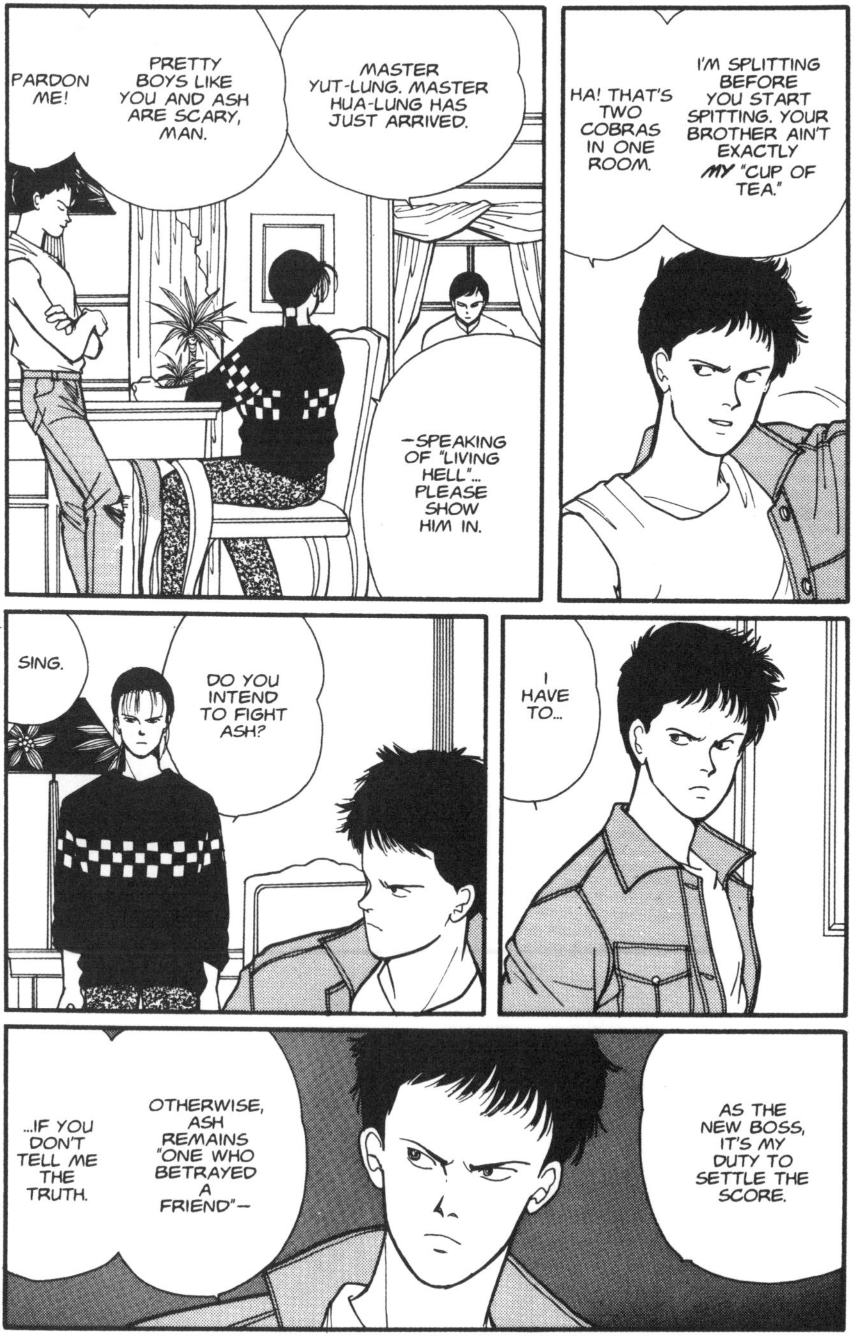
PARDON ME!
PRETTY BOYS LIKE YOU AND ASH ARE SCARY, MAN.
MASTER YUT-LUNG. MASTER HUA-LUNG HAS JUST ARRIVED.
—SPEAKING OF "LIVING HELL"... PLEASE SHOW HIM IN.
HA! THAT'S TWO COBRAS IN ONE ROOM.
I'M SPLITTING BEFORE YOU START SPITTING. YOUR BROTHER AIN'T EXACTLY MY "CUP OF TEA."
SING.
DO YOU INTEND TO FIGHT ASH?
I HAVE TO...
...IF YOU DON'T TELL ME THE TRUTH.
OTHERWISE, ASH REMAINS "ONE WHO BETRAYED A FRIEND"—
AS THE NEW BOSS, IT'S MY DUTY TO SETTLE THE SCORE.

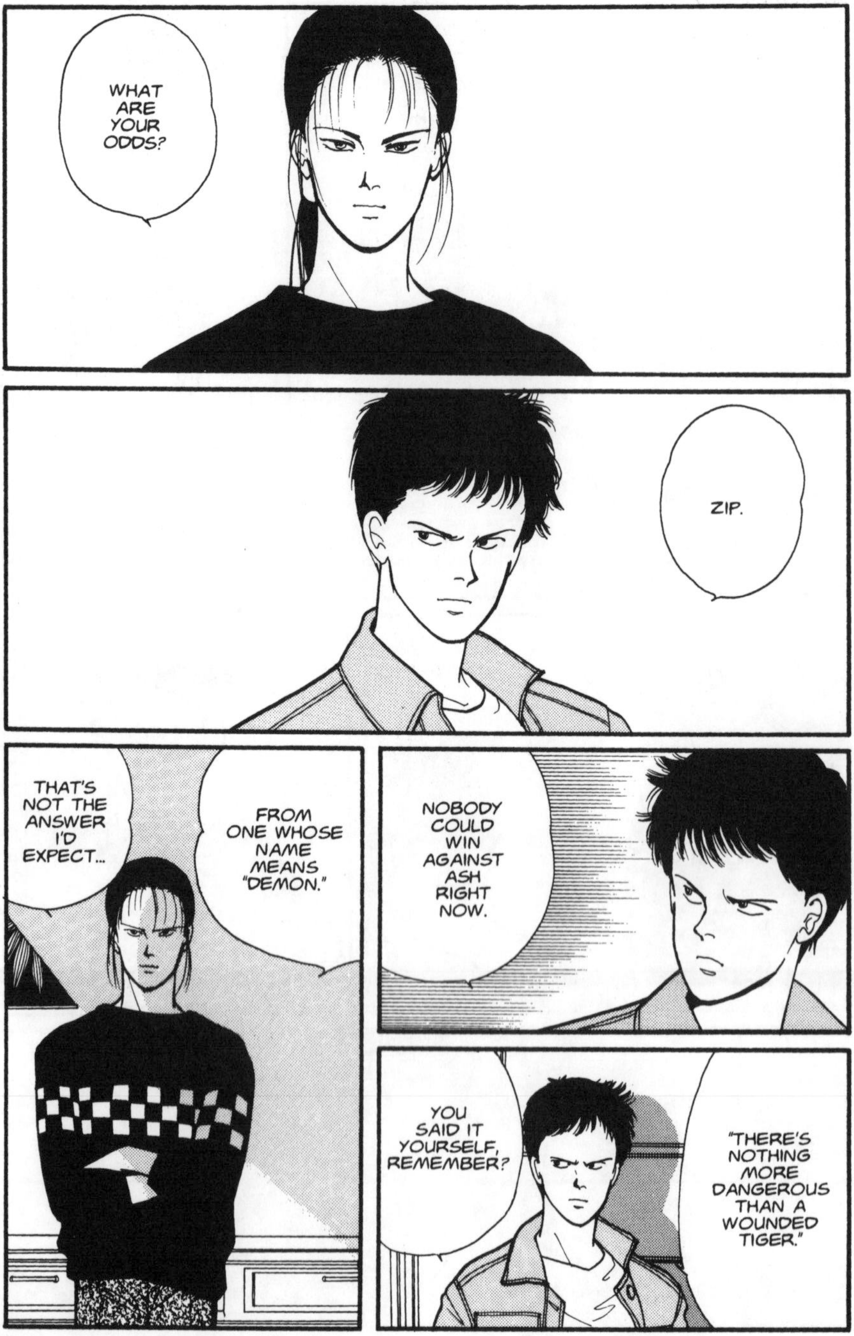
WHAT ARE YOUR ODDS?
ZIP.
THAT'S NOT THE ANSWER I'D EXPECT...
FROM ONE WHOSE NAME MEANS "DEMON."
NOBODY COULD WIN AGAINST ASH RIGHT NOW.
YOU SAID IT YOURSELF, REMEMBER?
"THERE'S NOTHING MORE DANGEROUS THAN A WOUNDED TIGER."

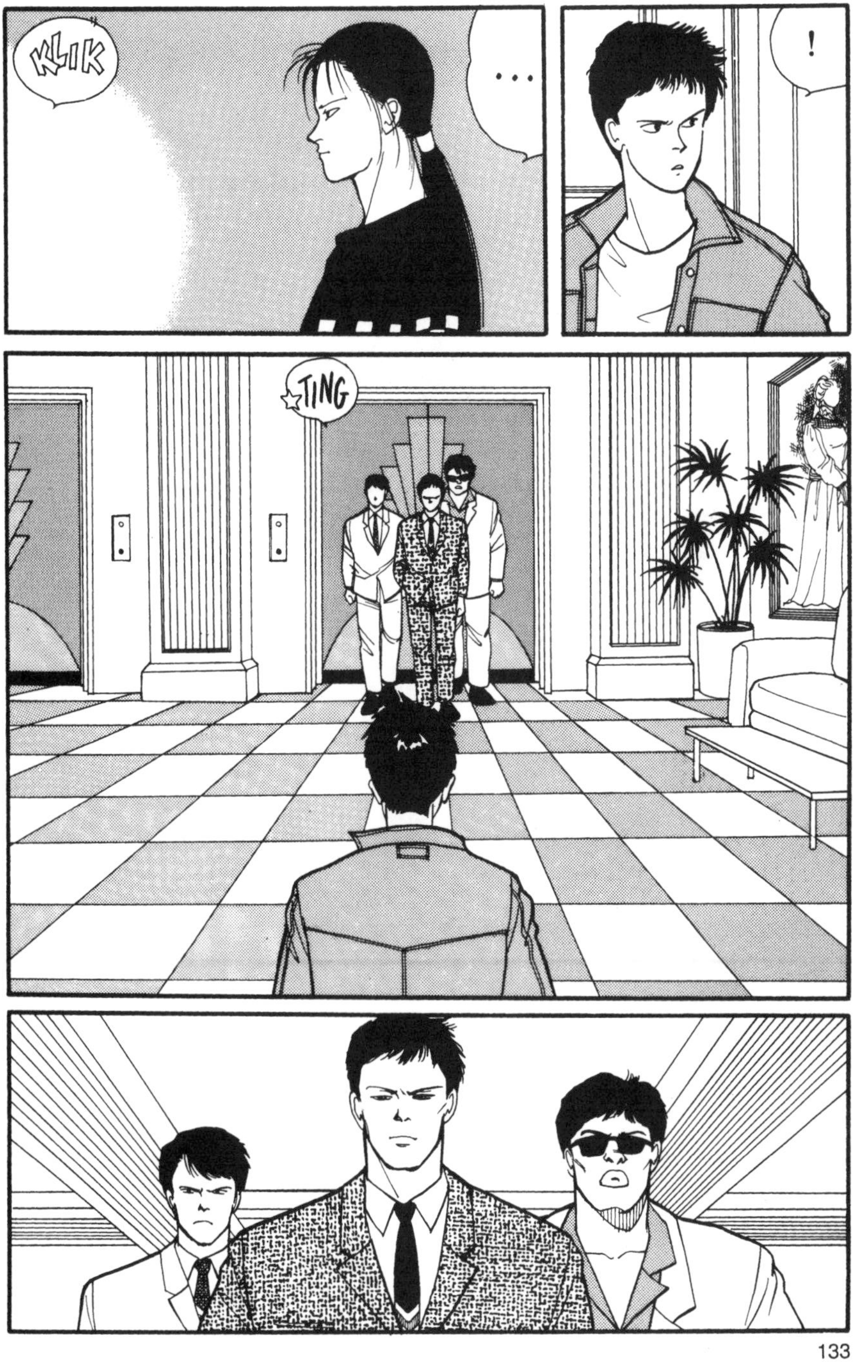
KLIK
...
!
TING

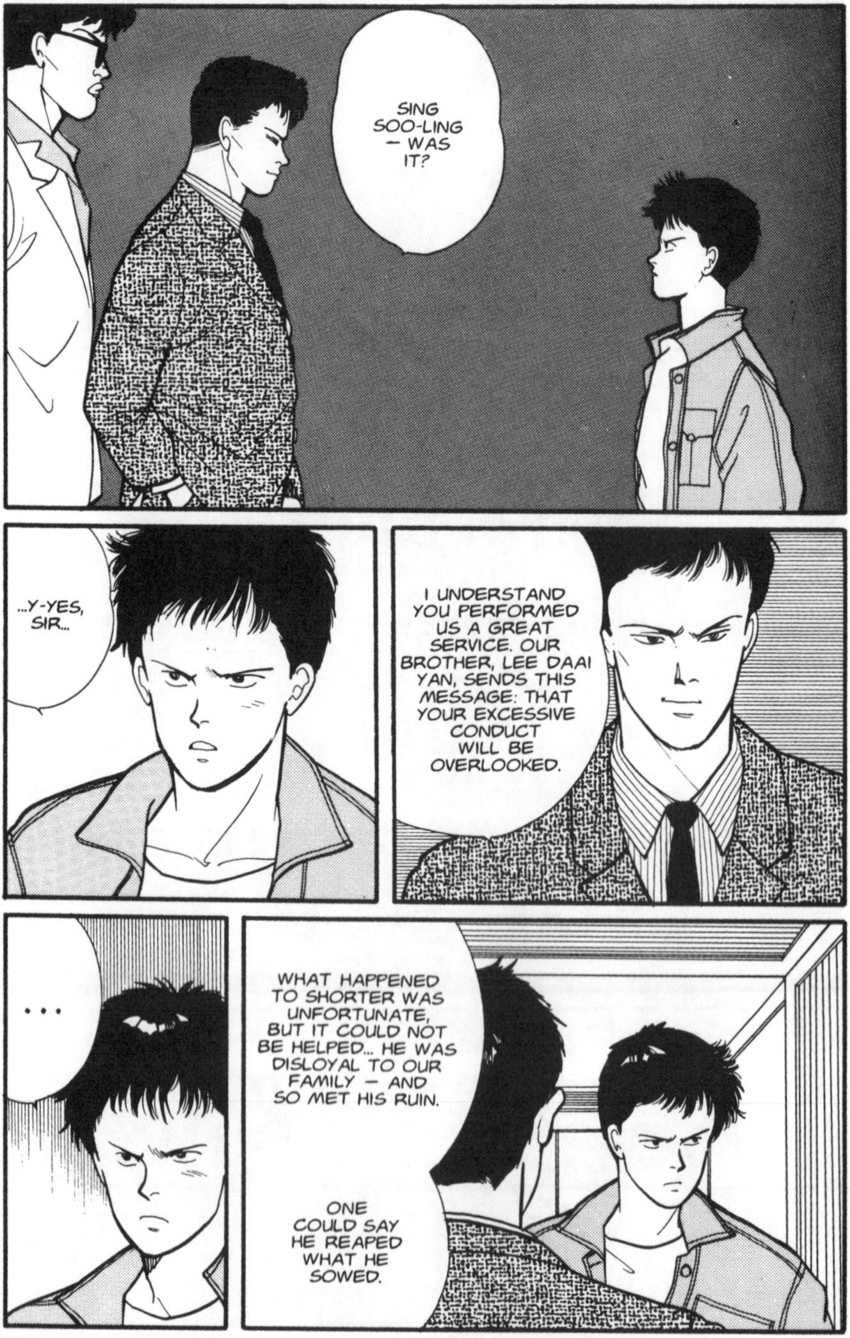
SING SOO-LING — WAS IT?
...Y-YES, SIR...
I UNDERSTAND YOU PERFORMED US A GREAT SERVICE. OUR BROTHER, LEE DAAI YAN, SENDS THIS MESSAGE: THAT YOUR EXCESSIVE CONDUCT WILL BE OVERLOOKED.
...
WHAT HAPPENED TO SHORTER WAS UNFORTUNATE, BUT IT COULD NOT BE HELPED... HE WAS DISLOYAL TO OUR FAMILY — AND SO MET HIS RUIN.
ONE COULD SAY HE REAPED WHAT HE SOWED.

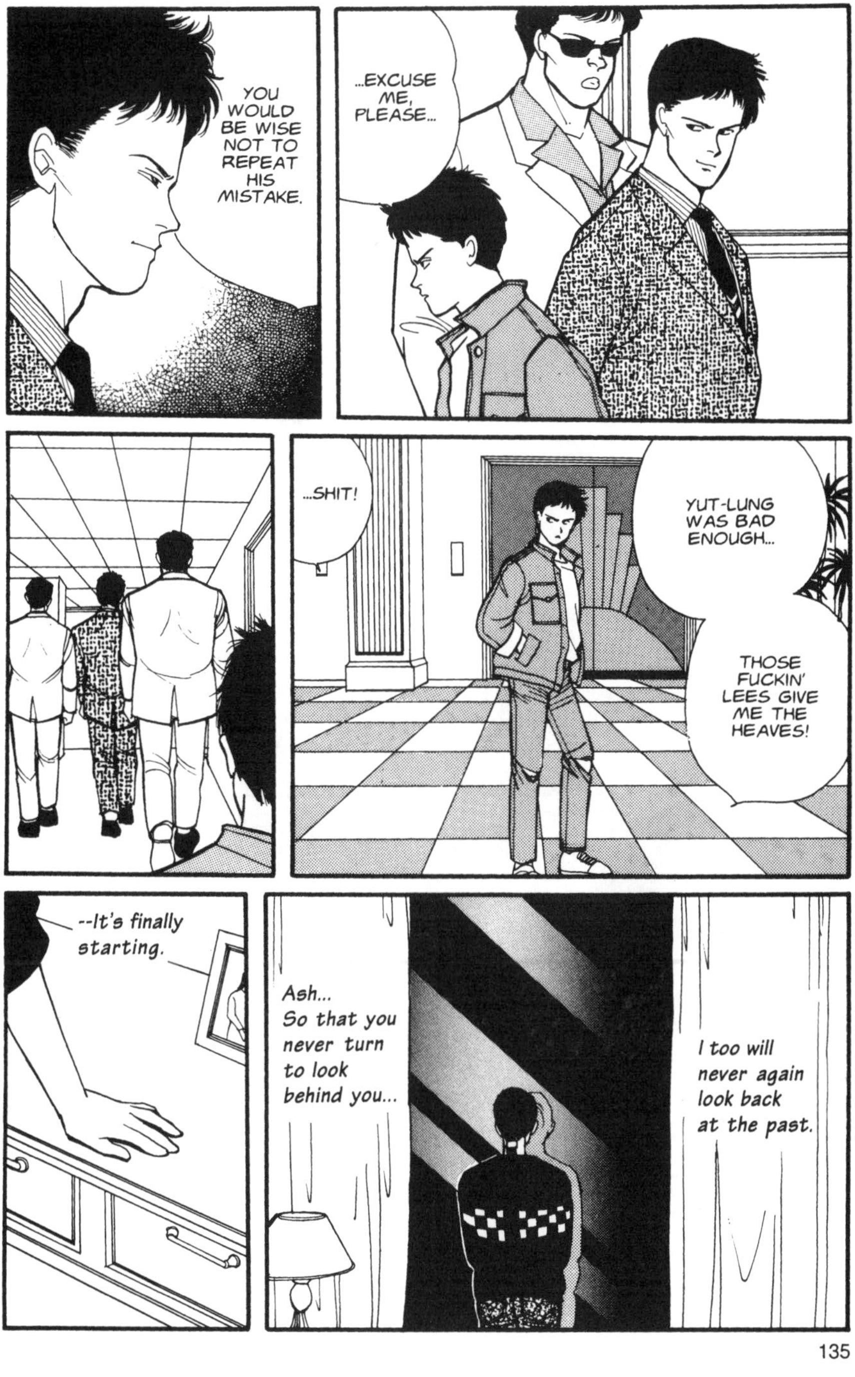
YOU WOULD BE WISE NOT TO REPEAT HIS MISTAKE.
...EXCUSE ME, PLEASE...
...SHIT!
YUT-LUNG WAS BAD ENOUGH...
THOSE FUCKIN' LEES GIVE ME THE HEAVES!
--It's finally starting.
Ash... So that you never turn to look behind you...
I too will never again look back at the past.

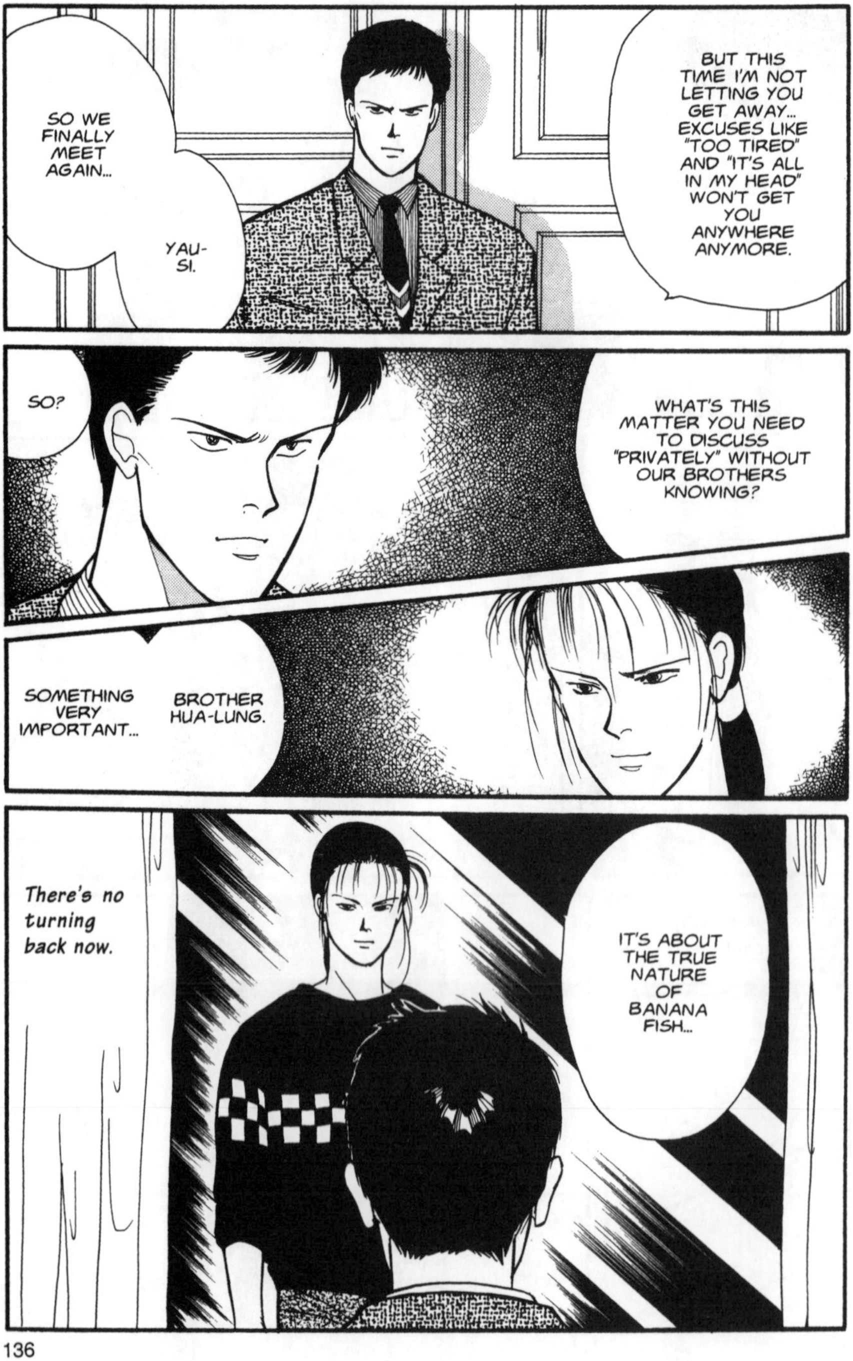
SO WE FINALLY MEET AGAIN...
YAU-SI.
BUT THIS TIME I'M NOT LETTING YOU GET AWAY... EXCUSES LIKE "TOO TIRED" AND "IT'S ALL IN MY HEAD" WON'T GET YOU ANYWHERE ANYMORE.
SO?
WHAT'S THIS MATTER YOU NEED TO DISCUSS "PRIVATELY" WITHOUT OUR BROTHERS KNOWING?
SOMETHING VERY IMPORTANT...
BROTHER HUA-LUNG.
There's no turning back now.
IT'S ABOUT THE TRUE NATURE OF BANANA FISH...

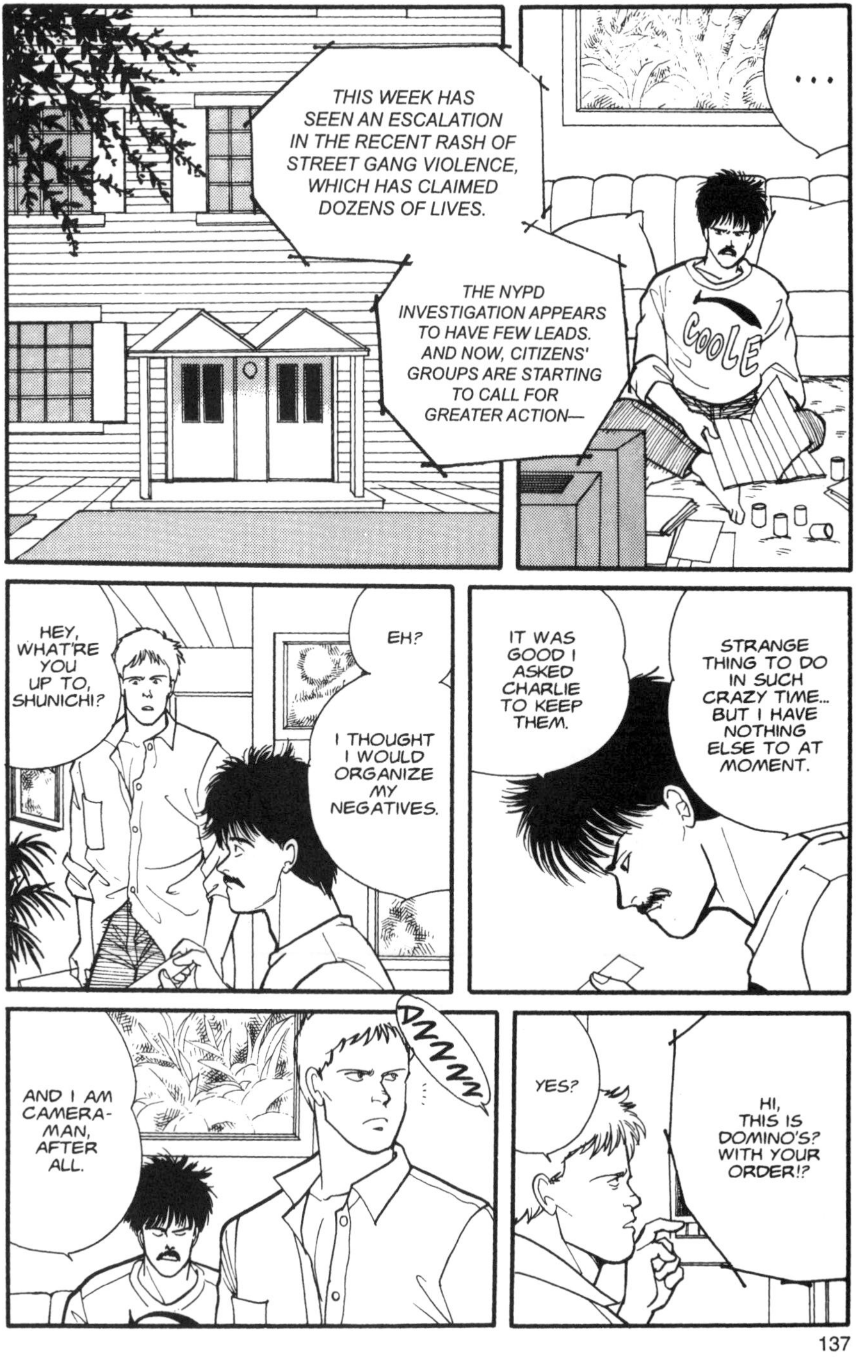
THIS WEEK HAS SEEN AN ESCALATION IN THE RECENT RASH OF STREET GANG VIOLENCE, WHICH HAS CLAIMED DOZENS OF LIVES.
THE NYPD INVESTIGATION APPEARS TO HAVE FEW LEADS. AND NOW, CITIZENS' GROUPS ARE STARTING TO CALL FOR GREATER ACTION—
...
COOLE
HEY, WHAT'RE YOU UP TO, SHUNICHI?
EH?
I THOUGHT I WOULD ORGANIZE MY NEGATIVES.
IT WAS GOOD I ASKED CHARLIE TO KEEP THEM.
STRANGE THING TO DO IN SUCH CRAZY TIME... BUT I HAVE NOTHING ELSE TO AT MOMENT.
AND I AM CAMERA-MAN, AFTER ALL.
YES?
HI, THIS IS DOMINO'S? WITH YOUR ORDER!?

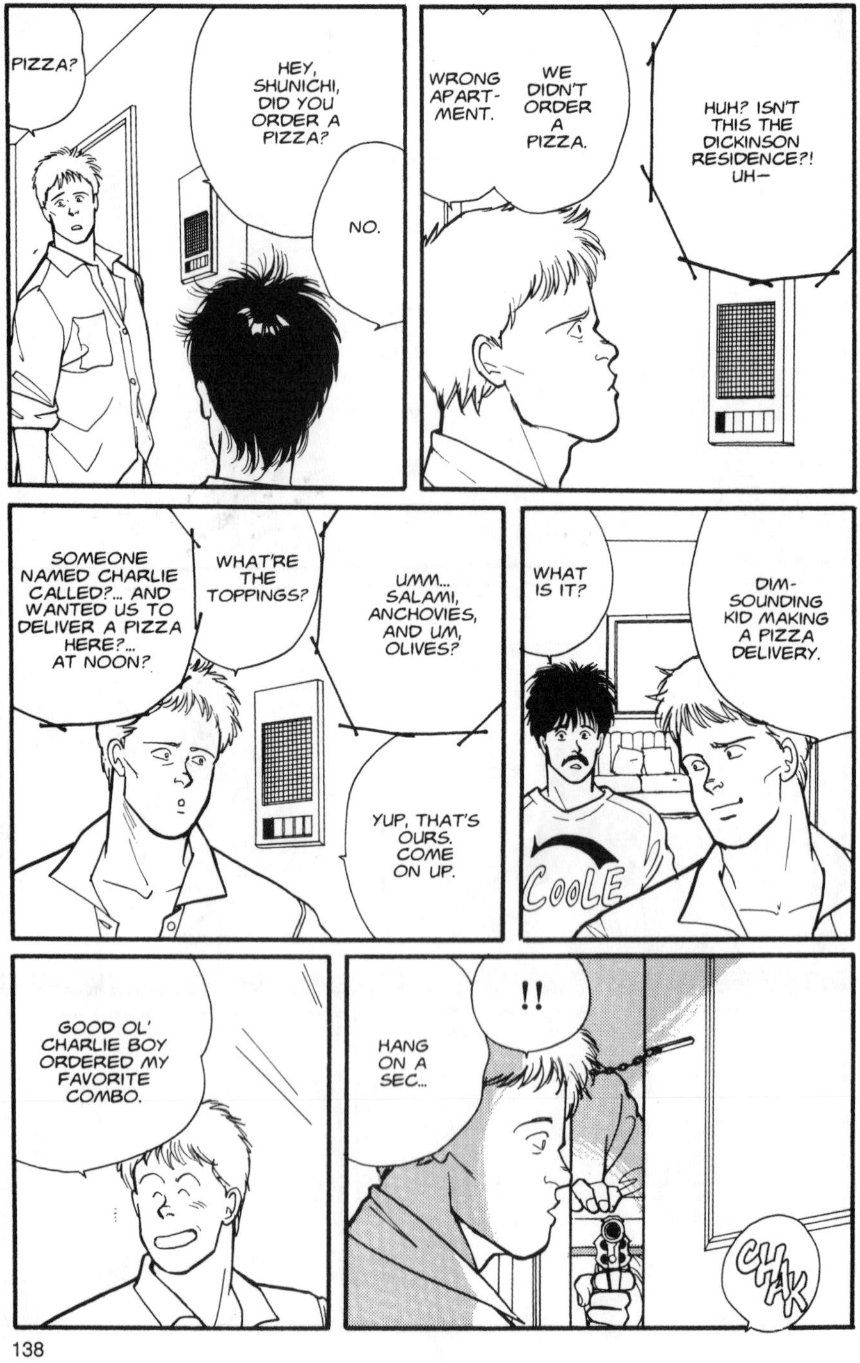
PIZZA?
HEY, SHUNICHI, DID YOU ORDER A PIZZA?
NO.
WRONG APART-MENT.
WE DIDN'T ORDER A PIZZA.
HUH? ISN'T THIS THE DICKINSON RESIDENCE?! UH—
SOMEONE NAMED CHARLIE CALLED?... AND WANTED US TO DELIVER A PIZZA HERE?... AT NOON?
WHAT'RE THE TOPPINGS?
UMM... SALAMI, ANCHOVIES, AND UM, OLIVES?
YUP, THAT'S OURS. COME ON UP.
WHAT IS IT?
DIM-SOUNDING KID MAKING A PIZZA DELIVERY.
COOLE
GOOD OL' CHARLIE BOY ORDERED MY FAVORITE COMBO.
!!
HANG ON A SEC...
CHAK

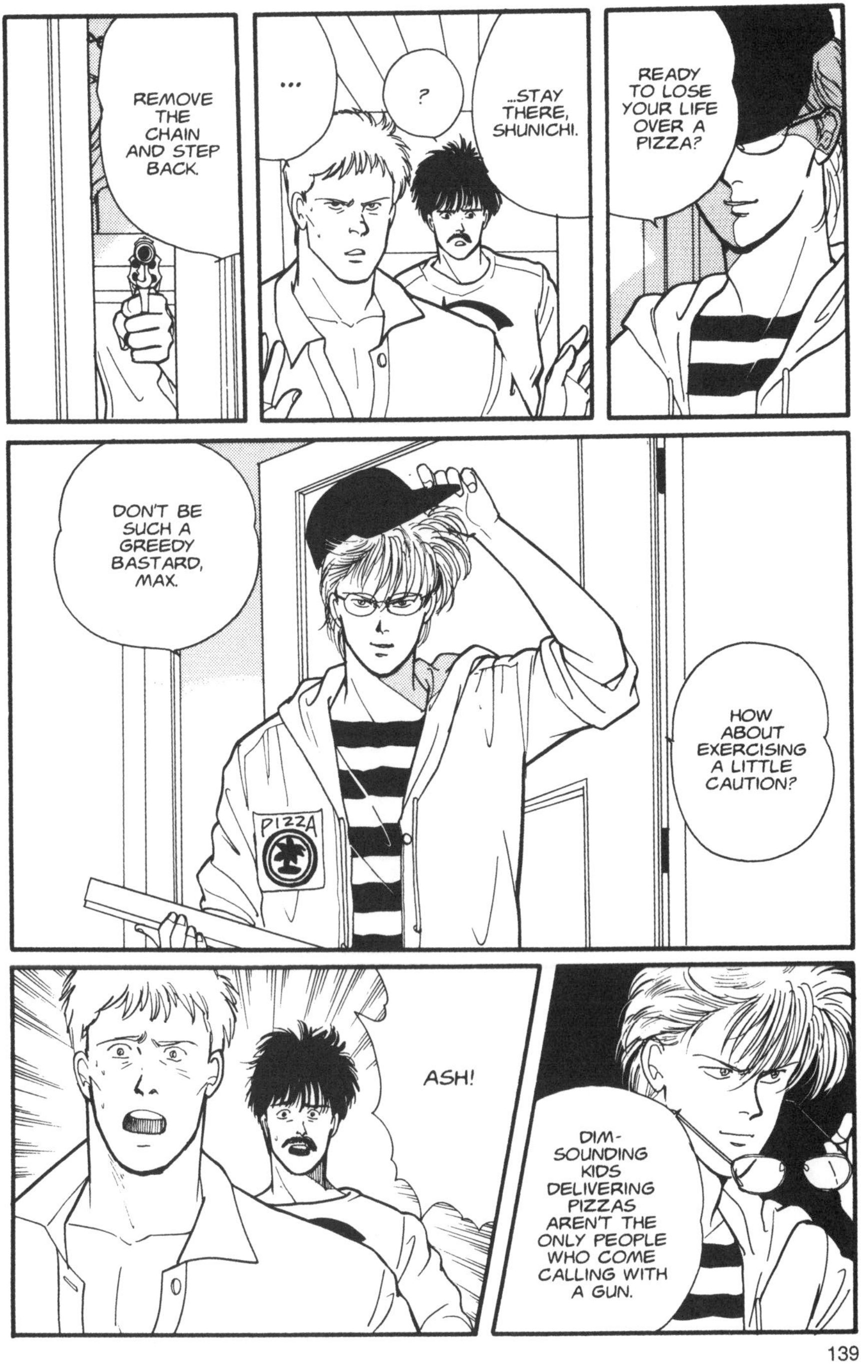
REMOVE THE CHAIN AND STEP BACK.
...
?
...STAY THERE, SHUNICHI.
READY TO LOSE YOUR LIFE OVER A PIZZA?
DON'T BE SUCH A GREEDY BASTARD, MAX.
PIZZA
HOW ABOUT EXERCISING A LITTLE CAUTION?
ASH!
DIM-SOUNDING KIDS DELIVERING PIZZAS AREN'T THE ONLY PEOPLE WHO COME CALLING WITH A GUN.

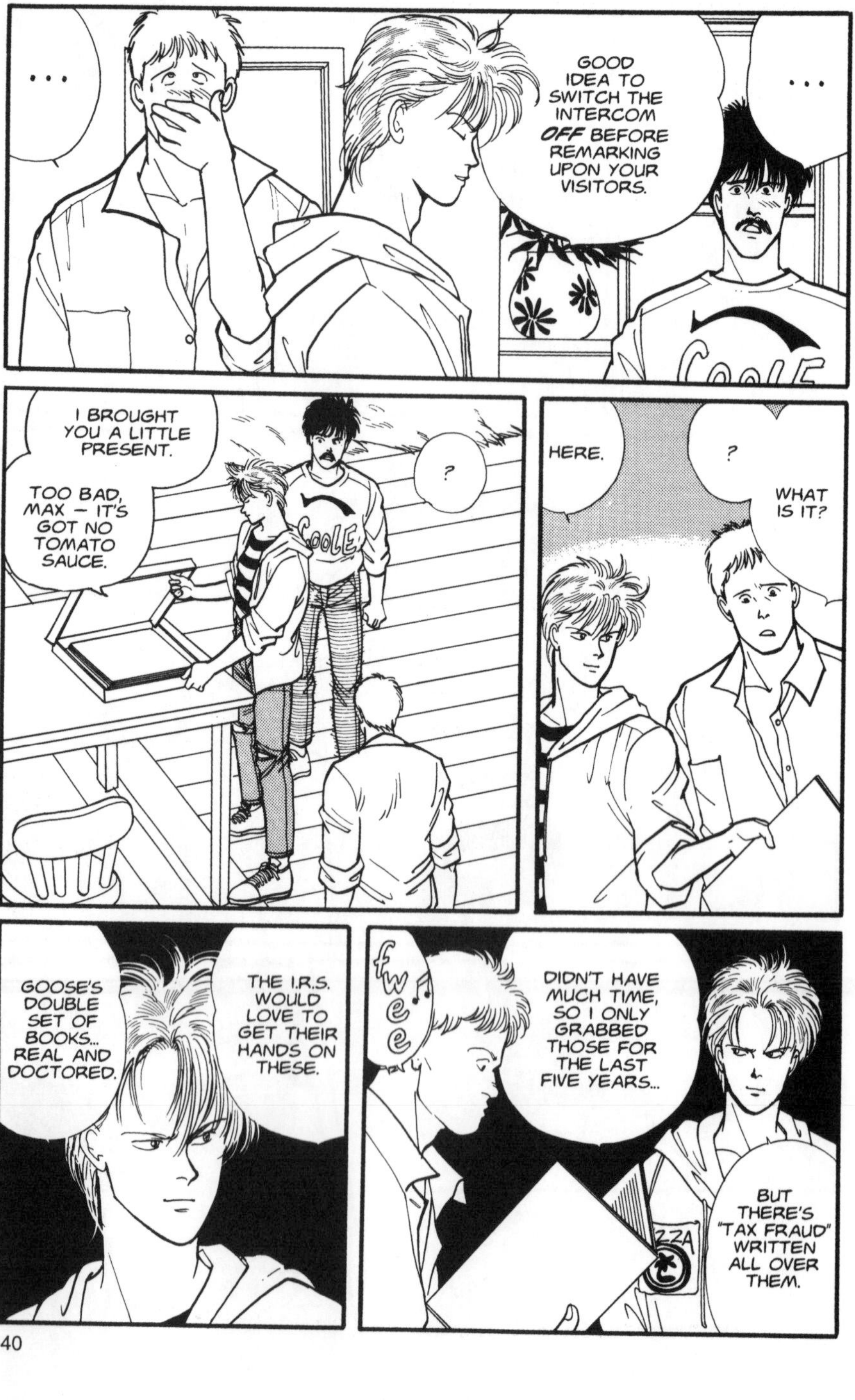
...
GOOD IDEA TO SWITCH THE INTERCOM OFF BEFORE REMARKING UPON YOUR VISITORS.
...
I BROUGHT YOU A LITTLE PRESENT.
TOO BAD, MAX – IT'S GOT NO TOMATO SAUCE.
?
HERE.
?
WHAT IS IT?
GOOSE'S DOUBLE SET OF BOOKS... REAL AND DOCTORED.
THE I.R.S. WOULD LOVE TO GET THEIR HANDS ON THESE.
fwee
DIDN'T HAVE MUCH TIME, SO I ONLY GRABBED THOSE FOR THE LAST FIVE YEARS...
BUT THERE'S "TAX FRAUD" WRITTEN ALL OVER THEM.

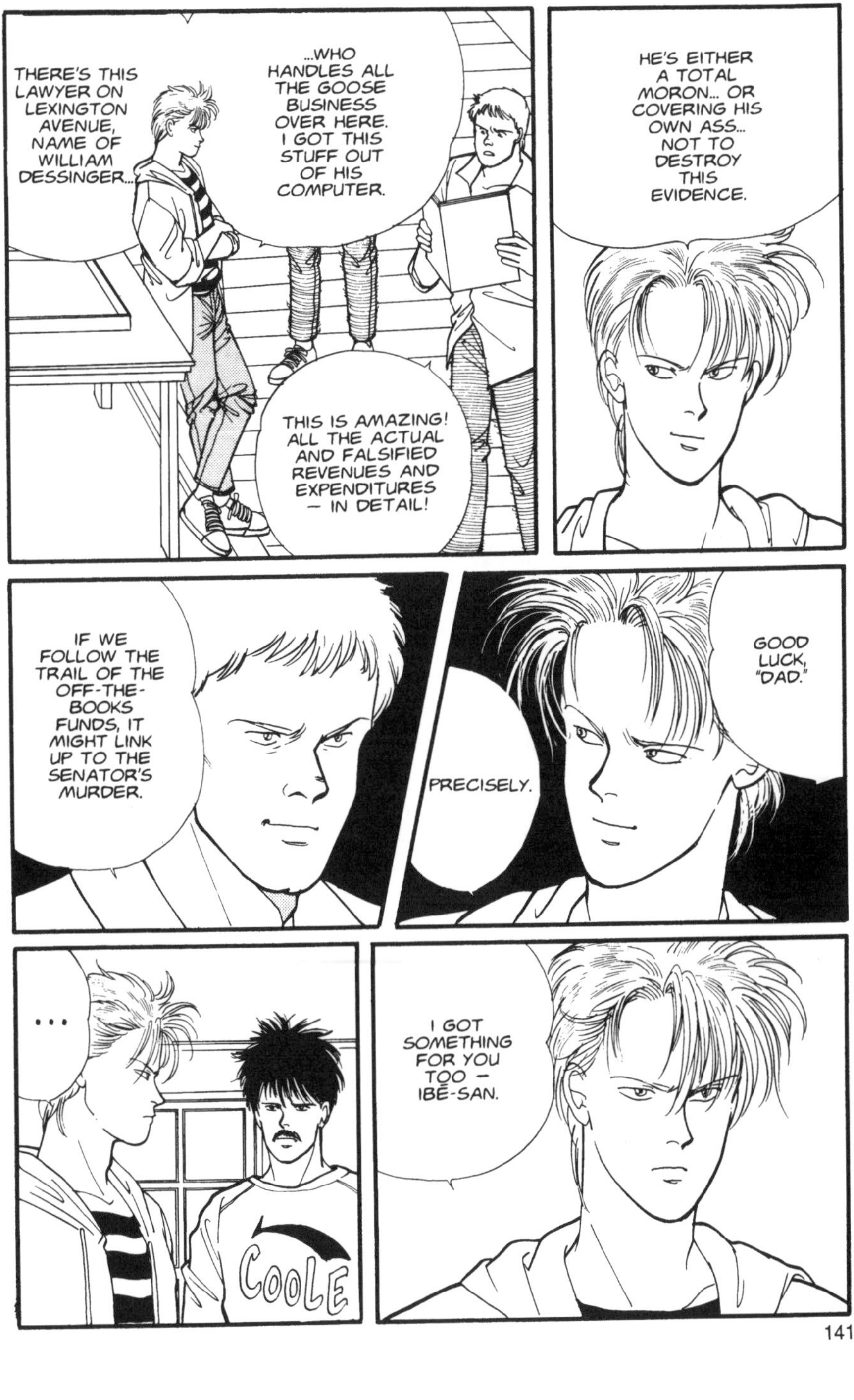
THERE'S THIS LAWYER ON LEXINGTON AVENUE, NAME OF WILLIAM DESSINGER...
...WHO HANDLES ALL THE GOOSE BUSINESS OVER HERE. I GOT THIS STUFF OUT OF HIS COMPUTER.
THIS IS AMAZING! ALL THE ACTUAL AND FALSIFIED REVENUES AND EXPENDITURES – IN DETAIL!
HE'S EITHER A TOTAL MORON... OR COVERING HIS OWN ASS... NOT TO DESTROY THIS EVIDENCE.
IF WE FOLLOW THE TRAIL OF THE OFF-THE-BOOKS FUNDS, IT MIGHT LINK UP TO THE SENATOR'S MURDER.
PRECISELY.
GOOD LUCK, "DAD."
...
COOLE
I GOT SOMETHING FOR YOU TOO – IBĒ-SAN.

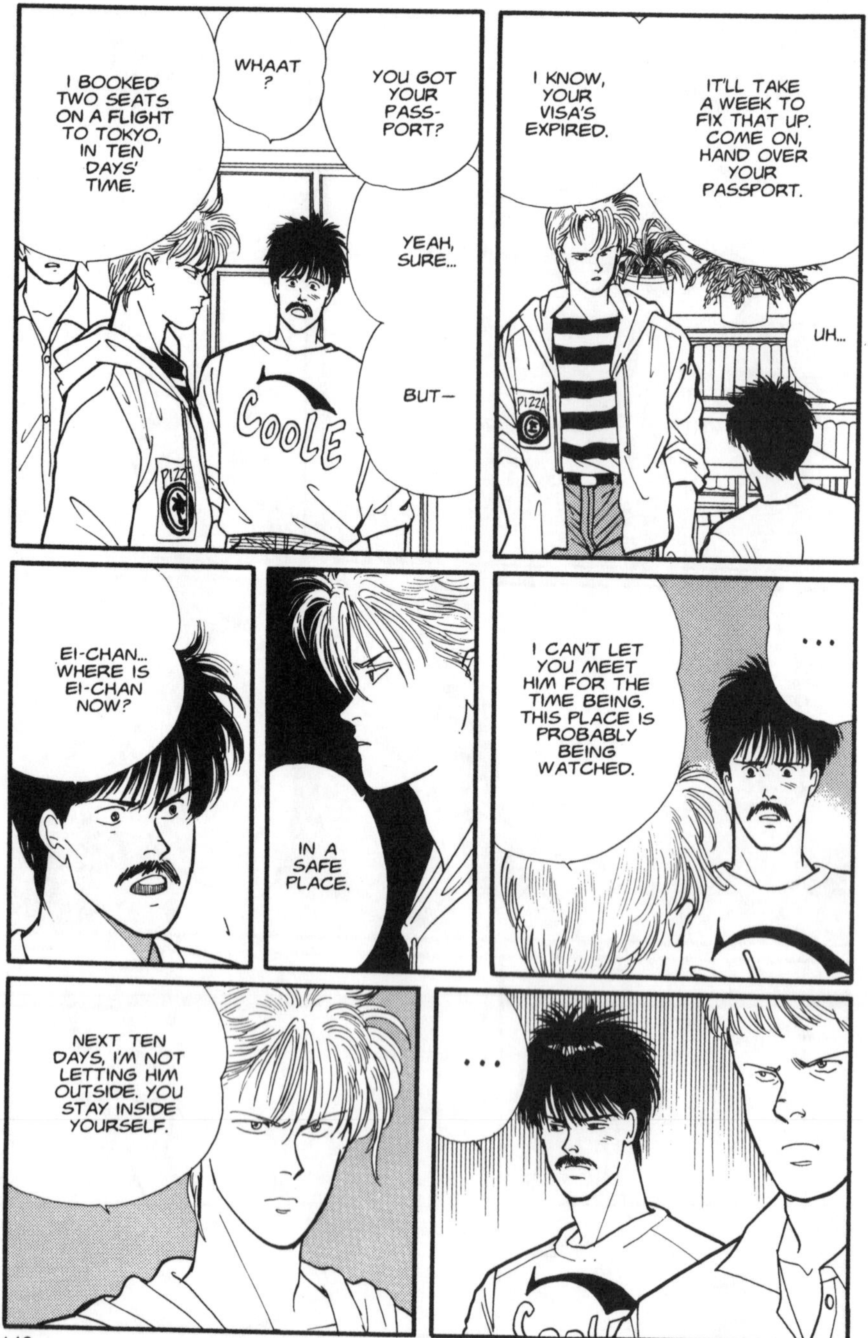

I BOOKED TWO SEATS ON A FLIGHT TO TOKYO, IN TEN DAYS' TIME.
WHAAT ?
YOU GOT YOUR PASS-PORT?
YEAH, SURE...
BUT—
I KNOW, YOUR VISA'S EXPIRED.
IT'LL TAKE A WEEK TO FIX THAT UP. COME ON, HAND OVER YOUR PASSPORT.
UH...
EI-CHAN... WHERE IS EI-CHAN NOW?
IN A SAFE PLACE.
I CAN'T LET YOU MEET HIM FOR THE TIME BEING. THIS PLACE IS PROBABLY BEING WATCHED.
...
NEXT TEN DAYS, I'M NOT LETTING HIM OUTSIDE. YOU STAY INSIDE YOURSELF.
...

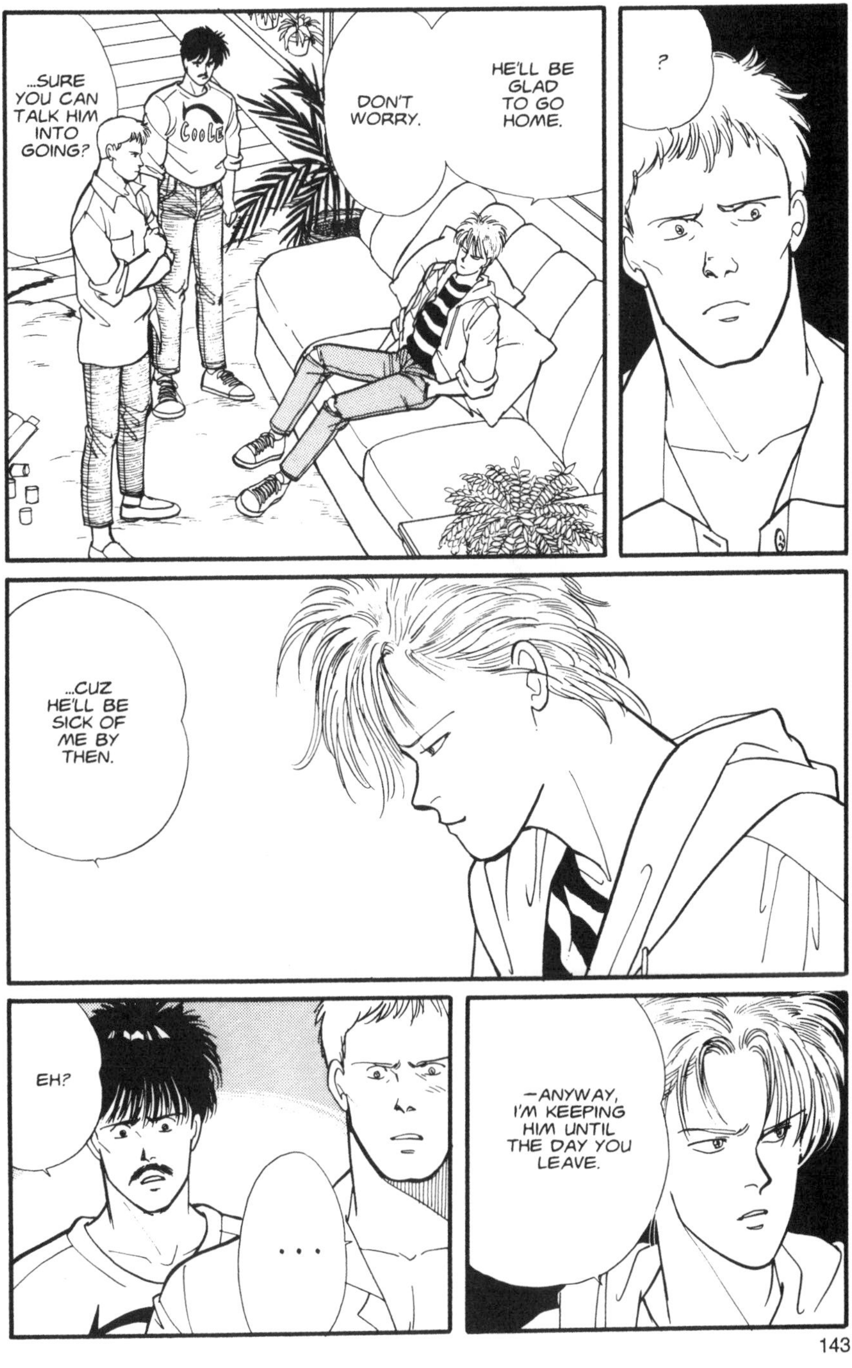
...SURE YOU CAN TALK HIM INTO GOING?
DON'T WORRY.
HE'LL BE GLAD TO GO HOME.
?
...CUZ HE'LL BE SICK OF ME BY THEN.
EH?
. . .
—ANYWAY, I'M KEEPING HIM UNTIL THE DAY YOU LEAVE.

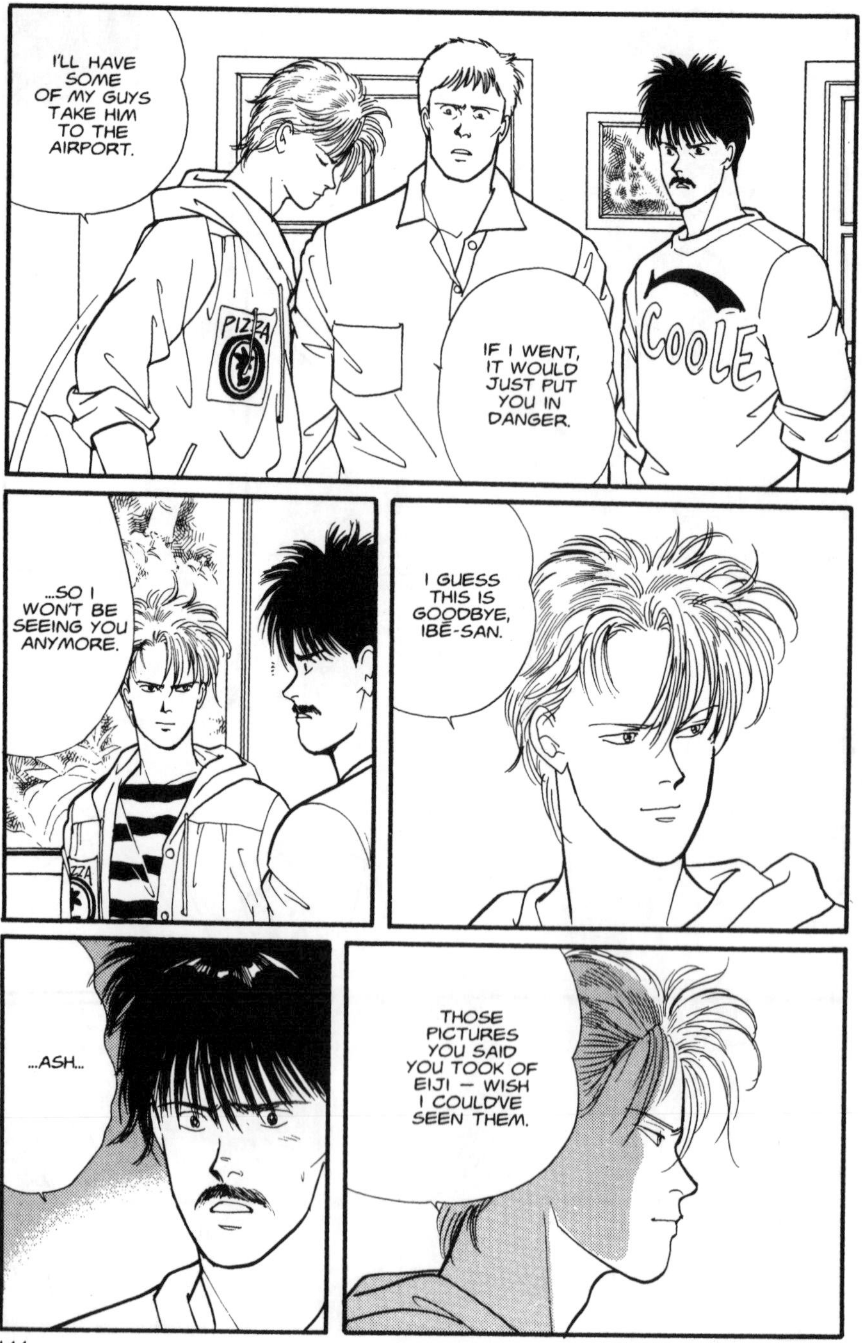
I'LL HAVE SOME OF MY GUYS TAKE HIM TO THE AIRPORT.
PIZZA
COOLE
IF I WENT, IT WOULD JUST PUT YOU IN DANGER.
...SO I WON'T BE SEEING YOU ANYMORE.
I GUESS THIS IS GOODBYE, IBE-SAN.
...ASH...
THOSE PICTURES YOU SAID YOU TOOK OF EIJI — WISH I COULD'VE SEEN THEM.

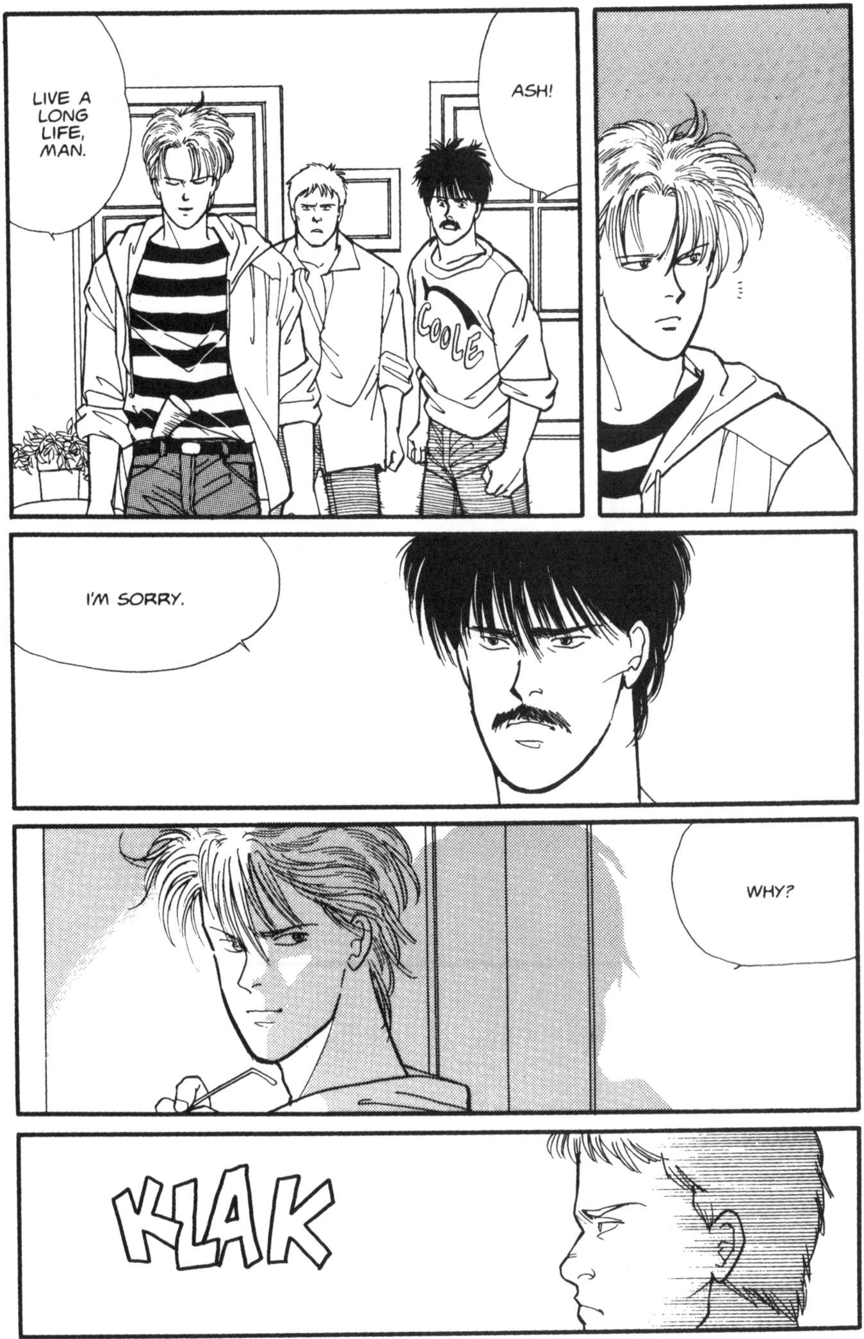
LIVE A LONG LIFE, MAN.
ASH!
I'M SORRY.
WHY?
KLAK

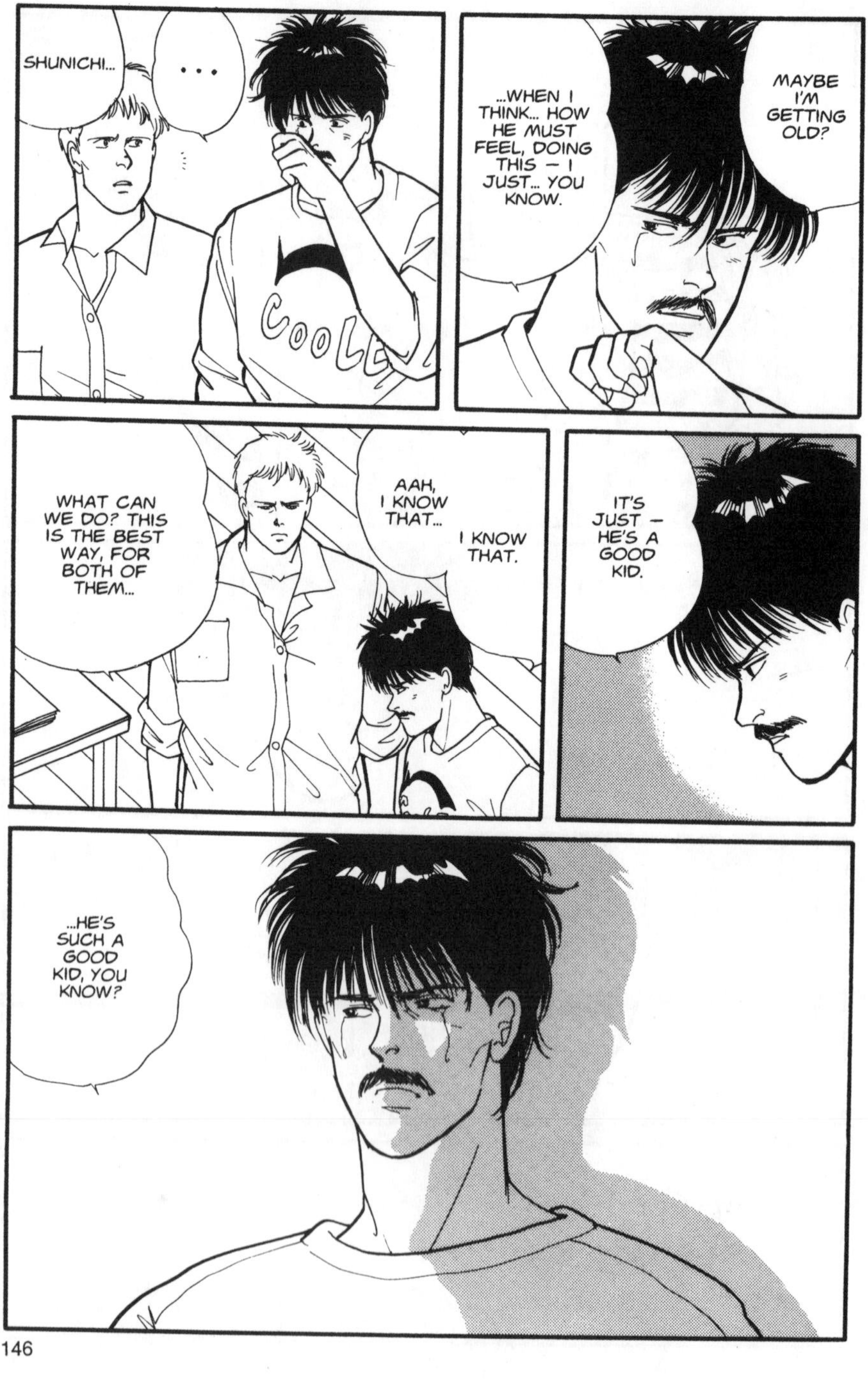
SHUNICHI...
. . .
...WHEN I THINK... HOW HE MUST FEEL, DOING THIS — I JUST... YOU KNOW.
MAYBE I'M GETTING OLD?
WHAT CAN WE DO? THIS IS THE BEST WAY, FOR BOTH OF THEM...
AAH, I KNOW THAT...
I KNOW THAT.
IT'S JUST — HE'S A GOOD KID.
...HE'S SUCH A GOOD KID, YOU KNOW?

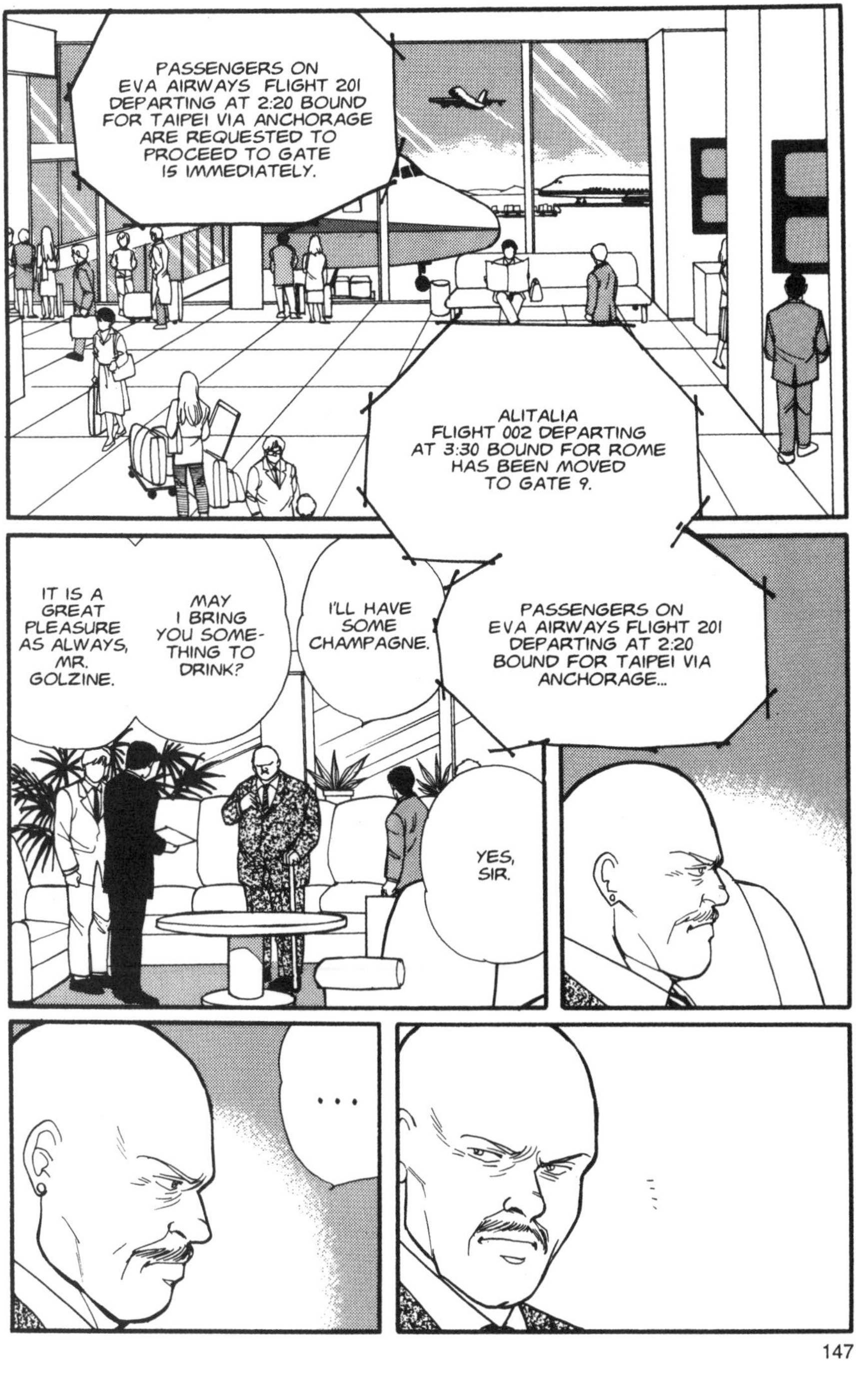
PASSENGERS ON EVA AIRWAYS FLIGHT 201 DEPARTING AT 2:20 BOUND FOR TAIPEI VIA ANCHORAGE ARE REQUESTED TO PROCEED TO GATE 15 IMMEDIATELY.
ALITALIA FLIGHT 002 DEPARTING AT 3:30 BOUND FOR ROME HAS BEEN MOVED TO GATE 9.
IT IS A GREAT PLEASURE AS ALWAYS, MR. GOLZINE.
MAY I BRING YOU SOME-THING TO DRINK?
I'LL HAVE SOME CHAMPAGNE.
PASSENGERS ON EVA AIRWAYS FLIGHT 201 DEPARTING AT 2:20 BOUND FOR TAIPEI VIA ANCHORAGE...
YES, SIR.
...

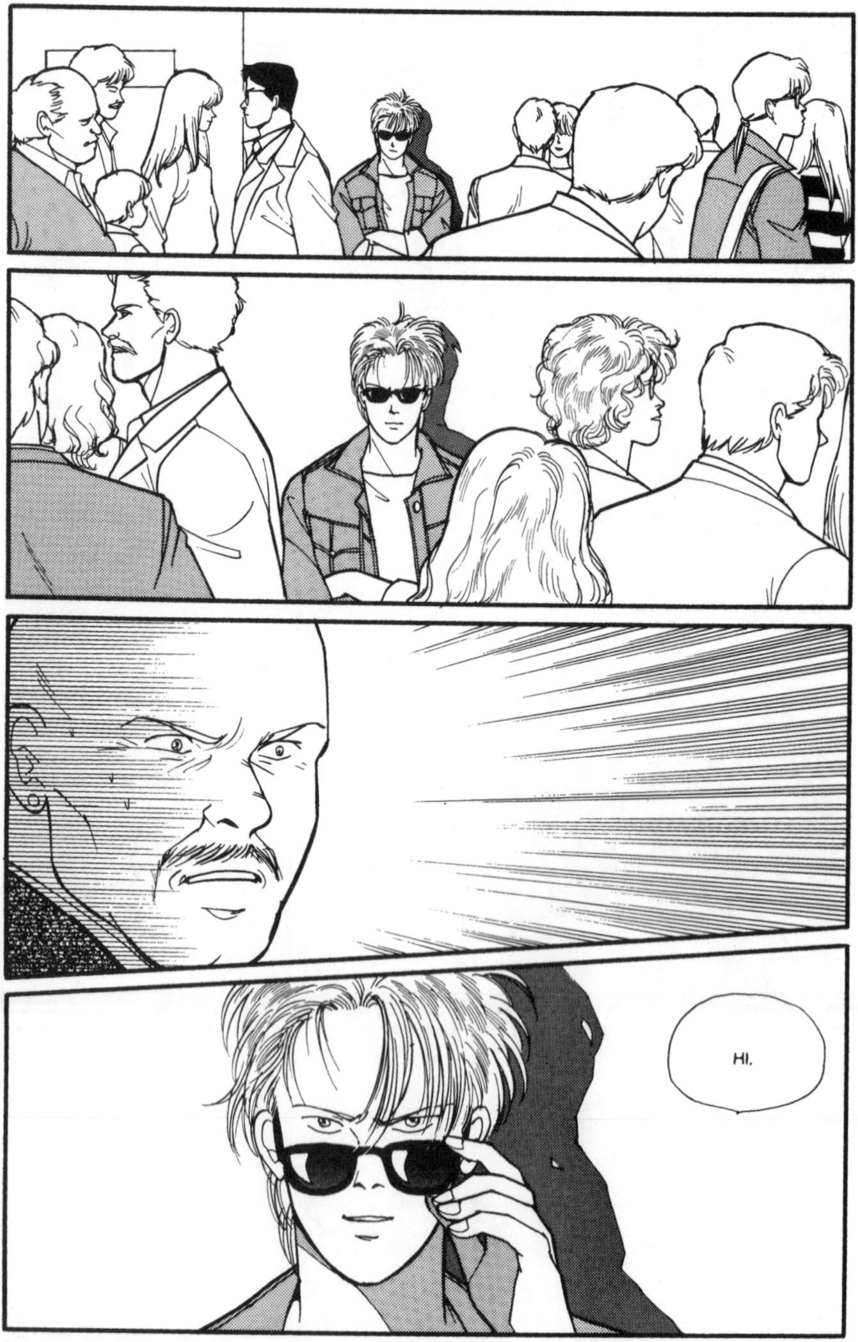
HI.

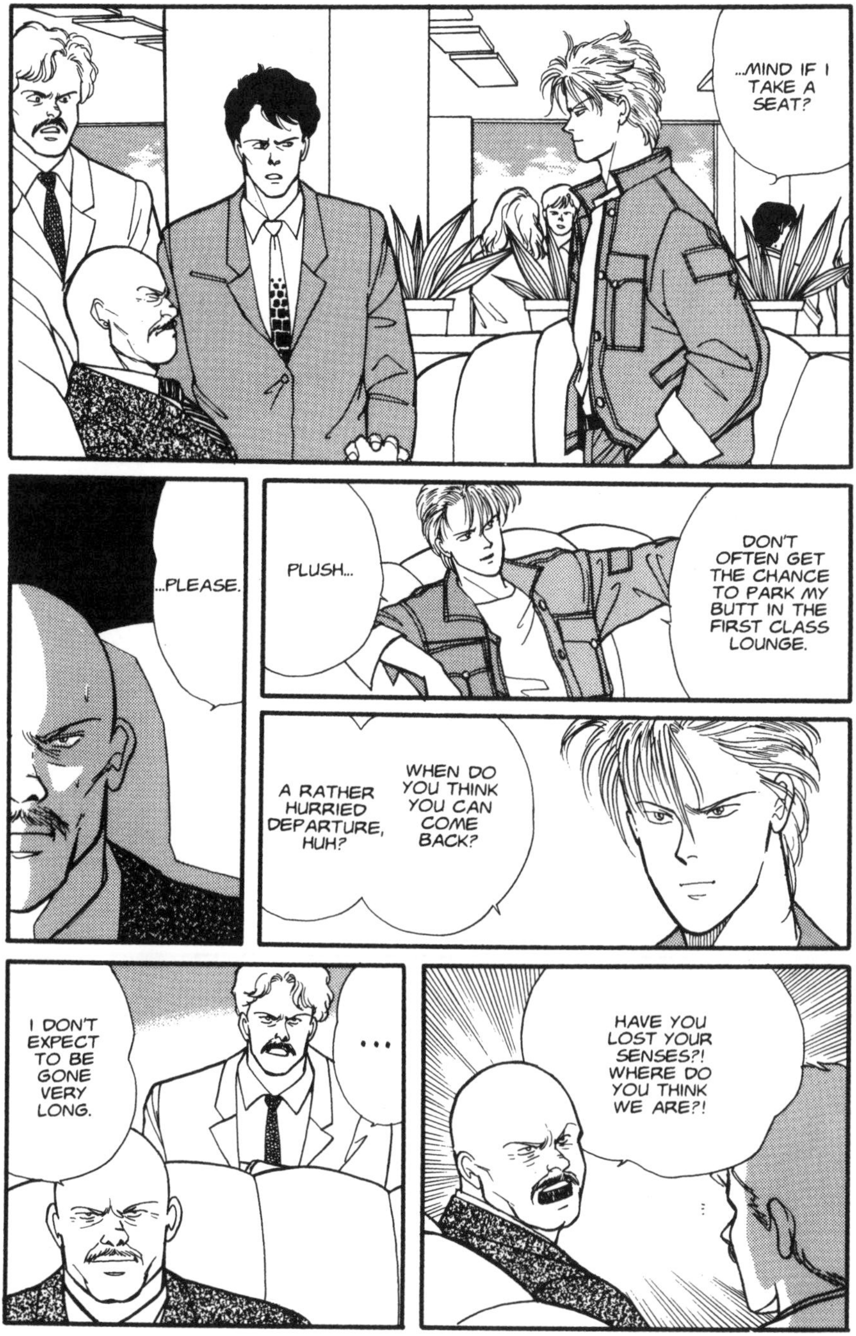
...MIND IF I TAKE A SEAT?
...PLEASE.
PLUSH...
DON'T OFTEN GET THE CHANCE TO PARK MY BUTT IN THE FIRST CLASS LOUNGE.
A RATHER HURRIED DEPARTURE, HUH?
WHEN DO YOU THINK YOU CAN COME BACK?
I DON'T EXPECT TO BE GONE VERY LONG.
...
HAVE YOU LOST YOUR SENSES?! WHERE DO YOU THINK WE ARE?!

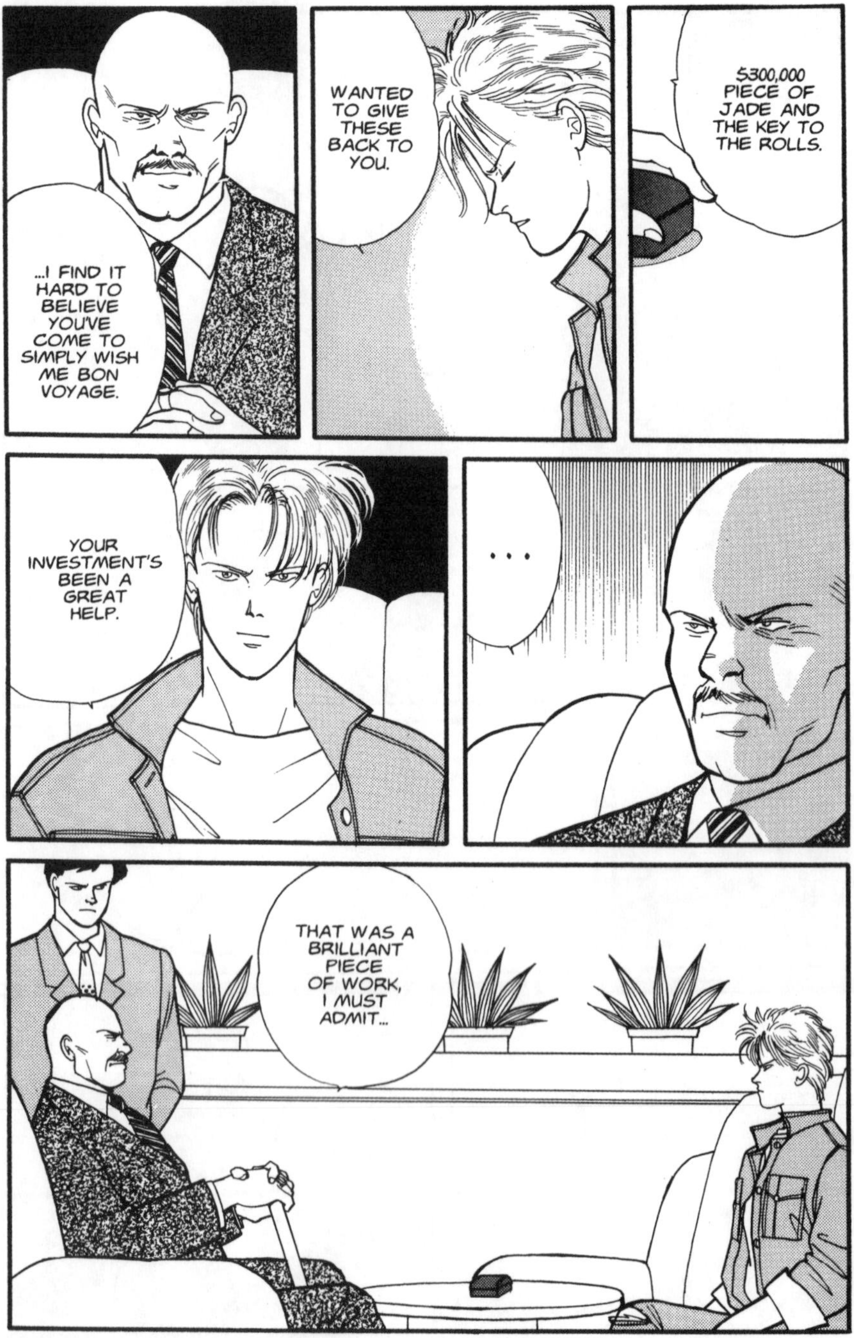
...I FIND IT HARD TO BELIEVE YOU'VE COME TO SIMPLY WISH ME BON VOYAGE.
WANTED TO GIVE THESE BACK TO YOU.
$300,000 PIECE OF JADE AND THE KEY TO THE ROLLS.
YOUR INVESTMENT'S BEEN A GREAT HELP.
. . .
THAT WAS A BRILLIANT PIECE OF WORK, I MUST ADMIT...

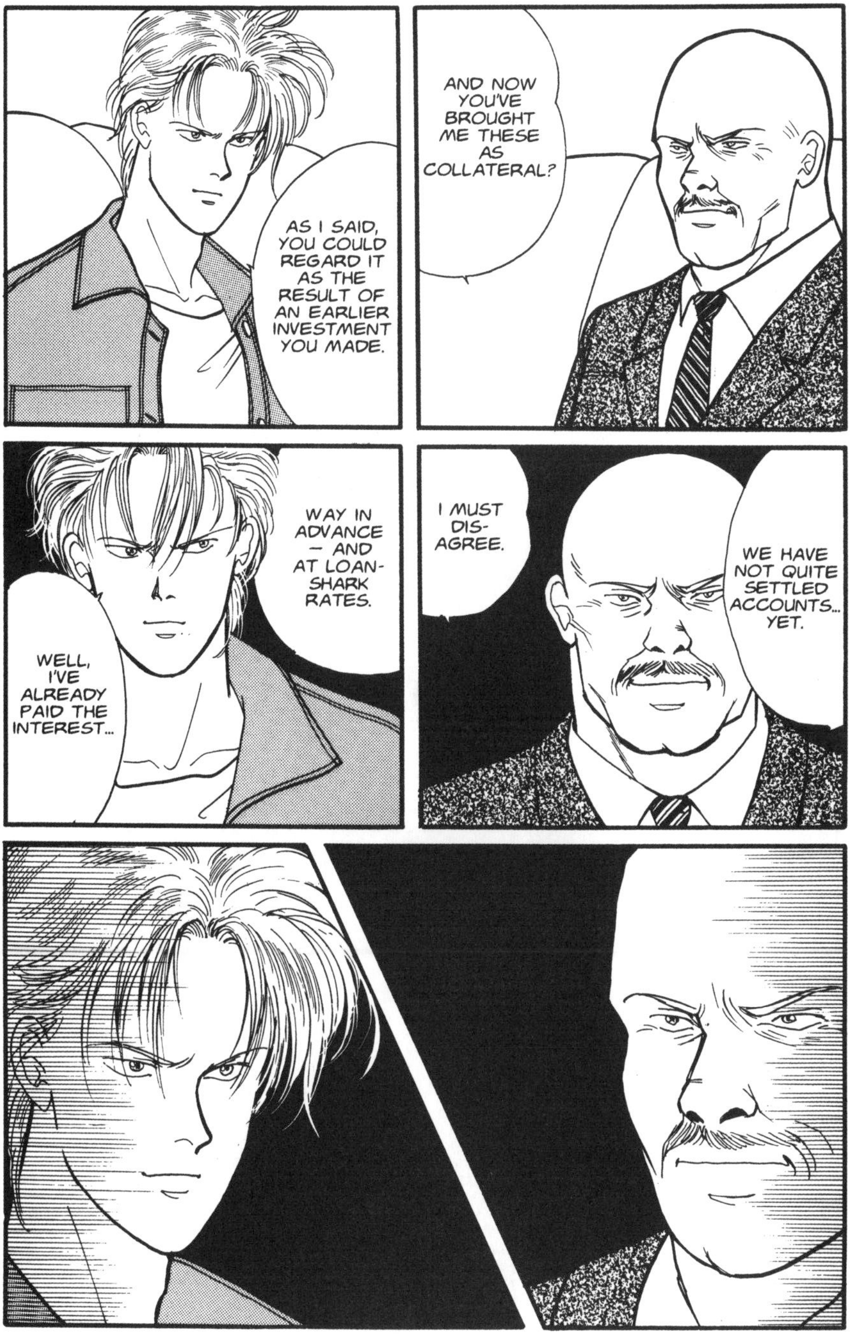
AS I SAID, YOU COULD REGARD IT AS THE RESULT OF AN EARLIER INVESTMENT YOU MADE.
AND NOW YOU'VE BROUGHT ME THESE AS COLLATERAL?
WELL, I'VE ALREADY PAID THE INTEREST...
WAY IN ADVANCE — AND AT LOAN-SHARK RATES.
I MUST DIS-AGREE.
WE HAVE NOT QUITE SETTLED ACCOUNTS... YET.

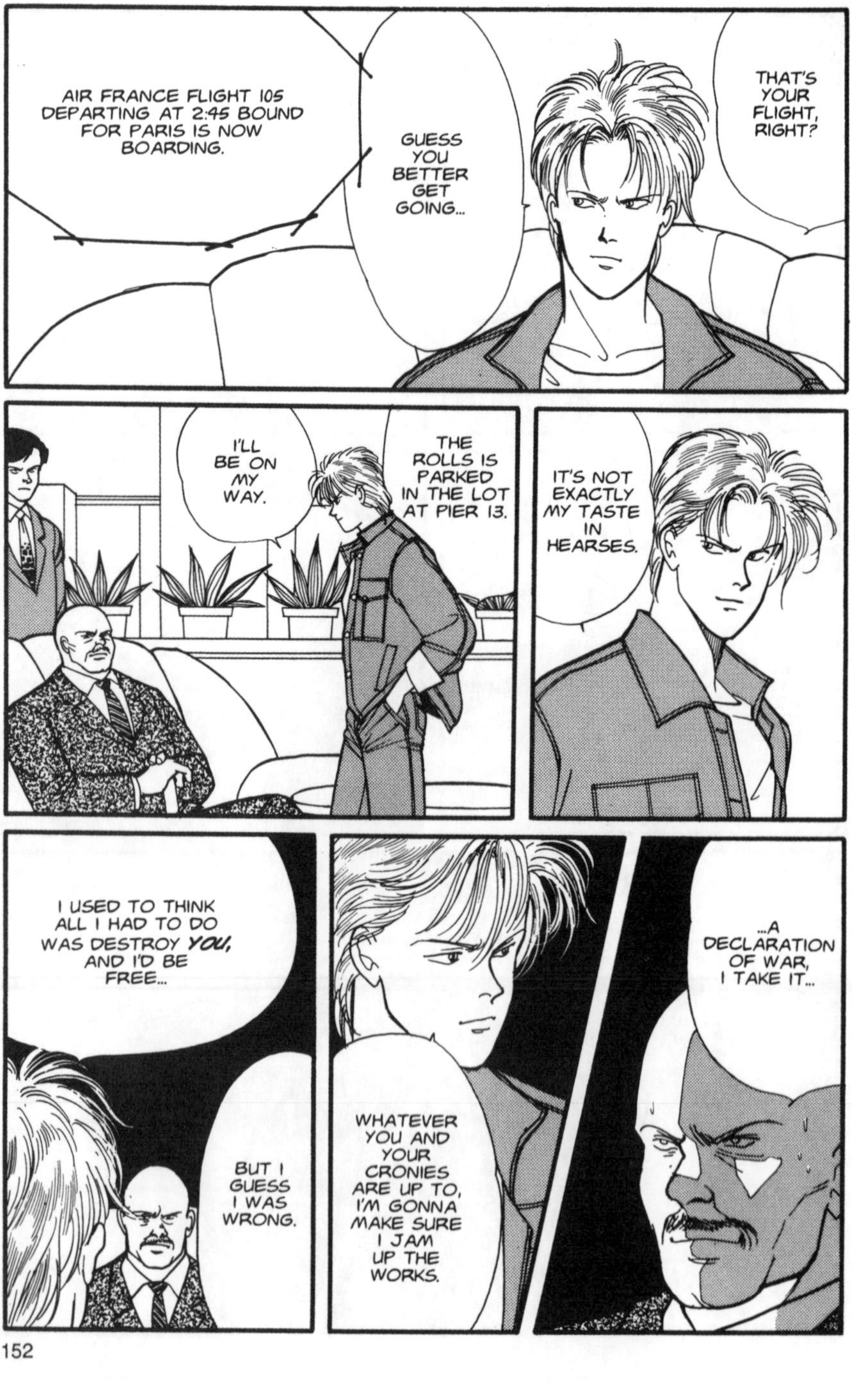
AIR FRANCE FLIGHT 105 DEPARTING AT 2:45 BOUND FOR PARIS IS NOW BOARDING.
GUESS YOU BETTER GET GOING...
THAT'S YOUR FLIGHT, RIGHT?
I'LL BE ON MY WAY.
THE ROLLS IS PARKED IN THE LOT AT PIER 13.
IT'S NOT EXACTLY MY TASTE IN HEARSES.
I USED TO THINK ALL I HAD TO DO WAS DESTROY *YOU,* AND I'D BE FREE...
BUT I GUESS I WAS WRONG.
WHATEVER YOU AND YOUR CRONIES ARE UP TO, I'M GONNA MAKE SURE I JAM UP THE WORKS.
...A DECLARATION OF WAR, I TAKE IT...

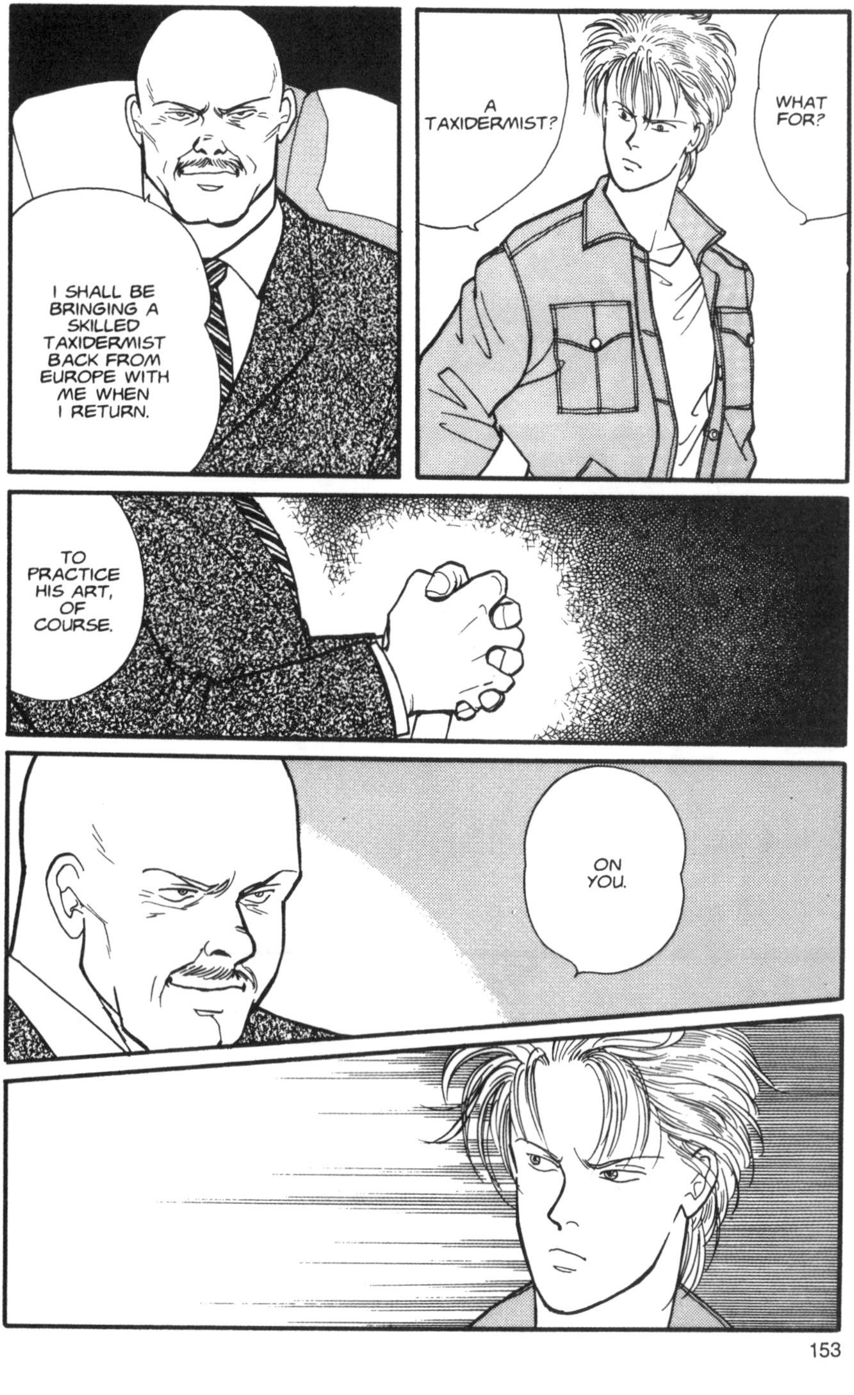
I SHALL BE BRINGING A SKILLED TAXIDERMIST BACK FROM EUROPE WITH ME WHEN I RETURN.
A TAXIDERMIST?
WHAT FOR?
TO PRACTICE HIS ART, OF COURSE.
ON YOU.

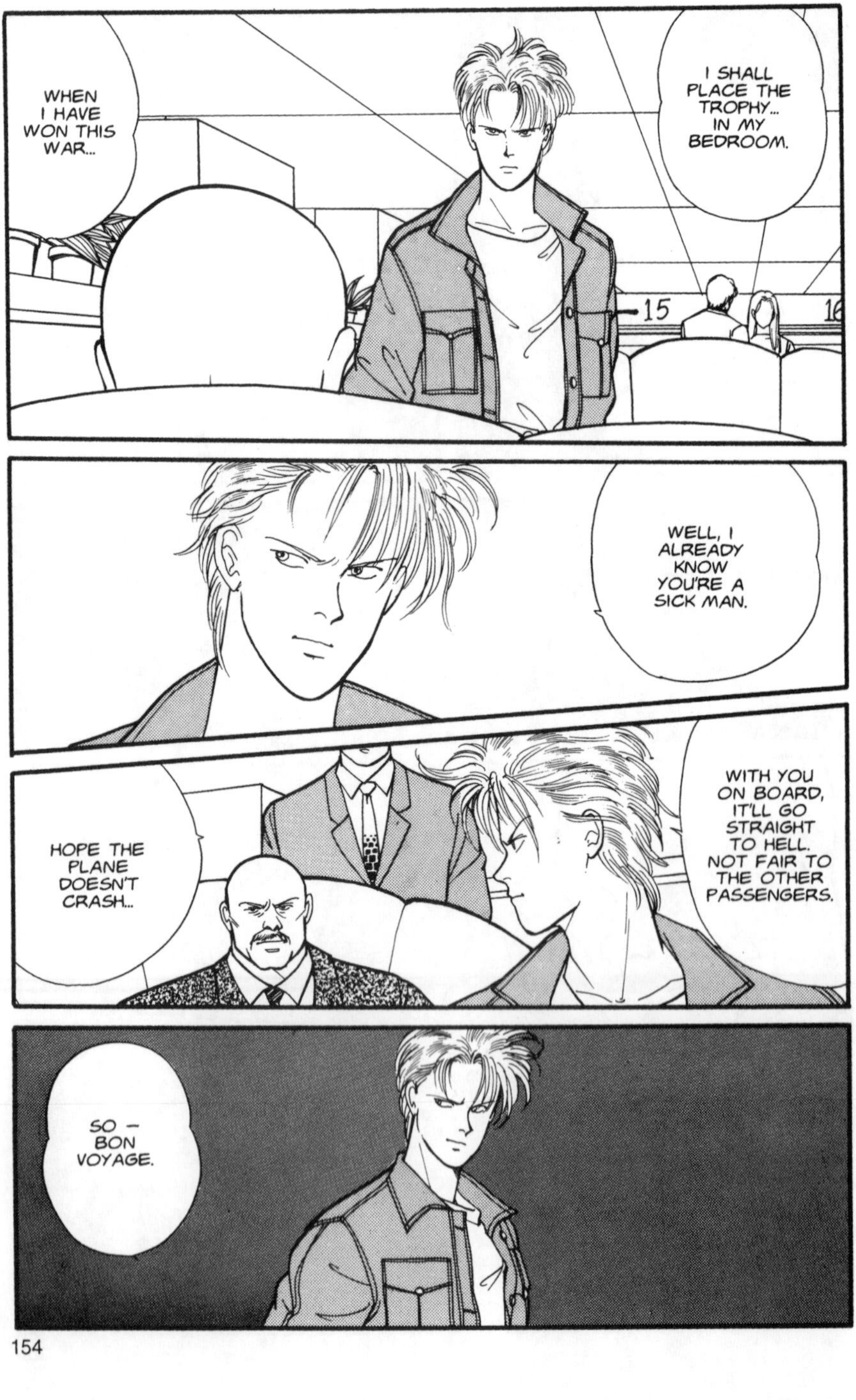

WHEN I HAVE WON THIS WAR...
I SHALL PLACE THE TROPHY... IN MY BEDROOM.
15
16
WELL, I ALREADY KNOW YOU'RE A SICK MAN.
HOPE THE PLANE DOESN'T CRASH...
WITH YOU ON BOARD, IT'LL GO STRAIGHT TO HELL. NOT FAIR TO THE OTHER PASSENGERS.
SO — BON VOYAGE.

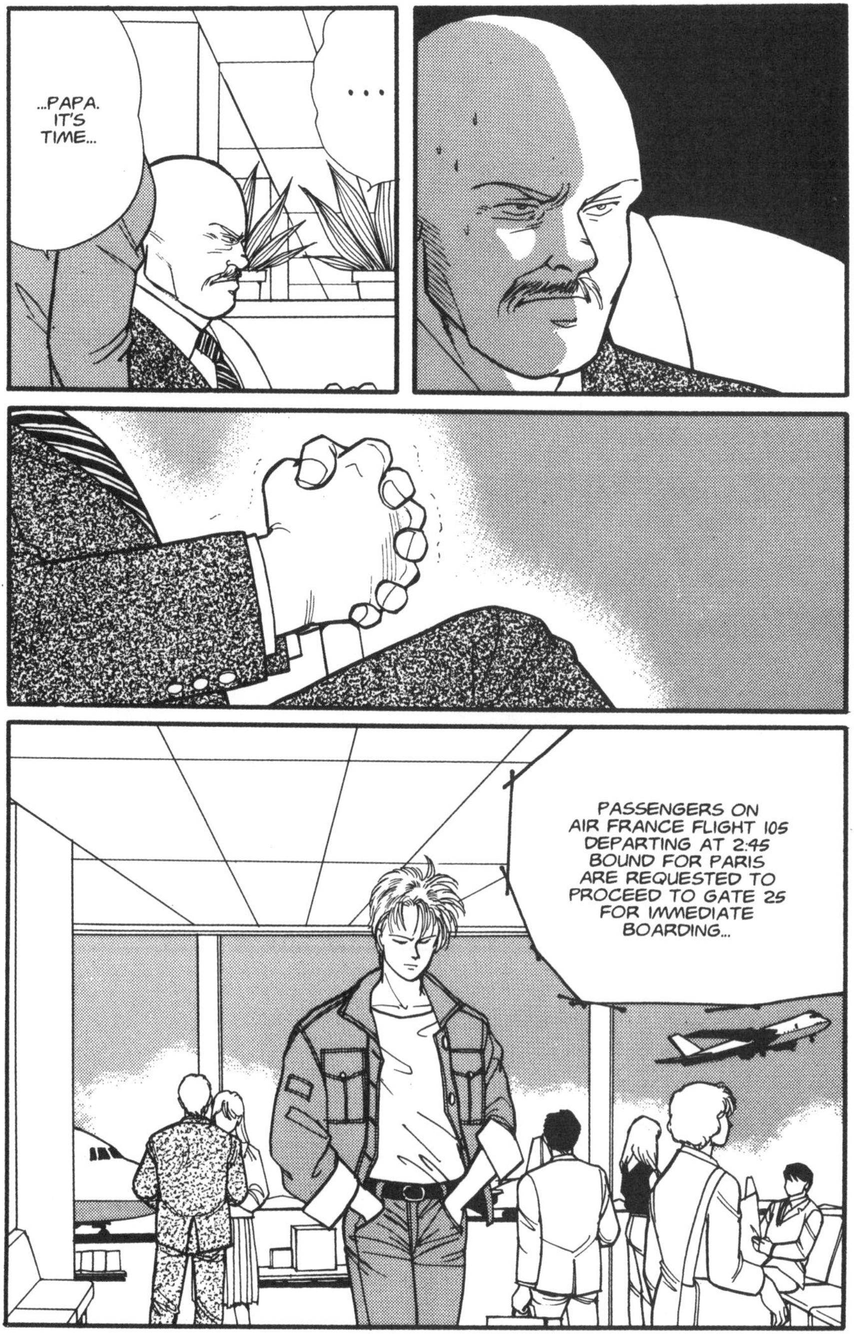
...PAPA. IT'S TIME...
...
PASSENGERS ON AIR FRANCE FLIGHT 105 DEPARTING AT 2:45 BOUND FOR PARIS ARE REQUESTED TO PROCEED TO GATE 25 FOR IMMEDIATE BOARDING...

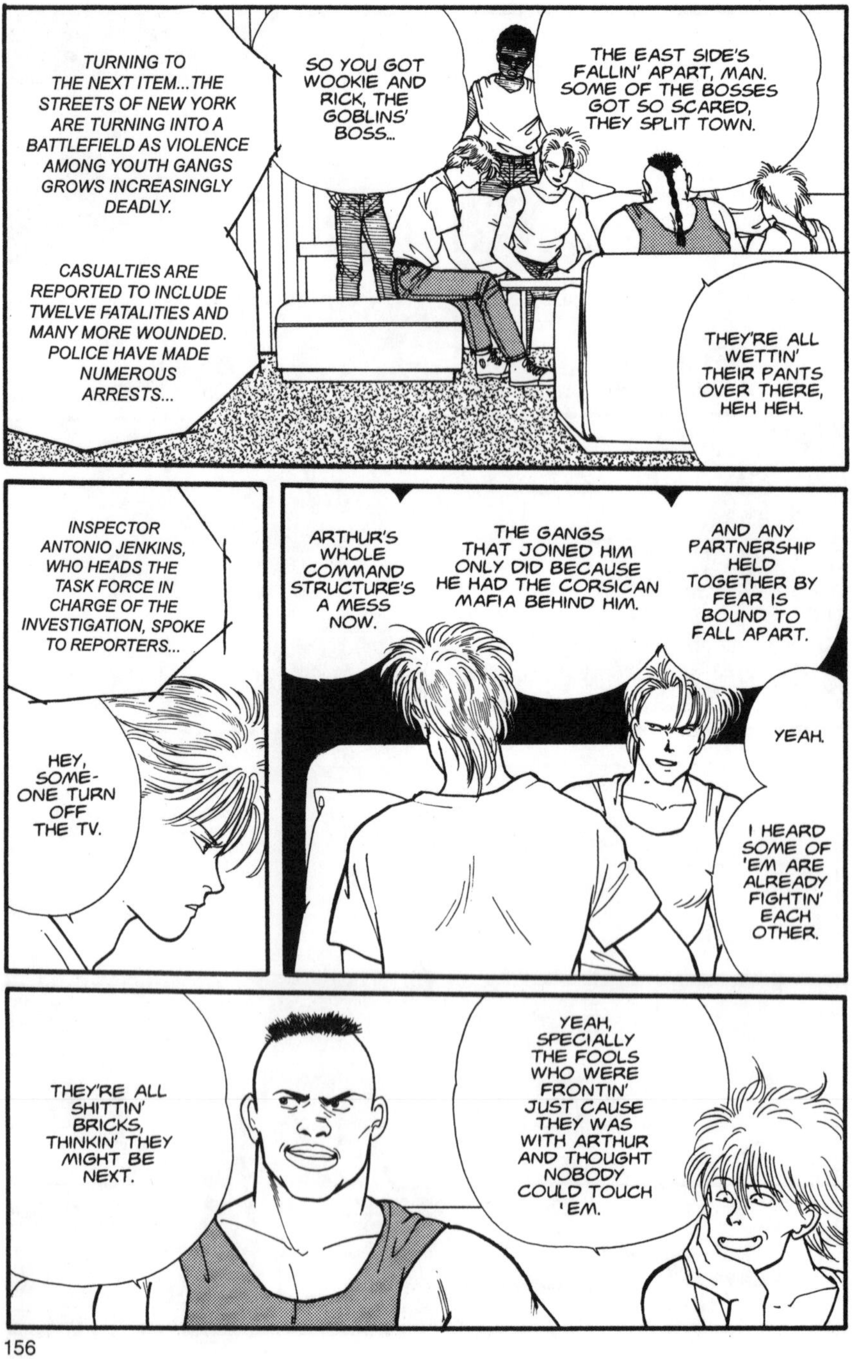
TURNING TO THE NEXT ITEM...THE STREETS OF NEW YORK ARE TURNING INTO A BATTLEFIELD AS VIOLENCE AMONG YOUTH GANGS GROWS INCREASINGLY DEADLY.
CASUALTIES ARE REPORTED TO INCLUDE TWELVE FATALITIES AND MANY MORE WOUNDED. POLICE HAVE MADE NUMEROUS ARRESTS...
SO YOU GOT WOOKIE AND RICK, THE GOBLINS' BOSS...
THE EAST SIDE'S FALLIN' APART, MAN. SOME OF THE BOSSES GOT SO SCARED, THEY SPLIT TOWN.
THEY'RE ALL WETTIN' THEIR PANTS OVER THERE, HEH HEH.
INSPECTOR ANTONIO JENKINS, WHO HEADS THE TASK FORCE IN CHARGE OF THE INVESTIGATION, SPOKE TO REPORTERS...
HEY, SOME-ONE TURN OFF THE TV.
ARTHUR'S WHOLE COMMAND STRUCTURE'S A MESS NOW.
THE GANGS THAT JOINED HIM ONLY DID BECAUSE HE HAD THE CORSICAN MAFIA BEHIND HIM.
AND ANY PARTNERSHIP HELD TOGETHER BY FEAR IS BOUND TO FALL APART.
YEAH.
I HEARD SOME OF 'EM ARE ALREADY FIGHTIN' EACH OTHER.
THEY'RE ALL SHITTIN' BRICKS, THINKIN' THEY MIGHT BE NEXT.
YEAH, SPECIALLY THE FOOLS WHO WERE FRONTIN' JUST CAUSE THEY WAS WITH ARTHUR AND THOUGHT NOBODY COULD TOUCH 'EM.

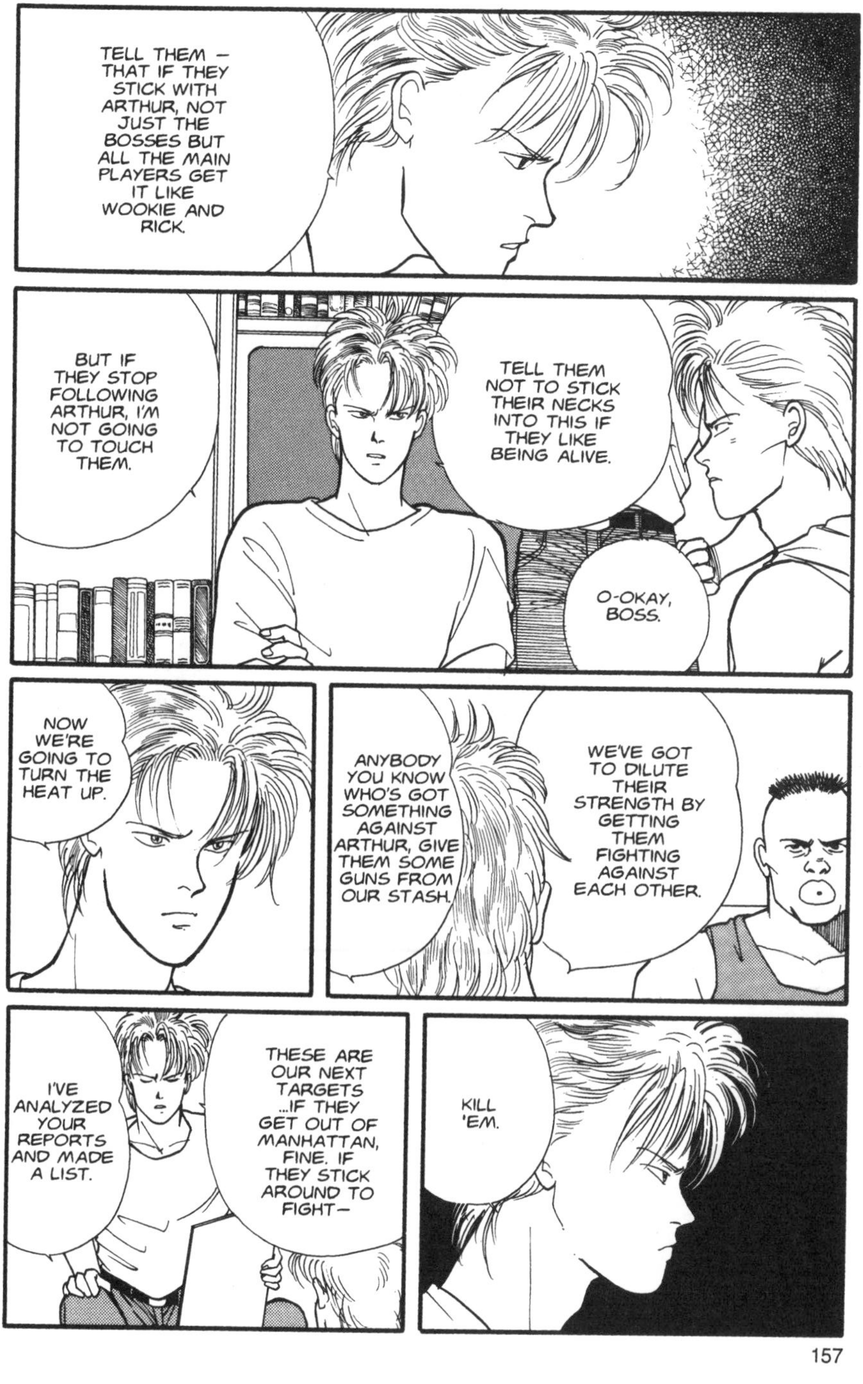
TELL THEM — THAT IF THEY STICK WITH ARTHUR, NOT JUST THE BOSSES BUT ALL THE MAIN PLAYERS GET IT LIKE WOOKIE AND RICK.
BUT IF THEY STOP FOLLOWING ARTHUR, I'M NOT GOING TO TOUCH THEM.
TELL THEM NOT TO STICK THEIR NECKS INTO THIS IF THEY LIKE BEING ALIVE.
O-OKAY, BOSS.
NOW WE'RE GOING TO TURN THE HEAT UP.
ANYBODY YOU KNOW WHO'S GOT SOMETHING AGAINST ARTHUR, GIVE THEM SOME GUNS FROM OUR STASH.
WE'VE GOT TO DILUTE THEIR STRENGTH BY GETTING THEM FIGHTING AGAINST EACH OTHER.
I'VE ANALYZED YOUR REPORTS AND MADE A LIST.
THESE ARE OUR NEXT TARGETS ...IF THEY GET OUT OF MANHATTAN, FINE. IF THEY STICK AROUND TO FIGHT—
KILL 'EM.

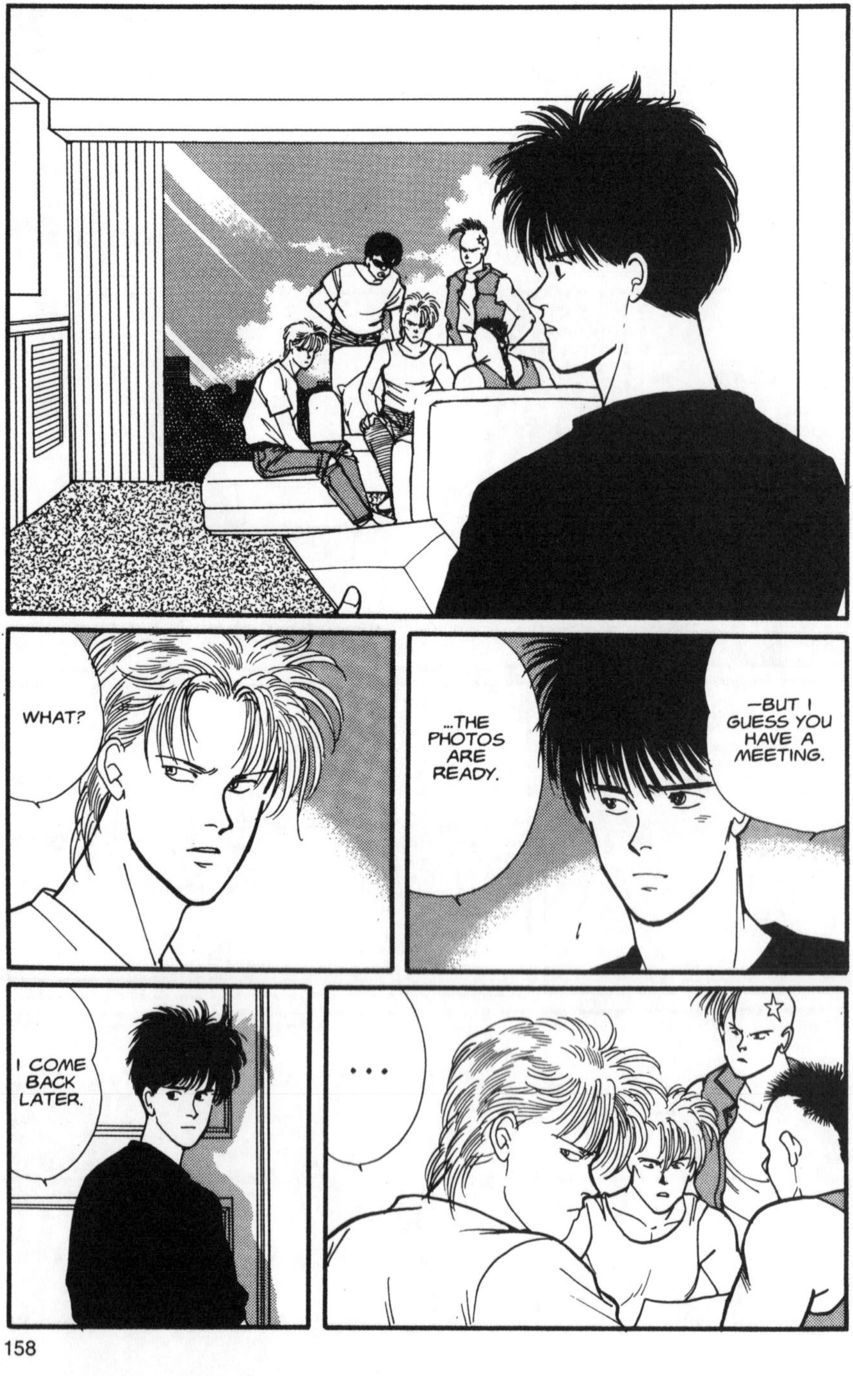
WHAT?
...THE PHOTOS ARE READY.
—BUT I GUESS YOU HAVE A MEETING.
I COME BACK LATER.
...

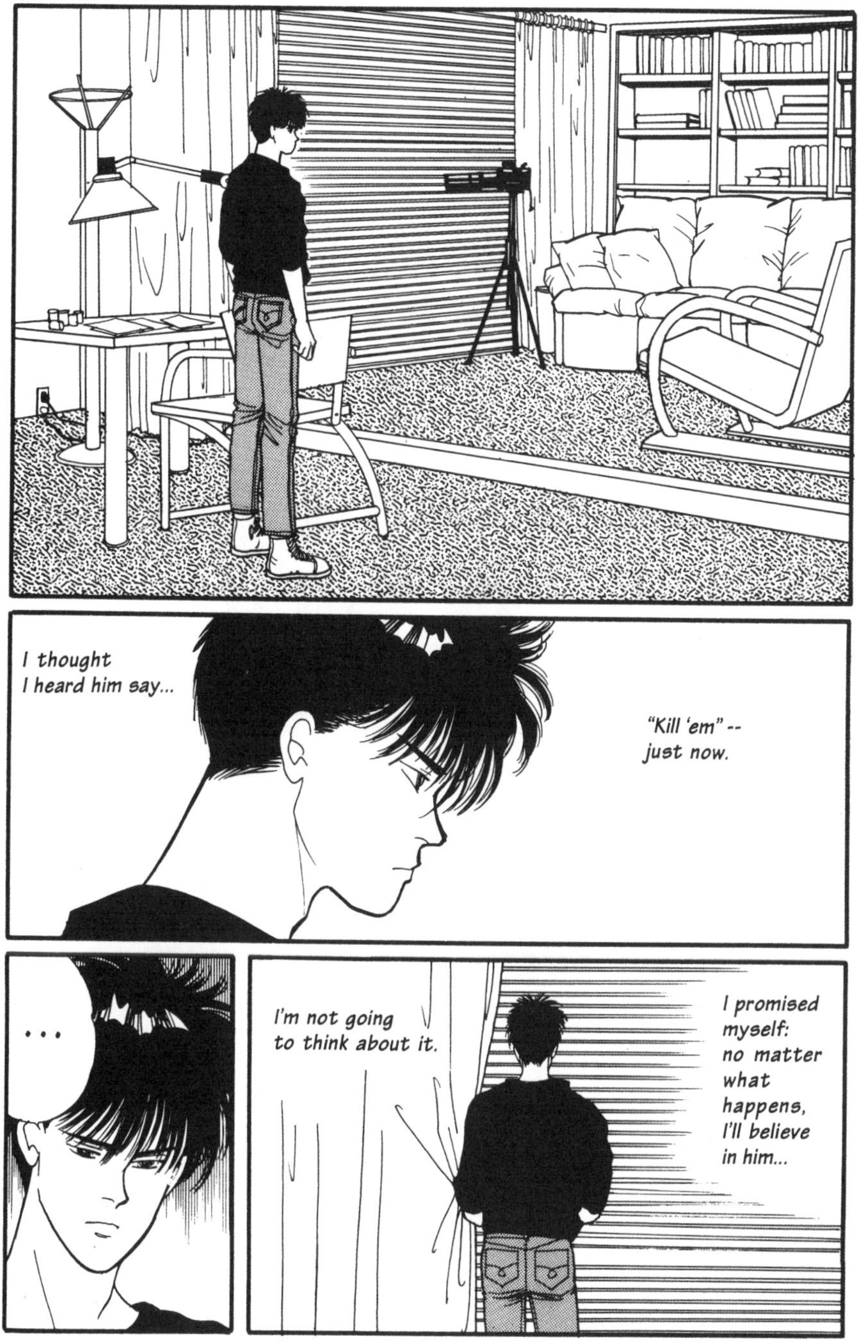
I thought I heard him say...
"Kill 'em" -- just now.
...
I'm not going to think about it.
I promised myself: no matter what happens, I'll believe in him...

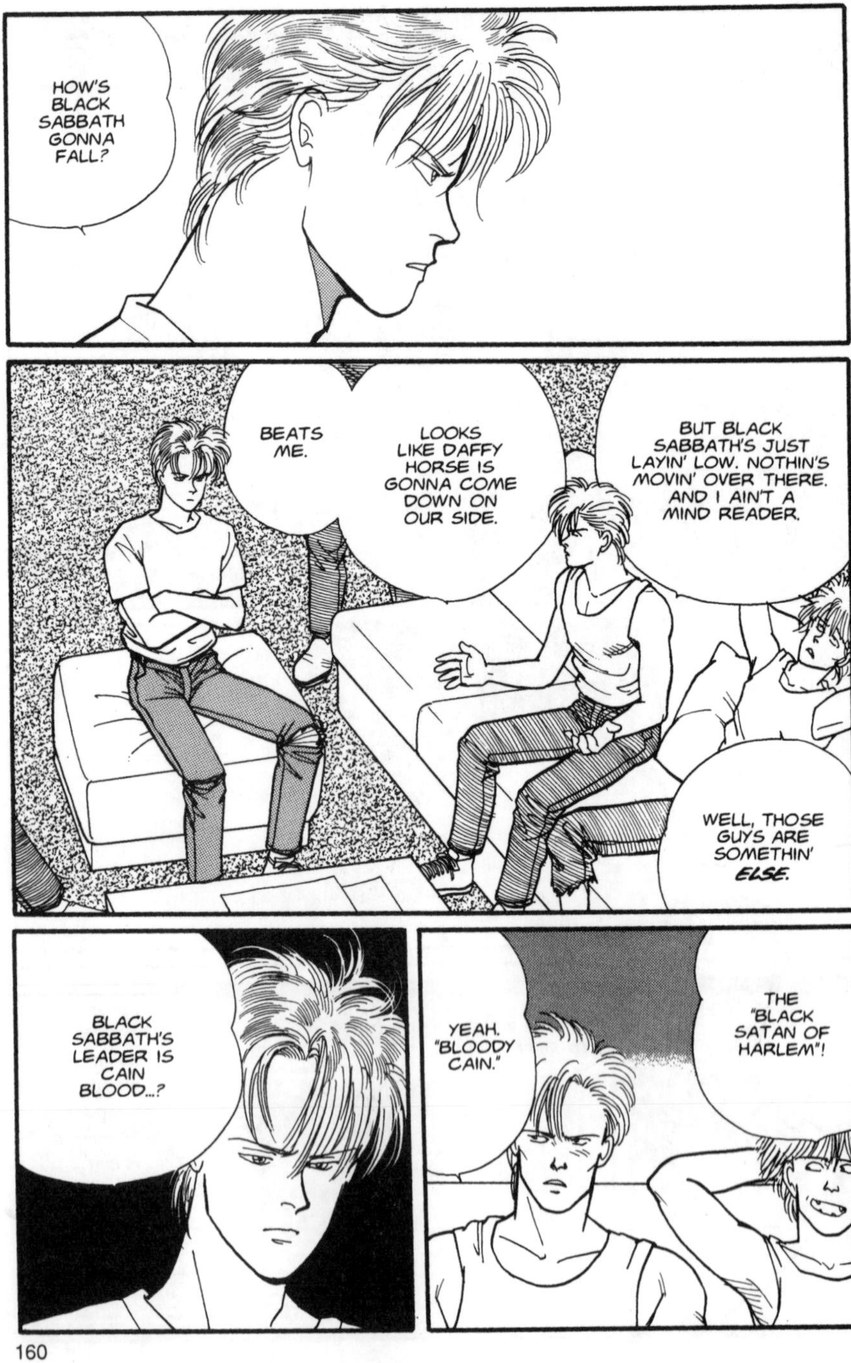
HOW'S BLACK SABBATH GONNA FALL?
BEATS ME.
LOOKS LIKE DAFFY HORSE IS GONNA COME DOWN ON OUR SIDE.
BUT BLACK SABBATH'S JUST LAYIN' LOW. NOTHIN'S MOVIN' OVER THERE. AND I AIN'T A MIND READER.
WELL, THOSE GUYS ARE SOMETHIN' *ELSE*.
BLACK SABBATH'S LEADER IS CAIN BLOOD...?
YEAH. "BLOODY CAIN."
THE "BLACK SATAN OF HARLEM"!

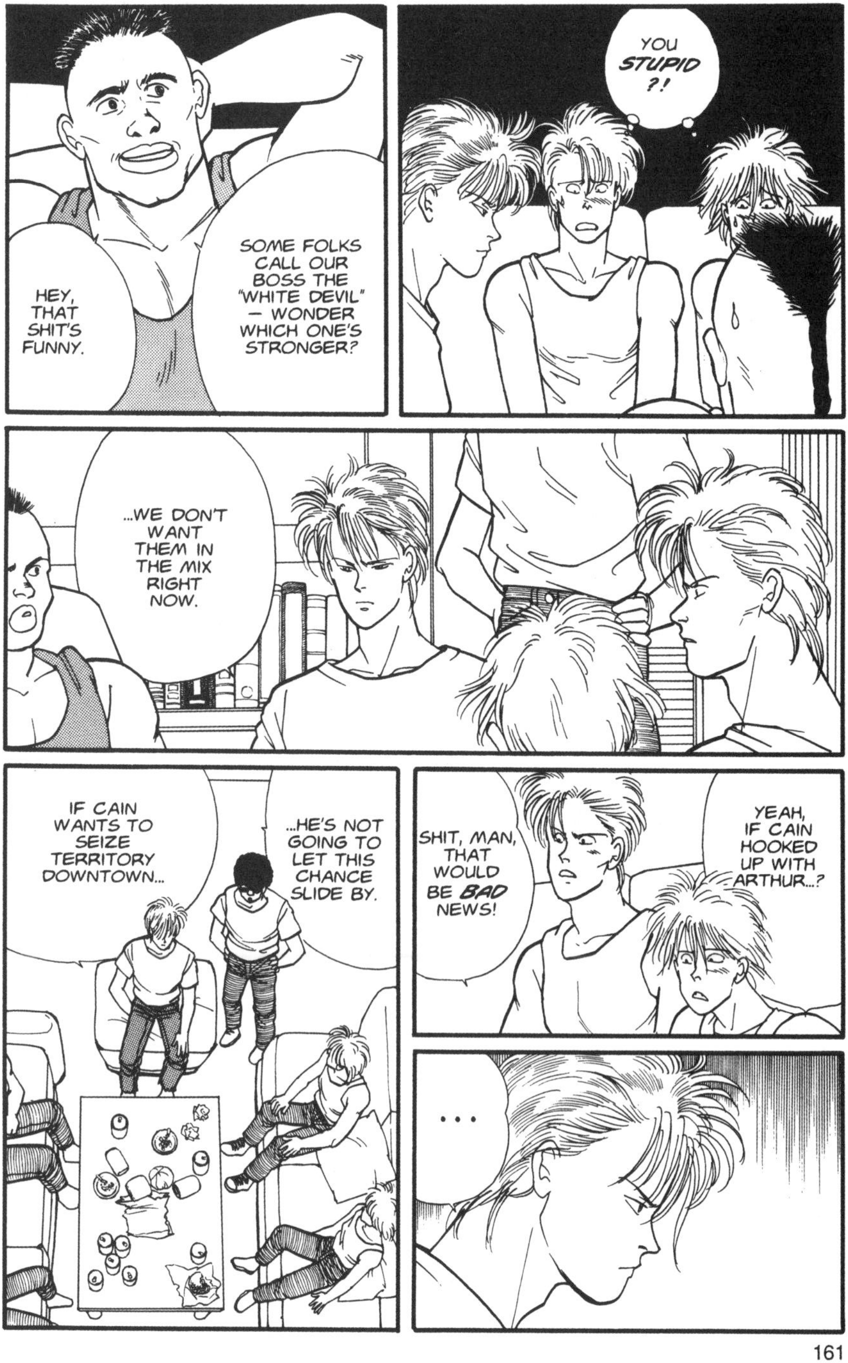
HEY, THAT SHIT'S FUNNY.
SOME FOLKS CALL OUR BOSS THE "WHITE DEVIL" — WONDER WHICH ONE'S STRONGER?
YOU STUPID ?!
...WE DON'T WANT THEM IN THE MIX RIGHT NOW.
IF CAIN WANTS TO SEIZE TERRITORY DOWNTOWN...
...HE'S NOT GOING TO LET THIS CHANCE SLIDE BY.
SHIT, MAN, THAT WOULD BE BAD NEWS!
YEAH, IF CAIN HOOKED UP WITH ARTHUR...?
...

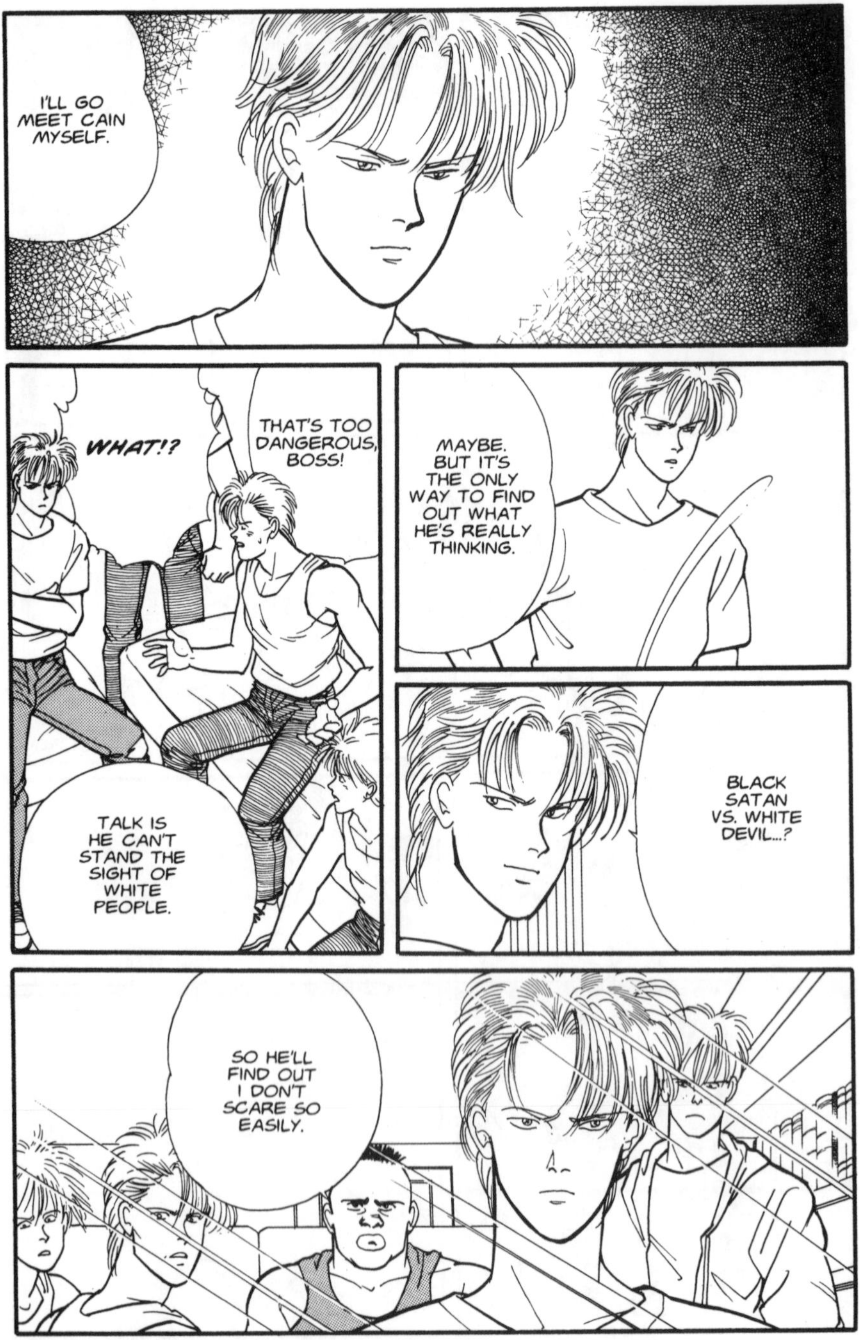
I'LL GO MEET CAIN MYSELF.
WHAT!?
THAT'S TOO DANGEROUS, BOSS!
TALK IS HE CAN'T STAND THE SIGHT OF WHITE PEOPLE.
MAYBE. BUT IT'S THE ONLY WAY TO FIND OUT WHAT HE'S REALLY THINKING.
BLACK SATAN VS. WHITE DEVIL...?
SO HE'LL FIND OUT I DON'T SCARE SO EASILY.

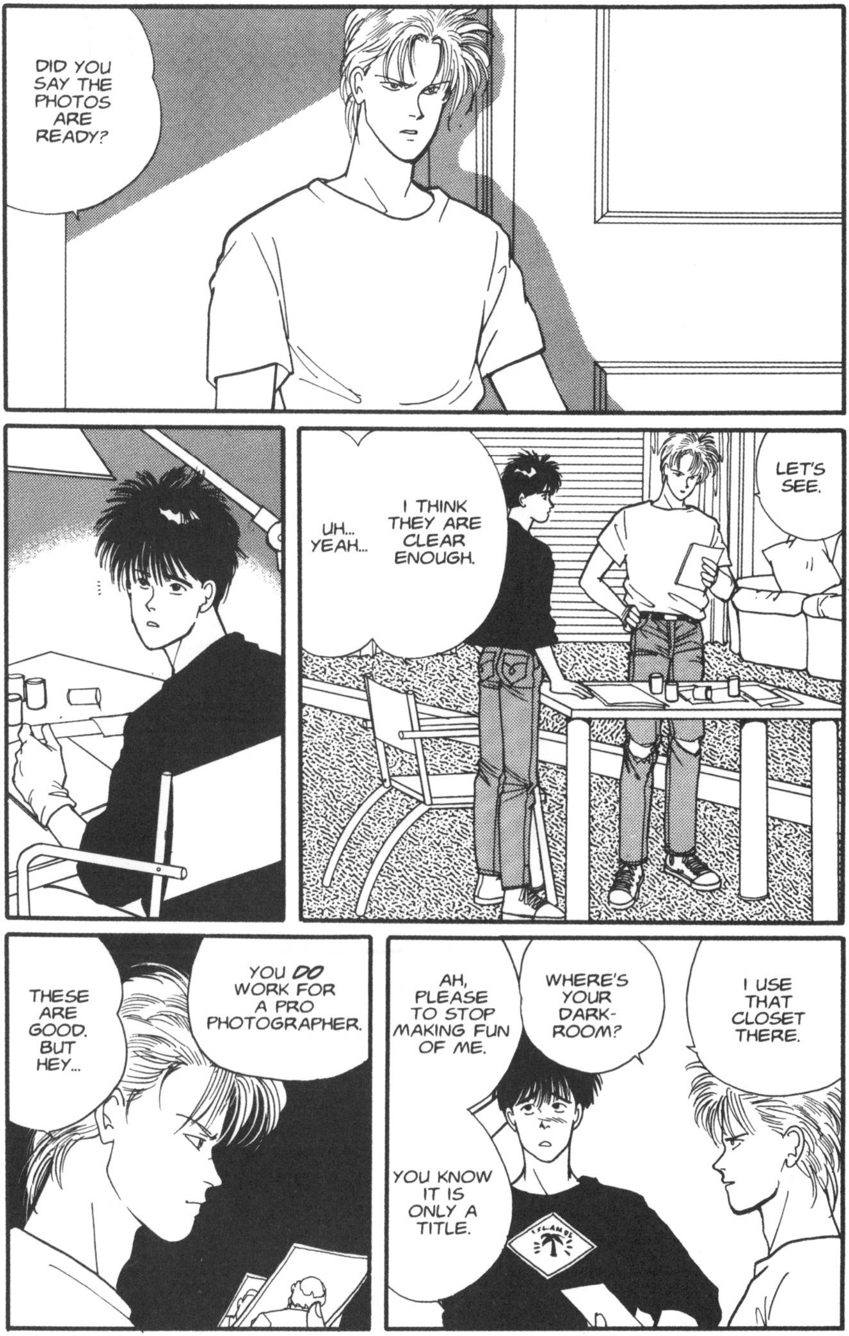
DID YOU SAY THE PHOTOS ARE READY?
UH... YEAH...
I THINK THEY ARE CLEAR ENOUGH.
LET'S SEE.
THESE ARE GOOD. BUT HEY...
YOU *DO* WORK FOR A PRO PHOTOGRAPHER.
AH, PLEASE TO STOP MAKING FUN OF ME.
YOU KNOW IT IS ONLY A TITLE.
WHERE'S YOUR DARK-ROOM?
I USE THAT CLOSET THERE.

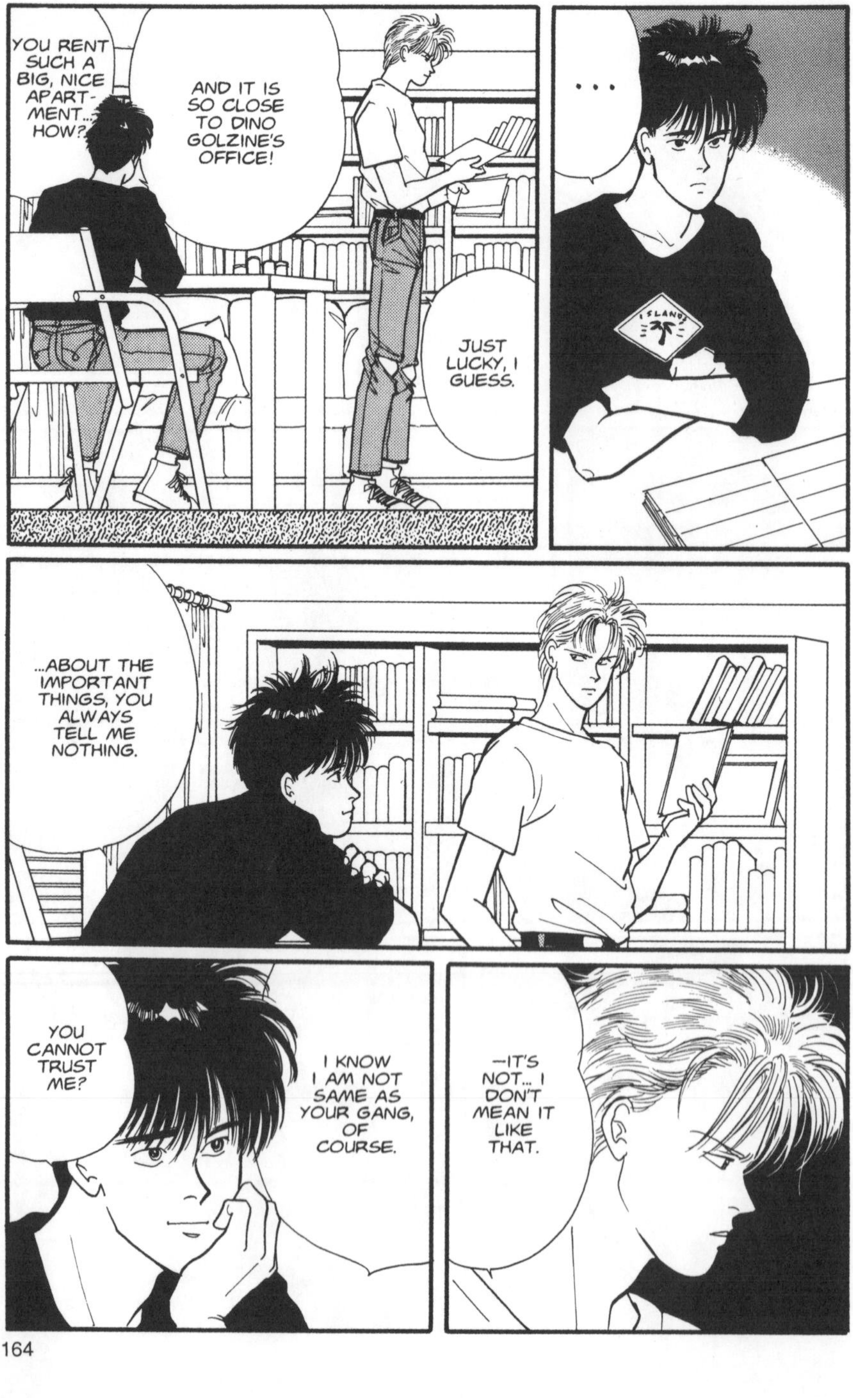
YOU RENT SUCH A BIG, NICE APART-MENT... HOW?
AND IT IS SO CLOSE TO DINO GOLZINE'S OFFICE!
JUST LUCKY, I GUESS.
...
...ABOUT THE IMPORTANT THINGS, YOU ALWAYS TELL ME NOTHING.
YOU CANNOT TRUST ME?
I KNOW I AM NOT SAME AS YOUR GANG, OF COURSE.
—IT'S NOT... I DON'T MEAN IT LIKE THAT.

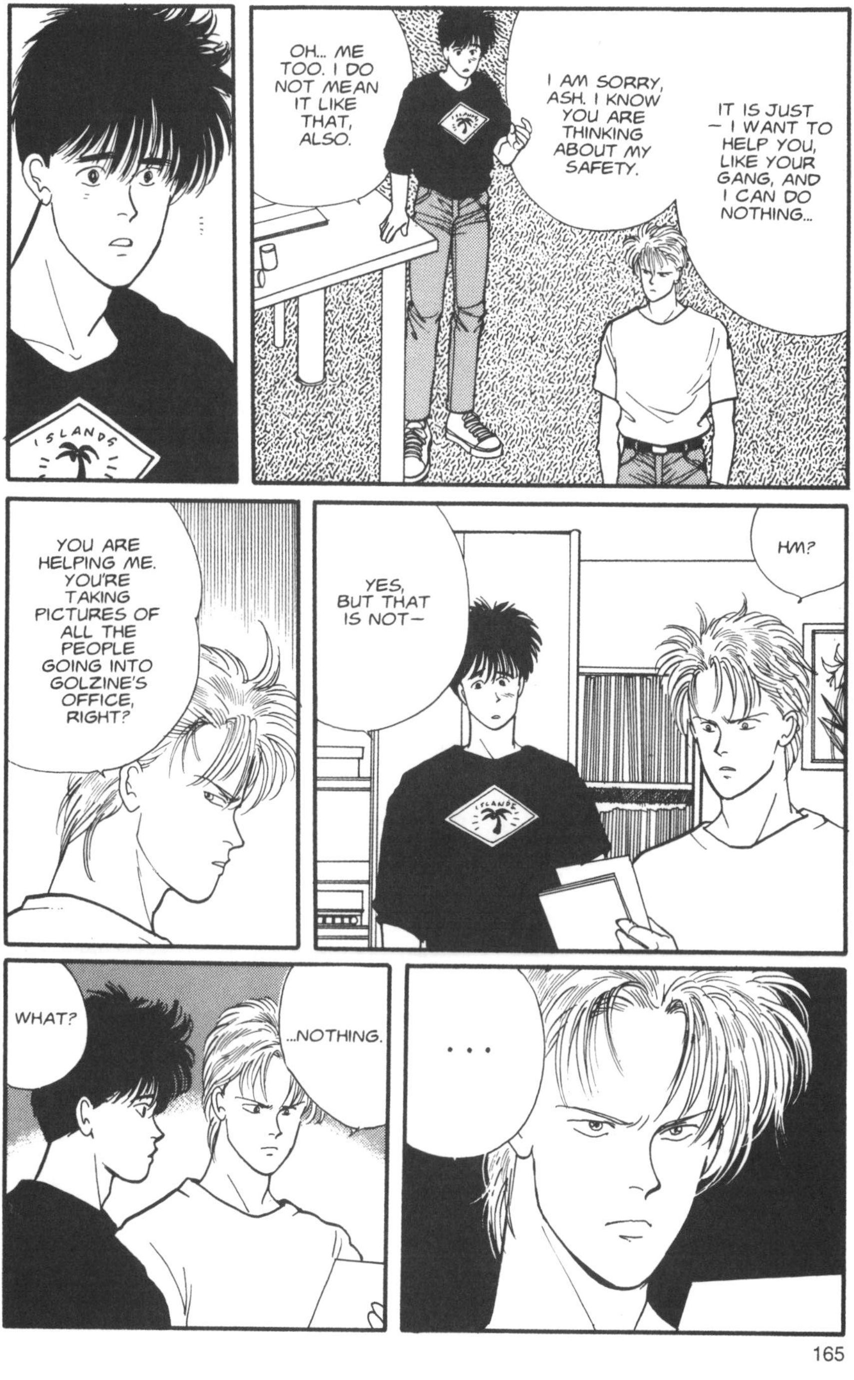
OH... ME TOO. I DO NOT MEAN IT LIKE THAT, ALSO.
I AM SORRY, ASH. I KNOW YOU ARE THINKING ABOUT MY SAFETY.
IT IS JUST — I WANT TO HELP YOU, LIKE YOUR GANG, AND I CAN DO NOTHING...
YOU ARE HELPING ME. YOU'RE TAKING PICTURES OF ALL THE PEOPLE GOING INTO GOLZINE'S OFFICE, RIGHT?
YES, BUT THAT IS NOT—
HM?
WHAT?
...NOTHING.
. . .

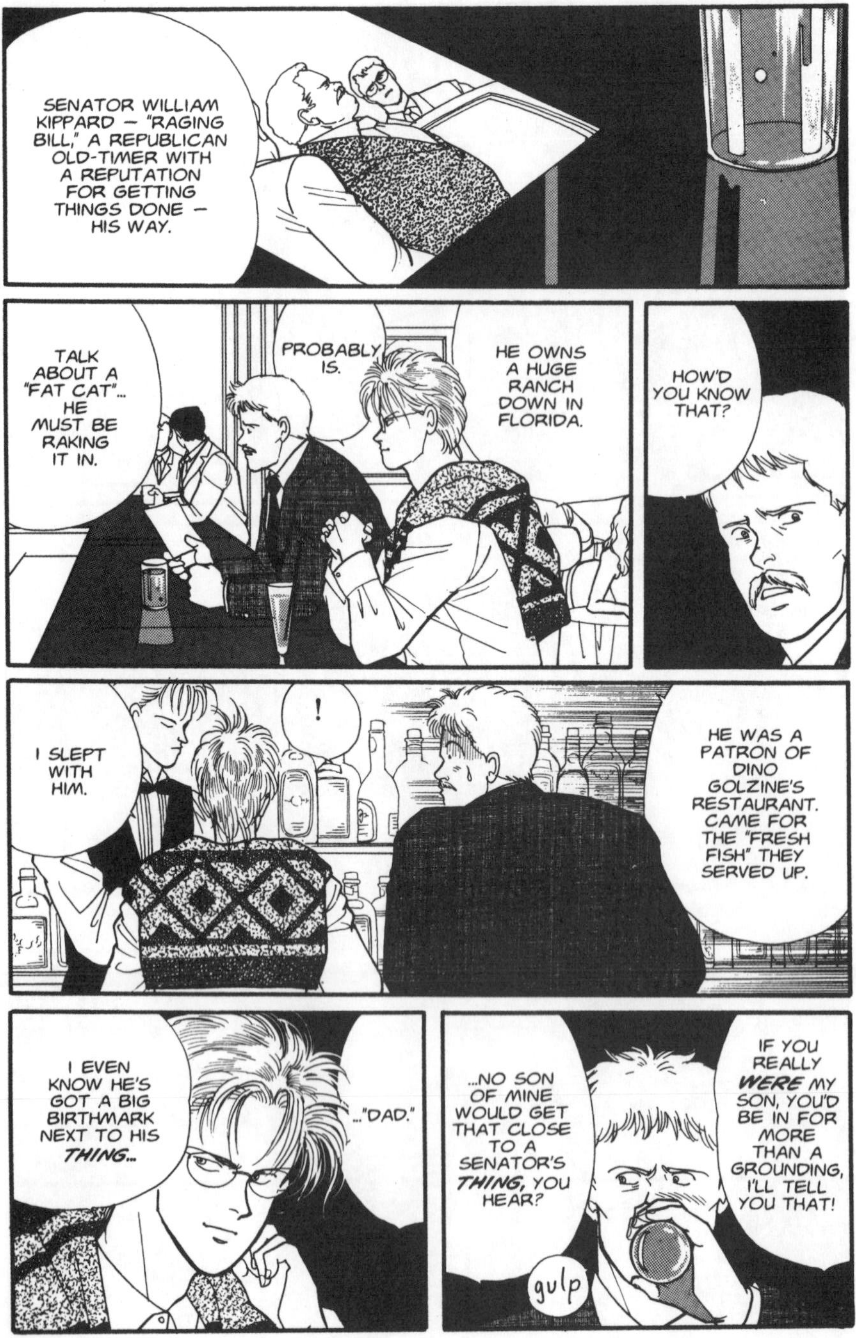

SENATOR WILLIAM KIPPARD — "RAGING BILL," A REPUBLICAN OLD-TIMER WITH A REPUTATION FOR GETTING THINGS DONE — HIS WAY.
TALK ABOUT A "FAT CAT"... HE MUST BE RAKING IT IN.
PROBABLY IS.
HE OWNS A HUGE RANCH DOWN IN FLORIDA.
HOW'D YOU KNOW THAT?
I SLEPT WITH HIM.
!
HE WAS A PATRON OF DINO GOLZINE'S RESTAURANT. CAME FOR THE "FRESH FISH" THEY SERVED UP.
I EVEN KNOW HE'S GOT A BIG BIRTHMARK NEXT TO HIS *THING*...
..."DAD."
...NO SON OF MINE WOULD GET THAT CLOSE TO A SENATOR'S *THING*, YOU HEAR?
IF YOU REALLY ***WERE*** MY SON, YOU'D BE IN FOR MORE THAN A GROUNDING, I'LL TELL YOU THAT!
gulp

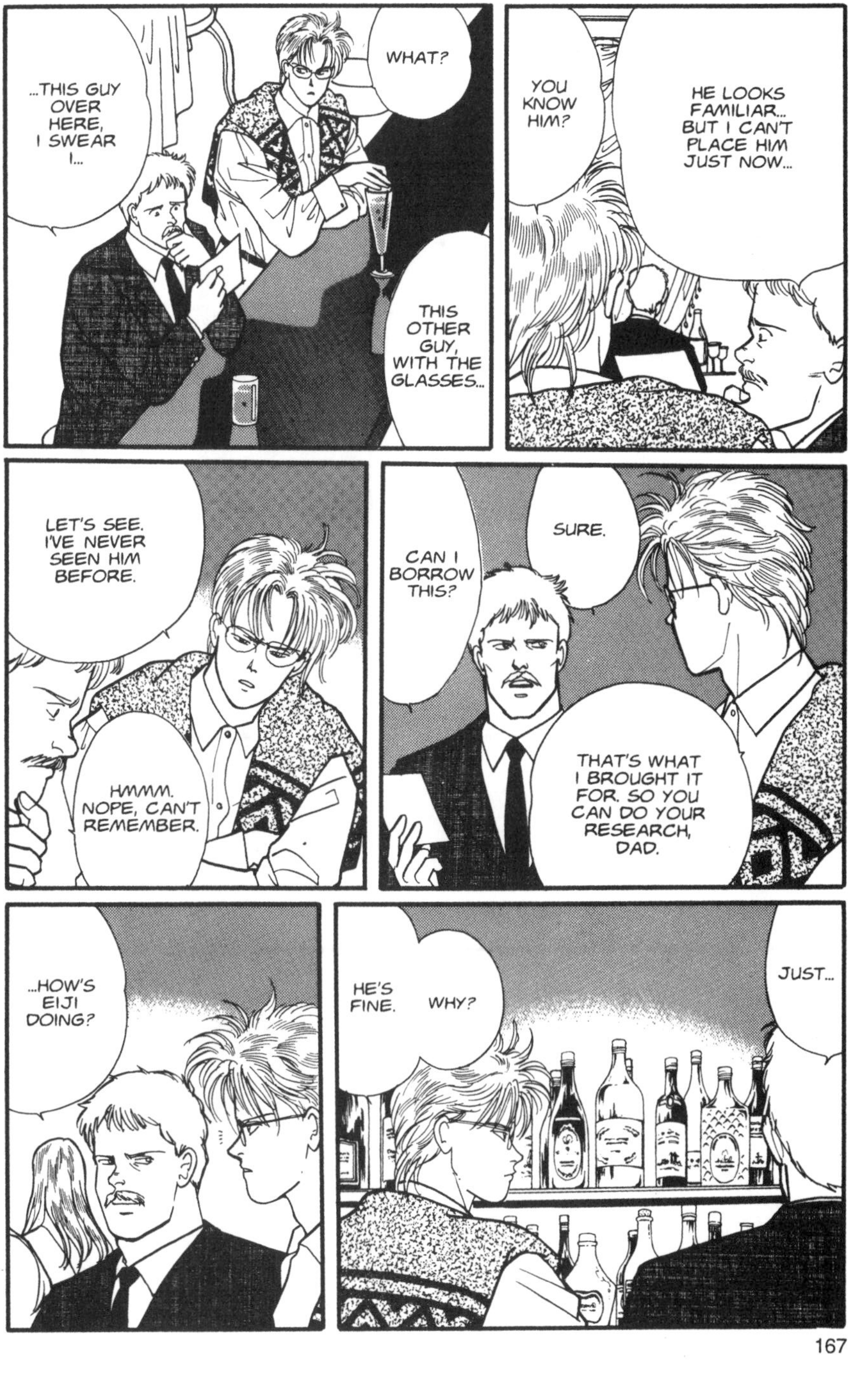
...THIS GUY OVER HERE, I SWEAR I...
WHAT?
THIS OTHER GUY, WITH THE GLASSES...
YOU KNOW HIM?
HE LOOKS FAMILIAR... BUT I CAN'T PLACE HIM JUST NOW...
LET'S SEE. I'VE NEVER SEEN HIM BEFORE.
HMMM. NOPE, CAN'T REMEMBER.
CAN I BORROW THIS?
SURE.
THAT'S WHAT I BROUGHT IT FOR. SO YOU CAN DO YOUR RESEARCH, DAD.
...HOW'S EIJI DOING?
HE'S FINE.
WHY?
JUST...

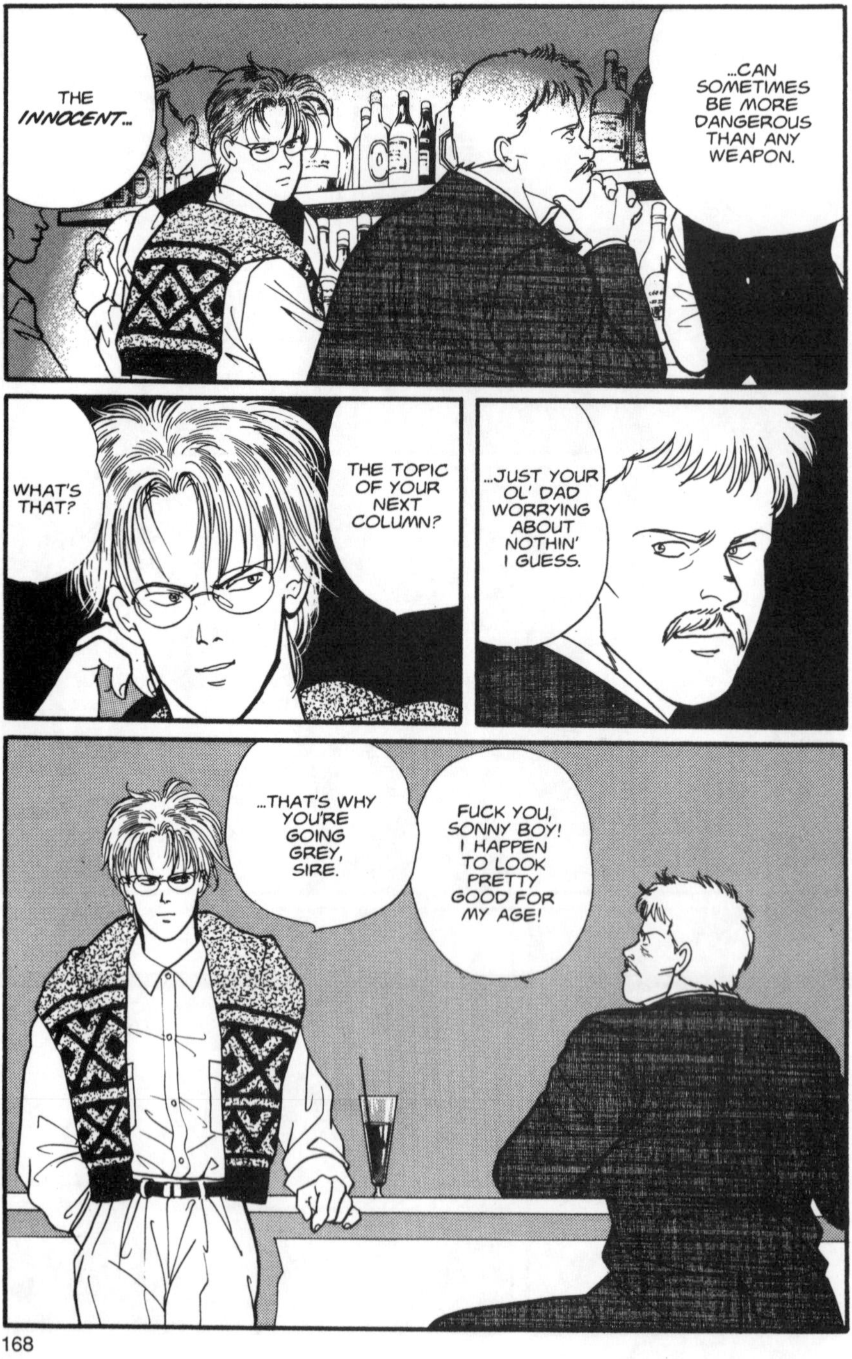
THE *INNOCENT*...
...CAN SOMETIMES BE MORE DANGEROUS THAN ANY WEAPON.
WHAT'S THAT?
THE TOPIC OF YOUR NEXT COLUMN?
...JUST YOUR OL' DAD WORRYING ABOUT NOTHIN' I GUESS.
...THAT'S WHY YOU'RE GOING GREY, SIRE.
FUCK YOU, SONNY BOY! I HAPPEN TO LOOK PRETTY GOOD FOR MY AGE!

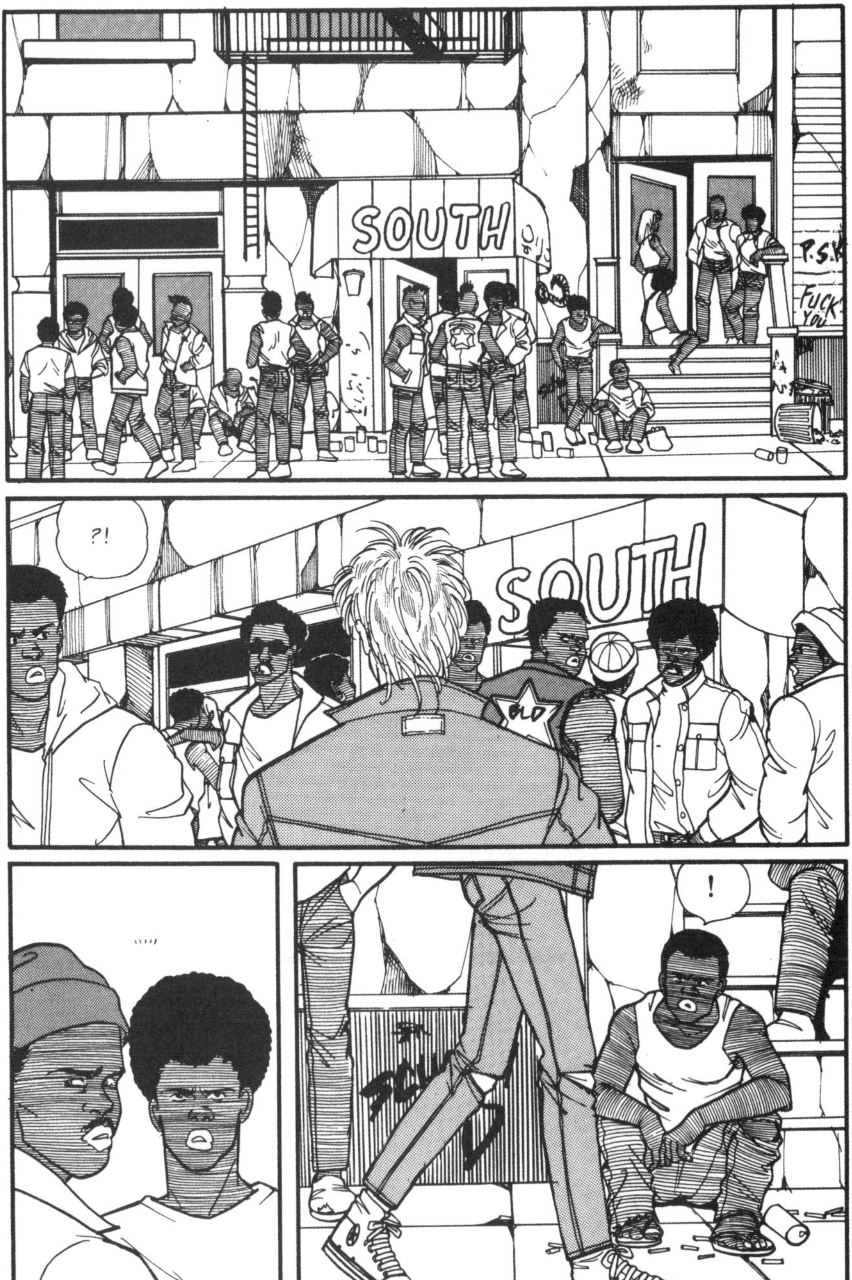
SOUTH
P.S.K
FUCK YOU
?!
SOUTH
!

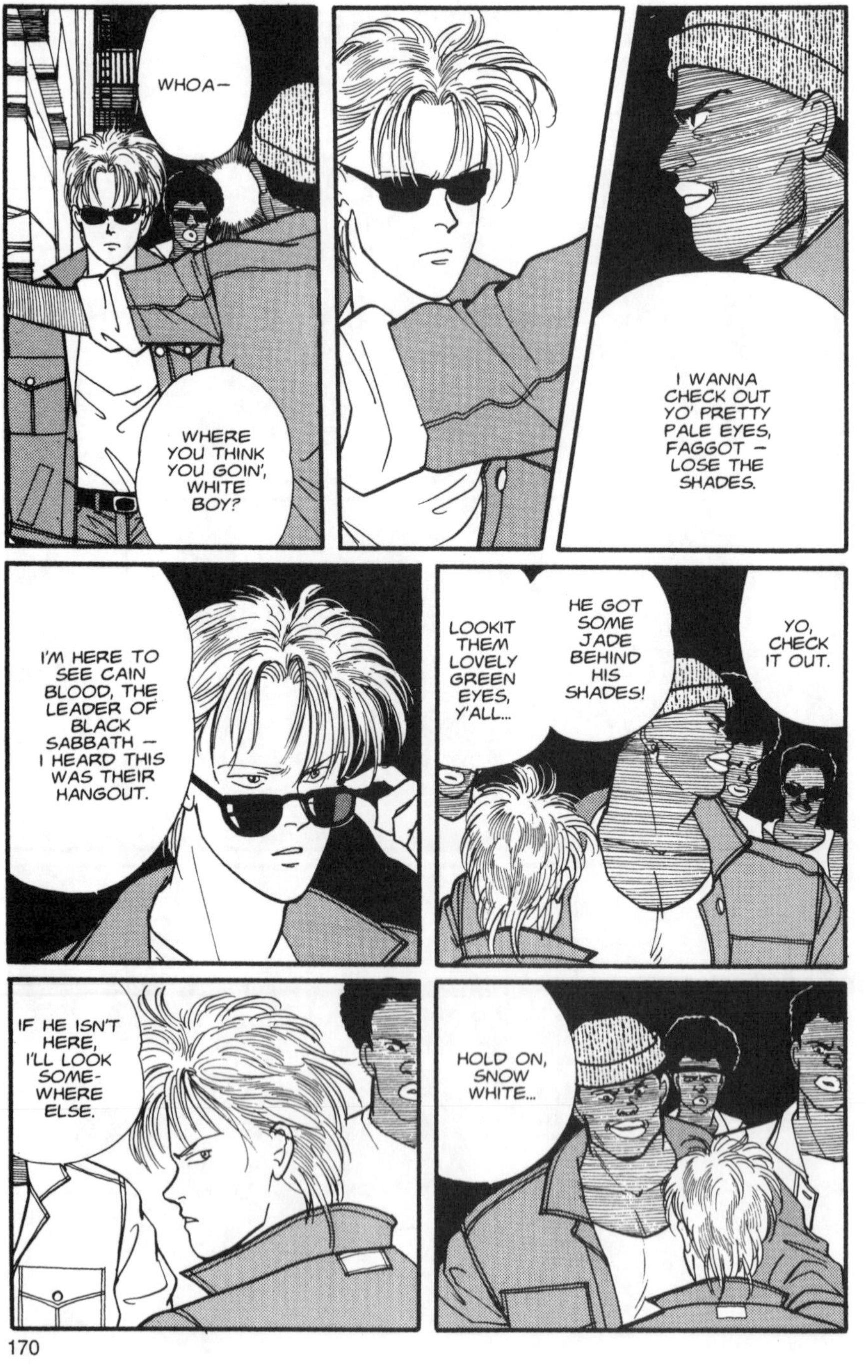
WHOA—
WHERE YOU THINK YOU GOIN', WHITE BOY?
I WANNA CHECK OUT YO' PRETTY PALE EYES, FAGGOT — LOSE THE SHADES.
I'M HERE TO SEE CAIN BLOOD, THE LEADER OF BLACK SABBATH — I HEARD THIS WAS THEIR HANGOUT.
LOOKIT THEM LOVELY GREEN EYES, Y'ALL...
HE GOT SOME JADE BEHIND HIS SHADES!
YO, CHECK IT OUT.
IF HE ISN'T HERE, I'LL LOOK SOME-WHERE ELSE.
HOLD ON, SNOW WHITE...

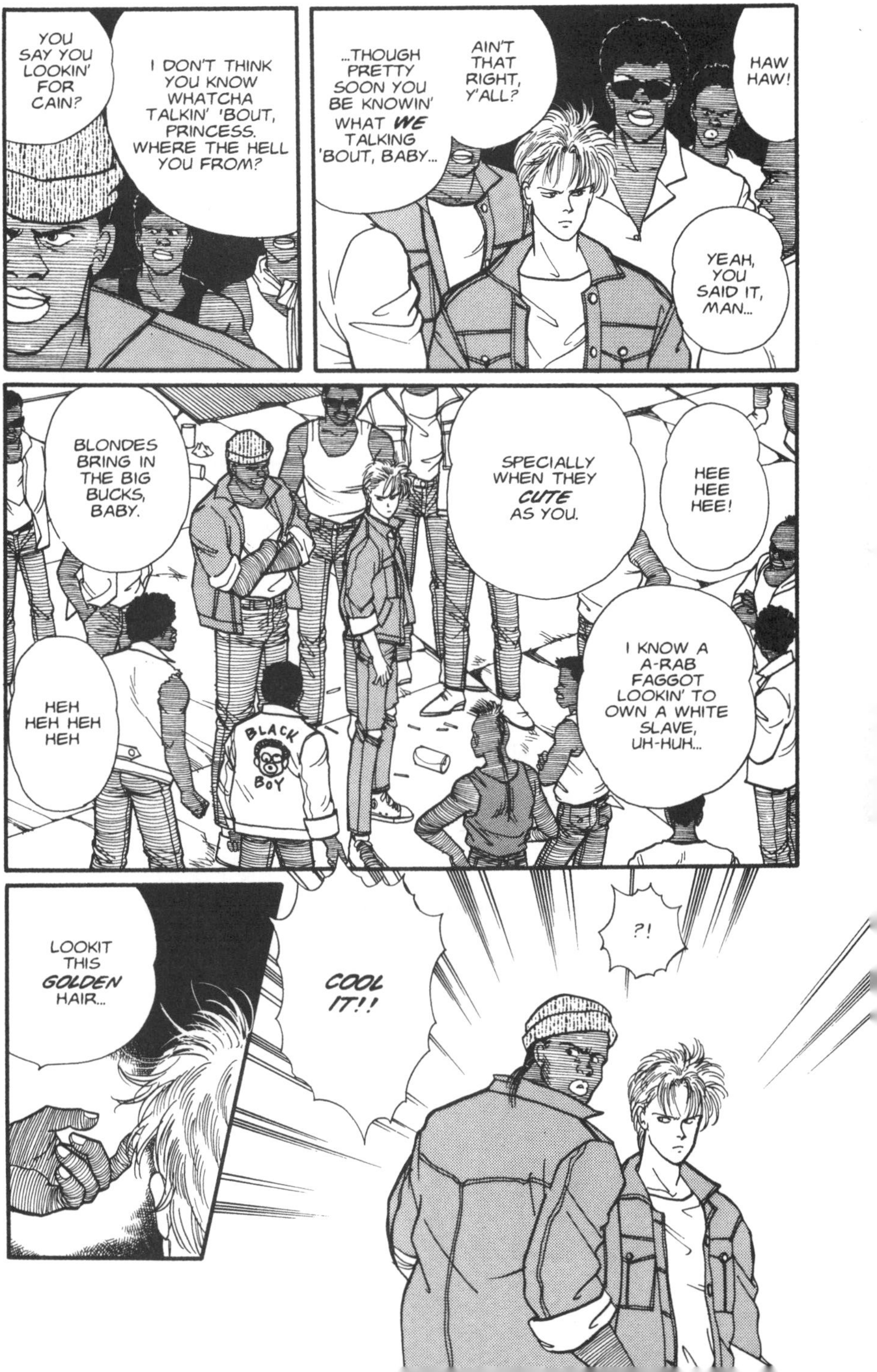
YOU SAY YOU LOOKIN' FOR CAIN?
I DON'T THINK YOU KNOW WHATCHA TALKIN' 'BOUT, PRINCESS. WHERE THE HELL YOU FROM?
...THOUGH PRETTY SOON YOU BE KNOWIN' WHAT WE TALKING 'BOUT, BABY...
AIN'T THAT RIGHT, Y'ALL?
HAW HAW!
YEAH, YOU SAID IT, MAN...
BLONDES BRING IN THE BIG BUCKS, BABY.
SPECIALLY WHEN THEY CUTE AS YOU.
HEE HEE HEE!
HEH HEH HEH HEH
BLACK BOY
I KNOW A A-RAB FAGGOT LOOKIN' TO OWN A WHITE SLAVE, UH-HUH...
LOOKIT THIS GOLDEN HAIR...
COOL IT!!
?!

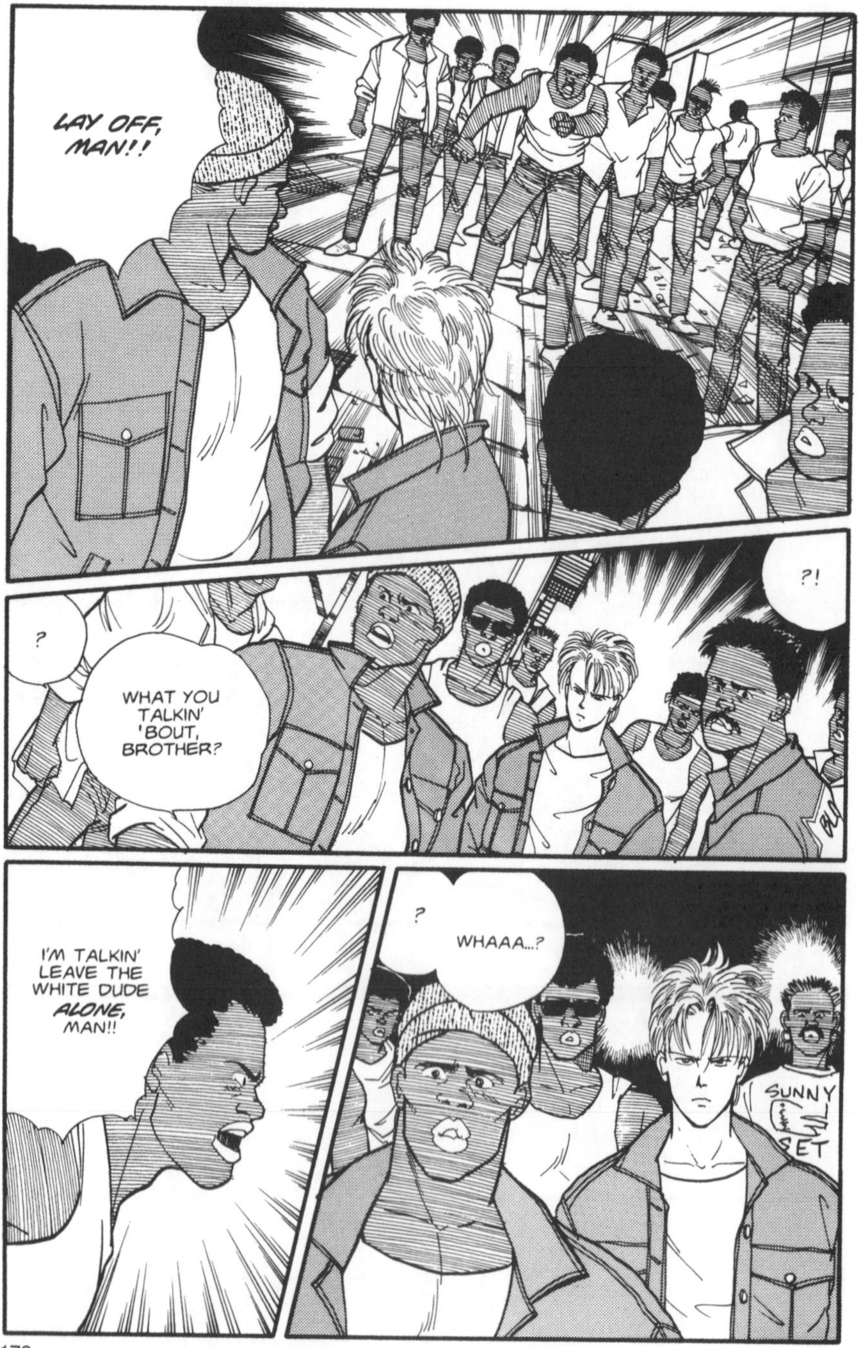
LAY OFF, MAN!!
?
WHAT YOU TALKIN' 'BOUT, BROTHER?
?!
I'M TALKIN' LEAVE THE WHITE DUDE ALONE, MAN!!
?
WHAAA...?
SUNNY SET

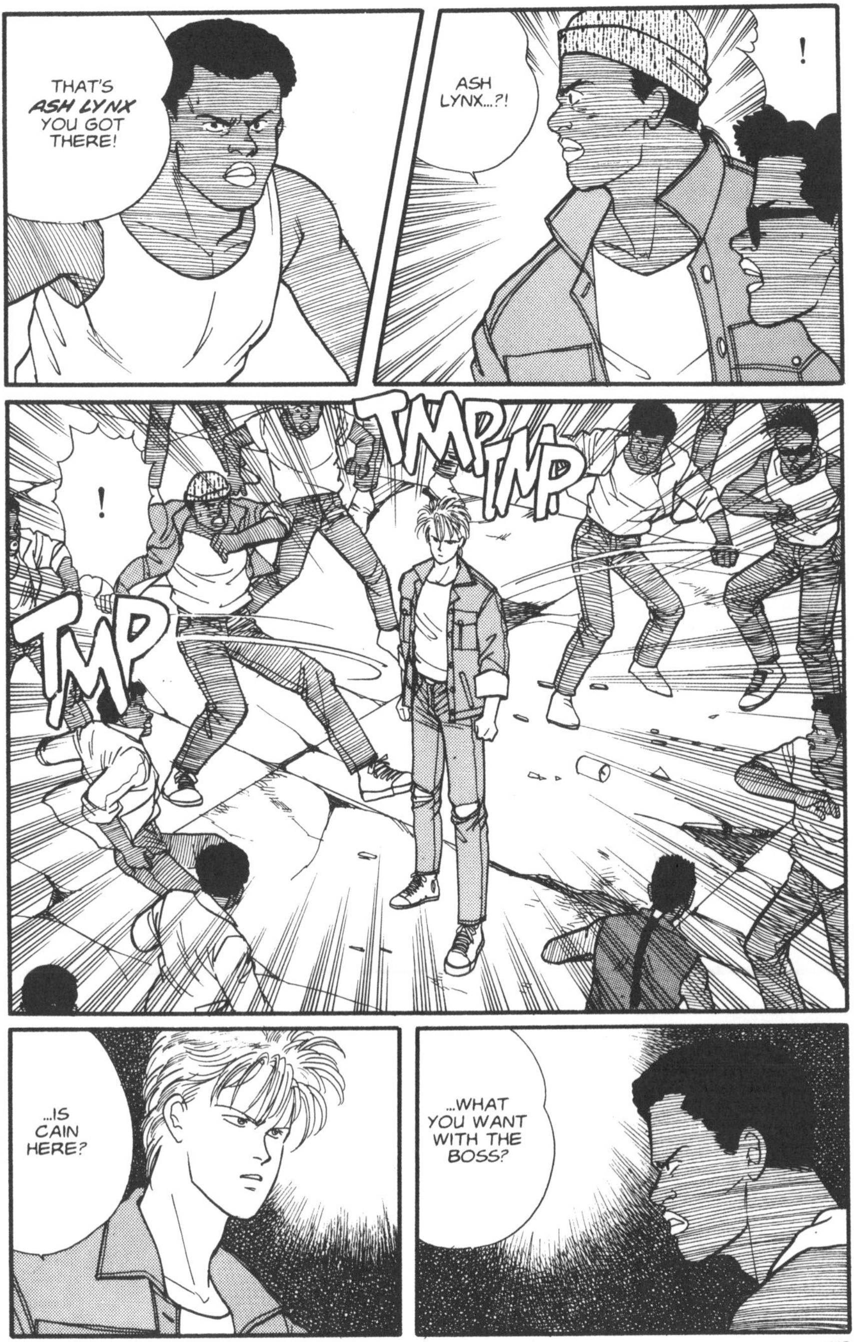
THAT'S ASH LYNX YOU GOT THERE!
ASH LYNX...?!
!
TMP TMP
!
TMP
...IS CAIN HERE?
...WHAT YOU WANT WITH THE BOSS?

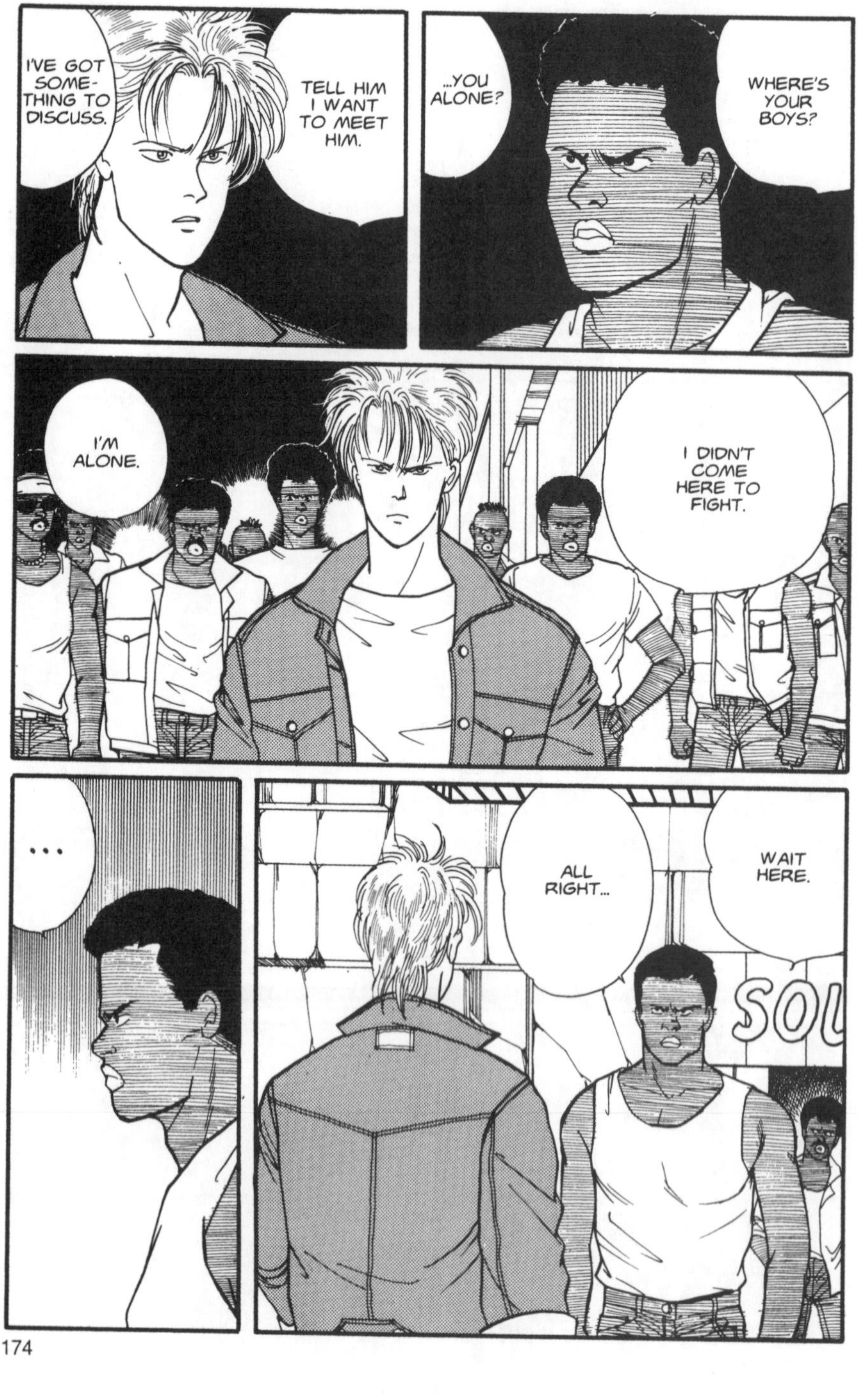
I'VE GOT SOME-THING TO DISCUSS.
TELL HIM I WANT TO MEET HIM.
...YOU ALONE?
WHERE'S YOUR BOYS?
I'M ALONE.
I DIDN'T COME HERE TO FIGHT.
...
ALL RIGHT...
WAIT HERE.
SOU

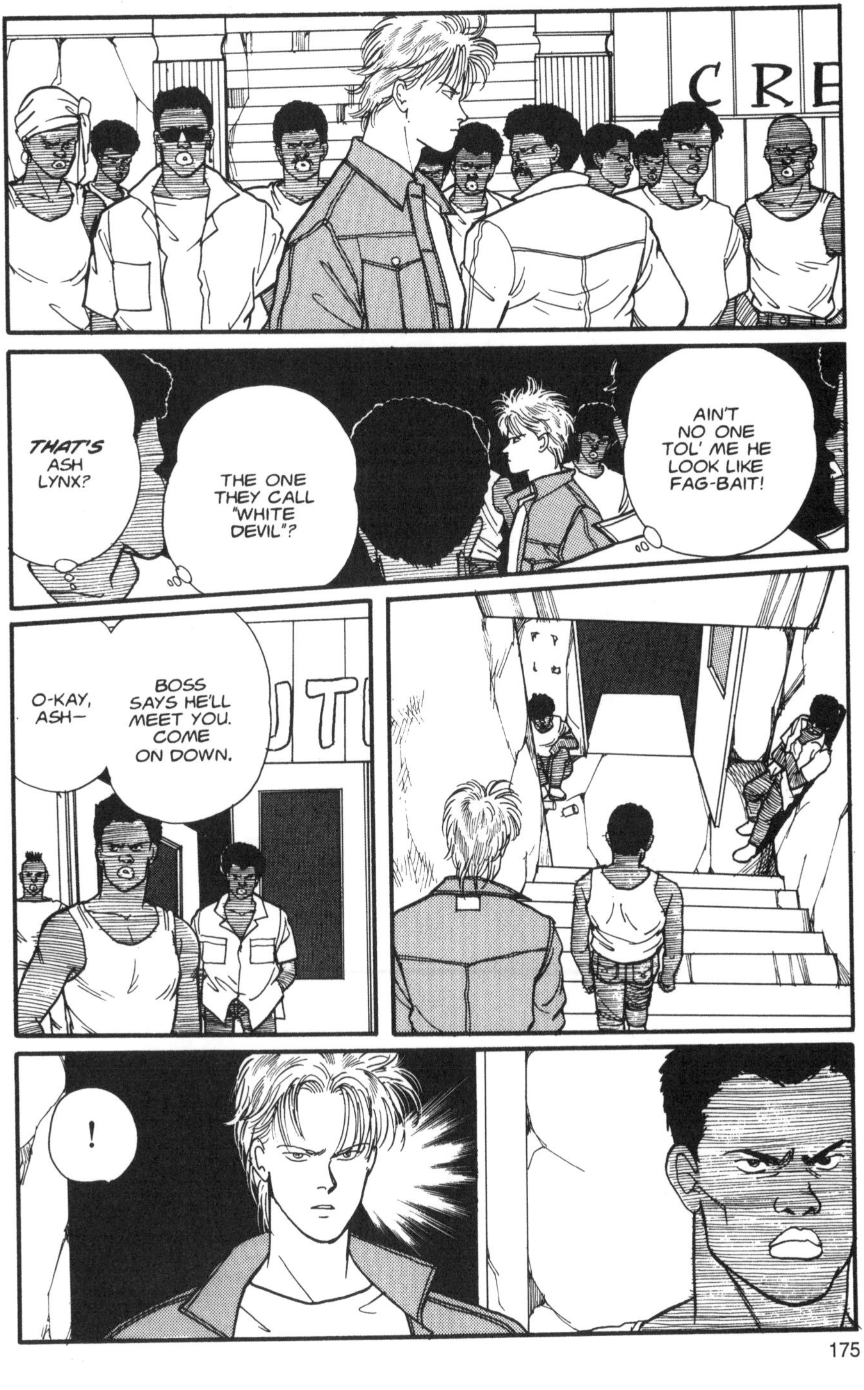
CRE
THAT'S ASH LYNX?
THE ONE THEY CALL "WHITE DEVIL"?
AIN'T NO ONE TOL' ME HE LOOK LIKE FAG-BAIT!
O-KAY, ASH—
BOSS SAYS HE'LL MEET YOU. COME ON DOWN.
!

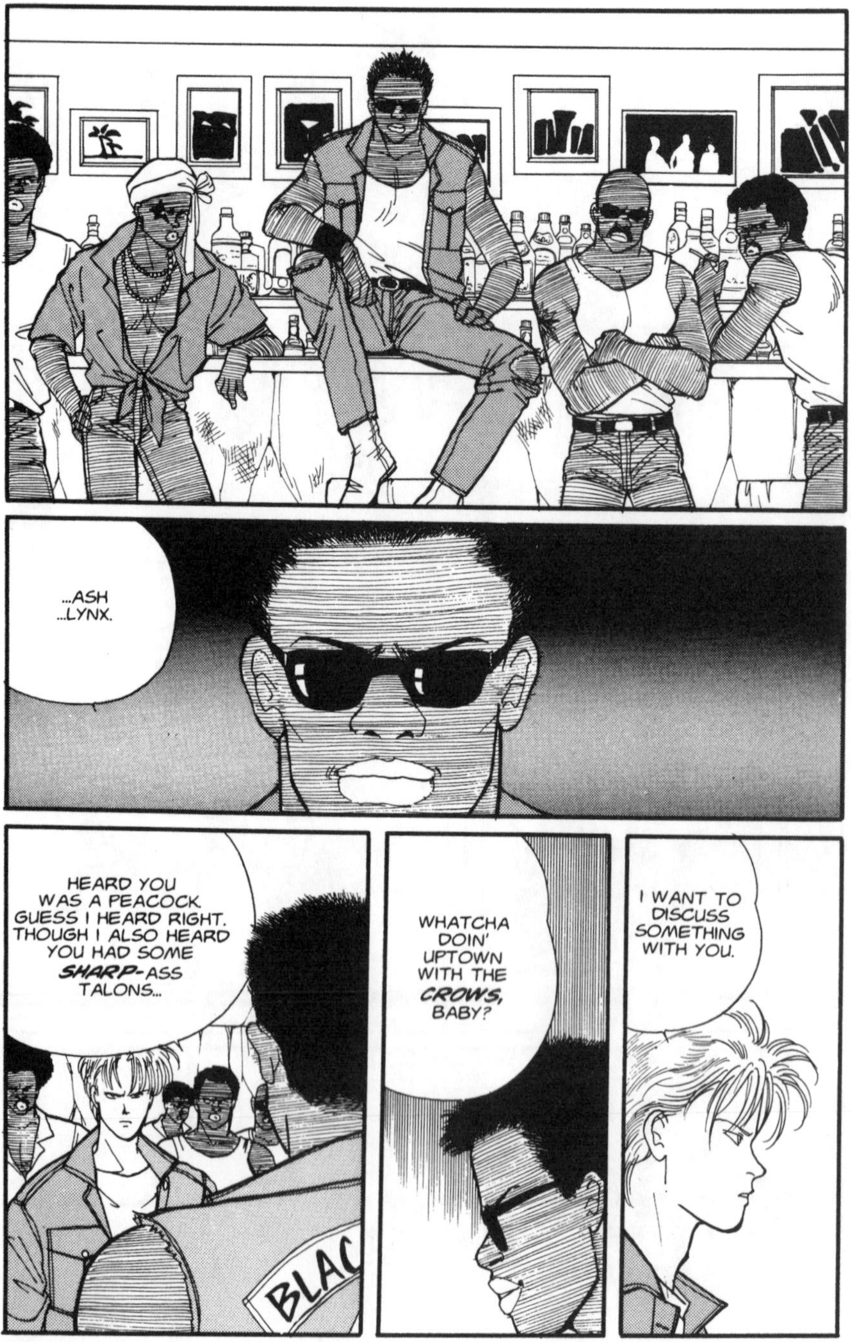
...ASH
...LYNX.
HEARD YOU WAS A PEACOCK. GUESS I HEARD RIGHT. THOUGH I ALSO HEARD YOU HAD SOME ***SHARP-***ASS TALONS...
WHATCHA DOIN' UPTOWN WITH THE ***CROWS,*** BABY?
I WANT TO DISCUSS SOMETHING WITH YOU.
BLAC

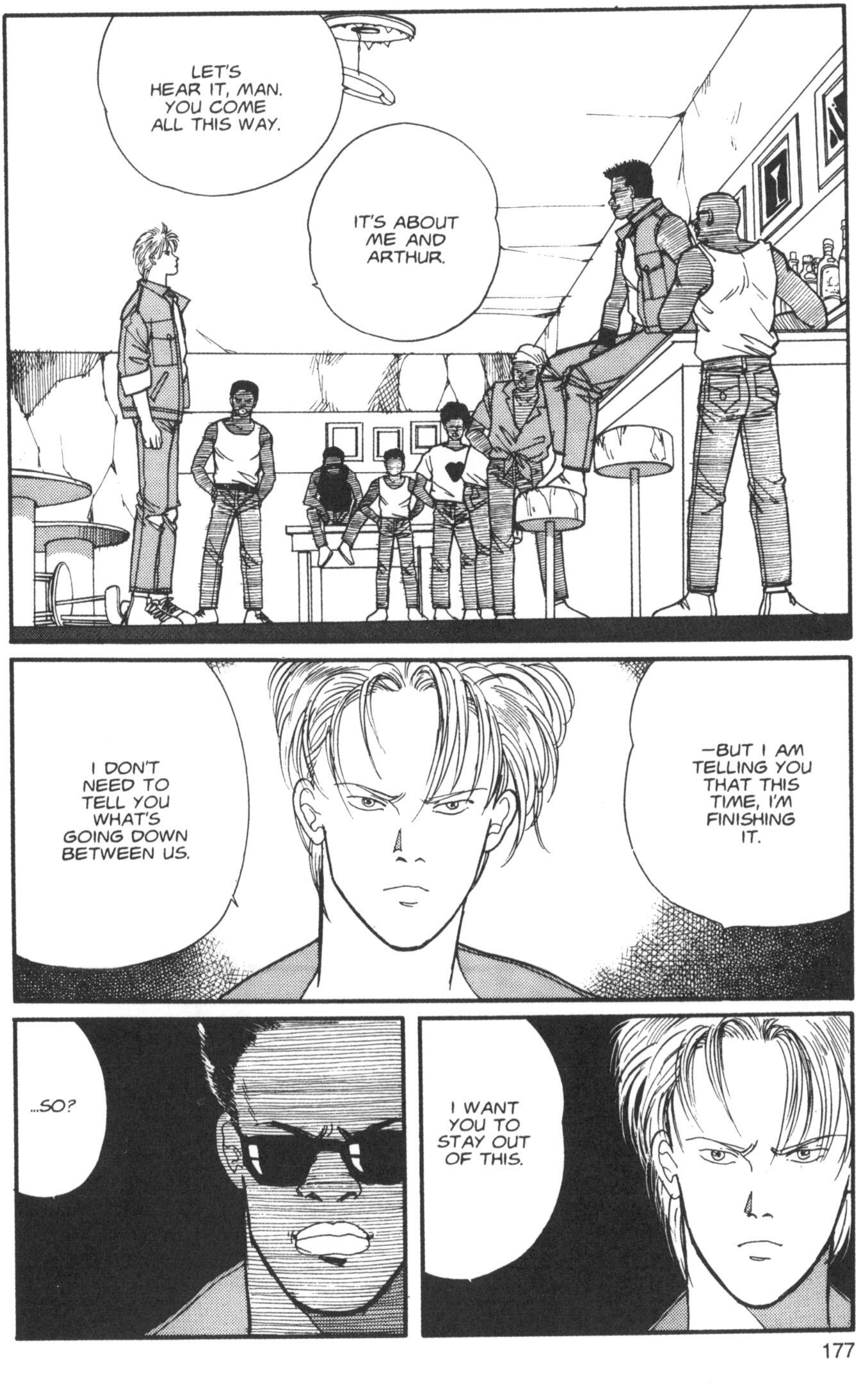
LET'S HEAR IT, MAN. YOU COME ALL THIS WAY.
IT'S ABOUT ME AND ARTHUR.
I DON'T NEED TO TELL YOU WHAT'S GOING DOWN BETWEEN US.
—BUT I AM TELLING YOU THAT THIS TIME, I'M FINISHING IT.
...SO?
I WANT YOU TO STAY OUT OF THIS.

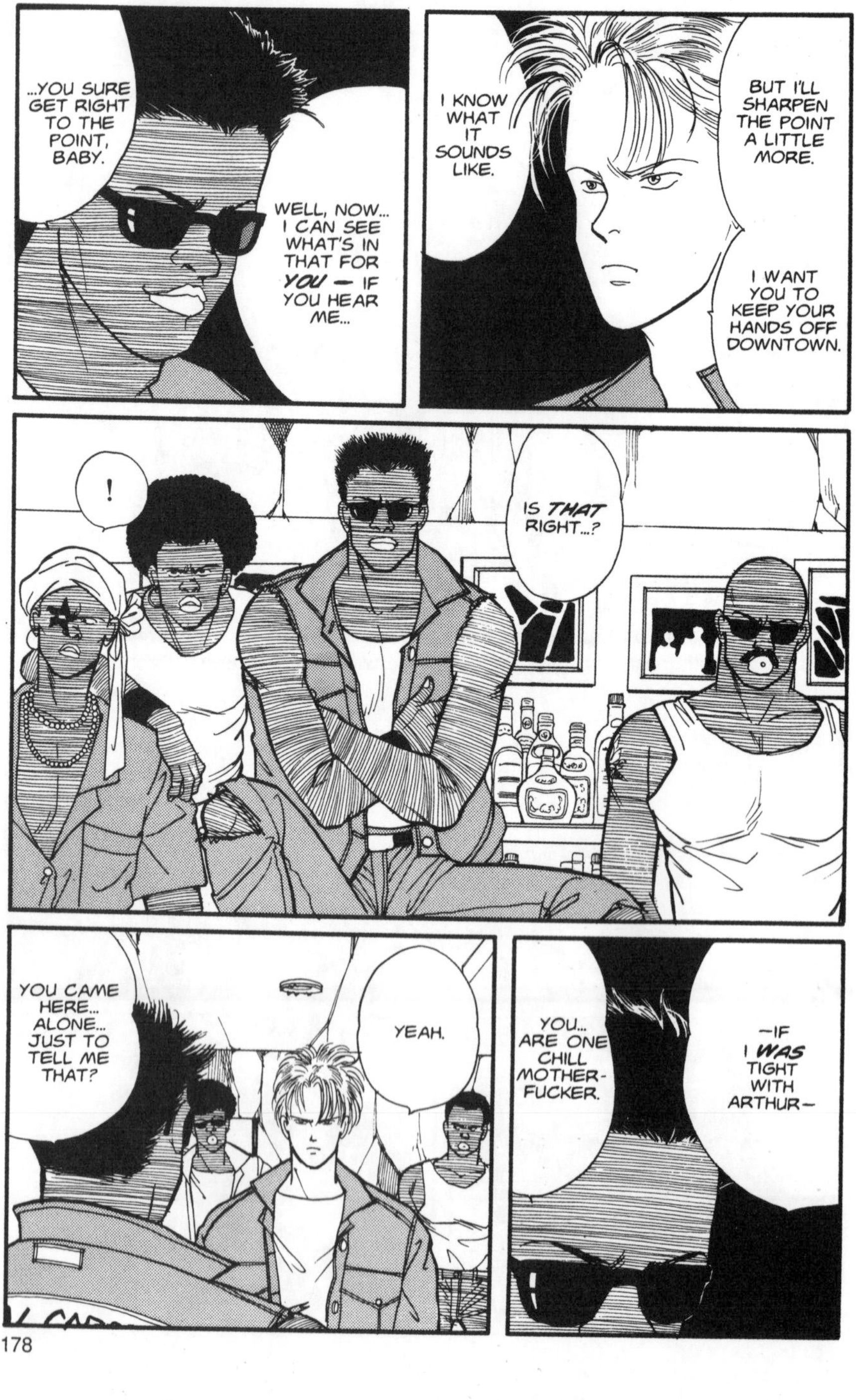
...YOU SURE GET RIGHT TO THE POINT, BABY.
WELL, NOW... I CAN SEE WHAT'S IN THAT FOR YOU — IF YOU HEAR ME...
I KNOW WHAT IT SOUNDS LIKE.
BUT I'LL SHARPEN THE POINT A LITTLE MORE.
I WANT YOU TO KEEP YOUR HANDS OFF DOWNTOWN.
!
IS THAT RIGHT...?
YOU CAME HERE... ALONE... JUST TO TELL ME THAT?
YEAH.
YOU... ARE ONE CHILL MOTHER-FUCKER.
—IF I WAS TIGHT WITH ARTHUR—

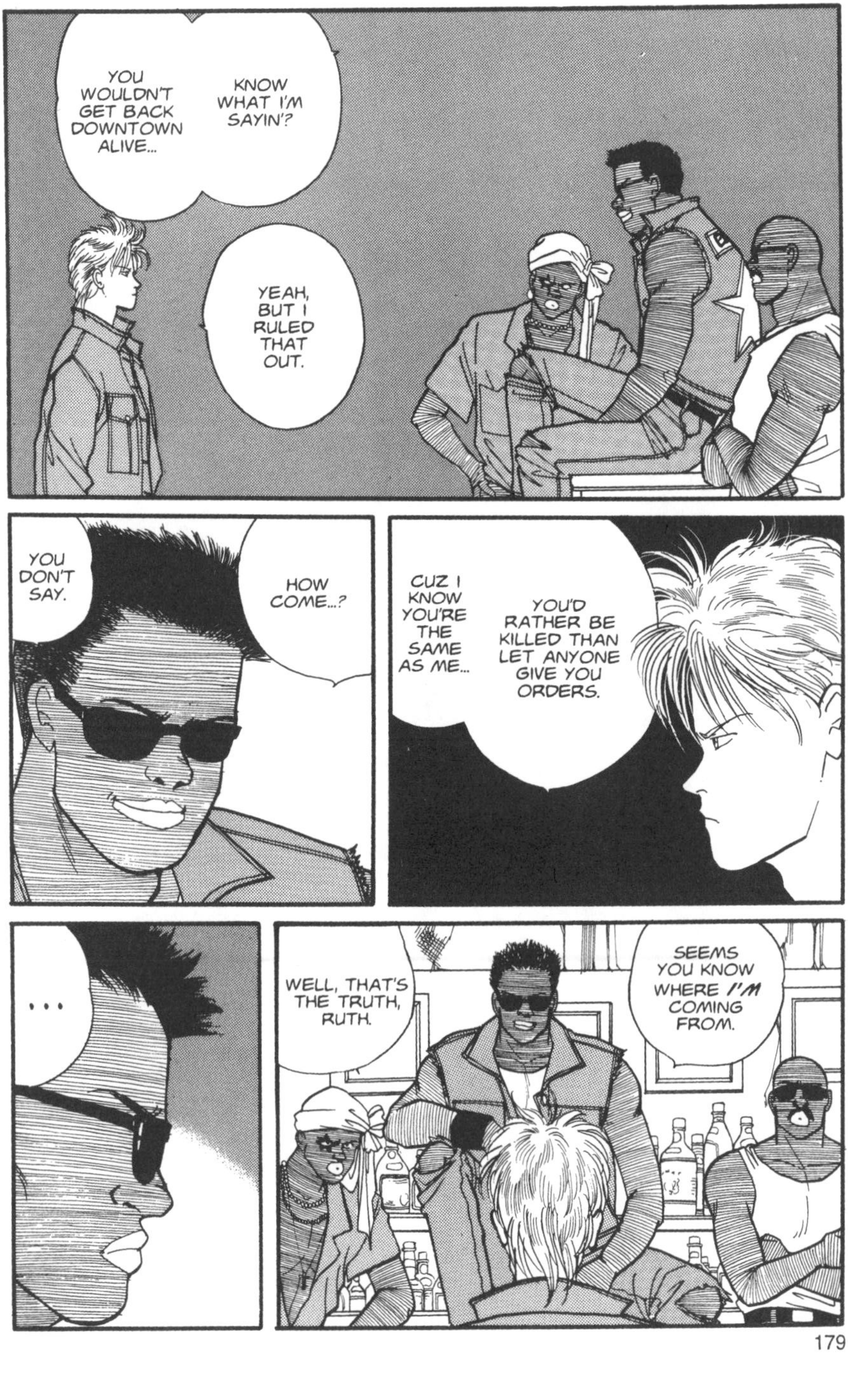
YOU WOULDN'T GET BACK DOWNTOWN ALIVE...
KNOW WHAT I'M SAYIN'?
YEAH, BUT I RULED THAT OUT.
YOU DON'T SAY.
HOW COME...?
CUZ I KNOW YOU'RE THE SAME AS ME...
YOU'D RATHER BE KILLED THAN LET ANYONE GIVE YOU ORDERS.
...
WELL, THAT'S THE TRUTH, RUTH.
SEEMS YOU KNOW WHERE *I'M* COMING FROM.

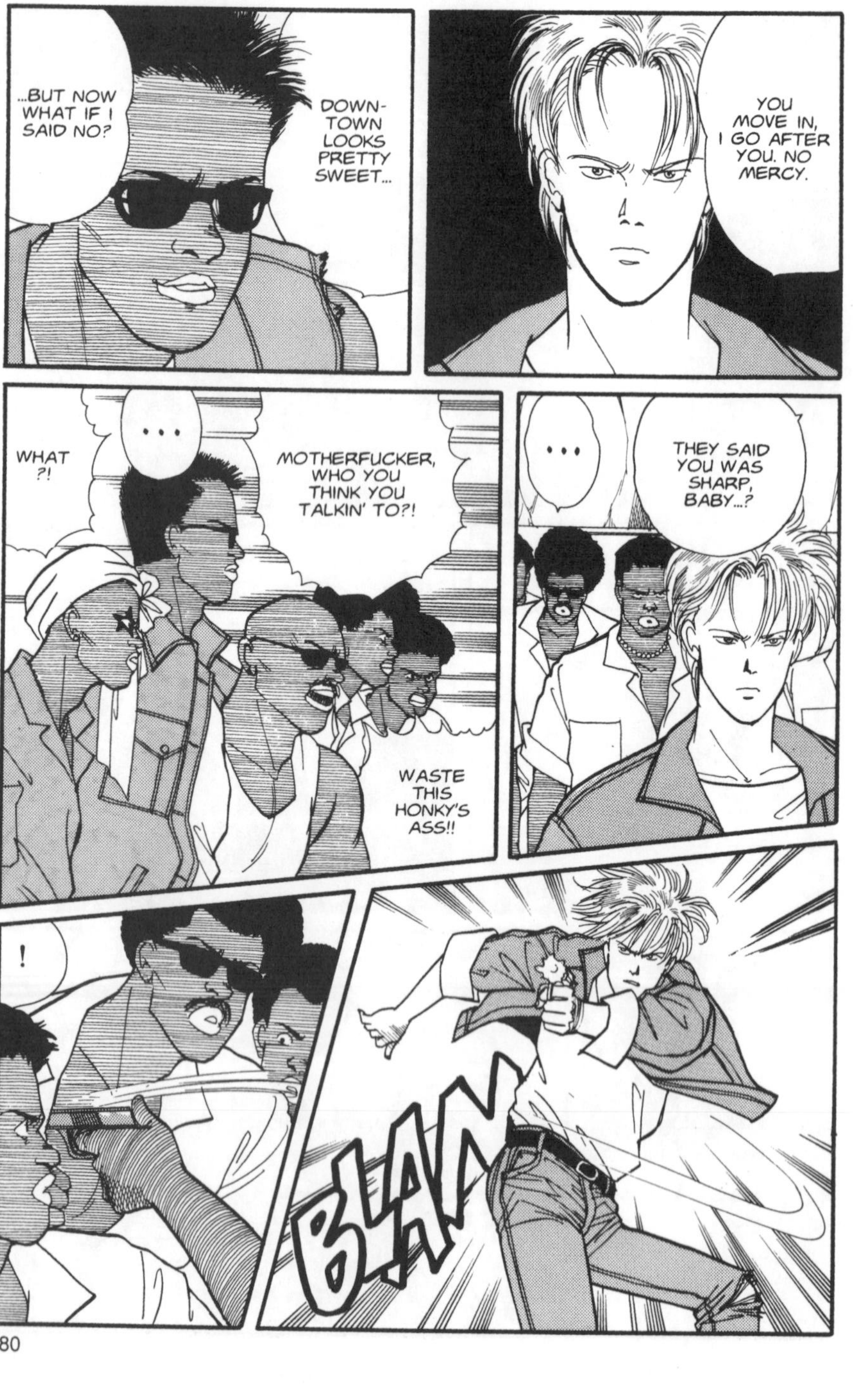

...BUT NOW WHAT IF I SAID NO?
DOWN-TOWN LOOKS PRETTY SWEET...
YOU MOVE IN, I GO AFTER YOU. NO MERCY.
WHAT ?!
...
MOTHERFUCKER, WHO YOU THINK YOU TALKIN' TO?!
WASTE THIS HONKY'S ASS!!
...
THEY SAID YOU WAS SHARP, BABY...?
!
BLAM

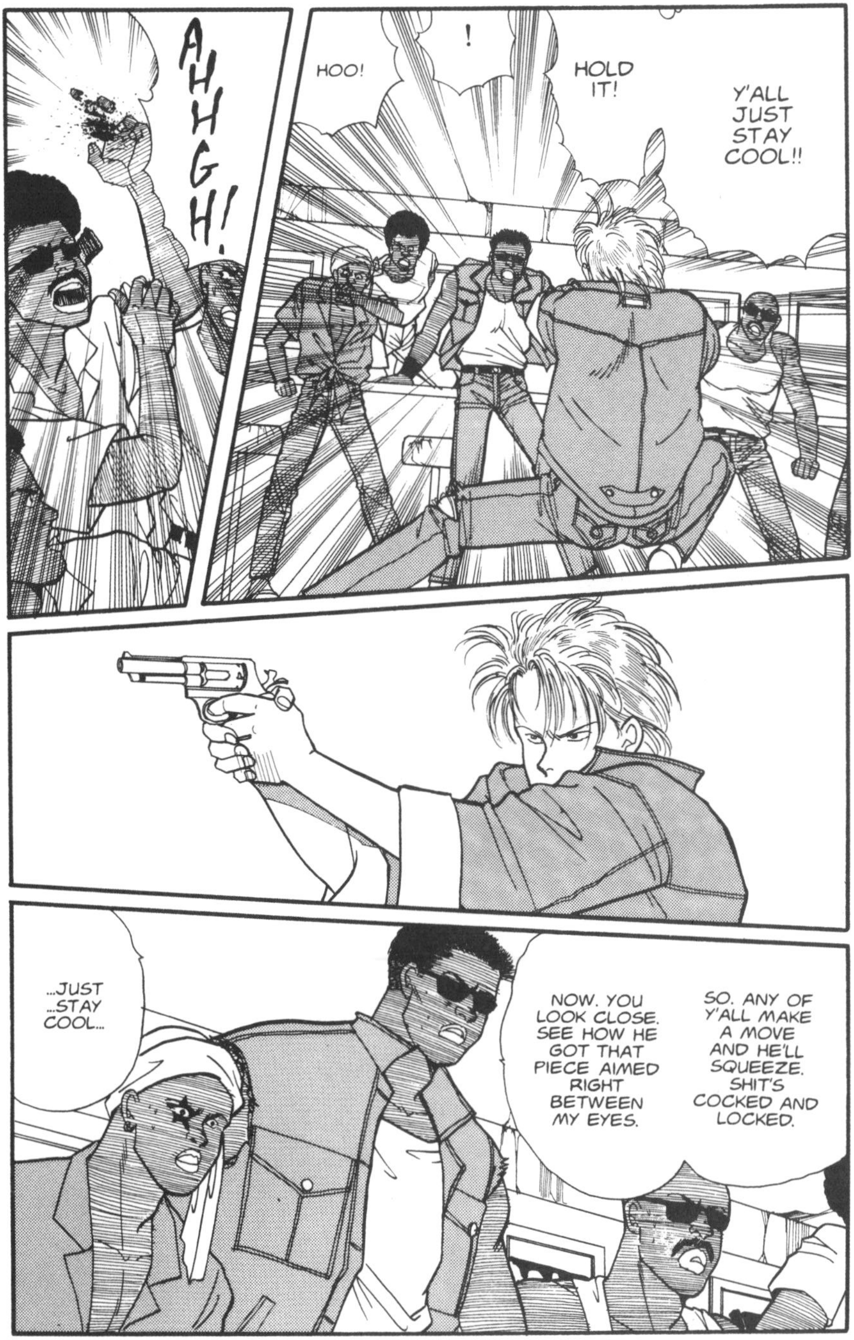
AHHGH!
HOO!
!
HOLD IT!
Y'ALL JUST STAY COOL!!
...JUST ...STAY COOL...
NOW. YOU LOOK CLOSE. SEE HOW HE GOT THAT PIECE AIMED RIGHT BETWEEN MY EYES.
SO. ANY OF Y'ALL MAKE A MOVE AND HE'LL SQUEEZE. SHIT'S COCKED AND LOCKED.

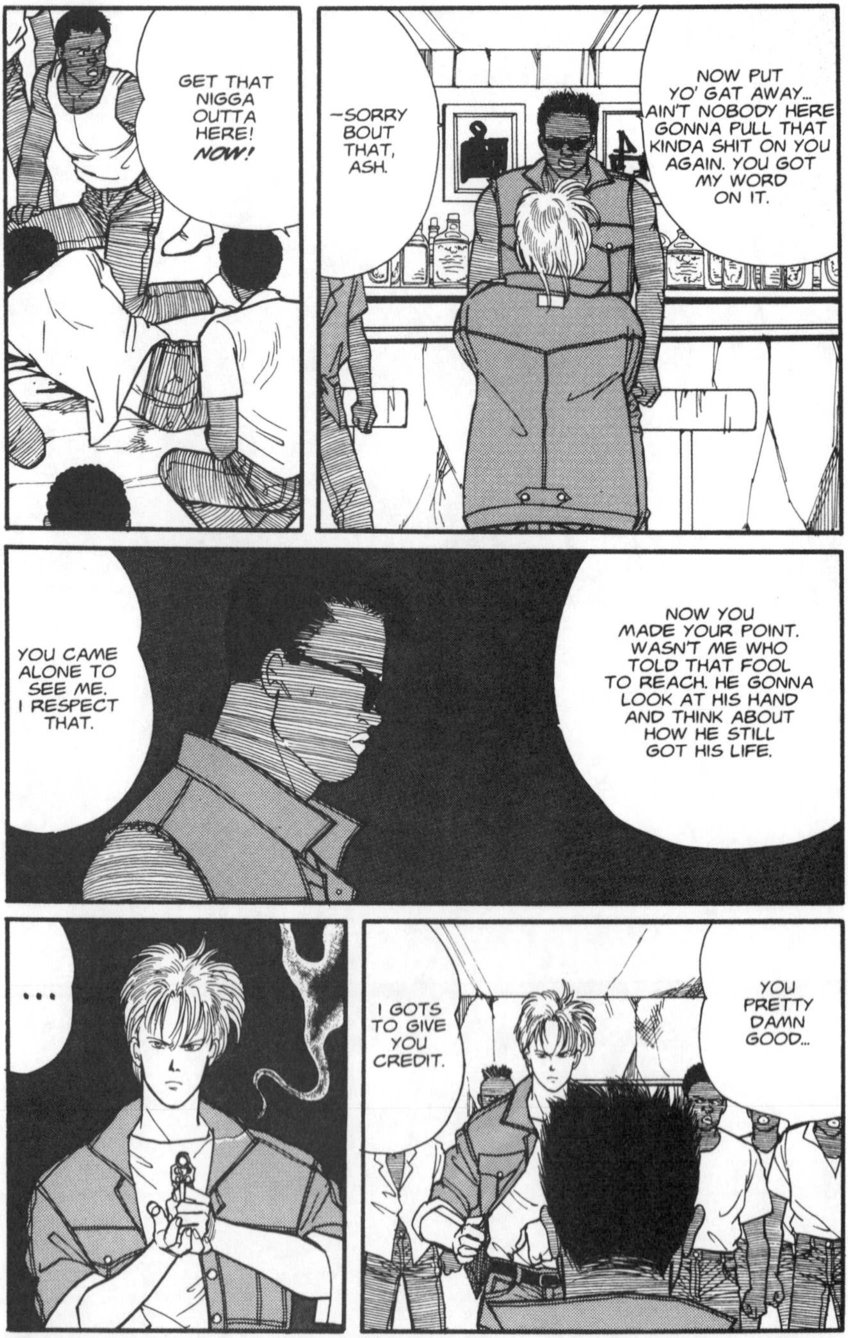
GET THAT NIGGA OUTTA HERE! *NOW!*
—SORRY BOUT THAT, ASH.
NOW PUT YO' GAT AWAY... AIN'T NOBODY HERE GONNA PULL THAT KINDA SHIT ON YOU AGAIN. YOU GOT MY WORD ON IT.
YOU CAME ALONE TO SEE ME. I RESPECT THAT.
NOW YOU MADE YOUR POINT. WASN'T ME WHO TOLD THAT FOOL TO REACH. HE GONNA LOOK AT HIS HAND AND THINK ABOUT HOW HE STILL GOT HIS LIFE.
...
I GOTS TO GIVE YOU CREDIT.
YOU PRETTY DAMN GOOD...

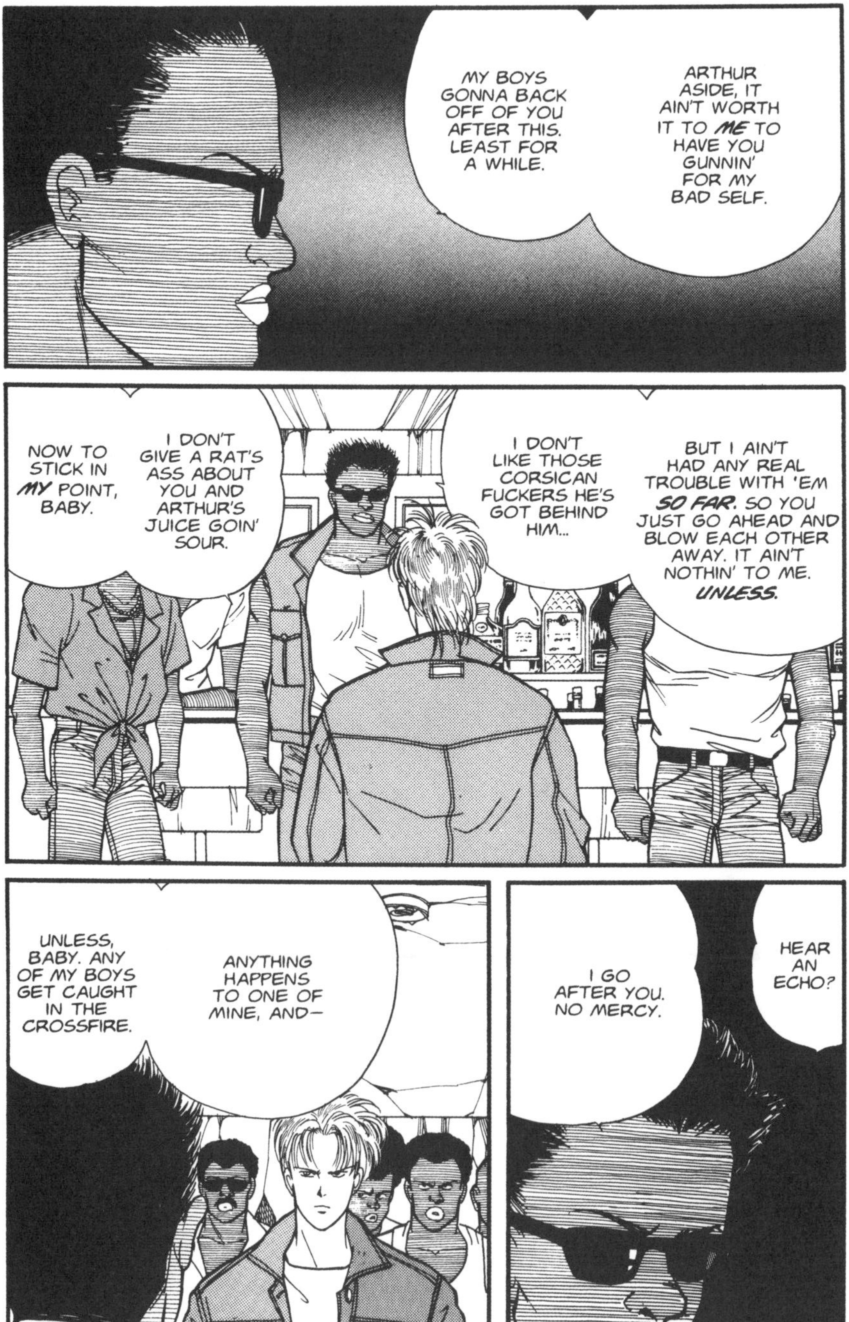
MY BOYS GONNA BACK OFF OF YOU AFTER THIS. LEAST FOR A WHILE.
ARTHUR ASIDE, IT AIN'T WORTH IT TO *ME* TO HAVE YOU GUNNIN' FOR MY BAD SELF.
NOW TO STICK IN *MY* POINT, BABY.
I DON'T GIVE A RAT'S ASS ABOUT YOU AND ARTHUR'S JUICE GOIN' SOUR.
I DON'T LIKE THOSE CORSICAN FUCKERS HE'S GOT BEHIND HIM...
BUT I AIN'T HAD ANY REAL TROUBLE WITH 'EM *SO FAR*. SO YOU JUST GO AHEAD AND BLOW EACH OTHER AWAY. IT AIN'T NOTHIN' TO ME. *UNLESS*.
UNLESS, BABY. ANY OF MY BOYS GET CAUGHT IN THE CROSSFIRE.
ANYTHING HAPPENS TO ONE OF MINE, AND—
I GO AFTER YOU. NO MERCY.
HEAR AN ECHO?

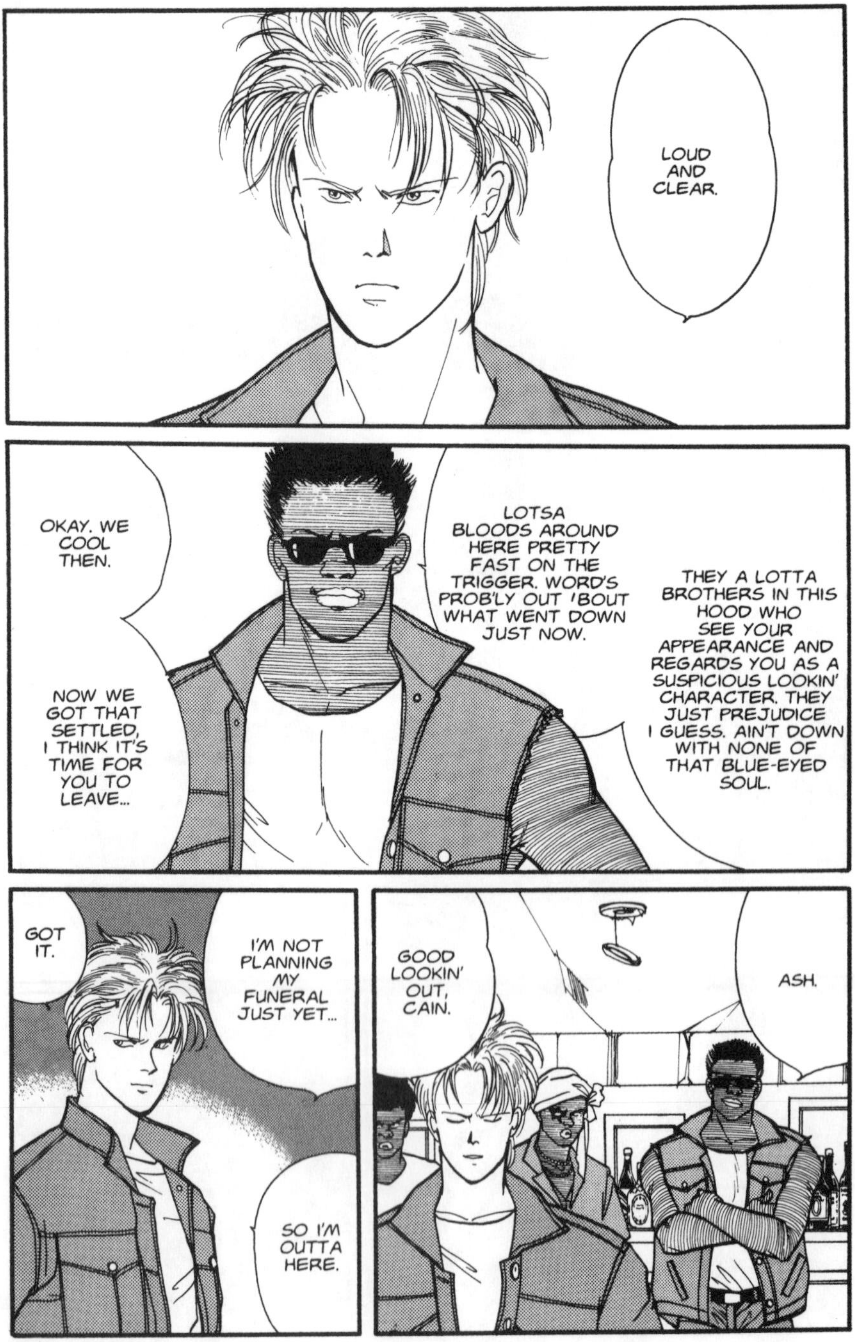
LOUD AND CLEAR.
OKAY. WE COOL THEN.
NOW WE GOT THAT SETTLED, I THINK IT'S TIME FOR YOU TO LEAVE...
LOTSA BLOODS AROUND HERE PRETTY FAST ON THE TRIGGER. WORD'S PROB'LY OUT 'BOUT WHAT WENT DOWN JUST NOW.
THEY A LOTTA BROTHERS IN THIS HOOD WHO SEE YOUR APPEARANCE AND REGARDS YOU AS A SUSPICIOUS LOOKIN' CHARACTER. THEY JUST PREJUDICE I GUESS. AIN'T DOWN WITH NONE OF THAT BLUE-EYED SOUL.
GOT IT.
I'M NOT PLANNING MY FUNERAL JUST YET...
SO I'M OUTTA HERE.
GOOD LOOKIN' OUT, CAIN.
ASH.

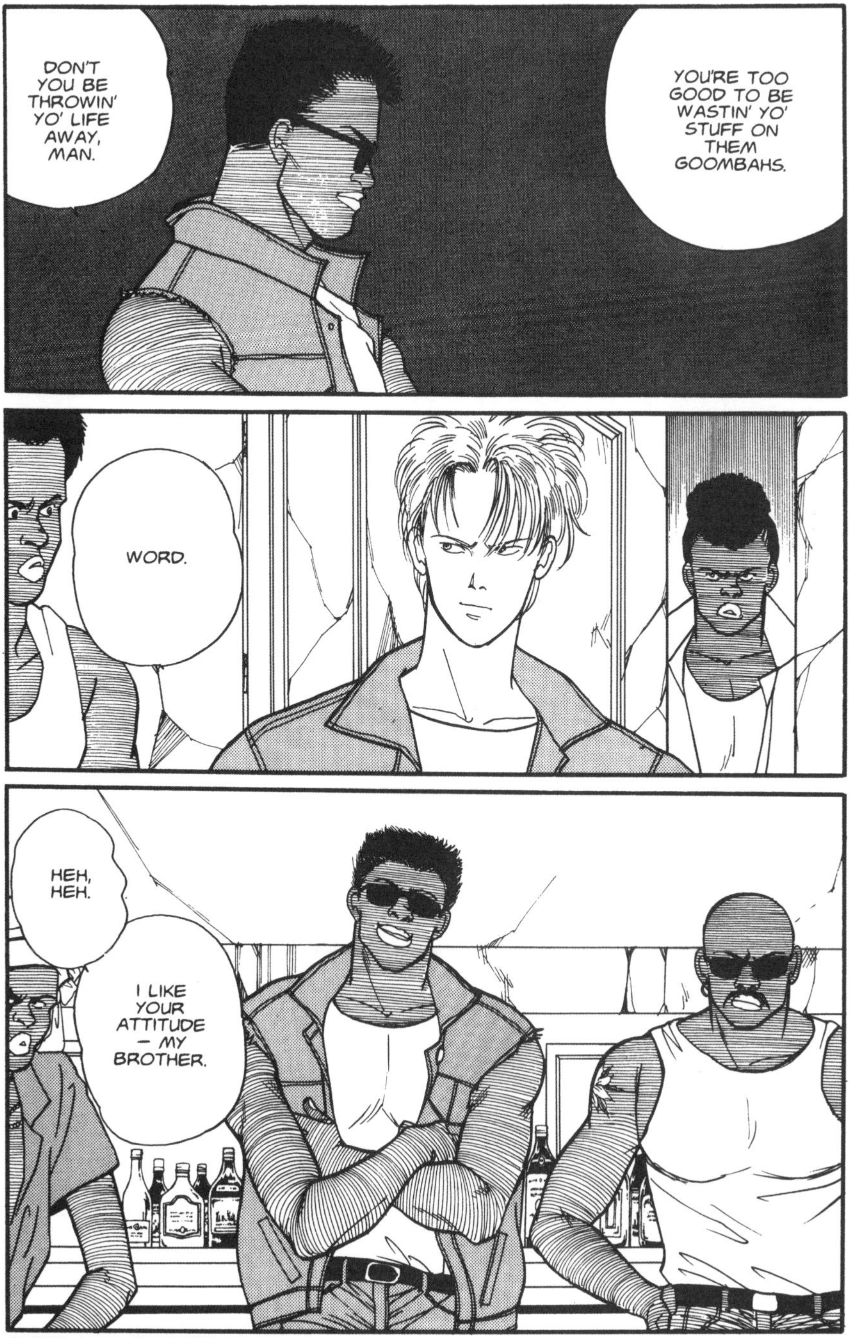
DON'T YOU BE THROWIN' YO' LIFE AWAY, MAN.
YOU'RE TOO GOOD TO BE WASTIN' YO' STUFF ON THEM GOOMBAHS.
WORD.
HEH, HEH.
I LIKE YOUR ATTITUDE – MY BROTHER.

BANANA FISH CONTINUES IN VOL. 8
AND EVERY MONTH IN **ANIMERICA EXTRA** MAGAZINE
STARTING DECEMBER 2002

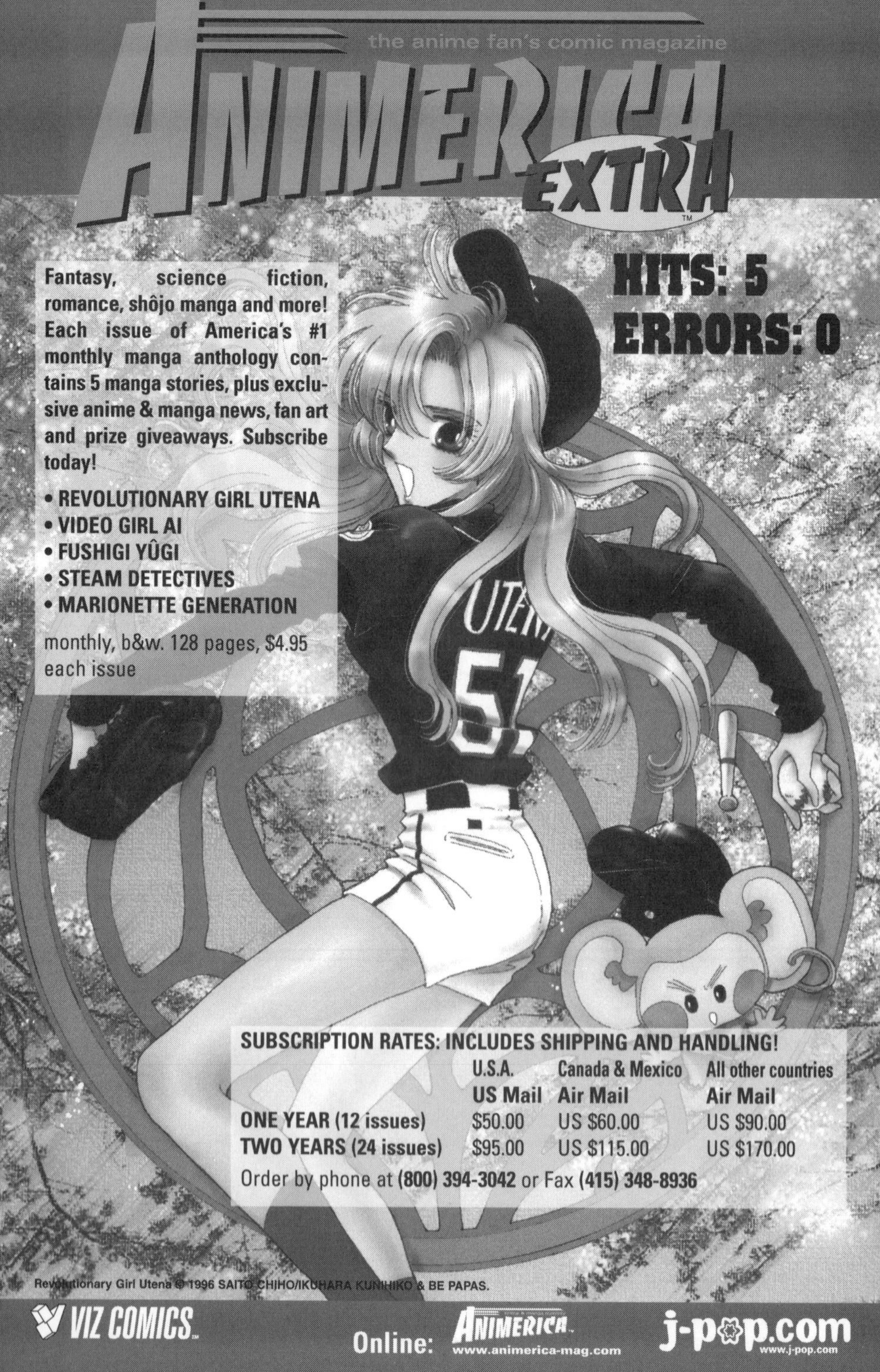
ANIMERICA EXTRA
the anime fan's comic magazine
HITS: 5
ERRORS: 0
Fantasy, science fiction, romance, shôjo manga and more! Each issue of America's #1 monthly manga anthology contains 5 manga stories, plus exclusive anime & manga news, fan art and prize giveaways. Subscribe today!
• REVOLUTIONARY GIRL UTENA
• VIDEO GIRL AI
• FUSHIGI YÛGI
• STEAM DETECTIVES
• MARIONETTE GENERATION
monthly, b&w. 128 pages, $4.95 each issue
UTENA
51
SUBSCRIPTION RATES: INCLUDES SHIPPING AND HANDLING!
U.S.A. US Mail
Canada & Mexico Air Mail
All other countries Air Mail
ONE YEAR (12 issues) $50.00 US $60.00 US $90.00
TWO YEARS (24 issues) $95.00 US $115.00 US $170.00
Order by phone at (800) 394-3042 or Fax (415) 348-8936
Revolutionary Girl Utena © 1996 SAITO CHIHO/IKUHARA KUNIHIKO & BE PAPAS.
VIZ COMICS
Online:
ANIMERICA
www.animerica-mag.com
j-pop.com
www.j-pop.com